DISCARDED

Reprints of Economic Classics

RAILWAY ECONOMY

RAILWAY ECONOMY

A TREATISE ON THE

NEW ART OF TRANSPORT

ITS

MANAGEMENT, PROSPECTS & RELATIONS

COMMERCIAL, FINANCIAL & SOCIAL

WITH AN EXPOSITION OF

THE PRACTICAL RESULTS OF THE RAILWAYS IN OPERATION IN THE UNITED KINGDOM, ON THE CONTINENT & IN AMERICA

BY

DIONYSIUS LARDNER

[1850]

REPRINTS OF ECONOMIC CLASSICS

AUGUSTUS M. KELLEY · PUBLISHERS
NEW YORK 1968

First Edition 1850
(London: Taylor, Walton & Maberly, 1850)

Reprinted 1968 by
AUGUSTUS M. KELLEY · PUBLISHERS
New York   New York   10010

From the Second American Printing
(New York: Harper & Brothers, Publisher,
Chatham Square, 1855)

Library of Congress Catalogue Card Number
67-29509

PRINTED IN THE UNITED STATES OF AMERICA
by SENTRY PRESS, NEW YORK, N. Y. 10019

RAILWAY ECONOMY;

A TREATISE ON THE

NEW ART OF TRANSPORT,

ITS

MANAGEMENT, PROSPECTS, AND RELATIONS,
COMMERCIAL, FINANCIAL, AND SOCIAL,

WITH AN EXPOSITION OF

THE PRACTICAL RESULTS OF THE RAILWAYS IN OPERATION IN
THE UNITED KINGDOM, ON THE CONTINENT,
AND IN AMERICA.

BY DIONYSIUS LARDNER, D.C.L., &c.

"There be three things which make a nation great and prosperous: a fertile soil, busy workshops, and easy conveyance of men and things from one place to another." —BACON.

"Let us travel over all the countries of the earth, and wherever we shall find no facility of passing from a city to a town, or from a village to a hamlet, there we may pronounce the people to be barbarians."—RAYNAL.

NEW YORK:
HARPER & BROTHERS, PUBLISHERS,
FRANKLIN SQUARE.
1855

ANALYTICAL TABLE

OF

CONTENTS.

CHAPTER I.

INFLUENCE OF IMPROVED TRANSPORT ON CIVILIZATION.

	Page
Art of transport essential to social advancement	25
Requisites of transport	26
Advantages of transport	26
Transport confers value on articles valueless and even nuisances	29
Transport stimulates consumption and production	29
Railway transport increases demand for labor	30
Advantages of increased speed by railway transport	31
Railway transport affords superior advantages	32
It increases the profit of the farmer, and the rent of the landlord	33
Importance of railway transport as regards persons	34
Its advantages to operative classes	34
Extends the area of supply of large cities and for residence of their population	35
Comparison of these advantages in England and on the Continent	36
Good means of communication advantageous in the diffusion of knowledge and the increase of civilization	38
Electric telegraph, its advantages and results	38
Journalism in England supplies a striking illustration of the effects resulting from improved transport	39

CHAPTER II.

RETROSPECT OF THE PROGRESS OF TRANSPORT.

Of the first construction and improvement of roads and carriages	41
Roads do not exist in more than two-sevenths of the inhabited parts of the globe	42
Roman and Egyptian roads	42
Roads constructed by order of Semiramis	43
Internal communication in ancient Greece	43
Roads of the Phenicians and Carthaginians	43
Roman military roads	44

CONTENTS.

	Page
Commercial intercourse during the middle ages	45
Influence of the crusades on the art of transport	45
Roads and intercommunication on the Continent to the middle of the seventeenth century	46
System of roads projected by Napoleon	46
Improvement in internal communication after the peace of 1815	47
Roads of France	47
First roads in England, those made by the Romans	48
Watling-street—Ermine-street—Fosse-way and Ikenald	48
First attempts to improve roads in Great Britain in reign of Charles the Second	49
Transport in Scotland to the middle of the eighteenth century	49
Slowness of traveling in Scotland	49
Arthur Young's account of the roads in England in 1770	50
Comparison between cost and speed of former and present modes of transport	51

CHAPTER III.

THE ORGANIZATION OF A RAILWAY ADMINISTRATION.

Its four principal departments	52
Their respective services explained generally	52

CHAPTER IV.

THE WAY AND WORKS.

Maintenance of way and works involves consideration of several kinds and degrees of wear and tear	53
Wear and tear classified and explained	53
Annual repairs of new railway greater than at later period	54
Wear and tear not made good by annual repairs	56
Erroneous opinion of engineers as to durability of rails	56
Mode of calculating the average duration of rails	56
Circumstances hitherto attending railways throw difficulties in the way of such inquiry	57
First English passenger railways laid with rails of 35 lbs. to the yard	57
Weight of engines successively augmented, carriages and goods wagons undergoing a corresponding increase	58
Rails originally laid thus rendered inadequate in strength	58
Speed and weight of trains also increased	59
From these circumstances, weight of rails increased	59
Railways at present laid with rails varying from 65 to 85 lbs. a yard	59
Messrs. Stephenson and Locke recommend rails of 85 lbs. a yard	59
Mode originally used for supporting rails	59
Now superseded for the most part by sleepers	59
Material of sleepers	60
Their preparation to insure durability	60
Distances between them	60
Their cubical magnitude	60
Wear of rails might have been ascertained	60

CONTENTS.

	Page
But their ultimate destination considered so remote — problem left without solution	61
In Belgium circumstances more favorable to investigation of questions more remote than immediate	61
Official reports of Belgian railways throw considerable light on this point	61
Durability of sleepers depends solely on intrinsic qualities	61
Duration of sleepers of white wood averages eight years, of oak not ascertained	61
Average duration of sleepers on Belgian railways	61
On Belgian lines about 8 per cent. renewed annually	61
Calculations by Belgian engineers as to advantage of oak exclusively	61
Result, that cost nearly the same ultimately	61
Cost affected by local circumstances	61
Durability of rails independent of time, and exclusively consequent on quantity of work	62
Observations of wear of rails on Belgian lines	62
Belgian engineers have endeavored to ascertain proportion of wear assignable to engines, vehicles, and load	62
Have arrived at conclusion of quantities abraded from rails by engine, vehicles, and load	62
Such quantities are in fact in the ratio of the weights of these objects	62
Directors of Northwestern directed investigation in 1849	63
Report of Captain Huish	63
Comparison of report of Captain Huish with conclusions of Belgian engineers	64
Financial expedient necessary to meet the exigency	65
Cost of relaying permanent way	65
Annual reserve necessary to meet such cost	65
Extent of railways in United Kingdom	65
Distribution of railways between England, Scotland, and Ireland	66
Rate of construction of railways	66
Table showing, for the railways authorized previously to the end of 1843 and in each succeeding year, the proportion opened for traffic during each year, and the proportion remaining to be completed at the end of 1848; and also showing the length of railway opened for traffic in each year since 1843	67
Railways sanctioned by parliament on January 1, 1849	67
Length likely to be constructed	68
Financial condition of railway companies to May 1, 1848	68
State of execution of recently opened railways	69
Probable cost of construction, stock, &c.	69
Tabular analysis of the number and description of persons employed on May 1, 1848, on 4253 miles of railway open, and 2958 in progress, by 170 companies	69
Railways then supplied means of living to two per cent. of population	70
State of railways since May 1, 1848, as to labor employed on them	70

CHAPTER V.

LOCOMOTIVE POWER.

Its economical importance	71
Stock divided into that of passenger and goods traffic	71
Passenger and goods engines	71
Register should be kept of locomotive engines	71

CONTENTS.

	Page
Kept by establishment of Belgian railways	72
Number of engines employed on Belgian lines at end of 1847	72
None had then been superannuated	72
Circumstances of locomotives on English railways	73
Mode of ascertaining the average mileage of each engine	73
Example deduced from Belgian railways	73
Although mileage might be augmented should not exceed certain limits	74
Expenses of cleaning, lighting, and raising steam should be charged on its mileage	74
Important to ascertain proportion of mileage to times cleaned and lighted	74
Mode of determining average number of miles run by each engine after cleaning and lighting	75
Examples deduced from official reports of Belgian railways	75
And of the Orleans railway	75
Expense incurred by engine standing with steam up	75
Reserve engines and assistant engines described	75
Separate account of reserve engines, &c., should be kept	76
Mode of ascertaining actual mileage of each working engine	76
Average distance run by each engine lighted and worked	76
Reserve engines, if included, would reduce this	77
A record of number of hours each engine has been lighted and standing should be kept	77
Example of this deduced from Belgian railway, in 1846, 1847	77
For every 10 miles of practical work, each engine kept one hour standing	77
Fuel consumed in working	77
Its classification—in lighting and steaming—in standing with steam up, or in reserve, and in drawing trains	77
Quantity of coke consumed in drawing trains depends on their magnitude, weight, and speed	78
Economy of fuel on Belgian railways	78
Rules established on these railways for allowance of coke to engine drivers for different purposes	78
Quantity consumed per engine per mile on Belgian railways	79
Register should be kept of fuel consumed under the three heads of lighting, standing, and working, with hours standing, engines lighted, and mileage worked	79
Statement of fuel consumed on Belgian railways	79
Sources from which economy of fuel may be expected	80
Manner of fabricating coke	80
Small coke unfit for locomotive engines	81
But useful for fuel	81
Quantities of large and small coke produced on Belgian railways	81
On English railways no data for similar calculations	81
Extract from report of Great Western of coal and coke	81
Return of Northwestern of coke consumed by locomotives and mileage of engines produced thereby	82
Examples from Brighton and South Coast for 1848 and 1849	82
Mode of ascertaining the number of times per annum each engine lighted	82
Examples from Belgian railways	82
Three days a week required on average for rest, cleaning, and repair of engine	83
Striking result of calculations.—Small amount of useful service of locomotives	83
Table of service of engines, deduced from returns of several continental railways	84
Result of investigation	85

CONTENTS. vii

	Page
Data supplied by English railways afford no means of comparison	84
But as to Northwestern, comparison instituted	84
Hence conclusion that engines worked, one with another, 1½ hour a day	85
Distances worked by engine drivers and firemen on Northwestern line and time of their performance	85
Distance in each trip run by each engine on Northwestern line, and time of its performance	85
Locomotive power worked more advantageously on these than on continental lines generally	85
Comparisons between railways sometimes instituted in reports on relation between locomotive stock and length of line	86
Afford no consequence of importance	86
Quantity of locomotive power does not depend on length of railway, but on quantity of traffic and its mileage	86
Test of comparison should be quantity of work executed by given power	86
Comparison between mileage of engines on Northwestern and North of France	86
Determination of number of engines necessary to work a given mileage	87
Amount of locomotive stock necessary may be assumed to be in direct proportion to receipts	88
Number and Mileage of locomotives in the United Kingdom	88
Consumption of fuel for twelve months ending June 30, 1849	89
Quantity of coal consumed in its fabrication	89
Quantity of coal consumed annually on the railways	89

CHAPTER VI.

CARRYING STOCK.

	Page
Vehicles of two classes for passengers and goods	89
Trains propelled by different engines and under different circumstances	90
Doubtful whether separate lines of rails for each traffic would not have been advantageous	90
Carrying stock of railways an important item in movable capital	92
Quantity on Belgian, North of France, and English Northwestern lines	92
In carrying department, register should be kept of mileage of each vehicle	94
Mode of ascertaining average mileage of each vehicle	94
Table of number and mileage of vehicles on Belgian railways	95
Daily duty of carriages smaller than expected	95
Table of mileages and quantities of carrying stock on five foreign railways	96
No data for similar calculations as to English railways	97
Table of vehicles of passenger traffic and their mileage on Northwestern railway during half-year ending December, 1848	97
Mode of calculating necessary amount of carrying stock	98
Table of goods-carrying stock and its mileage on six continental railways	98
Approximate estimate of mileage of goods carrying stock of Northwestern Company for half-year ending December, 1848	99
Small amount of daily useful mileage of goods-carrying stock explained	99
Average time of stock in carrying transport on continental lines about one hour per day	99
On English lines each vehicle worked one hour and a half daily	99
Necessary to ascertain composition of each train	99

viii CONTENTS.

	Page
Mode of determining this, and examples	90
Mileage account should be kept of passenger traffic carried with goods train	100
Table exhibiting the mileage of the goods vehicles, the average number of vehicles per engine, and of vehicles per train, with their designation, on Orleans railway	101
Deductions of composition of trains, as to passenger coaches, on English railways from data of Northwestern	101
But such data insufficient, and conclusions only approximate	102
Mode of obtaining number of wagons composing goods train, and results	102
In near accordance with the estimate of Captain Huish	102
Mode of exhibiting average extent to which railway has been used by rolling stock	103
As to locomotive stock	103
As to mileage of goods engines and other vehicles	103
Example from Belgian railways, for 1844	104
Table showing the quantity of locomotive and carrying stock which, being moved the whole length of the Belgian railways, consisting of 347 miles, would have the same mileage as the actual stock	104
Where traffic uniform, average distribution of traffic over entire line may be adopted as basis of general reasoning	104
But different parts of line unequally used by traffic	104
Desirable to obtain estimate of extent of each section used by rolling stock	104
Weights of vehicles on Belgian railways	105
Mode of finding average amount of dead weight drawn by each engine	105
Table of average dead weight drawn by each class of engine	105
No satisfactory data to ascertain proportion of dead weight to profitable load on English railways	106
Weights of passenger coaches on English railways	106

CHAPTER VII.

MAINTENANCE AND REPRODUCTION OF THE ROLLING STOCK.

Question raised as to wear and tear of rolling stock	107
Analogies suggested between this and permanent way	107
Only lately that question raised, whether rolling stock in condition analogous to permanent way	107
Economical principles on which solution of question depends	107
First projectors of lines contemplated themselves only as mere proprietors of the railway	107
Intended to offer it to the public to be run upon, receiving a toll	108
Proprietors compelled to become carriers	108
Provide apparatus for transport, and erect works for fabrication of engines and carriages	108
Establishments of Northwestern for fabrication of rolling stock	108
Capital absorbed in them	109
Factory at Wolverton	109
Establishment at Crewe	109
Stock of engines on Northwestern	110
Statement showing quantity and estimated actual value of articles included in amount charged to capital for "working stock" of £1,462,901—January 1st, 1848	110
Number of passenger coaches in progress at Crewe	111

CONTENTS.

	Page
Statement of Captain Huish of carrying stock of railways in England and Scotland, on 1st January, 1848	111
Former and present cost of railway carriages	112
Estimate of total carrying stock used for working railway traffic in United Kingdom in 1848, 9	113
Aggregate value of such stock	114
Question of annual reserve fund for future replacement of rolling stock discussed	114
Discussion of question between revenue and capital	115
Reported malpractices in railway management, by drafts of revenue on capital	116
Discussion of question as to closing capital account	116
Shown to be impracticable	116
Question as to taking annual valuation of stock discussed	117
Propriety of measure tested by examining its consequences	117
If made, must be on principle of estimating it by its quantity and efficiency only, and not its marketable value	119

CHAPTER VIII.

STATIONS.

Transport constitutes only a part of the railway business	119
Theatre of many operations preliminary, subsequent, and during transport—the stations	119
They consist of four departments:	
1. The passenger station:	
2. The goods station:	
3. The dépôt of the locomotive power:	
4. The carriage dépôt	120
General description of passenger station	121
Quantity of baggage allowed on continental railways	122
Parcels, important branch of traffic of passenger trains	123
Reception offices for parcels established at various places in large towns	123
Distinct department for parcels at chief stations	123
Mode of dealing with "light" parcels	124
Majority of parcels "light"	124
Heavier parcels generally sent by goods trains	124
Rates for transport of parcels vary	124
In England, charge for light parcels sometimes as low as 6d. including delivery	124
Penny postage greatly reduced this branch of traffic	125
Not above one parcel in 400,000 lost	125
Horses and carriages also composed traffic of passenger station	126
Arrangement of passenger trains	126
Carriages forming train screwed together to avoid collision	126
And provided with buffers	126
Arrangement of platform for passengers	127
Fixed engines of the Northwestern and Liverpool Railways	127
Lost luggage office	128
General description of goods stations	131
Goods wagons of the Northwestern, the York and Newcastle, the Belgian, and North of France Railways, and their performance	131

CONTENTS.

	Page
Average number of goods wagons of Northwestern arriving and departing daily at London station	132
Average load per wagon	132
And total weight of goods	132
Parcels of goods collected throughout capital by vans, and brought by them and other vehicles to station	132
Mode of dealing with such goods at station	132
Change effected by railways in management of business of retail dealers	133
Rates for transport by goods trains	133
Goods trains on Northwestern	133
Description of engine stable	134
In larger class of railways, expedients adopted for economy in consumption of fuel	135
Water heated in reservoirs and introduced into boilers	135
Coke prepared by ignition, and thrown into fire-box	135
Workshops for smaller repairs attached to engine department	135
Larger repairs conducted in larger establishments	135
General description of carriage and wagon station	136
Construction of wheels in railway carriages explained	136
Yellow grease described	137
Its composition on English railways	137
On Belgian railways	137
Quantity used on Belgian railways in 1844	137
And cost	137
Sheds for reception of carriages	137
Workshops for smaller repairs of carriages	138
Number of stations on English railways	138
Railway refreshment rooms	138

CHAPTER IX.

CLEARING HOUSE.

After several railways had been opened, inconveniences arose menacing railway establishments with insurmountable difficulties	140
In consequence of separate railway administrations, passenger compelled to change carriage	140
Trans-shipment of goods graver inconvenience	140
Inconvenience so enormous, and clamor so irresistible, that traffic of all descriptions carried without interruption from lines of one company to another	141
Produced great difficulties among companies	141
Difficulty removed by expedient suggested by London bankers' clearing house	141
Analogy led M. K. Morrison to suggest railway clearing house	141
Description of operations in clearing house of London bankers	141
Reciprocal interchange of business creating mutual debits and credits between railway companies explained	143
Number of companies which have combined their operations	143
Number of their stations	143
In adjusting accounts, clearing house regarded as common creditor and common debtor of all the companies	146
Mode of adjustment as to goods, traffic, and live stock	146
From each station, goods may be forwarded daily to all other stations	146

CONTENTS.   xi

	Page
Account of such goods forwarded daily to central clearing house	146
Account of goods received forwarded to central clearing house	146
Mode of rectifying errors	147
Debtor companies having liquidated balances, clearing house distributes them between creditor companies	147
Mode of adjusting accounts of passenger traffic	147
Clearing house debits companies for receipts, and credits companies interested	148
Accounts balanced monthly, and dealt with as in case of goods	148
Separate account kept of government duty	148
Weekly abstract of accounts sent by clearing house to companies	149
Mode of adjusting accounts of carrying stock	149
Account as to rolling stock opened with companies	149
Questions respecting lost luggage or parcels arranged by clearing house	150
Extent of transactions settled by agency of clearing house	150
Number of communications made daily from central clearing house to stations	150
Number of monthly accounts furnished to companies	150
Clearing house statistics for year ending June, 1849	151
Principle of clearing house admits of more extensive application	151
Interchange limited to vehicles of transport	151
Nothing to prevent same interchange of locomotive power	151
Clearing house may ultimately grow into establishment for maintenance of general locomotion and carrying stock for all railways	151
Nothing to limit operation of clearing house to United Kingdom	152
Same reciprocal conveniences as to traffic booked through might be extended to entire continent of Europe	152

CHAPTER X.

PASSENGER TRAFFIC.

Movement of passenger traffic expressed by mileage	152
Mileage easily calculated from records of booking office	152
Tabular analysis of the movement of passengers on the railways of the United Kingdom during the six years and a half terminating December 31, 1848	153
Mode of ascertaining average distance traveled by each passenger booked in the successive periods	154
Mode of determining average number of passengers booked per day	154
Tabular analysis of the daily mileage distance traveled and numbers booked on the railways of the United Kingdom	154
Average distances traveled much smaller than might have been supposed	155
Through traffic produces little effect	157
Passengers generally travel short distances	157
Tabular analysis of the passenger traffic of the railways of the United Kingdom, during the twelve months which terminated on June 30, 1847	158
Tabular analysis of the proportion of business supplied to the railways of the United Kingdom by the several classes of passengers respectively, during the seven years ending June 30, 1849	159
Second and third classes supply chief business of railway	160
Business of stations proportional to number of passengers booked, irrespective of distance	160
Business of the road proportional to mileage, irrespective of number booked	160

CONTENTS.

	Page
Ratio of business supplied to stations by several classes of passengers	160
Causes of augmentation of third class passengers from 1845 to 1847	160
Necessary to classify passengers according to distances	161
Tendency to augmentation in numbers and mileage of lower classes	162
Comparison between railway and stage coach traveling	162
Table showing the rate at which the average daily passenger traffic has augmented on the railways of the United Kingdom during the six years and a half ending December 31, 1848	163
Tabular analysis of the progressive development of the railways of the United Kingdom, and of the movement of passengers upon them during the seven years ending June 30, 1849	166
Increase of passenger traffic has not kept pace with increase of railways	166
Tabular analysis of the passenger traffic per mile of the railways during 1846, 7	167
Tabular comparison of the annual rates of increase of the railways in operation, the total traffic in passengers, and the average traffic per mile of railway	167
Cause of decreased traffic per mile	168
Mode of ascertaining the average load of each carriage	168
Estimate of Captain Huish	168
Average on some French and Belgian railways	169
Estimate of carriages on English railways	169
To estimate the necessary carrying stock of railways	170
Table showing the average number of passengers of each class carried by each passenger train on the Belgian and North of France railways	171
Tabular analysis showing the relation between the movement of the engines and the movement of the passengers on the Northwestern, Great Western, and London, Brighton, and South Coast Railways	172
Average composition of trains	173
To compute average load of horse boxes and carriage trucks	174
Advantages of frequency of departure	174
Departures from London stations	175
Expedition depends more on few stoppages than speed	175
Reflections on the enormous speed of locomotion on railways	176
Tabular analysis of the movement of the passenger traffic on the principal lines of railway diverging from London, showing the average speed, stoppages, &c., of each class of trains	177
Damage to railway and stock by extreme speeds	179
Danger of express trains	180
Necessity of checking tendency of public to demand excessive speed	181

CHAPTER XI.

GOODS TRAFFIC.

Importance of goods traffic	182
Subject to more difficult conditions than passenger traffic	182
Graduations of tariff	182
Data necessary for complete analysis of goods business	183
Tabular analysis of the quantity of goods and live stock traffic on the railways of the United Kingdom for twelve months ending June 30, 1847	184
Tabular analysis of the daily traffic in goods, and of the distance carried on the railways of the United Kingdom for twelve months ending June 30 1847	184

CONTENTS. xiii

Page

Tabular analysis of the average distances which each ton of goods was transported on the railways of the United Kingdom during twelve months ending June 30, 1847 185
Tabular analysis of the goods traffic on the railways of the United Kingdom during the six years and a half ending December 31, 1848 186
Table showing the comparative rates at which the average daily traffic in passengers and goods has augmented on the railways of the United Kingdom during the six years and a half ending December 31, 1848 186
Striking results of this table... 186
Captain Huish's estimate of loads of goods wagons 187
Tabular analysis showing the total daily mileage of the goods wagons, and of the goods engines of the English railways for six years and a half ending December 31, 1848.. 187
Estimate of equivalent business by goods wagons on common roads............. 188
Tabular comparison of the progressive development of the railways of the United Kingdom and of the movement of goods upon them during the six years and a half ending December 31, 1848 188
Increase of goods greater than passengers...................................... 189
Tabular analysis showing the average daily mileage of tons of goods, and the average number of tons carried daily per mile, on the railways of the United Kingdom during the twelve months ending June 30, 1847 190
Numerical estimate of men and horses employed by Northwestern 190

CHAPTER XII.

THE EXPENSES.

Introduction.. 191
Analysis of the past expenses of a railway has two objects—retrospective and prospective 194
Considered prospectively, supplies grounds of estimate of future expenses and basis of future tariff 194
Tariff may increase receipts, and yet be unjust and disadvantageous 195
Profits should separately be made on each class of objects 195
Past expenses should be classified, and each branch dissected 195
Cost of transport of each object should be known........ 195
Such cost supplies data for ameliorations 196
Belpaire's investigation of Belgian railways 197
Jullien and Teisserenc on French railways 197
To ascertain how much of expenses should be debited to each object of traffic ... 198
Details of expenses included under direction and management.................. 201
Expense of direction and management on Belgian railways in 1844 201
Charge per mile on each vehicle... 202
Expenses of direction and management of Northwestern Railway................ 202
Their distribution among vehicles of transport................................. 202
Comparison of these expenses on Belgian and Northwestern Railways.......... 203
To estimate cost of direction of a projected railway............................. 203
Estimating by length of line a fallacy... 203
Expenses of way and works classified 204
Portions of expenses of repairs, of wear produced by time and weather, and by other agencies 204

CONTENTS.

	Page
May be shared among carrying stock	205
Example from Belgian railways	205
These expenses augment for several years after a railway opened	206
Cause of this	206
Correct estimate of expenses of maintenance can only be obtained after road permanently consolidated	206
Expenses of maintenance of Northwestern	206
Compared with those of Belgian railways	207
Annual reserve fund	207
Experiments to determine expenses made on Belgian railways	207
Formula by which expense of wear of one ton passing over road may be ascertained	209
Example from Belgian railways	209
Expenses of maintenance of road resolved into four items	210
To what accounts chargeable	211
Expenses of locomotive power classified	211
To be brought to accounts of carrying expenses, traffic, and mileage of engines	212
Portion of expenses chargeable to each class of engines	213
Mode of finding charge per mile on each vehicle drawn	213
Another mode by which cost of locomotive power may be distributed among vehicles	213
Subdivision of expenses primarily chargeable on mileage of engines	214
Formula for finding expenses chargeable per mile for each engine	215
Cost per mile of driving train	215
Approximate calculations made as to some English railways	218
Comparison of results on Belgian and English railways	218
Average cost for locomotive power on English railways in working trains	220
Definition and classification of carrying expenses	220
Table of expenses per mile of each object of traffic, the average number of such objects of traffic carried by each vehicle, and the expenses per vehicle per mile produced by the load on Belgian railways	223
Table showing the share of expenses, the share by equal division among vehicles and the difference of overcharge and undercharge	224
Table showing the actual share of the total expenses of transport, per mile, of each object of traffic, and the amount per cent. of the overcharge or undercharge, by a uniform distribution among the vehicles	224
Recapitulation of various heads of expenses before explained	225
Expense per mile chargeable on each vehicle of passenger train and goods train	226
The expenses of the stations are chargeable on traffic without reference to distance	226
Classification of expenses of stations	226
Some common measure must be selected	228
Difference of expense of each class of objects	229
Estimated expenses of stations on Belgian railways	230
Practical example of application of analysis of general expenses in case of Belgian railways	230
Illustrates the economy of working with full trains	230
Table showing expenses of stations and of transport for each class of objects on Belgian railways	231
Process of computation of this table suggests means of economy of transport	231
Tabular analysis extracted from published reports of thirteen English companies of approximate proportion, in which the working expenses of railways were distributed under the several specified heads	233

CONTENTS. xv

Page
Statement of principal measures tending to increased economy of expenses in working railways 232

CHAPTER XIII.

RECEIPTS—TARIFFS—PROFITS.

Relation of receipts to services... 235
Tabular analysis of the revenue arising from the passenger traffic on the railways of the United Kingdom during the six years and a half ending December 31, 1846 235
Tabular analysis of the proportions in which each class of passengers contributed to every £100 of gross revenue in the six years and a half ending December 31, 1848 237
Increase of inferior classes of passengers 237
Tabular analysis of the revenue proceeding from the passenger traffic of the railways of the United Kingdom during the twelve months ending June 30, 1847 238
Table subject to correction owing to through passengers....................... 239
Statement of the gross receipts proceeding from merchandise, cattle, carriages, parcels, mails, &c., on the railways of the United Kingdom during the six years and a half ending Dec. 31, 1848 239
First projectors of railways contemplated traffic in merchandise exclusively..... 239
Tabular analysis of the receipts produced from the traffic in merchandise on the railways of the United Kingdom during the twelve months ending June 30, 1847 240
Table showing the total receipts for passengers and goods on the British railways during six years and a half ending Dec. 31, 1848........................... 240
Share per cent. of gross revenue contributed by goods traffic 241
Recent railway returns supply no data to ascertain proportion of revenue from different classes of traffic 241
Tabular analysis, deduced from reports of 1847, showing approximate proportion in which the gross revenue proceeding from railways of the United Kingdom arose from certain classes of traffic during twelve months ending June, 1847... 241
No data for exhibiting relations between receipts, expenses, and profits on English railways 241
Gross receipts on all the railways collectively do not appear to have ever amounted to 8 per cent. on capital 242
Table, calculated on hypothesis, showing the proportion of the receipts on the railways of the United Kingdom to their length, to the movement of the traffic upon them, and to the capital expended on them 243
Tabular analysis showing the proportion which the increase of receipts has borne to the increase of railways open during the six years and a half ending Dec. 31, 1848 244
Goods and third class passengers supply a more steady revenue than the other classes 245
No data to exhibit analysis of receipts, expenses, and profits on English railways 245
Tabular classification of the receipts, expenses, and profits of the Belgian railways during the year 1844... 246
Chief financial object to render ratio of gross receipts to expenses as great as possible 247
Elements on which gross receipts depend... 247

CONTENTS.

	Page
Problem for solution to investigate manner in which quantity of traffic and distance of transport can be influenced by tariff	247
Diagram illustrating the relation between the variations of tariff and receipts	249
Problem railway manager has to solve—discovery of the point at which net profits are a maximum	250
But involves the necessity of having regard to the expenses	250
Of what the gross expenses consist	250
Relations of receipts and expenses considered and illustrated by diagram	250
The point of maximum receipts not the point of maximum profits	252
To determine point of maximum profits, necessary to express arithmetical relation between tariff and traffic	252
Different on every railway, and only to be determined by tentative means	252
Practical illustrations of the principles proposed, and examples	253
Table showing the cost of transport per mile, the expenses per ton independent of distance, the tariff per ton per mile, the average distance carried, the total receipts and expenses per ton booked, and the total expenses per ton per mile	256
If average distance of transport doubled a tariff, 50 per cent. less would yield same profit	256
Proportional expenses could be diminished by reduction of tariff	257
Rate of charge per mile on traffic liable to variation	257
An important question in railway economy	257
Advantage to railways from graduated tariff favoring transport to greater distances	258
Table showing rates at which expenses of transport per mile are decreased corresponding to increase of distance	259
Tariff graduated on principle of diminishing as distance increases, source of largely augmented profits	259
Great encouragement on Belgian railways to secure complete loads	261
Difficulties in case of passenger traffic	261
May be partially obviated by careful classification of passengers in carriages, and by proper distribution of carrying stock	261
Table exhibiting relation between mileage of engines and receipts on some English and foreign railways	262
Average receipts per engine on English railways 7s. per mile	263
Mode of diminishing expense in goods and passenger traffic	263
Table exhibiting proportion which receipts have borne to capital of railways of the United Kingdom, during 6½ years, ending December, 1848	264

CHAPTER XIV.

ACCIDENTS ON RAILWAYS.

Chances of accident	266
From causes beyond the control of sufferer	266
Agents and servants of railways more exposed to accident	266
Analysis of railway accidents for two years ending December, 1848	267
Number of accidents to passengers from causes beyond their own control	269
Amount of risk to which railway passengers expose agents of transport	269
Number of accidents to railway servants from causes beyond their own control, in two years ending with 1848, fatal to life and resulting in personal injury	269
Number of passengers who must travel one mile to cause the death or injury of a railway servant	271

CONTENTS. xvii

	Page
Table showing the number of chances to one against accidents producing loss of life or bodily injury to a railway passenger in traveling distances from 10 miles to 10,000 miles; and also the chances against his being the cause of loss of life or bodily injury to a railway servant in such a journey	271
Accidents on foreign railways	272
On Belgian railways	272
Ratio of risks on Belgian and English lines	272
Accidents on French railways	272
Contrasted with accidents by stage coaches in and near Paris	272
Frequent departures, great expedition, and numerous stoppages create danger of collision	274
Liability to collision with express trains	275
Accidents by escaping rails	275
Neglect of points and switches	275
Analytical table of proportion of causes of accident in 100 cases	276
Number of brakes	276
Accident near Wolverton in 1847	276
Rule proposed by the Board of Trade	277
Similar rule in France	277
Greater number of brakes necessary with fast trains	277
Danger of bringing train to rest too suddenly	277
Danger of reversing action of engine	277
Fog signals	278
Consequences of collision aggravated by manner of connecting vehicles	278
Derailment of carriages	279
Necessity of adopting means of watching train	280
Proposals of Great Western and Northwestern	280
Investigation of circumstances producing accidents arising from imprudence or want of vigilance or care	282
Instances from reports of railway commissioners	282
Analysis of 100 accidents produced by imprudence of passengers	282
Precautions against accidents	283
PLAIN RULES FOR RAILWAY TRAVELERS TO AVOID ACCIDENTS	284

CHAPTER XV.

ELECTRIC TELEGRAPH.

Electric Telegraph suggested in early part of present century	296
Only within twenty-five years invention reduced to practice	296
Electric effects now used as signals	297
In what manner signals may be multiplied so as to indicate letters, &c.	300
Principle of American telegraph explained	302
By this system correspondence may be kept secret	305
Mode of forwarding message and receiving answer	306
Charge for transmission	306
Intelligence of the morning received by 8 A.M. in the country	307
Modes of constructing wires	307
Extent of electric communication in England and America	308
East India Company propose to lay down 10,000 miles	308
Cost of construction in England and America	308

xviii   CONTENTS.

CHAPTER XVI.

INLAND TRANSPORT IN THE UNITED STATES.

	Page
Natural apparatus of internal communication in United States	308
Canal navigation	309
Erie Canal	310
Extent of canals	311
Total cost, and cost per mile	311
Extent of canals as compared with population	311
River and coast navigation in United States	311
Steam navigation on Hudson	312
Table of nine Hudson steamers recently built	315
Explosions on eastern rivers rare	317
Description of paddle-boards and mode of working steam in steamers of eastern rivers	317
Increased dimension of vessels attended with increased economy	318
Resistance not increased by increased length	319
Fares reduced with increased size of vessels	319
Form and structure of Hudson steamers	320
Steam navigation of other American rivers	323
Mississippi steamboats	323
Ericsson's propellers	325
Table of sea-going American steamers recently built	326
Railway system introduced	327
Principally in Atlantic States	327
Description of lines constructed, in progress, and projected	328
Management of steam ferries	331
Curves of small radius and gradients of rapid acclivity adopted	335
Great economy in constructing and working railways	335
Ordinary speed	336
Railway carriages described	337
Mode of moving vehicles through curves	338
Proportion of dead to profitable weight	338
Railways carried to centre of cities	338
Mode of turning corners of streets	339
Tabular report of the extent of the lines completed and under traffic in June, 1849; the length of lines projected but not completed; the cost of construction and plant, where such particulars can be ascertained; the last dividends, and the average prices of shares	339
Tabular analysis of the movement of the traffic on twenty-eight principal railways in the States of New England and New York in 1847	343
Proportion of railways to population	345
Proportion in United Kingdom	345
Greater in United States than the United Kingdom	345
Basis of comparison should be capital expended	345
Effects of easy means of communication in United States	346
Passengers not classed on American railways	346
Small transport of goods on American railways	347
Means of obtaining act for railway	348
State generally offers inducements to companies	348

CONTENTS.   xix

CHAPTER XVII.

BELGIAN RAILWAYS.

	Page
History of their construction	349
Constructed at national expense	351
Tabular statement of the progressive increase of the commerce of Belgium during ten years ending December 31, 1845	351
Value of imports and exports at Antwerp	351
Increase in production of coal	354
And in other branches of commerce	352
Character of the country as regards construction of railways	352
High gradients and curves of small radius sometimes adopted	353
Railways pass roads on level, where practicable	353
Cause of the expedition of their construction	353
Cost of construction and stock	353
Tabular analysis of the receipts, expenses, and profits arising from the traffic carried on the Belgian railways during the seven years ending December 31, 1847	354
Synopsis of the movement on the Belgian railways, computed from official documents, during the four years ending December 31, 1847	355
Table showing the average amount of traffic carried daily over each mile of the Belgian railways during the four years ending December 31, 1847	358
Diagram of local variation of traffic	359
Diagram of variation of daily traffic with change of seasons	360
Table showing the number of each class of passengers in every 100 booked, the share of each class in every 100 miles traveled, and the share contributed by each class to every £100 receipts on the Belgian railways during the four years ending December 31, 1847	361
Tabular analysis of the traffic on the Belgian railways, classified according to the distances over which the objects of transport were severally carried, showing the proportion of 1000 objects booked of each class which was carried over each specified distance, and also showing the proportion per 1000 of the mileage of each class assignable to each specified distance	361
Table showing the share of every £100 of gross revenue contributed by each class of traffic on the Belgian railways, during the four years ending December 31, 1847	363
Analysis of the proportion in which the working expenses of the Belgian railways were distributed, under the specified heads, in the four years ending 1847	363
Synopsis of the proportion between the receipts, expenses, and profits, and the length of line worked, the movement of the trains, and the amount of capital on the Belgian railways during the seven years ending December 31, 1847	364
Tabular analysis of the movement of the passenger traffic on the principal Belgian lines of railway, showing the average speed, stoppages, &c. of each class of trains	365
Railways completed and in progress, by companies	364
Estimated cost of them	367

CHAPTER XVIII.

FRENCH RAILWAYS.

	Page
Introduction of passenger railways into France by M. Emile Pereire	367
Commission appointed by Chambers to prepare project of law for railways—concession to Paris and Orleans Company—concession of line from Paris to Rouen—law of 11 June, 1842	368
Railways contemplated by this law	370
Railways constructed, in progress, and projected	374
Synopsis of the length, and cost of construction of fifteen of the principal French railways	376
Capital required for French railways	377
Railway companies tenants of the State	377
State executed principal portion of works	377
Mode of offering leases to public competition	377
Locomotive and carrying stock	378
Tabular synopsis of the average daily movement of the locomotive stock of the North of France Railway during 1848	379
Tabular synopsis of the average daily movement of the carrying stock on the North of France Railway during 1848	379
Tabular synopsis of the average daily movement of the passenger traffic, and the revenue proceeding from it on the principal French railways during 1848	380
Table showing the proportion of business supplied to the principal French railways by the several classes of passengers, and the proportion in which they contributed to the receipts	382
Tabular analysis of the daily movement and daily average receipts of the passenger traffic on ten of the principal French railways for 1848	383
Table showing the share of every £100 of gross revenue contributed by each class of traffic on four of the principal French railways	384
Tabular analysis of the movement of the goods traffic, and the receipts proceeding from it, on some of the principal French railways	384
Tabular analysis of the total average daily receipts, expenses, and profits on the principal French railways during 1848, showing the proportion due to passengers and goods	385
Tabular analysis of the proportion of the receipts, expenses, and profits on the French railways chargeable per mile run by the trains per mile of the lines worked, and per cent. of the capital expended	385
Tabular analysis of the movement of the passenger traffic on the French lines of railway, showing the average speed, stoppage, &c., of each class of trains	386

CHAPTER XIX.

GERMAN RAILWAYS.

German railways completed, in progress, and projected	387
Table showing the progress of the railways in the Germanic States during the five years ending December 31, 1849	392
Table showing the railways of the Germanic States, distinguishing those which were in operation, those which were in progress, and those which were projected but not commenced in 1849	393

CONTENTS. xxi

	Page
Table showing the proportions in which the German railways on January 1, 1847, were distributed among the several states	395
Some railways constructed by Government, some by companies	395
Prussian Government has not interfered with railways	396
But has reserved a power of redemption	396
Railways have been constructed with view to economy	396
Curves of short radius admitted	396
Table showing the prevailing gradients and curves on the principal railways of the Germanic States, as well as the exceptional gradients of steeper acclivities, the exceptional curves of shorter radius where they occur	397
No difficulty in working lines with exceptional gradients and curves	398
Self-acting planes adopted	398
Mode of working traffic on them	398
Narrow gauge generally adopted	399
Form and weight of rails	399
Table of details of construction of principal German lines	400
Table showing the estimated cost of construction of the railways of the Germanic States to be completed, in progress, and projected	401
Average annual expenditure	401
Causes of low rate of cost of German railways	402
Table showing the average cost of land per acre, and the average wages of earthwork laborers per day on the principal German railways	402
Table showing the cost of construction per running mile of each of the principal German railways, with the share of the total expenses assigned to each head.	403
Traffic small as compared with English and other continental lines	403
Mode of working traffic	403
Three classes of passengers	403
No classification of trains	404
Mixed trains, which generally take goods	404
Table showing the number of trains daily which depart from each of the termini of the principal German railways, distinguishing those which go from terminus to terminus from those which ply to intermediate stations	404
Locomotive engines first supplied by foreign manufacturers	405
But now extensive factories in Germany	405
Table showing the dimensions of the locomotive engines used on the principal German railways	406
Table showing the magnitude and average cost of the vehicles of transport used on the principal German lines	406
Vehicles of transport described	407
Tabular analysis of the average daily traffic in passengers and goods on the German railways during the year 1846	407
Table showing the average distance carried, and the average receipts obtained, per head or per ton per mile, from the passengers and goods transported on the principal German railways during the year 1846	409
Third class a large proportion of passengers	409
Tabular analysis, showing the number of passengers belonging to each class in every 100 booked on sixteen of the principal German railways	410
Average fares	410
Average Tariffs	410
Table showing the average receipts per mile and per cent. of cost of construction on several railways during the four successive years ending December, 1846	411
Gross receipts on 2000 miles of railway in 1845 and 1846	411

CONTENTS.

	Page
Do not exceed 6 per cent. on capital	411
Tabular analysis of the expenses, receipts, and profits on several German railways during the year 1844	412
Tabular analysis showing the receipts, expenses, and profits compared with the length of railway worked and the cost of construction on several German railways during the year 1844	412
Tabular analysis of the movement of the traffic on the principal German railways, showing the average speed, stoppages, &c. of each class of train	413

CHAPTER XX.

RAILWAYS IN RUSSIA, ITALY, AND SPAIN.

Railways in Russia	414
Advantages offered to companies	414
Railway from St. Petersburgh to Moscow constructed by the State	415
Other railways	415
Railways in Italy	415
Railways in Spain	416

CHAPTER XXI.

COMPARISON OF RAILWAY TRANSPORT IN DIFFERENT COUNTRIES.

Comparative progress made in railways in different countries	416
Table showing the population, extent of territory, and extent of railway in operation and in progress, in the several countries of the world where railways have been constructed	417
Comparison of the extent of railways in operation, and the amount of railway capital, with the population and territorial extent of the countries which possess them	418
Remarkable results of this table	418
Comparative view of the movement of the traffic on a portion of the railways in operation in the United Kingdom, the United States, Belgium, France, and the Germanic States	420

CHAPTER XXII.

RELATION OF RAILWAYS TO THE STATE.

Monopolies necessarily consequent on the system of railways	422
Some states have assumed entire construction and working of lines, in others a mixed system prevails	423
In almost all the authority of the State asserted	423
The case of English railway companies peculiar	424
Whence a demand for control met by directors by denial of right of Parliament to interfere	424
This question discussed	425

CONTENTS.   xxiii

	Page
Necessity of control by an independent body admitted by all but railway directors and persons influenced by them	426
And even by some directors	426
Question of the authority from which nomination of such a body should emanate discussed	426
Absurdity of directors and impracticability of shareholders making nomination demonstrated	426
Parliamentary evidence as to usual audit system	427
Board of railway control properly constituted	427
Such a board would represent interests of public at large	428
And must be perfectly independent of directors	428
Objects of control	428
Views of the House of Lords	428
Parliamentary evidence and Lords' report as to question of capital and revenue	430
Powers hitherto conferred on shareholders insufficient to guard against abuses	431
Necessity of ample and unreserved publicity in railway management insisted on	431
By which means public at large would become one great and unquestionable board of control	432
Details necessary in well organized system of railway accounts	433
Most of such details furnished in annual reports of continental railways	435
Advantage of employing a self-acting *counter* to register mileage	436
Necessity of a statistical bureau in each railway administration	437

RAILWAY ECONOMY.

CHAPTER I.

INFLUENCE OF IMPROVED TRANSPORT ON CIVILIZATION.

1. The Art by which the products of labor and thought, and the persons who labor and think, are transferred from place to place, is, more than any other, essential to social advancement. Without it no other art can progress. A people who does not possess it can not be said to have emerged from barbarism. A people who has not made some advances in it can not yet have risen above a low state of civilization. Nevertheless, this art has been, of all others, the latest in attaining a state of perfection, so late, indeed, that the future historian of social progress will record, without any real violation of truth, that its creation is one of the events which have most eminently signalized the present age and generation. For, although transport by land and water was practiced by our forefathers, its condition was so immeasurably below that to which it has been carried in our times, that a more adequate idea of its actual state will be conveyed by calling it a new art, than by describing it as an improvement on the old one.

But if human invention have been late in directing its powers to this object, it must be admitted to have nobly compensated for the tardiness of its action by the incomparable rapidity of advancement it has produced, when once they have been brought into play. Within an hundred years more has been accomplished in facilitating and expediting intercommunication than was effected from the creation of the world to the middle of the last century. This statement may, perhaps, appear strained and exaggerated, but it will bear the test of examination.

The geographical conditions of the world, the distribution of the people who inhabit it, and the exclusive appropriation of its natural productions destined for their use, to the various countries of which it consists, have imposed on mankind the necessity of intercommunication and commerce. Commerce is nothing more than the interchange of the productions of industry between people and people. Such interchange presupposes the existence of the art of transport by land and water. In proportion to the perfection of this art will be the extent of commerce.

A people incapable of communicating with others must subsist exclusively upon the productions of its own labor and its own soil. But nature has given us desires after the productions of other soils and other climates. Besides this, the productions of each particular soil or country are obtainable in superfluity. They are infinitely more in quantity than the people by whom and amid whom they are produced have need of; while other and distant peoples are in a like situation, having a superfluity of some products and an insufficiency or a total absence of others. The people of South Carolina and Georgia have a superfluity of cotton, the people of the West India Islands have a superfluity of coffee and tobacco, the people of Louisiana have a superfluity of sugar, the people who inhabit the vast valley of the Upper Mississippi and Missouri have a superfluity of corn and cattle, the people of civilized Europe have a superfluity of the products of mechanical labor, those of France have a superfluity of silk goods, those of England of manufactured cotton, porcelain, and hardware. Each of these various peoples is able and willing to supply the others with those productions in which themselves abound, and to receive in exchange those of which they stand in need, and which abound elsewhere.

But, to accomplish such interchanges, means of transport must be provided, and this transport must be sufficiently cheap, speedy, safe, and regular, to enable these several productions to arrive with their consumers, and be delivered on such terms and conditions as will be compatible with the ability of the consumer to purchase them.

Among the advantages which attend improved means of transport, one of the most prominent is that of lowering the price of all commodities whatever in the market of consumption, and thereby stimulating production. The price paid for an article by its consumer consists of two elements: 1st, the price paid for the article to its producer at the place of its production; and,

2dly, the expense of conveying it from that place to the consumer. In this latter element is included the cost of its transport and the commercial expenses connected with such transport. These last include a variety of items which enter largely into the price of the commodity, such as the cost of the transport, properly so called, the interest on the price paid to the producer proportionate to the time which elapses before it reaches the consumer, the insurance against damage or loss during the transport. This insurance must be paid directly or indirectly by the consumer. If it be not effected by those who convey the commodity to the consumer, the value of the goods which may be lost or damaged in the transport will necessarily be charged in the price of those which arrive safe. In either case the consumer pays the insurance. There are also the charges for storage, packing, transhipment, and a variety of other commercial details, the total of which forms a large proportion of the ultimate price paid by the consumer.

In many cases, these expenses incidental to transport amount to considerably more than half the real price of the article; in some they amount to three-fourths or four-fifths, or even a larger proportion.

Let us take the example of raw cotton produced on the plains of South Carolina or Georgia. This article is packed in bales by the producer at the place of production. These are then transported to Charleston or Savannah, whence they are exported to Liverpool. Arriving at Liverpool, they are transferred upon the railway, by which they are transported to Manchester, Stockport, Preston, or some other seat of manufacture. The raw material is there taken by the manufacturer, spun into thread, woven into cloth, bleached and printed, glazed, and finished for the consumers. It is then repacked, and again placed on the railway and transported once more to Liverpool, when it is re-embarked for Charleston and Savannah, for example. Arriving there, it is again placed on a railway or in a steam-boat, and is transported to the interior of the country, and finally returns to the very place at which it originally grew, and is repurchased by its own producer. Without going into arithmetical details, it will be abundantly apparent how large a proportion of the price thus paid for the manufactured article is to be placed to the account of the transport and commercial expenses. The article has made the circuit of almost half the globe before it has found its way back in its manufactured state.

The products of agricultural labor have, in general, great

bulk with proportionately small value. The cost of transport has consequently a great influence upon the price of these in the market of consumption. Unless, therefore, this transport can be effected with considerable economy, these products must be consumed on the spot where they are produced.

In the case of many animal and vegetable productions of agriculture, speed of transport is as essential as cheapness, for they will deteriorate and be destroyed by the operation of time alone. Without great perfection, therefore, in the art of transport, objects of this class must necessarily be consumed in the immediate neighborhood of the place where they are raised. Such are, for example, the products of the dairy, the farm-yard, and the garden.

In countries where transport is dear and slow, there consequently arises great disadvantage, not only to the rural, but also to the urban population. While the class of articles just referred to are at a ruinously low price in the rural districts, they are at a ruinously high price in the cities and larger class of towns. In the country, where they exist in superfluity, they fetch comparatively nothing: in the towns, where the supply is immeasurably below the demand, they can only be enjoyed by the affluent.

But if sufficiently cheap and rapid means of transport be provided, these productions find their way easily to the great centres of population in the towns, and the rural population which produces them receives in exchange innumerable articles of use and luxury of which they were before deprived.

France, one of the most civilized states of Europe, exhibits a deplorable illustration of this. Notwithstanding the fertility of her soil, the number, the industry, and intelligence of her population, the products of every description, animal and vegetable, which abound in her territory, yet, from the absence of sufficiently easy means of intercommunication, these advantages have been hitherto almost annihilated. All these productions, in the place where they are raised, can be obtained at a lower price than in most other countries; and yet, in consequence of the cost of transport, they would attain, if brought to the place where they are in demand, a price which would amount to a prohibition on their consumption. From this cause the industry of France has long been to a great extent paralyzed.

In some cases the price of an article at the place of consumption consists exclusively of the cost of transport. An article has frequently no value in the place where it is found, which nevertheless would have a considerable value transported elsewhere. Numerous instances of this will occur in the case of manures used in agriculture. Every reduction, therefore, which can be made in the cost of the transport of these, will tend in a still greater proportion to lower their price to those who use them.

Cases even occur in which the cost of transport is actually greater than the price paid for an article by the consumer. This, which would seem a paradox, is nevertheless easily explained. An article in a given place may be a nuisance, and its possessor may be willing to pay something for its removal. This article, however, transported to another place, may become eminently useful, and even be the means of stimulating profitable production. The cleansing the common sewers of a city affords a striking example of this. The filth and offal which are removed are a nuisance where they exist, and may even be the cause of pestilence and death. Transported, however, to the fields of the agriculturalist, they become the instruments of increased fertility. Cases may be cited where the whole cost of transport will be more than covered by the sum paid for the removal of the nuisance.*

Every improvement in the art of transport having a tendency to diminish cost, and augment speed and safety, operates in a variety of ways to stimulate consumption and production, and thereby advance national wealth and prosperity. When the price of an article in the market of consumption is reduced by this cause, the demand for it is increased: 1st, by enabling former consumers to use it more freely and largely; and, 2dly, by placing it within the reach of other classes of consumers who were before compelled to abstain from it by its dearness. The increase of consumption from this cause is generally in a larger ratio than the diminution of price. The number of consumers able and willing to pay one shilling for any proposed article is much more than twice the number who are able and willing to pay two shillings for the same article.

But consumption is also augmented in another way by this diminution of price. The saving effected by consumers who, before the reduction, purchased at the higher price, will now be appropriated to the purchase of other articles of use or enjoyment, and thus other branches of industry are stimulated.

* In Aberdeen the streets are swept every day, at an annual cost of £1400, and the refuse brings in £2000 a year. In Perth the scavenging costs £1300 per annum, and the manure sells for £1730.

The improvements which cheapen transport, necessarily including the expenditure of less labor in effecting it, might seem, at first view, to be attended with injury to the industry employed in the business of transport itself, by throwing out of occupation that portion of labor rendered superfluous by the improvement. But experience shows the result to be the reverse. The diminished cost of transport invariably augments the amount of commerce transacted, and in a much larger ratio than the reduction of cost; so that, in fact, although a less amount of labor is employed in the transport of a given amount of commodities than before, a much larger quantity of labor is necessary by reason of the vast increase of commodities transmitted. The history of the arts supplies innumerable examples of this. When railways were first brought into operation it was declared, by the opponents of this great improvement (for it had opponents, and violent ones), that not only would an immense amount of human industry connected with the business of land carriage be utterly thrown out of employment, but also that a great quantity of horses would be rendered useless. Experience was not long in supplying a striking proof of the fallacy of this prevision.

The moment the first great line of railway was brought into operation between Liverpool and Manchester, the traffic between those places was quadrupled, and it is now well known that the quantity of labor, both human and chevaline, employed in land carriage where railways have been established, has been increased in a vast proportion, instead of being diminished.

In 1846 there were seventy-three stage-coaches or lines of omnibus employed in the transport of passengers to and from the several stations of the North of France Railway, which supplied 176 arrivals and departures, had 5776 places for passengers, and employed daily 979 horses. In the six months ending 31st December, 1846, these coaches transported 486,948 passengers.

Improvements in transport which augment the speed, without injuriously increasing the expense or diminishing the safety, are attended with effects similar to those which follow from cheapness.

A part of the cost of transport consists of the interest on the cost of production chargeable for the time elapsed between the departure of the article from the producer and its delivery to the consumer. This element of price is clearly diminished in the exact proportion to the increased speed of transport.

But increased speed of transport also operates beneficially on commerce in another way. Numerous classes of articles of production become deteriorated by time, and many are absolutely destroyed, if not consumed within a certain time. It is evident that such articles admit of transport only when they can reach the consumer in a sufficiently sound state for use ; various classes of articles of food come under this condition.

While the Houses of Parliament were occupied with the numerous railway acts which had been brought before them, a great mass of evidence was produced illustrating the advantages which both producer and consumer would obtain by the increased cheapness and expedition of transport which railways would supply. It was shown that the difficulties attending transport by common roads affected, in an injurious manner, the grazier who supplied the markets with veal and lamb. Lambs and calves were generally sent by the road; and when too young to leave the mothers for so long a time as the journey required, the producer was obliged to send the ewes or cows with them for at least a part of the way. This also rendered it impossible to send them to market sufficiently young, which it would have been advantageous to do, that the mothers might feed off earlier.

But, independently of this, the animals of every species driven to market on the common roads were proved to suffer so much from the fatigue of the journey, that when they arrived at market their flesh was not in a wholesome state. They were often driven till their feet were sore. Sheep frequently had their feet literally worn off, and were obliged to be sold on the road for what they would fetch. Extensive graziers declared that, in such cases, they would be gainers by a safe and expeditious transport for the animals, " even though it cost double the price paid to the drovers."

Butchers engaged in large business in London proved that the cattle driven to that market from considerable distances sustained so much injury that their value was considerably lessened, owing to the inferior quality of the meat, arising from the animal being slaughtered in a diseased state; that the animal, being fatigued and overdriven, " became feverish, his looks became not so good, and he lost weight by the length of the journey and the fatigue."

It was shown further, that even steam-vessels, when they could be resorted to, did not altogether remove this objection. Cattle arriving from Scotland in steam-vessels are found in

London to be in an unnatural state; "they seem stupefied, and in a state of suffering from fatigue."

It is not merely the fatigue of traveling which injures the animal, but also the absence from its accustomed pasture. The injury from this cause is more or less, under different circumstances, but always considerable: in order to obviate this, a large portion of the meat supplied to the London market was slaughtered in the country, and came in this state, in winter, from distances round London to the extent of one hundred miles. In warm weather a large quantity of it was spoiled. The transport of calves and lambs from a distance greater than thirty miles is altogether impracticable by common roads, and even from that distance is attended with difficulty and injury.

To convey these and other live cattle from a great distance, not only speed but evenness of motion is indispensable. Now these two requisites can not be combined by any other means than the application of steam-engines upon a railroad.

The whole of the evidence showed that the supply of animal food to the metropolis was not only defective in quantity, but of unwholesome quality—comparatively, at least, with what it might be, if the tract from which it could be supplied were rendered more extensive.

But, forcibly as the evidence bore on this species of agricultural produce, it was still stronger respecting the produce of the dairy and the garden. Milk, cream, and fresh butter, vegetables of every denomination, and certain descriptions of fruit, are usually supplied exclusively from a narrow annulus of soil which circumscribes the skirts of great cities. Every artificial expedient is resorted to, in order to extort from this limited portion of land the necessary supplies for the population. The milk is of a quality so artificial, that we know not whether, in strict propriety of language, the name milk can be at all applied to it. The animals that yield it are fed, not upon wholesome and natural pasturage, but, in a great degree, on grain and similar articles. It will not be supposed that the milk which they yield is identical in wholesome and nutritious qualities with the article which could be supplied if a tract of land, of sufficient extent for the pasturage of cattle, was made subservient to the wants of such cities. Add to this that, inferior as must be under such circumstances the quality of the milk, there exists the strongest temptations to the seller who retails it, to adulterate it still further before it finds its way to the table of the consumer.

Since the introduction of transport by railways, we see attached to the fast trains, morning and afternoon, numerous wagons loaded with tier over tier of milk-cans for the supply of the metropolitan population. Milk is thus brought from pastures at great distances from the cities where it is consumed. In Paris the benefits of this have been very conspicuous.

The benefits which would accrue to farmers and landlords, as well as to the inhabitants of towns, by carrying extensive lines of railroad through populous districts, connecting them with those places from which supplies of food and other necessaries might be obtained, are always considerable. The factitious value which tracts of land immediately surrounding the metropolis and large towns acquire from the proximity of the markets, is thus modified, and a portion of their advantages transferred to the more remote districts; thus equalizing the value of agricultural property, and rendering it, in a great measure, independent of local circumstances. The profit of the farmer and the rent of the landlord are augmented by the reduced cost of transport, while the price paid by the customer is diminished; the advantages of centralization are realized without incurring the inconvenience of crowding together masses of people within small spaces, and the whole face of the country is brought to the condition, and made to share the opportunities of improvement which are afforded by a metropolis and by towns of the larger class.

Steam navigation affords many striking examples of like advantages obtained in the transport of perishable productions.

Pines are now sold in the markets of England which are brought from the West Indies; various sorts of fruit are likewise brought from the countries on the coast of Europe which could not be transported in sailing vessels, as they would not keep during the voyage. Oranges are sent in large quantities from the Havanna to New Orleans and Mobile, in the United States: when they are brought by sailing vessels, a large proportion of the cargo is lost by the destruction and deterioration of the fruit; when sent by steamers, they arrive sound.

The utility of an article often depends on its place. Thus, what is useless at one part of the world will become eminently valuable if transmitted to another. We have already given examples of this in the case of agricultural manures. Others present themselves. Ice, at mid-winter, in Boston, Halifax, or St. John's, has no value; but this ice, properly packed and embarked, is transmitted to the Havanna or Calcutta, where a price is readily obtained for it which pays with profit the cost of the voyage.

Like all the other effects of improved transport, this reacts and produces collateral benefits. The ships thus enabled to go to Calcutta with a cargo which costs nothing and produces a considerable profit, instead of going in ballast, which would be attended with a certain expense, return with cargoes which again become profitable in the port from which they sailed, and which they could not have bought with profit unless aided by the expedient just mentioned.

Important as are improvements in the transport of the products of industry, they are less so than those which facilitate the transport of persons. Here speed becomes of paramount importance. In the case of the products of industry, the time of the transport is represented only by the interest on the cost of production of the article transmitted.

In the case of the transport of persons, the time of transport is represented by the value of the labor of the travelers, and their expenses on the road; and as travelers in general belong to the superior and more intelligent classes, their time is proportionally valuable.

When cheapness can be sufficiently combined with speed, considerable advantage is gained by the operative classes.

The demand for labor in the several great centres of population varies from time to time, sometimes exceeding, and sometimes falling short of the supply. In the latter case, the operative having little other capital save his bodily strength, is reduced to extreme distress, nay, often even to mendicancy.

In the former case, the producer is compelled to pay an excessive rate of wages, which falls disadvantageously on the articles produced, in the shape of an undue increase of price, and thereby checks consumption. But although the equilibrium between supply and demand in the labor market is liable to be thus deranged, it rarely or never happens that it is subject to the same derangement in all the centres of population. Supply is never in excess every where at once, nor is it in all places at once deficient. Improvements in transport which will render traveling cheap, easy, and expeditious, so as to bring it within the means of the thrifty and industrious operative, will enable labor to shift its place and seek those markets in which the demand is greatest. Thus, the places where the supply is in excess will be relieved, and those where the demand is in excess will be supplied.

INFLUENCE OF IMPROVED TRANSPORT.

The extent of soil by which great cities are supplied with perishable articles of food, is necessarily limited by the speed of transport. A ring of country immediately about a great capital, is occupied by market-gardens and other establishments for supplying the vast population collected in the city with their commodities. The width of this ring will be determined by the speed with which the articles in question can be transported. It can not exceed such a breadth as will enable the products raised at its extreme limit to reach the centre in such a time as may be compatible with their fitness for use.

It is evident that any improvement in transport which will double its speed will double the radius of this circle; an improvement which will treble its speed will increase the same radius in a threefold proportion. Now, as the actual area or quantity of soil included within such a radius is augmented, not in the simple ratio of the radius itself, but in the proportion of its square, it follows that a double speed will give a fourfold area of supply, a triple speed a ninefold area of supply, and so on. How great the advantages therefore are, which in this case attend increased speed, are abundantly apparent.

So far as relates to the transport of persons, the advantages of increased speed are equally remarkable. The population of a great capital is condensed into a small compass, and, so to speak, heaped together, by the difficulty and inconvenience of passing over long distances. Hence has arisen the densely populated state of great cities like London and Paris. With easy, cheap, and rapid means of locomotion, this tendency, so adverse to physical enjoyment and injurious to health, is proportionally neutralized. Distances practically diminish in the exact ratio of the speed of personal locomotion. And here the same arithmetical proportion is applicable. If the speed by which persons can be transported from place to place be doubled, the same population can, without inconvenience, be spread over four times the area; if the speed be tripled, it may occupy nine times the area, and so on.

Every one who is acquainted with the present habits of the population of London, and with those which prevailed before the establishment of railways will perceive the practical truth of this observation. It is not now unusual for persons whose place of business is in the centre of the capital, to reside with their families at a distance of from fifteen to twenty miles from that centre. Nevertheless, they are able to arrive at their respective shops, counting-houses, or offices, at an early hour of the morning, and to return without inconvenience to their residence at the usual time in the evening. Hence in all directions round the metropolis in which railways are extended, habitations are multiplied, and a considerable part of the former population of London has been diffused in these quarters. The same will, of course, be applicable to the country which surrounds all other great towns. It is felt at Paris, Brussels, and other capitals of Europe, just in the same proportion in which they are supplied with railway communication.

This principle of diffusion, however, is not confined to the towns only. It extends to an entire country when well intersected by lines of easy, rapid, and cheap communication.

The population, instead of being condensed into masses, is more uniformly diffused; and the extent of the diffusion which may be thus effected, compatibly with the same degree of intercourse, will be, to use an arithmetical phrase, in the direct proportion of the square of the speed of locomotion.

The common average of the speed of diligences in France and other parts of the Continent, is two leagues, or about five miles an hour. The speed of stage-coaches in England, before the establishment of railways, did not average eight miles an hour. According to the principle just explained, it would follow that the same degree of intercourse could be kept up in England in a space of sixty-four square miles, which in France could be maintained only within twenty-five square miles. Since the establishment of railways the average speed upon these lines of communication, on most parts of the Continent and in America, is fifteen miles an hour. By this improvement, so far as it has been carried, as compared with diligences, the area of practical communication, or, what is the same, of the diffusion of the population compatible with a given degree of intercourse, has been augmented in the ratio of the square of five to the square of fifteen; that is, in a ratio of twenty-five to two hundred and twenty-five. In other words the same degree of intercourse can be maintained by means of the present railways within an area of two hundred and twenty-five square miles, as could be previously maintained by diligences within an area of twenty-five square miles.

But in England, where the average speed of railway transit is much greater, this power of diffusion is proportionally increased. Assuming the average speed on English railways at twenty-five miles an hour, which is less than its actual amount, the power of intercommunication thus obtained will bear to that obtained on the continent of Europe where railways are in operation, the ratio of the square of twenty-five to the square of fifteen; that is, of six hundred and twenty-five to two hundred and twenty-five, or of twenty-five to nine.

Thus, the English railways afford the same facilities of communication within an area of twenty-five square miles as is afforded by the continental railways within an area of nine square miles; and thus, by augmenting the speed from fifteen to twenty-five miles an hour, the practical convenience to the public is augmented in the ratio of nine to twenty-five, or very nearly as three to one.

The importance of good internal communications in military affairs has long been acknowledged. By the possession of such means of transport as may enable a body of troops, with their arms and ammunition, to be transported promptly and rapidly from one part of the country to another, the standing army, maintained as well for the purpose of order at home as for the defense of the frontiers, may be diminished in proportion to such facilities.

Instead of maintaining garrisons and posts at points of the country within short distances of each other, it will be sufficient to maintain them at such points that they can, at need, be transported with promptitude to any other point that may be desired. In case of invasion, or any foreign attack on the frontier, by good internal communications, the troops quartered throughout the interior can be rapidly transferred and concentrated upon the point attacked.

If, however, such improvements in the art of transport facilitate the means of maintaining order at home and of defense against a foreign enemy, on the one hand, they also happily, on the other, greatly diminish the probability of a necessity for such expedients. "The natural effect of commerce," says Montesquieu, "is to tend to and consolidate peace." Two nations who trade with each other soon become respectively dependent. If one have an interest to buy, the other has an interest to sell, and a multitude of ties, commercial and social, spring out of their mutual wants.

Nothing facilitates and develops commercial relations so effectually as cheap and rapid means of intercommunication. When, therefore, all nations shall be found more intimately connected with each other by these means, they will inevitably multiply their exchanges, and general commerce will undergo great extension, mutual interest will awaken moral sympathies and will lead to political alliances. After having for ages approached each other only for war, peoples will henceforward visit each other for purposes of amity and intelligence, and old antipathies, national and political, which have so long divided and ruined neighboring states, will speedily vanish.

But if, in spite of this general tendency toward pacific progress and peace, war should occasionally break out, the improved means of intercommunication will aid in bringing it to a prompt close. A single battle will decide the fate of a country, and the longest war will be probably circumscribed within a few months.

The advantages of good means of communication in the diffusion of knowledge, and the increase of civilization by intellectual means, are not less considerable. While the means of intercommunication are slow, difficult, and costly, great cities have a tendency to monopolize intelligence, civilization, and refinement. There genius and talent are naturally attracted, while the rural districts are left in a comparatively rude and almost barbarous state. With easy and rapid means of locomotion, however, the best part of the urban population circulates freely through the country. This interfusion improves and civilizes the rural population. The highest intelligence will be occasionally found, both in public and in private, diffusing knowledge and science in the remotest villages. We can not now take up a London journal without observing announcements of men distinguished in the various branches of knowledge and art, visiting the various towns and villages of the provinces, and delivering there lectures on science, and entertainments and exhibitions in the fine arts. So rapid are the communications, that it is frequently announced that this or that professor or artist will, on Monday evening, deliver a lecture or entertainment in Liverpool, on Tuesday in Manchester, on Wednesday in Preston, on Thursday in Halifax, on Friday in Leeds, and so forth.

Nor is this all. The aspirations of the present generation after the spread of knowledge and the advancement of mind, unsatisfied with a celerity of transmission so rapid by the railway, which literally has the speed of the wind, has provoked from human invention still greater wonders. The Electric Telegraph for the transmission of intelligence, in the most literal sense of the term, annihilates both space and time. The interval which elapses between the transmission of a message from London and its delivery at Edinburgh, provided the line is uninterrupted, is absolutely inappreciable.

This system is now spreading throughout the whole civilized

world. The United States of America are overspread with a net-work of electricity. The President's message delivered at Washington, was transmitted from thence to St. Louis, on the confines of the state of Missouri, a distance of about 1200 miles, in an hour. The news from Europe arriving at Boston by the Cunard steamers, is often transmitted to New Orleans, over almost the entire territory of the United States from north to south, a distance of nearly 2000 miles, in less time than would be necessary to commit it to paper. Even the small delay that now exists arises, not from any imperfection in the instrument of transmission, but merely from the line of electric communication being interrupted from point to point, and transferred from one system of telegraphs to another, at several intermediate stations. After improvements shall remove such delays as these, we shall probably see intelligence conveyed in an instant over a quadrant of the globe.

But if we would seek for a striking illustration of the effects of the rapid transmission of intelligence by the combination of all the various expedients supplied by science to art, it is in the practice of Journalism that we are to look for them, and more especially in the great enterprises of the London newspapers. The proprietors of a single morning journal are able to maintain agencies, for the transmission of intelligence to the central office in London, in all the principal cities of Europe, besides roving correspondents wherever the prevalence of war, revolution, or any other public event exerts a local interest. These various agents or "correspondents" as they are called, not only transmit to the centre of intelligence in London regular dispatches by the mails, but also, on occasion of emergency, by special couriers.

These dispatches are first received by an agent at Dover, by whom they are forwarded to London by a special messenger. But in cases where intelligence arrives of adequate importance, this Dover agent sends it to London, in an abridged form, by the electric telegraph, thus anticipating the detailed dispatches by about three hours. Within two hours of its arrival the intelligence is in the hands of the London public.

That portion of the journal intended for the provinces is sent to press at 3 A. M.; and by the activity of the editors, reporters, and compositors, all of whom work during the night, it includes not only the detailed reports of the Houses of Parliament, which often sit to a late hour in the morning, but also the foreign news received from Dover, as above explained, by electric telegraph.

This earliest impression is printed and delivered to the news-venders, in sufficient time to be dispatched to the provinces by the early railway trains, and it is thus delivered at all the stations along the road.

The part of the impression intended for London circulation is worked off and delivered later.

Thus we see that, by these combinations of enterprise, intellectual and material, the intelligence which arrives in London at 3 A. M., is written, composed, printed, and distributed within a radius of one hundred miles round London, and in the hands of the population before their customary hour of breakfast.

Even before the present improved methods of transport were brought into operation, wonders in this way were effected.

Thus, in some cases where debates of adequate public interest took place in Parliament in the evening, the evening mails (for there were then no other) carried to the provinces the first part of an important speech, reported and printed before the remaining part was spoken. Thus it was related that the commencement of Mr. (since Lord) Brougham's celebrated speech on the reform of the laws was read at tea-tables twenty miles from London before he had pronounced the peroration.

Few of the numerous readers of newspapers have the least idea of the immense commercial, social, and intellectual powers wielded, and benefits conferred, by these daily publications, a large portion of which influence is to be ascribed to the cheapness, promptitude, and rapidity with which they are transmitted from the capital to all parts of the country.

It is commonly estimated, that the average number of copies of the most widely circulating London journal which are daily issued amounts at present to little less than forty thousand. Each of these forty thousand copies, according to common estimation, passes under the eyes, upon an average, of at least ten persons. Thus we have four hundred thousand daily readers of one organ of information and intelligence. But the effects do not end there. These four hundred thousand *readers*, long before the globe completes a revolution on its axis, become four hundred thousand *talkers*, and have vastly more than four hundred thousand *hearers*. Thus they spread more widely by the ear the information, the arguments, and the opinions they have received through the eye. We shall certainly not be overstating the result if we assume, that this influence of a single journal, directly and indirectly, reaches daily a million of persons.

CHAPTER. II.

RETROSPECT OF THE PROGRESS OF TRANSPORT.

IN the first attempts at an interchange of the products of industry, which mark the incipient commerce of a people emerging from barbarism, human labor and the strength of the inferior animals, applied in the most rude and direct manner to transport, are all the means brought into play. The peddler and the pack-horse perform all the operations of interchange which take place in an infant society. Pathways are formed over the natural surface of the ground, in a course more or less direct, between village and village. The beds of streams following, by the laws of physics, the lowest levels, serve as the first indication to the traveler how to avoid steep acclivities, and by deviating from the most direct and shortest course, to obtain his object with a diminished amount of labor.

As industry is stimulated and becomes more productive, invention is brought more largely into play, and these rude expedients are improved. Wheel carriages are invented, but the earliest theatre of their operations is the immediate surface of the soil from which the products of agriculture are raised. They are used to gather and transport these to a place where they may be sheltered and secured.

But to enable wheel carriages to serve as the means of transport between places more or less distant, the former horse-paths are insufficient. A more uniform and level surface, and a harder substratum, become indispensable. In a word, a ROAD, constructed with more or less perfection, is necessary.

These roads, at first extremely rude and inartificial, and rendered barely smooth and hard enough for the little commerce of an infant people, are gradually improved. The carriages, also, which serve as the means of transport undergo like improvement, until, after a series of ages, that astonishing instrument of commerce, the modern road, results, which is carried on an artificial causeway, and reduced, at an enormous expense, to a nearly level surface by means of vast excavations, extensive embankments, bridges, viaducts, tunnels, and other expedients supplied by the skill and ingenuity of the engineer.

Between the pack-horse, used in the first stages of growing commerce, and such a road with its artificial carriages, there is a prodigious distance. The first step, from the pack-horse to the common two-wheel cart, was, in itself, a great advance.

It is calculated that a horse of average force, working for eight or ten hours a day, can not transport on his back more than two hundred weight, and that he can carry this at the rate of only twenty-five miles a day over an average level country. The same horse, working in a two-wheel cart, will carry through the same distance per day twenty hundred weight, exclusive of the weight of the cart. By this simple expedient, therefore, the art of transport was improved in the ratio of one to ten; in other words, the transport which before was effected at the cost of ten pounds, was, with this expedient, reduced to the cost of one pound.

The adoption of expedients for the maintenance of commerce so obvious as roads, would seem to be inevitable among a people who are not actually in a state of barbarism. Nevertheless, we find, that not only was the construction of good roads for commercial purposes of comparatively recent date, but that, even at the present day, a very large portion of that part of the world called civilized is unprovided with them. With the exception of certain parts of Europe, the French colony of Algeria, and the United States, the entire surface of the world is still without this means of intercourse.

It is calculated that, of the entire inhabited part of the globe, roads do not exist in more than *two-sevenths*. The extensive empire of Russia, with the exception of one or two main communications, such as that between Petersburg and Moscow, is without them. In general, the only practicable communications through this vast territory are effected in winter on the surface of the frozen snow by sledges. On the return of summer, when the snow has disappeared, the communications become extremely difficult, slow, and expensive. Spain is scarcely better supplied with roads than Russia, nor do we find much improvement in the practice of transport in Italy. Until recently, Corsica possessed no communications of this sort; horses and mules were the common means of communication and interchange in that island until the French government constructed some roads.

The roads constructed by the Romans and Egyptians will probably be referred to as instances of an early advance in this art. But these great monuments of antiquity, though serving incidentally, to some extent, as means of commerce, were constructed for exclusively military purposes.

The most ancient roads which are recorded in history, are those constructed by order of Semiramis, throughout the extent of her empire. It would seem, however, that the commerce of that day did not find these communications suitable to its objects; for it is certain that, at the epoch at which Tyre and Carthage were signalized for their enterprise, their commerce was almost exclusively carried on by the coasting navigation of the Mediterranean.

Notwithstanding the advanced stage to which civilization had arrived in Greece, the means of internal communication in that country remained in a state of great imperfection. This may in part be explained by the multitude of small states which formed that confederation, by their conflicting interests, and their want of any moral or social sympathies. The common sentiment of nationality slumbered, except when it was awakened by the strong stimulus of foreign attack. The intercourse between one centre of population and another was then very restrained, and although the public ways were placed under the protection of the gods, and the direction of the most considerable men of the respective states, they were suffered to fall into neglect. The exigencies of internal commerce were never sufficiently pressing to excite the people to contribute to the maintenance of good means of intercommunication and exchange.

The earliest roads which were really rendered conducive to the purposes of commerce on any considerable scale, were those constructed by the Phenicians and Carthaginians. To the latter is ascribed, by Isidore, the invention of paved roads.

When imperial Rome attained the meridian of her power, and her empire extended over a large portion of Europe and Asia, colossal enterprises were entered upon for the construction of vast lines of communication, extending over the immensity of her territory. These roads, however, like those of the Egyptians, were constructed without the slightest view to commercial objects. It concerned imperial Rome but little that her provinces should be united by commercial or social interests. What she looked to was to be enabled to convey with celerity her powerful legions, at all times, from one extremity of her dominions to another. With this purpose, she availed herself of her vast resources to construct those military roads intersecting her territory, the remains of which have excited the admiration of succeeding generations.

The first of these great monuments of the enterprise and art of the Roman people, were those so well known by the names of the Via Appia, the Via Aurelia, and the Via Flaminia. Under Julius Cæsar, communications were made by paved roads between the capital of the empire and all the chief towns. During the last African war, a paved road was constructed from Spain, through Gaul, to the Alps. Subsequently similar lines of communication were carried through Savoy, Dauphiné, Provence, through Germany, through a part of Spain, through Gaul, and even to Constantinople.

Asia Minor, Hungary, and Macedonia were overspread with similar lines of communication, which were carried to the mouths of the Danube. Nor was this vast enterprise obstructed by the intervention of seas. The great lines which terminated on the shores of continental Europe were continued at the nearest points of the neighboring islands and continents. Thus Sicily, Corsica, Sardinia, and England, and even Africa and Asia, were intersected and penetrated by roads, forming the continuation of the great European system.

These colossal works were not paths rudely prepared for the action of the feet of horses and the wheels of carriages, by merely removing the natural asperities from the surface of the soil. They were constructed, on the contrary, on principles in some respects as sound and scientific as those which modern engineering has supplied. Where the exigencies of the country required it, forests were felled, mountains excavated, hills leveled, valleys filled up, chasms and rivers bestridden by bridges, and marshes drained, to an extent which would suffer little by comparison with the operations of our great road-makers of modern times.

On the fall of the empire, these means of communication, instead of subserving the purposes of the commerce of the people through whose territory they were carried, were, for the most part, destroyed. When the barbarians conquered Rome, and a multitude of states were formed from its ruins, the victors shut themselves up, and fortified themselves in these several states, as an army does in a citadel; and, far from constructing new roads, they destroyed those which had already existed, as a town threatened with siege breaks those communications by which the enemy may approach it.

From this epoch, through a long series of ages, the nations of Europe, animated only by a spirit of reciprocal antagonism, thought of nothing but war, and entered each other's territories only for the purposes of conflict. The history of the intercommunications of nations during the middle ages is only a history of their wars.

When Europe emerged from this state, and when commerce began to force itself into life, its operations were in a great measure monopolized by Jewish and Lombard merchants, who carried them on subject to the greatest difficulty and danger.

The provincial nobles and lords of the soil, through whose possessions the merchants necessarily passed, in carrying on the internal commerce of the country, were nothing better than highway robbers. They issued with their bands from their castles, and arrested the traveling merchant, stripping him of the goods which he carried for sale.

The sovereigns of France endeavored in vain, by penal enactments, to check this enormous evil. Dagobert I. established a sort of code to regulate the public communications through his dominions, and decreed heavy fines against such provincial lords as might obstruct the freedom of communication, by interrupting or plundering travelers. These decrees, however, remained a dead letter, no adequate power in the state being able to carry them into practical effect.

Under the successors of Charlemagne, this abuse, which it was found impossible to repress, was in some measure recognized and regularized. Tolls of limited amount were allowed to be exacted by the local proprietors from those who passed through the provinces for purposes of trade, on the condition that such travelers and merchants should be otherwise unmolested.

The prevalence of all these vexatious impediments soon rendered intercommunication by land almost impracticable. The roads, such as they were, became accordingly deserted, and were suffered to fall into utter disrepair. During a series of ages, internal communication and internal commerce became almost suspended; a journey even of a few leagues being regarded as a most serious and dangerous undertaking.

The crusades had a favorable influence on the art of transport. The population of Western and Northern Europe became by them acquainted with the productions and arts of the East. New desires were excited, and new wants created. Commerce was thus stimulated, and greater facility of intercourse becoming necessary, governments were forced to adopt expedients for the security of the traveler.

The same difficulties and dangers did not, however, affect

navigation. We find this art developed in a much higher degree than that of internal commerce. Hence arose the disproportionate commercial opulence of maritime people. The British, the Dutch, and the Portuguese rose into immense commercial importance, as well as the Genoese, the Tuscans, and the Venetians.

Even so late as the middle of the seventeenth century, the roads throughout the Continent continued in a condition which rendered traveling almost impracticable.

They are described by writers of this epoch as being absolute sloughs. Madame de Sevigny, writing in 1672, says, that a journey from Paris to Marseilles, which by the common roads of the present day is effected in less than sixty hours,* required a whole month.

Besides the material obstacles opposed to the growth of internal commerce on the Continent by the want of roads in sufficient number, and the miserable state of those which did exist, other impediments were created and difficulties interposed by innumerable fiscal exactions, to which the trader was exposed, not only in passing the confines of different states, but even in going from province to province in the same state, and in passing through almost every town and village. Hence the cost of every commodity was enormously enhanced, even at short distances from the place of its production.

The disorganization of society and the destruction of the institutions of feudalism which followed the French Revolution of 1789, caused some improvement in the means of internal commerce in Europe, and would have caused a much greater development in this instrument of civilization, but for the wars which immediately succeeded that political catastrophe, and which only terminated with the battle of Waterloo.

Indeed Napoleon, conscious of the vast importance of a more complete system of roads, had actually projected one, which he intended to spread over Europe. His fall, however, intercepted the realization of this magnificent design, and the *Simplon* remains as the only monument of his glory in this department of art.

After the re-establishment of peace, the nations of Europe, directing their activity to industry and commerce, soon became impressed with the necessity of effecting a great improvement

---

* The projected railway from Paris to Marseilles is not completed at the time of writing these pages (October, 1849).

in the means of internal communication. Western Europe, accordingly, soon began to be covered with roads and canals. The obstructions arising from fiscal causes, if not removed, were greatly diminished.

The advance made by France, especially, in this department, is deserving of notice. That country possesses at present four or five times the extent of roads which were practicable under the Empire; a sum of nearly four millions sterling was, until lately, expended annually upon the completion and maintenance of these great lines of communication.

The roads of France consist of three classes; the first, until the late revolution, were called *royal roads*, and are now called *national roads*. These are the great arteries of communication carried from one chief town to another throughout the territory, and being used indifferently, or nearly so, by the whole population, are constructed and maintained at the general expense of the nation. The second class are *departmental roads*, or what would be called in England *county roads*. These are chiefly the branches running into the royal roads, by which the local interests of the departments are served, and are accordingly maintained at the expense of the departments. Finally, the third class is called *vicinal roads*, which would correspond to our *parish roads*.

The rate at which these improved communications have contributed to augment the internal commerce and national wealth, may be estimated in some degree from the statistical results which have been published. In 1810, the various stage-coach establishments in Paris transported each day from the capital into the departments, two hundred and twenty passengers, and twenty-one tons of merchandise. Before the establishment of railways, they transported nearly one thousand passengers and forty-five tons of merchandise. Thus the passengers were augmented in a fourfold, and the merchandise in a twofold proportion.

In 1815, the length of roads in operation in France was as follows: there were three thousand leagues of royal roads, and two thousand leagues of departmental roads. In 1829, there were four thousand two hundred and five leagues of royal roads, and three thousand leagues of departmental roads. In 1844, there were eight thousand six hundred and twenty-eight leagues of royal roads, and nine thousand one hundred and forty-six leagues of departmental roads, independently of twelve thousand leagues of vicinal roads. Thus, it appears that between

1815 and 1844, the total length of roads of the first and second classes was augmented from five thousand leagues to nearly eighteen thousand, or in the proportion of three and a half to one.

Although the practice of road making in England attained a certain degree of perfection at a much earlier period than in other parts of Europe, and the united kingdom was overspread with a noble network of internal communications, while continental Europe remained in a comparatively barbarous condition, the art of transport nevertheless, even in England, remained for a long series of ages incalculably behind what would seem to be the commercial wants of the population.

The first English roads of artificial construction were those made by the Romans, while England was a province of that empire. The island was then intersected by two grand trunk roads running at right angles to each other, the one from north to south, and the other from east to west.

These main lines were supplied with various branches, extending in every direction which the conquerors found it expedient to render accessible to their armies.

The Roman road called *Watling Street* commenced from Richborough, in Kent, the ancient Ruterpiac, and, passing through London, was carried in a northwesterly direction to Chester. The road called *Ermine Street* commenced from London, and, passing through Lincoln, was carried thence through Carlisle into Scotland. The road called the *Fosse-way* passed through Bath in a direction N.E., and terminated in the Ermine Street. The road called *Ikenald* extended from Norwich in a southern direction to Dorsetshire.

But these great works, at the date of their construction, exceeded the wants of the population, who, unconscious of their advantage, allowed them to fall into neglect and disrepair. Nor were any new roads in other or better directions constructed. For a succession of ages the little intercourse that was maintained between the various parts of Great Britain was effected almost exclusively by rude footpaths, traversed by pedestrians, or at best by horses.

These were carried over the natural surface of the ground, generally in straight directions, from one place to another. Hills were surmounted, valleys crossed, and rivers forded by these rude agents of transport, in the same manner as the savages and settlers of the backwoods of America or the slopes of the Rocky Mountains now communicate with each other.

The first important attempt made to improve the communications of Great Britain took place in the reign of Charles II. In the sixteenth year of the reign of that monarch was established the first turnpike road where toll was taken, which intersected the counties of Hertford, Cambridge, and Huntingdon. It long remained, however, an isolated line of communication; and it was little more than a century ago that any extensive or effectual attempts were made, of a general character, to construct a good system of roads through the country.

Until the middle of the eighteenth century, most of the merchandise which was conveyed from place to place in Scotland was transported on pack-horses. Oatmeal, coals, turf, and even hay and straw, were carried in this manner through short distances; but when it was necessary to carry merchandise between distant places, a cart was used, a horse not being able to transport on his back a sufficient quantity of goods to pay the cost of the journey.

The time required by the common carriers to complete their journey seems, when compared with our present standard of speed, quite incredible. Thus, it is recorded that the carrier between Selkirk and Edinburgh, a distance of thirty-eight miles, required a fortnight for his journey, going and returning. The road lay chiefly along the bottom of the district called *Galawater*, the bed of the stream, when not flooded, being the ground chosen as the most level and easy to travel on.

In 1678, a contract was made to establish a coach for passengers between Edinburgh and Glasgow, a distance of forty-four miles. This coach was drawn by six horses, and the journey between the two places, to and fro, was completed in six days. Even so recently as the year 1750, the stage-coach from Edinburgh to Glasgow took thirty-six hours to make the journey. In this present year, 1849, the same journey is made, by a route three miles longer, in one hour and a half!

In the year 1763 there was but one stage-coach between Edinburgh and London. This started once a month from each of these cities. It took a fortnight to perform the journey. At the same epoch the journey between London and York required four days.

In 1835 there were seven coaches started daily between London and Edinburgh, which performed the journey in less than forty-eight hours. In this present year, 1849, the same journey is performed by railway in twelve hours!

In 1763, the number of passengers conveyed by the coaches

between London and Edinburgh could not have exceeded about twenty-five *monthly*, and by all means of conveyance whatever did not exceed fifty. In 1835 the coaches alone conveyed between these two capitals about one hundred and forty passengers *daily*, or four thousand monthly. But besides these, several steam-ships, of enormous magnitude, sailed weekly between the two places, supplying all the accommodation and luxury of floating hotels, and completing the voyage at the same rate as the coaches, in less than forty-eight hours.

As these steam-ships conveyed at least as many passengers as the coaches, we may estimate the actual number of passengers transported between the two places monthly at eight thousand. Thus the intercourse between London and Edinburgh in 1835 was one hundred and sixty times greater than in 1763.

At present the intercourse is increased in a much higher ratio, by the improved facility and greater cheapness of railway transport.

Arthur Young, who traveled in Lancashire about the year 1770, has left us in his Tour the following account of the state of the roads at that time. "I know not," he says, "in the whole range of language, terms sufficiently expressive to describe this infernal road. Let me most seriously caution all travelers who may accidentally propose to travel this terrible country to avoid it as they would the devil, for a thousand to one they break their necks or their limbs by overthrows or breakings down. They will here meet with ruts, which I actually measured, four feet deep, and floating with mud, only from a wet summer. What, therefore, must it be after a winter? The only mending it receives is tumbling in some loose stones, which serve no other purpose than jolting a carriage in the most intolerable manner. These are not merely opinions, but facts; for I actually passed three carts broken down in these eighteen miles of execrable memory."

And again he says (speaking of a turnpike road near Warrington, now superseded by the Grand Junction Railway), "This is a paved road, most infamously bad. Any person would imagine the people of the country had made it with a view to immediate destruction! for the breadth is only sufficient for one carriage; consequently it is cut at once into ruts; and you may easily conceive what a break-down, dislocating road, ruts cut through a pavement must be."

Nor was the state of the roads in other parts of the north of England better. He says of a road near Newcastle, now superseded by railway, "A more dreadful road can not be imagined. I was obliged to hire two men at one place to support my chaise from overturning. Let me persuade all travelers to avoid this terrible country, which must either dislocate their bones with broken pavements, or bury them in muddy sand. It is only bad management that can occasion such very miserable roads in a country so abounding with towns, trade, and manufactures."

Now it so happens that the precise ground over which Mr. Young traveled in this manner less than eighty years ago, is at present literally reticulated with railways, upon which tens of thousands of passengers are daily transported, at a speed varying from thirty to fifty miles an hour, in carriages affording no more inconvenience or discomfort than Mr. Young suffered in 1770, when reposing in his drawing-room in his arm-chair.

Until the close of the last century, the internal transport of goods in England was performed by wagon, and was not only intolerably slow, but so expensive as as to exclude every object except manufactured articles, and such as, being of light weight and small bulk in proportion to their value, would allow of a high rate of transport. Thus the charge for carriage by wagon from London to Leeds was at the rate of £13 a ton, being $13\frac{1}{2}d.$ per ton per mile. Between Liverpool and Manchester it was forty shillings a ton, or $15d.$ per ton per mile. Heavy articles, such as coals and other materials, could only be available for commerce where their position favored transport by sea, and, consequently, many of the richest districts of the kingdom remained unproductive, awaiting the tardy advancement of the art of transport. Coals are now carried upon railways at a penny per ton per mile, and, in some places, at even a lower rate. Merchandise, such as that mentioned above, which was transported in 1763 at from $14d.$ to $15d.$ per mile, is now carried at from $3d.$ to $4d.$, while those sorts which are heavier in proportion to their bulk, are transported at $2\frac{1}{2}d.$ per ton per mile.

But this is not all: the wagon transport formerly practiced was limited to a speed which in its most improved state did not exceed twenty-four miles a day, while the present transport by railway is effected at the rate of from twelve to fourteen miles an hour.

CHAPTER III.

THE ORGANIZATION OF A RAILWAY ADMINISTRATION.

The organization of the administrative machinery necessary for the conduct of the practical business of a railway, or a system of railways, brought under a common direction and management, includes the following four principal departments or services, more or less distinct from, and independent of each other. These are —
1st. The service of the way and works.
2d. The service of the draft.
3d. The service of carriage.
4th. The service of the stations.

Each of these departments has its separate staff, machinery, and stock.

The "service of the way and works" consists in the due maintenance and repair of the road structure, including rails, chairs, sleepers, ballasting, drains, the slopes of the embankments and cuttings, and the works of art, such as bridges, tunnels, and viaducts, the gates of level crossings, and, in a word, all that is necessary for the due maintenance of the line in a fit state to bear the rolling stock and traffic which pass over it. For this purpose a staff of superintendents, engineers, artificers, and operatives of various grades and classes, is necessary.

In the "service of draft" is included the entire staff of engineers and operatives employed in the maintenance, repair, management, and working of the locomotive stock, consisting of engines and tenders, with all their accessories, and including the means of cleaning and repairing them—sheds, workshops, tools, &c.—and due means for the supply of water and fuel. In this department is included, also, all the means provided by the establishment for the reproduction of the stock as it is worn.

In the "service of carriage" is comprehended all that is necessary for the proper preservation, management, and repair of the coaches used for the passenger traffic, the horse-boxes, baggage-vans, parcel-vans, and carriage-trucks, with all the accessories necessary for their maintenance, cleaning, and repair, and also all that appertains to the maintenance, cleaning, and repair of the wagons of every description used in the goods department.

The "service of the stations" consists of the staff of clerks, porters, and others, supplied with all the necessary means for the reception, weighing, booking, and embarkation, and for the disembarkation, discharge, and delivery of the passengers, baggage, and goods, of every class and description, which are transported on the road, together with the maintenance and repairs of the buildings in which the stations are established, consisting of booking-offices, baggage and parcel-offices, passengers' waiting-rooms, sheds, warehouses for the reception of goods, and the entire furniture and machinery necessary for the embarkation and disembarkation of passengers, baggage, and goods.

Each of these services is attended with arrangements of more or less complexity and importance, which it is necessary to explain in detail, and to reduce to such order and arithmetical statement as may supply the means of comparing the operations and results of different railways one with another, and the performances of the same railway with itself, during different and successive epochs. We shall, therefore, consider successively each of the above services.

CHAPTER IV.

THE WAY AND WORKS.

The subject of the maintenance of the way and works involves the consideration of different kinds and degrees of wear and tear:

1st. That wear and tear which, taking place at short intervals of time, is repaired and made good annually.

2dly. That wear and tear of the fixed materials which, though not strictly speaking insensible, takes place in a manner which does not admit of annual repair, and which, accumulating from year to year, after a period of greater or less duration, must render necessary the complete reconstruction and reproduction of the materials so worn.

3dly. That wear and tear which, being due to the slow operation of time acting upon the more solid structures, produces an effect altogether insensible when observed through short periods, but which, after a long interval of time, such, for example, as centuries, must necessitate the reconstruction of some or all even of the most solid structures.

These changes may not unaptly be assimilated to the periodical and secular inequalities which take place in the movements of the great bodies of the universe.

The operation of time upon the more massive works of art upon the railway, such as the bridges, tunnels, viaducts, &c., afford examples of what may be called the secular wear and tear. The more rapid and visible deterioration, which is made good by repairs or reconstruction effected at shorter intervals, is analogous to the periodic inequalities.

In the annual repairs is included the casual damage which the exterior of the more solid and durable works may from time to time sustain; but, independently of these repairs, age produces its effects even on these structures, and an epoch must arrive, however remote it be, at which they would be reduced to a state which will necessitate their reconstruction.

For financial and economical purposes such an epoch is, perhaps, too remote to render it necessary to bring it into practical calculation, and therefore it need here only be noticed in passing.

It might be expected that the annual repairs would, in the commencement of a well-constructed railway, amount to little, and that, as the establishment advances in age, they would increase.

The result of experience, however, shows the effects to be to some extent contrary, the annual repairs for the first years being invariably greater than at a later epoch.

The cause of this is easily explained.

In a newly constructed railway the earth works are fresh and unconsolidated, the embankments have had no other means of acquiring solidity than the gravity of their own materials, and the work of their own construction which has been conducted upon them.

When the road gets into operation, the traffic which is carried over the embankments gradually consolidates them. This produces a corresponding subsidence in the substratum of the road, and a consequent derangement of the position and level of the rails. Such derangement requires to be continually redressed, and this rectification will require to be constantly made until, after an interval of more or less duration, according to the materials composing the embankments, and the amount of traffic carried over them, a complete, consolidation takes place.

Although the same observations do not apply with equal force to the cuttings, they are, nevertheless applicable to them in a modified sense. When the natural bed of the road consists of solid and dry materials, the superficial structure, when once properly laid, will retain its position; but when the natural soil through which the cutting is carried, and upon which the road materials rest, is soft or yielding, then similar effects to those already described in the case of the embankments ensue.

Perhaps, in strictness of language, those operations which take place after the railway has been brought into use ought not to denominated *repairs*, but should be considered as an essential part of the construction of the railway, and in the financial accounts should be debited to capital, and not to revenue, not being expenses due to wear and tear, or to the legitimate operations of the traffic, but to the original and inevitable incompleteness of the construction of the line.

In like manner, in a newly constructed railway, the slopes both of the cuttings and embankments are liable to occasional *slips*, a term expressing the falling down of portions of the earth which forms the surface of these slopes.

In the case of cuttings, the earth which thus slips sometimes falls upon the road so as to obstruct the traffic, and it is therefore necessary to have means at hand at all times for its immediate removal.

In the case of embankments, these slips leave the crown of the embankment, constituting the road structure, with imperfect support, and they require therefore to be immediately repaired.

After wet weather, or during the vicissitudes of frosts and thaws in winter, such effects frequently ensue.

After, however, the road has been in operation for a sufficient length of time, the slopes of the cuttings and embankments become more or less covered with vegetation, which forms a sort of skin or coating, giving security and permanence to their surface.

The chief objects, however, of the annual repairs of a railroad are the iron and wood-work, which form the immediate materials of the road structure—the sleepers, chairs, pins, and rails.

Whatever care or skill may be used in the fabrication of these materials, and however severe the proofs to which they may have been subjected before being laid upon the road, they will be found in practice to be liable to casual defects, in consequence of which failures and fractures will from time to time take place. Individual sleepers will prove unsound, and exhibit premature decay; chairs will be fractured, pins displaced, rails exfoliated or broken. In all these cases, the broken or failing materials have to be removed and replaced by sound ones.

So far as these repairs depend on casual defects and flaws, their number and extent will be greater in the commencement of the operation of a railway than later; but, on the other hand, as the regular wear and tear of the road structure proceeds, its natural strength will be proportionally diminished, and the chances of fracture and failure multiplied.

It therefore often happens that this class of repairs, considerable within the first years, becomes less later, and later still increases; its excess at first being ascribable to casual and undiscovered defects and flaws, and its excess at a later epoch being due to the deterioration and diminished strength of the materials.

But, independently altogether of these annual repairs, which arise from the casual fracture and failure of the road structure, the rails and other iron-work of the road are subject to a gradual and slow, but not insensible wear and tear, arising from the continual operation of the vehicles rolled upon the road. Not one of these vehicles passes over a rail without detaching from its surface more or less of the metal which composes it; and when the enormous number of these vehicles which pass over a railway in active traffic is considered, the wonder will be, not that the rails are subject to wear, but that their durability is as great as it proves to be. Yet strange to say, the prevalent opinion, countenanced and supported by the most eminent practical engineers, was, until a late period, that the duration of a railway was secular, and that the wear and tear of the rails was so utterly insensible, that for all practical, financial, and economical purposes, it might be totally disregarded. Thus, it was said, that the rails of a properly laid line would last from one hundred to one hundred and fifty years. Such statements are examples of how small value are opinions of practical men not based upon their own immediate experience.

The only sure ground on which to calculate the average duration of the life of the rails would be from a careful record of the effects observed on railways under traffic for periods of time of sufficient length; but for this we should possess more extended experience than railways have yet furnished.

The modern railway may be dated from the opening ot the Liverpool and Manchester line in 1830. Its duration, consequently, has not yet covered a space of twenty years. Unless, therefore, the average life of the rails were less than twenty years, we could not determine as yet its duration from the immediate results of experience. No rails, in fine, have yet lived out their natural lives.

In the absence, however, of the direct evidence of experience, we may reason from analogy.

If, for example, the rails originally laid down on some of the lines first brought into operation be taken up and weighed, their weight having been accurately ascertained at the time they were laid, their loss of weight might be determined. The traffic which has passed over them might also be ascertained.

The cause and effect would thus be brought into immediate juxtaposition, and we should possess data, by which the wear and tear of a rail, produced by a given amount of traffic passing over it, might be known. This being determined, the only question remaining would be, what loss of weight a rail must sustain before it would be necessary to replace it by a new one.

The circumstances attending the construction and operation of the railways hitherto established have, however, thrown great difficulties in the way of such an inquiry. When the railways were first projected, the amount of traffic which they were destined to bear was not foreseen; still less was it known with what speed such traffic must be carried, or by what description or weight of engine it should be propelled. Nevertheless, all these circumstances vitally affected the duration of the rail. The engineers who constructed the roads were therefore obliged to provide a structure endowed with strength for a traffic unknown in amount. The conditions of weight and strength to be imparted to the rails were altogether conjectural.

The first railway for passenger traffic with locomotive engines was accordingly laid between Liverpool and Manchester, with rails of the description called fish-bellied, now out of use, weighing 35 lbs. per yard. The strength of these was at the time considered great to superfluity, and this form was regarded as eminently favorable to their durability.

Experience soon proved their weight to be utterly insufficient, and their form to be a source of weakness.

The first engine run upon the line thus constructed weighed $7\frac{1}{2}$ tons, including the tender.

It was soon found, however, that engines of this power were altogether insufficient for the traffic, which increased beyond all the estimates of the projectors of the line.

The capability of speed developed by the locomotive engine also vastly exceeded all previsions, and the appetite of the public for even augmented expedition appeared to increase with what fed it. Increased speed required increased power, and increased power necessarily inferred increased weight. It was, accordingly, not long before the weight of the engines was successively augmented to 10, 12, and 15 tons; and now there is actually an engine on one of the English railways which, with its tender, water, and fuel, weighs about 60 tons; and in the service of a single company there are at present more than 36 engines, weighing, with their tenders, about 40 tons each.

The weight of the carriages underwent a corresponding, though not proportionate increase. The first carriages placed on the railways weighed from 3 to $3\frac{1}{2}$ tons; their weight now sometimes exceeds $4\frac{1}{2}$ tons.

The strength and weight of the goods wagons have undergone a like increase.

But these were not the only circumstances which rendered the rails originally laid inadequate in strength. The quantity of traffic, and its speed, were gradually increased far beyond any limit which had entered into the contemplation of the engineers who projected and constructed the roads. Thus the average speed of the passenger trains, which in 1831 was 17 miles an hour, was gradually increased, until in 1848 it was 30 miles an hour; while the speed of the fastest trains, which in 1831 was 24 miles an hour, was in 1848, on the Liverpool and Manchester line, 40 miles an hour, and on the Grand Junction and the Liverpool and Birmingham, 50 miles an hour.

In 1837, the number of trains per day which arrived at and departed from the Stafford station, on the Grand Junction line, was 14; in 1848 it was 38. The number of trains per day which arrived at and departed from the Euston-square station of the Birmingham line in 1837 was 19; in 1848 it was 44.

In fine, the number of trains per day arriving at and departing from the Liverpool terminus of the Liverpool and Manchester Railway in 1831 was 26; in 1848 it was 90.

A corresponding augmentation took place in the weight of the trains. In 1831, the average weight of a passenger train, engine and tender included, was 18 tons. In 1848, the average weight of the engine and tender alone was considerably above

20 tons; and the average weight of the passenger trains, including the engine and tender, exceeded 75 tons.

In 1831, the average weight of a goods train, including engine and tender, was 52 tons; in 1848 it varied from 160 to 176 tons.*

Thus the number of trains on some railways was augmented 150, on others 250 per cent.; the weight of the engines was increased 114 per cent.; the weight of the carriages 30 per cent.; the average speed about 90 per cent.; and the average weight of the trains 350 per cent.

For such increased work the rails originally laid down at 35 lbs. a yard would have been totally inadequate, and they were accordingly soon replaced by others which weighed 50 lbs. These, again, under the gradually increasing traffic, being found insufficient, were taken up, and successively replaced by rails weighing 62 lbs. and 65 lbs. These were succeeded by others weighing 72 lbs. and 75 lbs.; and the latest rails laid down have weighed 85 lbs.

These changes were not made suddenly. The weight and strength of the permanent way were gradually increased, under the gradually increasing traffic; and, at present, the principal railways exhibit a motley arrangement of rails of various weights, the lightest being 60 lbs. and the heaviest 85 lbs. per yard.

Thus, on 438 miles of railway, placed under the direction of the Northwestern Company, there were, at the commencement of the present year (1849), about 150 miles laid down with rails of 75 lbs. per yard, 100 miles at 65 lbs. per yard, and the remainder, in detached lengths varying from 50 to 70 miles, with rails of weights varying from 60 lbs. to 85 lbs. per yard.

In a joint report of Messrs. Stephenson and Locke, dated April, 1849, the company is recommended to adopt for the future the heaviest description of rails, viz., 85 lbs. per yard.

The mode originally adopted for supporting the rails was upon square blocks of stone, measuring 2 ft. in the side and 1 ft. in depth, upon which a cast iron chair was fastened by wooden pegs driven into holes bored in the stone block, the rail being fixed in the chair by an iron pin.

After a time, these stone blocks were superseded by transverse beams of wood called sleepers, which served at once as supports for the chair and rails, and as ties for keeping the rails in gauge.

* Report of Captain Huish, manager of the Northwestern Railway. London, 1849.

The material selected for these sleepers, when first used, was larch, which was considered to be the most durable wood for the purpose, next to oak.

Later, the timber used for sleepers was prepared by impregnating it with certain saline substances, by a process variously denominated, according to the principle and mode of impregnation. Sleepers of soft wood thus prepared were regarded as having a durability equal to that of oak.

It has recently been proposed to substitute sleepers of cast iron for those of wood, and the plan has been already reduced to practice on a large scale.

The distances between sleeper and sleeper were subject to as much variation as were the strength and weight of the rails. At first, the sleepers were placed at 3 ft. asunder; the distance was afterward increased from 3 to 5 ft., according to the weight of the rails; and at present the rails are variously laid on supports at 3 ft., 3 ft. 6 in., 3 ft. 9 in., 4 ft., and 4 ft. 6 in. asunder.

The cubical magnitude of the sleepers has been subject to similar changes, according to the increasing amount of the traffic.

When these rapid and successive changes, spread over so brief a period as twenty years, are considered, it will be easily understood how difficult a problem is the solution by analogy of the average life of a rail. No rails hitherto laid down have ever been, strictly speaking, worn out. They have been successively taken up and replaced, not because they were worn out, but because their strength was insufficient for the increasing amount and speed of the traffic, and the consequently augmented weight of the engines.

If rails, selected in sufficient number, and in positions sufficiently various, had been accurately weighed when first laid down, and the amount and speed of the traffic passing over them had been accurately recorded, and if, after a sufficiently protracted interval, these rails had been taken up and weighed, the loss of weight corresponding to the traffic would have been ascertained; but directors and engineers were too actively engaged in the practical working of the lines, and too deeply involved in the present interests of their respective concerns, to give themselves much trouble about a problem which was regarded as affecting the interests of their remote successors rather than their own. Few scientific men devoted themselves to these practical questions, and those few could scarcely expect that the directors of railways would allow their current business to be interfered with by experiments and observations.

which would necessarily involve labor, cost, inconvenience, and even the danger of the temporary displacement of the rails. The problem was therefore left, without solution, to vague conjecture.

In Belgium, where the railway system was first adopted on the Continent, it was placed under the superintendence of the government, and was therefore in circumstances more favorable to the investigation of questions having an interest more remote than immediate. We find, accordingly, in the official reports of the Belgian railways, observations on the circumstances which determine the duration of the permanent way, which throw considerable light on this point.

The durability of the sleepers depends solely upon their intrinsic qualities, without reference to the traffic carried on upon the road. Their deterioration is produced by the gradual destruction of the timber, by the vicissitudes of moisture and temperature to which it is exposed. The sleepers of the Belgian railways are partly of oak and partly of white wood.

The average duration of the white wood sleepers has been found not to exceed eight years, but the duration of oak sleepers, though much more considerable, does not appear to be ascertained with the same accuracy. The average duration of the entire system of sleepers used on these lines, partly white wood and partly oak, has been found, however, from observations of sufficient extent and accuracy, to be twelve years. No sleepers impregnated with chemical principles have been used on these lines.

It appears to be the result of experience that the sleepers do not all perish at the same rate, but that a portion require to be replaced year by year; and the experience of the Belgian lines shows that each year about eight per cent. of the sleepers are renewed. Thus, in the course of twelve years, by the gradual annual repairs, all the sleepers are renewed.

Calculations have been made by the Belgian engineers as to the economical advantages derivable from the use of oak sleepers exclusively, instead of the more perishable description of wood. The result of this calculation was, that the ultimate cost is nearly the same, whether the sleeper used be more perishable and cheaper, or more durable and dearer, the increased expense being very nearly equal to the augmented durability. These calculations, however, must vary in their results, according to local circumstances, and according to the market price of the material of the sleepers.

The durability of the rails, on the other hand, is altogether independent of time, and exclusively consequent on the quantity of work which they have performed. Rails, laid under various circumstances, and in various positions, on the Belgian railways, have been previously weighed with great accuracy, and, being taken up after the lapse of a certain time, have been again weighed, and the loss of weight ascertained, the quantity of work performed meanwhile having been accurately recorded. The result of these observations has been, that, taking into account the wear and fracture of the rails, a railway composed of well-manufactured rails, weighing 27 kilogrammes per current metre, which is equal to $55\frac{1}{2}$ lbs. per yard, and giving passage annually to 3000 trains, of 14 coaches or wagons per train, would last 120 years before it required to be relaid.

The rails from which these calculations have been deduced were of English manufacture, and they were taken in every variety of position which could be supposed to influence the rate of their wear. Thus, some were taken near a station where the action of the brake in stopping the trains, and the action of the driving-wheels in starting them, necessarily augmented the wear; some were taken at an intermediate position between station and station, where such causes did not operate; some were taken on ascending and some on descending gradients, so as to efface from the calculation, by the various conditions of the data, the peculiar influences of each variety of position, and to obtain an average result.

The Belgian engineers have carried their investigations further, and have endeavored to ascertain the proportion of this wear assignable to the engine, the vehicles which it draws, and the load.

M. Belpaire has accordingly made an elaborate investigation, founded on the theory of the action of the driving-wheels of the engines, and the effects produced by the weight of the carriages and by the increased tractive power exacted from the engine; and, after a long and complicated calculation, has arrived at the conclusion that in passing over ten myriameters, or about 60 English miles, the engine abrades from the rails 2·2 lbs., each empty carriage or wagon abrades 4·5 oz., and each ton of load abrades 1·4 oz. of iron.

It appears to have escaped the notice of the Belgian engineer that these quantities of wear, which he has assigned respectively to the engines, the carriages, and the load, are as nearly as possible in the ratio of the weights of these objects severally;

CHAP. IV.]   THE WAY AND WORKS.   63

and his conclusions might have been obtained very simply, and more directly, and supported by reasoning equally cogent, by assuming that the wear produced by each object would be in the direct proportion of its weight. Such an hypothesis would be quite as admissible as those which are involved in his investigation.

The average weight of the vehicles of transport of various sorts may be taken at about 3 tons. Now 4·5 oz. is nearly three times 1·4 oz., the latter being the wear assigned to *one ton* weight of load, and the former the wear assigned to *three tons* of weight of vehicle. Again, 2·2 lbs. is 25 times 1·4 oz. very nearly, and the engine and tender weigh upon an average about 25 tons. Thus the wear assigned to the engine and tender is just so many more times the wear assigned to one ton as is expressed by the number of tons in their weight.

The reasoning upon which this distribution of the wear of the rails by the engine, the vehicles, and the load is based, is necessarily more or less theoretical, however conclusive. The most material point, however, is the total wear, which appears to have been very satisfactorily established.

It was incidentally observed in these inquiries, that, although the rails of 55 lbs. per yard were well adapted to the traffic of the Belgian lines, a railway having more active traffic would be more advantageously worked with heavier and stronger rails; and it was inferred, that rails weighing 80 lbs. per yard would be sufficient for a traffic ten times more active than the average traffic of the Belgian lines.

The Board of Directors of the Northwestern Railway Company, the largest and most important of the British railway establishments, ordered, at the commencement of the present year (1849), their manager and engineer to investigate the condition of the extensive system of railways, amounting to nearly 500 miles, placed under their direction, with a view to solve the same question as that to which the labors of the Belgian engineers were directed; that is to say, to ascertain the probable duration of the permanent way, and the future epoch at which it might require to be relaid. This investigation was accordingly made by Captain Huish, the manager of the railway, aided by the engineer and superintendent permanently engaged on the line. A report was made in April, 1849, in which it was stated, that the actual average age of the then permanent way was $7\frac{1}{2}$ years, and that, all things considered, the reporters concluded that its total duration might be estimated at 20 years, thus leaving $12\frac{1}{2}$ years of its present life to run, the railway being laid chiefly with rails weighing 65 lbs. and 75 lbs. per yard, as above stated.

Now, let us compare the conclusion arrived at by Captain Huish and his assistants, by means totally different from, and independent of, those used by the Belgian engineers, with the conclusion obtained by the latter, as already stated.

It appears by the report of Captain Huish, that the number of trains passing daily over the principal sections of the line was as follows: the Liverpool and Manchester, 90; the Grand Junction, 38; and the London and Birmingham, 44. He takes the average at 50 trains daily, which is equal to 18,250 trains annually; and this being continued for 20 years (the duration assigned by Captain Huish to the permanent way), we should have a total of 365,000 trains, as the traffic necessary to wear out the line, and render necessary its reconstruction.

Now, according to the conclusion of the Belgian engineers, 3000 trains per annum would wear out the Belgian lines in 120 years, which would give a total amount of work of 360,000 trains for the entire existence of the road.

The coincidence of these two conclusions is very remarkable, especially as Captain Huish himself does not seem to be aware of the striking manner in which his report is confirmed by the Belgian observations.

It must be observed here, that the Belgian rails are 55 lbs. per yard, while the rails upon which the English estimate is made range between 60 and 80 lbs. per yard, the average being 70 lbs.; but, on the other hand, the weight of the trains and engines, as well as their velocity, worked upon the English lines is proportionately greater than on the Belgian lines, so that the coincidence of the conclusion is not disturbed by this difference.

It may therefore be calculated, that, with a traffic equal to that now carried upon the system of railways under the direction of the Northwestern Company, rails laid down at the average weight of 70 lbs. per yard will have a duration of 20 years, after which the entire line must be relaid.

It is evident, that if from its nature the amount of wear which thus gradually takes place upon the rails from year to year could be included in the annual repairs, it ought to be comprised in them; but from the nature of the case it must necessarily be allowed to accumulate, so that at the end of a period of 20 years the entire expense of relaying the line would have to be incurred.

The financial expedient proper to meet this exigency is evident. Estimating as nearly as is possible the major limit of the cost of relaying at the end of the period just mentioned, the *amount* of an annuity (to use a term well understood), must be calculated which at the termination of 20 years would be equal to the estimated cost of relaying the rails; and an equivalent sum must be annually taken from the revenue, and invested at compound interest to meet the future exigency.

It appears by the tables of annuities, that an annuity of £1 reserved and improved at compound interest, would at the expiration of twenty years attain the following amounts:

$$\begin{array}{ll} \text{At 3 per cent.} & £26\cdot 870 \\ \text{At } 3\tfrac{1}{2} \text{ per cent.} & 28\cdot 280 \\ \text{At 4 per cent.} & 29\cdot 778 \\ \text{At } 4\tfrac{1}{2} \text{ per cent.} & 31\cdot 378 \end{array}$$

To find the annual reserve which ought to be invested, it is only necessary to divide the estimated cost of relaying a mile of the road by one or other of the above sums, according to the rate of interest at which the investments can be made. The quotient will be the annual reserve necessary for each mile of the road.

The cost of laying a mile of the permanent way with 80 lbs. rails, and suitable chairs and sleepers (the duration of the latter being taken at twelve years), is estimated in round numbers at £3000, after allowing for the value of the old rails and chairs.

Let us suppose that the investment can be made at 4 per cent., that the cost of relaying is £3000 per mile, and that the length of the line is 75 miles.

To find the necessary annual reserve, divide 3000 by 29·778, and the quotient is 100·75; multiply this by 75, and the product is 7556·75. The annual reserve would therefore be £7556 15s.

It now remains for us to explain, so far as the data before us will enable us to do, the extent of railways projected, executed, and in process of execution, in the United Kingdom, the cost of their construction, and the cost of their maintenance.

By an official report of the railway commissioners, published in June, 1849, it appears that on the 1st January, 1849, there were completed and in actual operation in the United Kingdom, 5007[*] miles of railway.

[*] Since the above was written, it appears by a more recent report, that the length of railways open on the 1st Jan., 1849, was $5126\tfrac{3}{4}$

This differs slightly from the reports of the different organs of the press devoted to railway affairs, their estimate being as much below 5000 as that of the railway commissioners is above it. We may take, therefore, 5000 miles in round numbers to express the actual length of railways which were in operation on 1st Jan., 1849.

According to the commissioners, this extent of railway communication is distributed between England, Scotland, and Ireland in the following proportions:

	Miles
England	3918
Scotland	728
Ireland	361
	5007

The rate at which the construction of railways has proceeded during the last seven years in these countries, may be estimated from the following statement, in the second column of which is given the number of miles of railway which were in operation on the first day of each of the years given in the first column. In the third column is given the number of miles of railway which were opened for traffic in the successive years, being the difference of the numbers given in the second column.

	Miles open on January 1.	Miles opened during the Year.
1843	1857	95
1844	1952	196
1845	2148	293
1846	2441	595
1847	3036	780
1848	3816	1191
1849	5007	

It further appears that acts had been obtained previously to 1st January, 1849, for other railways, and for branches and extensions, the total length of which was 7005 miles. Thus the total extent of lines constructed and projected to this date was 12,012 miles.

All the railways for which acts had been passed up to the close of 1844, with the exception of about 20 miles, had been completed and in operation by the end of 1848.

In 1845 Parliament passed acts sanctioning the construction

miles. But the additional miles consisted of lines leading to collieries and mines, and such as are not used for the general purposes of traffic.

of 2700 miles of railway. Of these not much more than one half was completed on the 1st January, 1849. In 1846, parliament passed acts authorizing the construction of a further extent of 4538 miles of railway, of which only 500 miles was completed and opened on 1st January, 1849.

The following table taken from the report of the railway commissioners of May, 1849, will exhibit the rate at which railway projects have been sanctioned by parliament, and the rate at which their execution has proceeded, up to the commencement of 1849.

TABLE showing, for the Railways authorized previously to the End of 1843 and in each succeeding Year, the Proportion opened for Traffic during each Year, and the Proportion remaining to be completed at the end of 1848; and also showing the Length of Railway opened for Traffic in each Year since 1843.

	Length of Line opened.						Total Length of Line opened to Dec. 31, 1848.	Length of Line authorized.	Length of Line remaining to be opened.
	Previously to Dec. 31, 1843.	During 1844.	During 1845.	During 1846.	During 1847.	During 1848.			
	Miles.	Miles.	Miles.	Miles.	Miles.	Miles.	Miles.	Miles.	Miles.
Of Lines authorized previously to Dec. 31, 1843.	1952	196	129	8	...	...	2285	2285	...
Of Lines authorized in 1844...	....	...	158	365	140	121	784	805	21
Of Lines authorized in 1845...	....	...	6	222	556	618	1402	2700	1298
Of Lines authorized in 1846...	....	...	...	...	84	398	482	4538	4056
Of Lines authorized in 1847...	....	...	...	...	...	54	54	1354	1300
Of Lines authorized in 1848...	....	...	...	...	...	...	...	330	330
Total....	1952	196	293	595	780	1191	5007	12,012	7005

On the 1st May, 1848, about 2960 miles of railway were in course of construction, of which 800 miles were opened by the end of the year, during which period no new works had been commenced. There were therefore in progress of construction, on the 1st January, 1849, only 2160 miles.

The account of the total amount of railways sanctioned by parliament on the 1st January, 1849, was therefore as follows:

	Miles.
Open for traffic	5007
In process of construction	2160
Not commenced	4845
Total sanctioned by Parliament	12,012

Of this extent of 4800 miles of railway sanctioned by the legislature, but not commenced, on 1st May, 1849, the railway commissioners considered that there was good reason for inferring that one half at least would never be constructed, so that the total amount of railways which were considered likely to be constructed, including those already in operation and in progress, on 1st January, 1849, was as follows:

	Miles.
Open for traffic	5007
In process of construction	2160
Not commenced, but likely to be executed	2400
	9567

The following particulars respecting the financial condition of the railway companies are also supplied by a parliamentary return, dated 1st May, 1848:

Capital paid up in cash by shareholders to January 1, 1848	£126,149,476
Capital paid by lenders on railway debentures and other securities	40,788,765
Total capital paid up to January 1, 1848	166,938,241
Paid up in shares during 1848	30,359,102
Paid up in loans during 1848	2,875,715
Total capital raised by shares and on loan to January 1, 1849	200,173,058
Balance of capital, to raise which, by existing shares, by new shares, and by loan, the actual companies possessed powers on January 1, 1849	143,717,773
	£343,890,831

Thus it appears that upon these works a sum expressed in round numbers by 200 millions sterling had been actually expended on 1st Jan., 1849, and the chartered companies had retained powers to expend a further sum, to be raised by shares or loan, of 140 millions, making a total of 340 millions to be expended on 12,000 miles of railway. But as 2400 miles of these were estimated as likely to be abandoned, a corresponding portion of the capital would not be raised or expended. This would authorize the supposition, that of the 340 millions above mentioned, 68 millions would not be required; but this computation rests on the supposition, that the railways in progress, and those to be abandoned, were estimated at the same average rate as those which are constructed. The estimates, however, being lower, the railway commissioners calculate that the probable abandonment of 2400 miles of the projected lines would cause a diminution of the estimated capital amounting only to 50 millions, leaving a total amount of capital of 290 millions to be absorbed by 9500 miles of railway. This would be at the average rate of £30,500 per mile.

Of the sum of 200 millions, which had been expended before the 1st Jan., 1849, a part had been absorbed by the lines which were in process of construction, but had not yet been opened. Against this, however, there remained an amount of capital still to be expended on the lines already open. On most of the more recently opened railways, the stations were still incomplete; in some cases, dépôts, workshops, and other permanent buildings, had not even been commenced. The full complement of the locomotive and rolling stock had not been provided. In the absence of exact data, then, if these latter expenses be placed against the former, the entire capital of 200 millions may be placed to the account of the 5000 miles open for traffic; which would give an average expense of construction, including the locomotive and carrying stock, and the workshops and dépôts for its repair, &c., of £40,000 per running mile.

An estimate of the actual quantity of labor of every class employed on this stupendous national enterprise may be obtained from a parliamentary return, showing the number of persons employed on the railways on the 1st May, 1848; the extent then open for traffic being 4253 miles, the extent in process of construction being 2958 miles, and the number of distinct companies by whom these works were directed being 170.

TABULAR ANALYSIS of the Number and Description of Persons employed on the Railways of the United Kingdom on May 1, 1848.		
	On Lines open for Traffic.	On Lines not open.
Secretaries	81	102
Managers	30	93
Treasurers	29	21
Engineers	95	405
Superintendents	343	1,897
Storekeepers	125	243
Accountants	70	145
Cashiers	48	88
Draughtsmen	106	306
Carry forward	927	3,300

	On Lines open for Traffic.	On Lines not open.
Brought forward	927	3,300
Clerks	4,360	887
Artificers	10,814	29,087
Laborers	14,297	147,325
Inspectors	---	119
Land surveyors	---	26
Miners, or quarrymen	---	6,250
Foremen or overseers	1,010	685
Policemen	2,475	71
Porters and messengers	7,559	10
Platelayers	4,391	256
Drivers and carters	---	45
Engine-drivers	1,752	
Engine-stokers	1,809	
Guards	1,464	
Switchmen	1,058	
Gatekeepers	401	
Wagoners	141	
Brakesmen	32	
Miscellaneous	197	
Total	52,687	188,071

It appears, therefore, that in 1848 a quarter of a million of persons were employed on the railways of the United Kingdom; and if it be considered that each of these must have contributed to the support, on an average, of one or more other persons, it will follow, that this vast enterprise must have, at that epoch, supplied means of living to at least two per cent. of the entire population of these countries.

Since the date of these returns, the extent of railway which has been completed is greater than the length which has been commenced, and the extent now in process of construction is therefore less than at the epoch just referred to. It is probable, therefore, that the quantity of labor employed in this branch of industry has been somewhat diminished; because, although the length of lines under traffic is greater than formerly, the length in process of construction is less, and the latter, for a given length, employs more industry than the former, in the proportion of three and a half to one.

CHAPTER V.

THE LOCOMOTIVE POWER.

WHEN the magnitude of the capital invested in the locomotive stock of a railway, and the large proportion of the annual revenue absorbed in maintaining it, are considered, its economical importance may be readily estimated.

The locomotive stock may be primarily resolved into two classes—that which is employed in working the passenger traffic, and that which is employed in drawing the goods trains.

The passenger engines are so constructed as to draw light loads at great speed, the goods engines heavy loads at a low speed. In the one, the driving wheels are large, so as to carry the train forward through a great space by each stroke of the piston; in the other they are of more limited magnitude, in order to give the moving power a greater leverage upon the load. In the one, they are single, rendering the engine light, so as to absorb less of the moving power in propelling itself; in the other, they are double and coupled, and sometimes even tripled, so as to give a greater purchase to the impelling power. In the one class of engine steam of small density is consumed rapidly and in great volume; in the other, steam of greater density is consumed at a slower rate.

These different mechanical requirements render it necessary, in general, to provide a locomotive stock for the goods service, separate from, and independent of, that provided for the passenger service.

In the locomotive department a register should be kept, containing a record of the past and current performances and condition of every engine in the service of the railway. Such a record should contain the following particulars of the past services of each engine:

1st. The day and year it was put upon the road.
2d. Its maker.
3d. The diameter and stroke of its cylinders.
4th. The diameter and number of its driving-wheels.
5th. The number of times it was cleaned, lighted, and had steam raised.

6th. The number of hours it was standing with steam raised.

7th. Its total mileage, from the commencement of its service to the current date.

8th. The total quantity of fuel it had consumed.

9th. Original cost of engine.

10th. Total sum expended on its repairs.

And, with respect to its current service during the past year, the following details should be given:

1st. The number of times it was lighted, and had steam raised.

2d. The number of hours it stood with steam raised.

3d. Its mileage by months, and its total mileage.

4th. The quantity of fuel consumed in lighting and raising steam.

5th. The quantity of fuel consumed in standing.

6th. The quantity of fuel consumed in working.

7th. A memorandum of any accident, or other notable circumstance, attending the performance of the engine.

Such a record as the above is neither impracticable nor unimportant. A register of this kind is kept by the establishment of the Belgian railways, and the principal results of it are published annually, in a tabulated form, in the "Compte Rendu," or official report of the service of the railways, delivered to the Chambers by the minister of public works every session. Such a table exhibits a "coup d'œil" of the condition and the past history of the entire locomotive stock.

On the Belgian lines, which consist of 347 miles of railway, there were employed, at the end of the year 1847, 154 locomotives, of the conditions and performance of which a tabular statement appears in the report of that year. The Belgian railways had been then 13 years in operation, and no engine had yet been superannuated.

The first engine placed upon the road was "La Flèche," constructed by Messrs. Stephenson & Co. This machine had performed, within the 13 years, a total mileage of 86,932 miles, and within the year 1847 had performed a mileage of 7292 miles. Thus, in its thirteenth year of service, it performed more than its annual average.

Another engine constructed by Messrs. Stephenson, called St. Hubert, which had been put on the road in December, 1838, had, at the end of 1847, completed a mileage of 130,962 miles, having performed within the year 1847 21,737 miles.

Another engine, called "Les Quatre Journées," constructed by Messrs. Cockerill, which had been put upon the road in

September, 1837, and had then been upward of ten years in service, had performed a total mileage of 130,160 miles, and within the year 1847 performed, in five months, a mileage of 11,537 miles.

In short, it appears from this register, that not only were none of the engines composing the stock of the Belgian railways, which had been accumulating for 13 years, superannuated, but that the current mileage of the oldest engine was equal to that of the youngest and most vigorous.

In the progress of the English railways, locomotives have been, from time to time, cast aside, and put, as it were, upon the retired list; but this has in general arisen, not from the circumstance of their being superannuated, but because the conditions of the traffic had undergone such a change that the natural powers of these engines were not suited to it. Immediately after the comencement of the operation of the railway system, the traffic augmented so rapidly as to exceed all the previsions of those who constructed and organized the first railways. The weight and strength of the rails were successively increased, as well as the weight and magnitude of the trains, and the weight and power of the engines underwent a corresponding augmentation.

A regularly kept journal of the life of some of the oldest locomotives working on the English railways would be a record of profound interest. Whether such a register exist, I am not aware; but none such has, I believe, ever been published.

From a comparison of the total mileage of each class of the locomotive stock with the number of engines in service, the average mileage of each engine can be ascertained.

Thus, if E express the number of passenger engines, and e express their total mileage, then $\frac{E}{e}$ will express the average mileage of each engine. In like manner, if E' express the number of goods engines, and e' their total mileage, $\frac{E'}{e'}$ will express the average mileage of each. Or, in fine, if $E + E'$ express the total number of engines of both kinds, and $e + e'$ their total mileage, then $\frac{E + E'}{e + e'}$ will express the general average mileage of each engine.

As an example of such a calculation, let us take the Belgian railways for 1847.

The total number of engines in active service was 154, and

their total mileage was 2,366,885; this divided by 154 gives 15,369 as the average annual mileage of each engine, the average daily mileage being therefore 42 miles.

It may be asked, whether a locomotive engine, once lighted, may not be worked almost indefinitely?

It is known that many steam-engines used in the manufactures and in mining are kept for several months together in unceasing action night and day; and the engines used in steam-ships are often kept in incessant operation throughout a voyage of 3000 miles. Why therefore, it may be said, may not a locomotive engine be worked for a much longer distance without interruption, and thus distribute the expense of lighting and cleaning over a greater extent of mileage, and thereby diminish the cost per mile?

Although the mileage of the engine might be augmented much beyond its present amount, it is nevertheless indispensable that it should not exceed a certain practical limit. The locomotive engine, an iron horse, requires intervals of repose as much as do the horses of flesh, blood, and bones. It becomes fatigued, so to speak, with its work, and its joints become relaxed by labor, its bolts loosened, its rubbing surfaces heated, and often unequally expanded and strained. Its grate-bars and fire-box become choked with clinkers, its tubes become charged with coke; and were its labor continued to a certain point, it would end in a total inability to move. The durability of the engine, therefore, requires that its work should be suspended before these causes of disability operate to an injurious extent.

When its labor ceases, the engine-cleaners, who are, as it were, its grooms, clean out its fire-place, scrape its grate-bars and the internal surface of the fire-box, clean out its tubes, tighten all its bolts and rivets, oil and grease all its moving parts, and, in a word, put it again into working order.

The expense of cleaning an engine, and the cost of the fuel consumed in lighting it and raising the steam, so as to prepare it for propulsion, must necessarily be charged upon the mileage which it performs; and the cost of this mileage will therefore be augmented in the inverse proportion of the ratio of the total mileage of the engine to the number of times it has been cleaned and lighted during the period of its service. It is therefore important, in the economy of the locomotive power, to ascertain with precision the proportion which the mileage of the engines bears to the number of times they have been cleaned and lighted.

Hence appears the importance of the record above mentioned, of the number of times each engine has been lighted and cleaned.

To determine the average number of miles run by each engine after such cleaning and lighting, it is only necessary to divide the total mileage of the locomotive stock, or of each class of it, by the total number of engines lighted; the quotient will give the distance run by each engine lighted. In general, if E'' express the number of engines lighted, then $\frac{e+e'}{E''}$ will express the average distance run by each engine lighted.

As examples of the application of this, we take, from the official reports of the Belgian railways, the number of engines lighted during 1846 and 1847. The number was 27,452 for 1846. Dividing this into the total mileage, 2,027,014, already given, the quotient is 73·8, which is therefore the average number of miles run by each engine cleaned and lighted.

In 1847 the number of engines lighted was 30,676. We have already seen that the total mileage was 2,366,885. Dividing this by the number of engines lighted, we find 77·6 miles as the distance run by each engine lighted, being an improvement on the performance of the previous year.

On the Orleans Railway, in 1847, there were 11,315 engines lighted, of which the total mileage was 853,505. Dividing the latter by the former, we find 76 miles as the average distance run. On the same railway, during the year 1848, there were 11,072 engines lighted. The total mileage of all the engines was 782,591. Dividing the latter by the former, we obtain 70·7 miles, the average distance run by each engine lighted.

In the practical working of the locomotive stock, it inevitably happens that engines, after they have been lighted, had their steam raised and prepared for starting, have to stand, keeping their steam up more or less time, waiting for trains which they are to draw; and thus an expense is incurred, not directly productive, for fuel and wages.

But, besides this, the service of the road requires that, at certain stations, engines shall be kept waiting with their steam up ready for work, for the mere purpose of providing for the contingencies of the active service of the road. Thus, if an accident occur to a train, by which the engine that draws it is disabled, notice is sent forward by the electric telegraph, by signals or otherwise, to the next engine station, summoning an engine to proceed to the spot to take on the train. If an engine were not prepared for such a contingency, with its steam up, the road would be obstructed for a considerable length of time by the train thus accidentally brought to a stand.

The engines thus kept prepared for accidents are called *Reserve Engines.*

Another cause which renders it necessary at certain points of the line to keep engines waiting with their steam up, is the existence of exceptional gradients.

Thus, if a railway be generally laid out with gradients of about 15 feet a mile, but at a particular point a natural elevation of the ground, or other cause, renders the construction of a gradient rising at the rate of 60 feet a mile necessary, then the engines which are adapted to the general character of the line become insufficient for such exceptional gradient; and, in such case, the expedient resorted to is to keep one or more powerful engines constantly waiting with their steam up at the foot of the incline, for the purpose of aiding in propelling the trains in their ascent. These engines are denominated *Assistant Engines* or *Bank Engines.* Their mode of operation is as follows. They wait near the foot of the incline in a siding provided for the purpose; and when a train arrives and begins to ascend, the assistant engine follows it, and, pushing from behind, aids the regular engine in front in propelling it up the plane. When it arrives at the summit, the assistant engine drops off, and, descending the plane, returns to its station.

In the above calculations of the proportion of the engines lighted to the actual mileage, these reserve and assistant engines, when such occur, are included; and the average mileage per engine lighted, which has been obtained as above, is less than the actual average performed by the *engines worked*, because the engines lighted for reserve enter into the divisor, which gives the mileage. It is convenient, therefore, in the records of the locomotive department, to keep an account of the engines *lighted for reserve*, &c., separate from the engines *lighted for work.*

On the Orleans Railway in 1848, of 11,072 which were lighted, 1825 were reserve engines, and 9247 only were worked.

To ascertain the actual average mileage of each of the *working engines* which were lighted, it would be therefore necessary to divide the total mileage by 9247, which will give 84·6 as the actual average distance run by each engine *lighted and worked.*

In like manner, in 1847, on the same railway, the number of reserve engines lighted was likewise 1825, and, therefore, the number of engines lighted and worked 9490. Dividing the mileage, which was 853,505, by 9490, we obtain 90 as the average distance run by each engine lighted and worked. Thus it appears that, if the reserve engines be included in the computation, they would reduce the average run of each engine lighted in 1848 from 84·6 to 70·7, and in 1847 from 90 to 76.

To estimate the time during which the locomotive stock is kept standing with steam up in reserve or waiting for work, a record of the number of hours each engine has been lighted and standing should be kept. By dividing this total number of hours by the number of engines lighted, we obtain the average number of hours which each engine lighted had been kept standing with steam up.

As an example of this, on the Belgian railways, in 1846 and 1847, the number of hours which engines were kept standing with steam up was 204,124 in 1846, while the number of engines lighted was 27,452. Dividing the former by the latter, the quotient is 7·43, which is the average number of hours each engine lighted was kept standing with steam up.

In like manner, in 1847, on the same railways, the number of hours the engines were kept standing was 214,610, and the number of engines lighted was 30,676. Dividing the former by the latter the quotient is 7. Hence it appears that the average number of hours each engine lighted was kept standing in this year was 7 hours. In this, however, are included the reserve engines.

As on the same railways the average distance run by each engine lighted was about 70 miles, it follows, that for every 10 miles of practical work performed by each engine the engine was kept one hour standing.

The fuel consumed in working a railway may be classed under three heads:

1st. That which is consumed in lighting the engines and raising their steam, to prepare them for work.

2d. That which is consumed while the engines stand with their steam up, waiting for the trains they are intended to draw, or standing in reserve, prepared for the contingency of accidents on the line.

3d. That which is consumed in drawing the trains.

When the engine has stopped work, its fire-box is cleared, preparatory to the engine being cleaned. A certain portion of coke, more or less, according to the state of the fire-box at the moment the engine is stopped, is collected in this way half consumed. This coke is to a certain extent available to aid in lighting the engine when next started. The small coke which has been rejected as unfit for the working engine is mixed, in a greater or less proportion, by the engineer with the large coke used for raising the steam, for in this process the draft is not so strong as to carry this small coke injuriously through the tubes. The small coke is also used, mixed in a certain proportion with the large coke, for keeping the steam up in the reserve engines.

The quantity of coke consumed in drawing a train will depend upon the magnitude and weight of the train, and the speed with which it is moved. The greater the resistance which it has to overcome, the greater will be the consumption of fuel in a given distance. The resistance increases in a high ratio with the speed. Now as the speed of passenger trains is usually greater than that of goods trains, the consumption of fuel, so far as it is affected by the speed, will be greater in the former than in the latter; but, on the other hand, goods trains consisting of a much greater number of vehicles and of a greater gross weight than passenger trains, the resistance due to the load is greater in the latter case than in the former.

On the Belgian railways the economy of fuel is very strictly attended to. Rules are established by which a certain weight of coke is allowed to the engineer for the different purposes:

For lighting and raising the steam, 280 kilogrammes, equal to 618 lbs., of coke are allowed.

For each passenger coach drawn, $\frac{3}{4}$ kilo. per kilometre, equal to 2·64 lbs. per mile, are allowed.

For each loaded goods wagon, $\frac{2}{3}$ of a kilogramme per kilometre, equal to 2·30 lbs. per mile, are allowed.

Two empty wagons are accounted as equal to a loaded one, and $2\frac{1}{2}$ kilogrammes per kilometre, equal to 8·82 lbs. per mile, are allowed for an engine without a load.

Ten kilogrammes, equal to 22 lbs., per hour, are allowed for keeping up the steam while the engine is standing.

These quantities are, however, understood to be average major limits which ought not to be exceeded. To stimulate the engineers and their superintendents to the observance of a due economy of fuel, premiums are awarded, in proportion to the extent of the saving effected upon these allowances; 5s. 6d. a ton is allowed to the engineer for every ton of coke by which his actual consumption falls short of these limits, and a further premium of one-fourth of this amount is allowed to the superintendents of the locomotive department.

In the year 1846 the amount of premiums paid for these

savings to the engine-drivers was £678, and to the superintendents £169.

The savings of fuel are not either alone or chiefly effected by the care bestowed on feeding the fire-box. Much more depends on the engine not being lighted at too early a moment before starting, and consequently not being kept standing with steam up needlessly.

In the year 1841 the engines upon the Belgian railways consumed, upon an average, 70 lbs. per mile, including the fuel consumed in lighting and standing.

In 1842 this was reduced to 45 lbs., and in 1844 and 1845 to 40 lbs.

This improved economy was not altogether owing to the increased vigilance of the engine-drivers and stokers, but was in part due to an improvement in the arrangement of the valves, by which the steam was allowed to escape from the cylinders, so that the economy was partially effected on the consumption of steam, and through that on the consumption of fuel.

In the locomotive department, a register should be kept of the fuel consumed, distinguishing such consumption under the three heads of standing, lighting, and working, together with which should be noted the hours standing, the engines lighted, and the mileage worked. There is nothing impracticable or difficult in the maintenance of such a register in every well-organized establishment, and such a one is regularly kept in the administration of the Belgian railways. It appears from these records, that the following was the fuel consumed for these purposes respectively on the Belgian railways during the years 1846 and 1847:

	1846.	1847.
Number of hours standing	204,124	214,610
Number of lbs. of coke consumed in standing	4,503,077	5,306,573
Average number of lbs. consumed per hour	22·0	24·7
Number of engines lighted	27,452	30·676
Total number of lbs. consumed in lighting	16,828,505	18,605,263
Average number of lbs. consumed per engine lighted	613·0	606·4
Total mileage worked	2,027,014	2,366,885
Total number of lbs. of coke consumed in working	60,698,538	71,500,965
Average number of lbs. consumed per mile worked	30·0	30·0
Average consumption per mile, including coke consumed in lighting and standing	40·5	40·3

It may then be stated in round numbers, that 600 lbs. of fuel are consumed in lighting an engine and raising the steam, and that every engine lighted travels, on an average, as worked upon the Belgian lines, 70 miles.

The fuel consumed in lighting adds, therefore, $8\frac{1}{2}$ lbs. per mile to the working consumption, which latter being 30 lbs., the proportion consumed in lighting is 28 per cent. The fuel consumed in standing with steam up, either as an engine of reserve or otherwise, adds $1\frac{1}{2}$ per cent. more to the working consumption per mile, the total amount of which may be taken in round numbers at 40 lbs., as these railways are worked.

To determine what part of this consumption is directly expended on the load, it would be necessary to ascertain the proportion which the dead weight bears to the profitable load. This will become the subject of inquiry in a succeeding chapter.

The sources, therefore, from which the economy of fuel may be expected, are the extending the mileage of each engine lighted, the keeping the engines waiting as short a time as possible for their loads, and securing as full a load as possible for the carriages.

It is well known that the fuel invariably used in locomotive engines on European railways is coke.

Weight for weight, this fuel develops a greater amount of heat, and develops it in a smaller space and more rapidly, than coal. It is therefore better adapted to produce the quick evaporation in a small space, which is indispensable to railways. Its combustion is not attended with the evolution of the black, sooty smoke produced by coal; and the engines, therefore, in passing through districts more or less populous, are not productive of the same nuisance.

Coke is fabricated by submitting coal to the process of baking or being heated in close retorts, by which means its volatile constituents are driven out of it, and little more than carbon remains. In this process, the magnitude of the fuel is considerably increased.

The augmentation of magnitude varies according to the quality of the coal. In some cases it is augmented 50 per cent. in bulk, and of course proportionally diminished in weight.

In the process of coking, coal loses the weight of the volatile elements expelled. This diminution of weight varies according to the quality and analysis of the coal, from 15 to 25 per cent. of the total weight.

Thus, it may be assumed, that, allowing for waste in incom-

CHAP. V.] THE LOCOMOTIVE POWER. 81

bustible matter, contained even in the best coal in greater or less proportion, the weight of coke derived from 100 tons of coal will be about 70 tons; but of this quantity a portion, more or less according to the mode and the skill of fabrication, will be produced in pieces of too small magnitude to be capable of being used in locomotive engines. The small coke, if burned in the locomotive engine, either falls through the grate-bars, or is drawn through the tubes unconsumed, and a portion of it remaining in them, obstructs the draft. The small coke is, nevertheless, useful as fuel, and is valued at its own weight of coal. On the Belgian railways, 65 per cent. of large coke, and $2\frac{1}{2}$ per cent. of small, is obtained from the coal.

By analysis, this coal contains from 17 to 25 per cent. of volatile matter, and consequently, even by distillation in close vessels, would yield, in coking, only from 75 to 83 per cent. A portion of the coal, however, in the common process of coking, is consumed in producing the necessary heat, and the remainder is waste and incombustible matter.

In the year 1844, 23,800 tons of large coke and 900 tons of small were produced on the Belgian railways from 36,500 tons of coal, the cost of the coal being 11s. 4d. per ton, and that of the coke 20s.

In 1846, 52,185 tons of coal were used in making 28,220 tons of large and 834 tons of small coke.

In 1844, 3·6 per cent. of the coke produced was small, and had only the value of its weight in coal.

In 1846, only 2·8 per cent. was small, an improvement in the fabrication having taken place, which effected a saving of nearly 1 per cent. in the coke produced.

In the reports of the English railways, no data are supplied by which similar calculations can be made.

According to the reports of the Great Western Railway, the cost of coke, its consumption, and the mileage of the engines during the last four years, had been as follows:

	Cost per Ton.		Coke consumed.	Mileage of Engines.
	s.	d.	Tons.	
1845	21	0	21,919	1,240,412
1846	23	8	19,731	1,346,341
1847	24	4	21,454	1,454,610
1848	21	4	25,346	1,582,672

The mileage here given includes that of the assistant engines, and of engines traveling without a train; and the consumption of fuel is the total quantity, including what was consumed in lighting the engines and in standing.

Hence it follows that the consumption in each year per engine per mile, including lighting and standing, was as follows:

	Coke consumed per Engine per Mile.
1845	$39\frac{1}{2}$ lbs.
1846	33 ,,
1847	33 ,,
1848	$35\frac{8}{10}$,,

By a return now before me, I find that, in the twelve months ending the 30th June, 1849, the total amount of coke consumed by the locomotive stock of the Northwestern Railway was 116,396 tons, or 260,727,040 lbs., which produced a total mileage of the engines amounting to 7,532,230. Dividing the former by the latter, we find the consumption per engine per mile to be 34·6 lbs.

As may be expected, considering that the consumption of fuel must depend on the magnitude and weight of the trains, as well as on the speed, the consumption per mile is found to vary considerably on different railways.

Thus, on the Brighton and South Coast Railway, in the half-year ending the 30th June, 1849, the total consumption of coke was 6345 tons, or 14,212,800 lbs., which produced a total mileage of the engines amounting to 593,844 miles. Dividing the former by the latter, it appears that the consumption per engine per mile was about 24 lbs.

On the same railway, during the half-year ending the 30th June, 1848, the fuel consumed was 9319 tons, or 20,874,560 lbs., which produced a mileage of the engines amounting to 668,785.ND Dividing the former by the latter, the consumption per mile proves to have been 31·21 lbs.

Since in this case it is not likely that any material change took place in the nature of the traffic, the increased economy must have been produced by improved management.

In comparing the total number of engines worked with the total number lighted, we obtain the number of times per annum that each engine in service was lighted.

As the number of engines worked on the Belgian railways in 1846 was 151, and in 1847, 154, by dividing these respectively into the total number lighted already given, we obtain the quotients 181 and 200 very nearly.

It appears, therefore, that in the year 1846 each engine, on an average, was lighted on 181 days, and in 1847 on 200 days. This is on four days per week very nearly.

From this it follows, that three days per week were required, upon an average, for the rest, cleaning, and repairs of an engine.

This result is in accordance with another obtained previously, viz., that the average daily mileage of the engines was 42 miles, which would give an average weekly mileage of about 300 miles, which would be four working days per week of 75 miles, nearly the amount of the average run of each engine lighted.

One of the most striking results of the preceding calculations is the apparently small amount of useful service obtained from the locomotive engines.

We have seen that in each run, an engine on the Belgian lines, at the most improved epoch of the service yet reported, did not quite average 78 miles, and that even this was performed only four days in seven. Thus the average daily work of an engine would appear to be only 42 miles.

But it also appears, that for 74 miles run the engine is kept, on an average, $7\frac{1}{2}$ hours standing. This being reduced to a daily average, leads to the conclusion, that the daily service of the engines consisted in 42 miles run and $3\frac{3}{4}$ hours standing with the steam up.

But as the average speed on the Belgian railways is about 20 miles an hour, the run of 42 miles would occupy about two hours.

The daily service of an engine, therefore, expressed in time, would be nearly 2 hours working and $3\frac{3}{4}$ waiting with steam up.

These inferences are so striking, that we naturally turn elsewhere to inquire how far the results of other railways vary from or corroborate them.

In general, the daily mileage of the engines employed in the service of a railway may be found by dividing the average annual mileage by 365. In all cases, therefore, where the reports supply the annual mileage and the number of engines, the daily mileage is a matter of easy calculation.

The results given in the subjoined table (see p. 84) are calculated from the returns of the several railway companies therein mentioned now before us.

From this table it appears that the useful daily service of an engine varies on the above railways between 28 miles as a minimum and 45 as a maximum. This variation depends partly on the degree of skillful management under which the locomotive power is placed, and partly on the nature of the traffic.

Name of Railway.	Year.	Number of Engines.	Total Mileage.	Average annual Mileage per Engine.	Average daily Mileage per Engine.
Belgian Railways	1844	143	1,584,532	11,080	30·4
	1845	148	1,694,203	11,447	31·4
	1846	151	2,027,014	13,490	37·0
	1847	154	2,366,885	15,369	42·0
North of France Railway	1847	175	1,789,152	10,224	28·0
	1848	177	1,917,855	10,835	29·7
Orleans Railway:					
Passenger traffic	··	43	483,206	11,237	30·8
Goods traffic	··	9	153,227	17,026	44·0
Paris and Rouen Railway:					
Passenger traffic	··	40	406,039	10,151	28·0
Goods traffic	··	10	147,174	14,717	40·0
Alsace Railway	··	29	335,405	11,565	31·6
Gard Railway:					
Passenger traffic	··	5	82,429	16,486	45·0
Goods traffic	··	13	191,814	14,755	40·0
Rhenish Railway	··	16	201,534	12,596	35·0
Totals and general averages	··	1113	13,380,469	12,022	32·9

The data supplied by the English railways are so scarce, and in general so vague, as to afford no adequate means of general comparison with the results above given. In the case of the London and Northwestern lines, however, a more detailed account has been published, which, considering the great extent and traffic of that system of railways, is entitled to much attention.

On these lines, during the twelve months ending June 30, 1849, there was a stock of 504 locomotives; but of this number, 47 were in store, newly-made, and not yet worked. The number of engines, therefore, actually worked during the year, was 457. These engines supplied the locomotive power, not only to the Northwestern lines, properly so called, but to the following railways:

	Miles.
Chester and Holyhead	80·50
Preston, Lancaster, and Carlisle	90·00
Kendal and Windermere	9·75
Shropshire Union (Shrewsbury and Stafford)	29·25
North Union (Parkside and Preston)	22·00
Total	231·50
London and Northwestern, main line and branches	438·00
Total	669·50

THE LOCOMOTIVE POWER.

The traffic of these lines was worked, during the twelve months ending June 30, 1849, by 457 locomotive engines, the total mileage of which was as follows:

	Mileage.
Passenger engines	4,649,556
Goods engines	2,882,674
Total	7,532,230

Hence the average daily run of each engine was 45 miles.

These results, obtained from services so various and numerous, leave no doubt that the average daily service of each locomotive engine is much less than would have been expected. If the average speed on the Northwestern lines be taken at 28 miles an hour, we shall obtain the singular and somewhat unexpected conclusion, that the engines, taken one with another, are each worked with traffic little more than one hour and a half a day.

By a return which I have obtained from the Northwestern Company, I find that, in the twelve months ending June 30, 1849, they had in active employment an average number of 275 engine-drivers, and an equal number of firemen. Now it has already been stated, that during the same period the number of engines employed was 457; there were thus 10 engine-drivers and firemen for every 16 engines.

By dividing the total annual mileage of the engines by the total number of engine-drivers and firemen employed, we shall find the total annual distance driven by each; and dividing this by 365, we shall obtain the average daily work of each engine-driver and fireman, expressed *in distance*. This distance, divided by the average speed in miles per hour, will give the daily work on the road in time. The following are the details of this for the lines worked by the Northwestern Company:

Total mileage of engines	7,532,230
Number of engine-drivers and firemen	275
Annual distance worked per head	27,390 miles.
Daily distance worked per head	75
Time daily on the road (at the average speed of 28 miles per hour)	$2\frac{3}{4}$ hours.

If it be assumed that the engines, one with another, work on alternate days, the actual distance run in each trip by each engine on the system of lines worked by the Northwestern Company will be 90 miles; which, in time, at 28 miles an hour, would be very nearly $3\frac{3}{14}$ hours.

It appears, therefore, that the locomotive power is worked to greater advantage on these than on the continental lines generally. We have seen that the average distance run by each engine lighted on the Belgian lines was about 75 miles.

It has been customary, in some of the reports presented to the railway companies, to institute comparisons between one line of railway and another, founded upon the relation between the locomotive stock and the length of the line.

Now such a mode of comparison can afford no legitimate consequence of the least importance, either in a financial or mechanical point of view. The quantity of locomotive power does not in any manner depend on the length of the railway. The locomotive power is used to draw the traffic, and for no other purpose. Its quantity, therefore, will depend on the quantity of the traffic, and the average distance to which it is carried, or, in other words, on the mileage of the goods and passengers.

Two railways having the same traffic mileage will require the same locomotive stock, be their length equal or unequal. If a million of tons of goods require to be annually transported an average distance of 500 miles, and ten millions of passengers also require to be annually transported 300 miles, it is manifest that the same locomotive power will be requisite to execute the traffic, whether the railway on which it is carried be 400 miles or 800 miles in length.

If the object be to compare the merits of the management of the locomotive power, then the test of comparison should be the quantity of work executed by a given quantity of this power; and the quantity of work must be decided by the useful mileage of the engines, and not by the length of the line.

Nevertheless, we find railway authorities in high repute announcing, that to stock a line requires so many engines per mile. To such a statement there can be no objection, provided it be made with the understanding that it applies to railways only which have a certain understood amount of average traffic.

But it is clear that, with every variation of the traffic upon the proposed railway, there must be a corresponding and proportional variation in the necessary amount of locomotive stock.

A legitimate mode of comparing the merits of the management of the locomotive department will be found in the estimate of the average daily mileage of the engines.

It is evident, that if we find on one railway—for example, the Northwestern—the engines performing a daily mileage of 45 miles, while on another—the North of France—we find them performing a daily service under 30 miles, that the locomotive stock in the one case was more profitably managed than the other in the ratio of 2 to 3, it being understood that other things are similar. But even in this comparison it would be necessary that the length and weight of the trains should be taken into account; for if it prove that the weight of the train drawn 30 miles is greater than the weight of the train drawn 45 miles in the proportion of 3 to 2, then the useful labor of the engines will, after all, be the same. In short, the test, and the only test, of the useful effect of the locomotive power is the actual mileage (including in that term the quantity) of the traffic which it executes in a given time.

It may be well here to repeat what is to be understood, through this work, by the term mileage.

The entire amount of traffic of a given kind is supposed to be reduced to another imaginary amount carried one mile; and the expression thus obtained will involve at once the consideration of weight and distance. Thus, for instance, if 10,000 tons be carried 100 miles, we assume it to be equivalent to a million of tons carried one mile, this last expression being denominated the mileage of the tons. It is evident that such an expression combines the consideration of both weight and distance.

The conditions which determine the amount of the locomotive stock necessary to work any given railway form a very important subject of inquiry in railway economy; but it is a subject upon which we as yet possess but scanty and unsatisfactory data. As has been already stated, railway authorities have, with more rashness than skill, given a sort of rough estimate of it at so much per mile. This must, however, be regarded as utterly unworthy of attention, for the very intelligible reasons already explained.

The amount of locomotive stock depends exclusively on the mileage of the traffic. We shall see, in a subsequent chapter, how, when the quantity and quality of the traffic is given, the number and mileage of the trains necessary for it can be ascertained. This being done, the mileage of the engines necessary to work these trains easily follows.

The question is thus reduced to the determination of the number of engines necessary to work a given mileage.

If we assume the results of the working of the Northwestern lines as a general modulus, it would follow, that to find the quantity of stock necessary for working a given daily mileage, it will be sufficient to divide this mileage by 45; the quotient will express the requisite number of locomotive engines.

But if there be any thing in the peculiar nature of the traffic to show the practicability of better economizing the locomotive power, and of obtaining from the engines a greater average amount of daily work; or, on the contrary, if there be any thing in the proposed service to render it impracticable to obtain so great an average amount of daily work, then the estimated average of 45 miles must be augmented or diminished, according to the proposed conditions.

It is found that the number of tenders ought to be equal to the number of engines.

In the absence of more certain and exact data, we may assume, as the means of an approximate calculation, that the amount of the locomotive stock necessary for each line of railway is in the direct proportion of the gross amount of its receipts, these receipts being taken as the modulus of the traffic.

We find by the official returns of the railway commissioners for the half-year ending December 31, 1848, that the receipts of the lines worked by the locomotive stock of the Northwestern Company was £1,320,819, while the total receipts of all the lines open for traffic was £5,744,964. It follows, therefore, that the ratio of the traffic of all the railways of the United Kingdom, taken collectively, to that of the lines worked by the Northwestern Company, was 43 to 10 nearly.

Since, then, the number of locomotive engines and tenders necessary to work the traffic of the Northwestern lines was 457, the number necessary for the traffic of all the railways collectively would be $457 \times \dfrac{43}{10} = 1965$.

It follows, therefore, from this approximate calculation, that the total work of the five thousand miles of railway open for traffic on Jan. 1, 1849, was performed by 1965 locomotives.

In the same manner, assuming that the mileage of locomotives, in performing this work, was proportional to that of the Northwestern engines, its total amount would be found by multiplying the mileage of the Northwestern engines by 4·3. Thus we have

$$7{,}532{,}230 \times 4\cdot 3 = 32{,}388{,}589.$$

The total distance run, therefore, by all the locomotives working the traffic of the railways of the United Kingdom for the twelve months ending June 30, 1849, was 32,388,589 miles.

This gives a total daily mileage of 88,736 miles.

To illustrate these stupendous results, let us compare them

with moduli more in accordance with their magnitude than are the ordinary phenomena witnessed around us.

The distance from the earth to the sun is ninety-six millions of miles.

The locomotives of the British railways would, at their present rate of work, pass over it in three years!

The circumference of the globe is twenty-five thousand miles.

The same engines, with their present work, would go seven times round it in two days; and, in doing so, each engine would work only $3\frac{1}{2}$ hours.

Taking the average consumption of fuel by the locomotives at 35 lbs. per mile, the total consumption for the twelve months ending June 30, 1849, would be found as follows:

32,388,589 miles at 35 lbs. per mile = 506,071 tons.

The traffic was therefore worked by half a million of tons of coke.

But ten tons of coal are required to make seven tons of coke. The quantity of coal consumed in making the coke was therefore 728,958 tons.

We may, therefore, conclude, that the railways consume at present nearly three quarters of a million of tons of coal annually.

CHAPTER VI.

THE CARRYING STOCK.

THE various forms of vehicle composing the carrying stock of a railway consist, like the locomotive stock, of two classes, corresponding to the two great divisions of railway traffic, the traffic in passengers and the traffic in goods.

By passenger trains are conveyed, besides passengers, certain other objects of transport which require expedition, and can bear a tariff of corresponding amount. These are principally carriages, horses, baggage, parcels, and the mails.

By the goods or merchandise trains are conveyed all descriptions of merchandise, of heavy goods and live stock, such as cattle, sheep, pigs, and calves.

These two species of traffic are conducted by a different set of agents, and in a great measure by a different establishment, though connected with the same company.

The trains are in general propelled by a different class and form of engine, at different speeds, and in some cases at different epochs in the 24 hours. In short, between these two classes of traffic there is very little in common, except the road on which they are transported; and it is doubtful whether the advantage of the railways would not have been better consulted, if a separate line of rails had been laid for the goods traffic.

It is true that on most of the continental lines, and occasionally on the English railways, one or two passenger carriages are often attached to goods trains, and goods wagons are occasionally attached to passenger trains; but these may be regarded as exceptions to the general rule. We shall therefore fall into no error of practical importance, if we consider the passenger trains as exclusively devoted to the one class of traffic, and the goods trains to the other.

To each of the objects composing the passenger traffic a particular form of vehicle is appropriated. The first-class passenger is accommodated with a spacious carriage, in which usually a separate seat is divided off for each passenger, the interior being luxuriously cushioned, lined, and carpeted. Convenient means of varying the ventilation at the will of the passenger are provided over the windows. A lamp is placed, in some of the best conducted railways, in the centre of the roof, with a reflector projecting the light downward, which illuminates the carriage in passing through tunnels, and at night. In some railways, also, a heater is placed in cold weather in first-class carriages under the feet of the passengers, and other accommodations of minor importance are provided.

Carriages are appropriated to the second-class passengers, in which the seats are not divided, and where less room is left for each passenger. On the continental lines these carriages are usually lined, and have the seats cushioned. Less space is also left between the seats; carpets are not provided; nor are they always lighted or ventilated; and never warmed.

The carriages appropriated to third-class passengers are still more contracted in the space allowed for a given number of passengers. They are neither cushioned, lined, carpeted, ventilated, nor illuminated, and in some cases are unprovided with any other means of closing the windows than wooden blinds or coarse curtains. These carriages are, however, usually roofed

These several arrangements vary much in different railways.

The carriages provided for the transport of horses are called *horse-boxes*. Each of them consists usually of three stalls, the animal standing across the road, and therefore being carried sideways, and being completely inclosed and covered in.

Private carriages are transported on flat trucks constructed for the purpose. They are rolled upon these, and when brought to their position, wedges are placed before and behind the wheels, and the carriages are lashed in their places.

Passengers' baggage, except such small baggage or packages as the passengers are enabled to take with them, is usually carried in baggage-vans appropriated to the purpose, which are placed under the superintendence of a baggage conductor. These vans are divided into compartments, so as to enable the conductor to sort the baggage according to its place of destination.

In some railways, including most of the English lines, passengers' baggage is placed on the roof of the passenger carriages.

Under the title of parcels is included that class of transport which, before the establishment of railways, was denominated coach parcels, and which on the Continent is called "Articles de Messagerie." This class of traffic, before the establishment of railways, was also extensively expedited in vans, which traveled at 5 or 6 miles an hour.

The increased powers of expeditious transport obtained by railways has augmented this class of transport in a very large ratio.

For the transport of the mails a special vehicle is provided, which is a moving post-office, being a bureau of considerable magnitude, provided with all the usual office furniture, and all the necessary means for the sorting of the correspondence as the train proceeds.

In this way a certain portion of the business of the post-office, formerly executed before the dispatch of the mails, is performed upon the road, whereby expedition is gained.

On some of the foreign railways, cattle, sheep, and pigs are also sent by the passenger trains. In England these are, however, sent by goods trains.

Commodities of consumption which are perishable are frequently sent by the passenger trains. Thus, on the continental railways, the produce of the dairy, the garden, and the farm-yard, as well as fish, are frequently sent by these trains.

The goods trains are appropriated to the transport of heavy commodities of every description. They consist of wagons of various forms, some closed, some open, some having sides and ends, but open at the top, and some being mere platforms on wheels.

These are appropriated to the transport of different classes of goods, according to their quality, and the degree of care and shelter necessary for them.

The roofs of close wagons are frequently covered with an awning prepared with caoutchouc, so as to render them waterproof.

The forms of the wagons appropriated to cattle vary according to the class of cattle they are intended to carry.

Beasts are carried in wagons having only a single tier. Pigs and sheep are often carried in the same wagon, tier above tier, and crowded very closely together, a wagon not unfrequently carrying 70 to 80. To facilitate the loading and discharge, these classes of animals are sometimes sent in cribs provided by their owners, which only require to be laid and fastened upon a platform wagon.

The carrying stock of a system of railways forms an important item in its movable capital.

On the Belgian railways, consisting, as has been stated, of 347 miles, there were, on 1st January, 1847, 724 passenger carriages and 2507 goods wagons.

On the North of France railway there were, on 1st January, 1848 (322 miles of railway being then open), the following carrying stock:

First-class passenger coaches	102
Second-class passenger coaches	183
Third-class passenger coaches	199
Baggage-wagons	97
Carriage-trucks	78
Horse-boxes	50
Milk-wagons	20
Goods-wagons	1459
Sugar-wagons	200
Cattle-wagons	410
Sheep-wagons	50
Post-offices	2
Total stock of vehicles	2850

According to the report of Captain Huish, the following was the amount and value of the carrying stock of the Northwestern Railway Company, on the 1st January, 1848

THE CARRYING STOCK.

Passenger Vehicles.	Southern Division.	Northern Division.	Manchester and Birmingham.	Total.	Value.	
					Average Price.	Total.
	No.	*No.*	*No.*	*No.*	£.	£.
State carriage	1	..	..	1	900	900
First class, 6 wheels	20	8	..	28	420	11,760
Do. 4 do.	154	136	38	328	320	104,960
Mails	16	16	..	32	250	8,000
Composite	25	6	4	35	200	7,000
Second class	178	178	45	401	220	88,220
Third class (closed)	52	80	18	150	170	25,500
Do. (open)	43	..	32	75	80	6,000
Post-offices	3	..	5	8	390	3,120
Horse-boxes	136	54	20	210	105	22,050
Carriage-trucks	149	56	12	217	88	19,096
Parcel-vans	13	6	7	26	180	4,680
Guard-vans	42	18	2	62	175	10,850
Bullion-vans	4	5	..	9	100	900
Post-office tenders	6	7	..	13	210	2,730
Luggage-vans	..	5	..	5	220	1,100
Parcel-carts	..	14	5	19	20	380
Milk-trucks	..	2	..	2	60	120
Brake-wagons	..	4	..	4	30	120
Convict carriage-truck	..	1	..	1	160	160
	842	596	188	1626		317,646
Goods Vehicles.						
6 Ton large goods wagons	} 831	100	29 }	2745		
4½ " ordinary do.		1593	192 }			
3½ " small do.	510	1077	542	2129		
Cattle-wagons	382	83	30	495		
Coal-trucks (iron)	..	..	653	653		
Timber-trucks	12	..	..	12		
Brake-wagons	53	24	..	77		
Sheep-vans	117	..	..	117		
Powder magazines	4	..	..	4		
Iron trolleys	4	..	..	4		
	1913	2877	1446	6236		

Viz.:	£	s.
Southern Division, 1913 at 72*l.* 10*s.* each, average	138,692	10
Northern Division, 2877 at 56*l.* each	161,112	0
Manchester and Birmingham, 1446 at 41*l.* 10*s.*	60,009	0

The carrying stock, like the locomotive power, of the North-western Company, was used to work the traffic of other lines which the company contracted to supply with rolling stock.

Passenger vehicles were supplied by the company for the entire traffic of the following lines during the twelve months, ending 30th June, 1849:

	Miles.
London and Northwestern, and its branches	438
Chester and Holyhead	$80\frac{1}{2}$
Kendal and Windermere	$9\frac{3}{4}$
Shrewsbury and Stafford (Shropshire Union)	$29\frac{1}{4}$*
Preston and Carlisle	90
Preston and Parkside (North Union)	22
Total supplied with passenger vehicles	$669\frac{1}{2}$

Goods vehicles were provided for all the above lines, except the Preston and Carlisle.

In the carrying department a register should be kept exhibiting the mileage of each individual vehicle, similar to the register already described in the drawing department; but inasmuch as the duty of the carrying stock is more simple than that of the drawing stock, there will be less complexity in such a register. All that can be required is, that the carrying stock shall be classed and properly designated by numbers, so that each vehicle may be distinguished and referred to.

In the register should be stated the total mileage from month to month, of each particular vehicle. By comparing the total mileage of all the vehicles, of any particular class, worked upon the railway with the number of such vehicles included in the carrying stock, the average mileage of each vehicle of that class can be ascertained.

Thus if C express in general the number of any particular class of vehicle, and c the total annual mileage of such class, then $\dfrac{c}{C}$ will be the average annual mileage of each vehicle of that class

As an illustration of this, I give in the following table the number, the total mileage, and the average annual mileage of the various classes of vehicles employed on the Belgian railways in the year 1844. In the first column is given the number of vehicles, in the second their total mileage, in the third their average annual mileage, and in the fourth their average daily mileage.

* The Shropshire Union was not opened for traffic until June, 1849.

THE CARRYING STOCK.

Description of Vehicle.	Number.	Total Mileage.	Average annual Mileage.	Average daily Mileage.
Passenger-coaches, 1st class	110	1,671,454	15,195	41·6
" 2d class	186	2,013,231	10,824	29·5
" 3d class	290	2,591,136	8,935	24·5
Baggage-vans	27	839,000	31,074	85·0
Parcel-vans	33	1,056,360	32,010	86·0
Horse-boxes	25	93,208	3,728	10·2
Carriage-trucks	75	310,700	4,143	11·0
Goods-wagons	1735	8,432,188	4,860	13·0
Cattle-wagons (beasts)	36	139,777	3,883	10·5
" (sheep, pigs, &c.)	12	46,604	3,882	10·5

It appears from this table that very considerable differences exist, in the case of the Belgian railways, betwen the extent to which the different classes of vehicles comprising the passenger-carrying stock have been utilized. That part of the stock, however, which appears most exceptional in this respect, viz., the horse-boxes and carriage-trucks, were comparatively little used. The baggage-vans and parcel-vans, on the other hand, were more largely utilized, having a daily mileage of more than double that of the first-class passenger coaches, while the latter had a considerably greater daily mileage than either the second or third class.

It is to be regretted that the railway reports, whether in England or on the Continent, supply extremely scanty materials for general conclusions as to the relative daily service of the different classes of vehicles employed in passenger trains. We have, however, some collective results, which afford conclusions that may pretend to generality.

I have arranged these in the following table (see page 96), in which is included also the aggregates of the preceding table.

The daily duty resulting from these calculations of the different classes of carriages employed is so much smaller than might have been expected, that, if we had not so large a basis as that given above, some distrust might be entertained of the accuracy of the results.

Although we can not command, at present, more extensive data for the calculations of the carrying stock *in classes*, we have some further means of estimating its collective amount, the results of which will further corroborate the above conclusions.

Name of Railway.	Number of Carriages.	Total Mileage.	Average annual Mileage.	Average daily Mileage.
First-Class Carriages.				
Belgian Lines, 1844	110	1,671,454	15,195	41·5
North of France, 1847	101	1,889,990	18,811	51·0
" 1848	102	1,544,011	15,137	41·5
Totals and averages	313	5,105,455	16,311	44·7
Second-Class Carriages.				
Belgian Lines, 1844	186	2,013,231	10,824	29·5
North of France, 1847	183	2,364,209	12,919	35·5
" 1848	183	2,330,800	12,731	35·0
Totals and averages	552	6,708,240	12,152	33·3
Third-Class Carriages.				
Belgian Lines, 1844	290	2,591,136	8,935	24·5
North of France, 1847	218	2,442,726	11,205	31·0
" 1848	200	2,197,287	11,042	30·5
Totals and averages	708	7,231,149	10,213	27·8

We have before us the collective mileages and quantities of the carrying stock used on five foreign railways, including the results of the year 1845 of the Belgian railways. We have given these in the following table:

Mileage of Passenger-carrying Stock.				
Names of Railways.	No. of Vehicles in carrying stock.	Total Mileage	Average annual Mileage.	Average daily Mileage.
Paris and Orleans	269	4,462,822	16,613	45·5
Paris and Rouen	207	4,817,792	23,274	64·0
Alsatian Railways	112	2,427,924	21,669	59·0
Rhenish Railways	63	1,084,373	17,212	47·0
Belgian Railways, 1845	940	10,030,078	11,202	31·0
Totals and averages	1591	22,828,989	14,349	39·0

The daily mileage obtained here, as the average for all classes of vehicles used in passenger traffic on the above railways, is greater than what would result from the previous calculations. This is explained by the particular character of the traffic on the principal lines included in the table. They pass, in general, through districts thinly peopled, having few important stations and few departures, the consequence of which is, that the distance traveled in a single trip, or the average mileage of the passengers, is greater than in the case of railways passing through a more densely peopled country. This is rendered manifest in the table itself, by the comparatively small daily mileage afforded by the vehicles on the Belgian railways.

As I have so often already stated, we are without the necessary data for making similar calculations with respect to English railways generally; but I have procured a return of the carrying stock on the lines worked by the Northwestern Railway during the half-year ending 31st December, 1848, which will supply inferences which are valuable in proportion to the great extent of railway to which they refer. I have already shown that these returns include the traffic on nearly seven hundred miles of the most active railway enterprise in the United Kingdom.

In the previous table I have given the number of vehicles employed in the passenger traffic, their total mileage, as calculated from the average loads estimated by Captain Huish, as being transported in each class of carriage, and the total mileage of the passengers, of which I possess a return.

TABULAR ANALYSIS of the Movement of the Passenger-carrying Stock on the Lines worked by the Northwestern Company during the Half-year ending December 31, 1848.

	Number of Vehicles.	Total Mileage.	Average Mileage per Vehicle.	Average daily Mileage per Vehicle.
Passenger coaches:				
1st class	451	4,834,324	10,719	58·8
2d class	416	3,448,364	8,289	45·5
3d class	229	1,606,760	7,016	38·6
Totals and averages	1096	9,889,448	9,023	49·5

The general accordance of these results is remarkable, and, considering the great extent of mileage, and the various sources from which they are derived, the conclusions deduced from them may be considered to be attended with much precision and generality. We may therefore be safe in assuming, as a fair approximate estimate of passenger traffic as now worked on British railways, that the average daily mileage of first, second, and third-class coaches is 59, 45, and 38 miles respectively.

In calculations, therefore, of the requisite amount of carrying stock of each class, it is only necessary to obtain an estimate of the mileage from the assumed traffic, the method of ascertaining which we shall explain hereafter. Let, then, the estimated daily mileage of the first-class carriages be divided by 59, that of the second-class carriages by 45, and that of the third-class carriages by 38, and the quotients will give the number of each of these classes of vehicles necessary to work the traffic.

Meanwhile, let us proceed to the examination of the merchandise-carrying stock.

For this purpose, we have data sufficiently extensive derived from foreign railways.

In the following table I have given the goods-carrying stock and its mileage on the undermentioned lines.

Mileage of the Goods-carrying Stock.				
Name of Railway.	Number of Vehicles.	Total Mileage.	Average annual Mileage.	Average daily Mileage.
Belgian Railways, 1844	1,783	8,618,569	4,883	14·0
" 1845	2,073	14,103,406	6,803	19·0
North of France, 1847	2,316	13,402,330	5,786	16·0
" 1848	3,069	14,505,689	4,739	13·0
Paris and Orleans	380	3,783,963	9,957	27·0
Paris and Rouen	420	4,237,034	10,088	28·0
Alsacian Railways	155	1,389,847	8,966	24·0
Rhenish Railways	304	2,267,962	7,460	20·5
Totals and averages	10,500	62,308,800	5,934	16·25

The discordance which prevails in some of these results admits of easy explanation. On lines which pass through a thinly peopled district, having but few stations, the distances to which the traffic is transported are proportionally great, and, accordingly, the average daily mileage of the wagons is increased. In the case of more busy traffic, as on the Belgian and North of France railways, the distances are less, and we find, accordingly, the average daily run of the wagons proportionally decreased.

The general average of 16 miles may be taken as a fair estimate, at least on the continental railways.

According to the reports of Captain Huish, given above, the

goods-carrying stock on the lines worked by the Northwestern Company, in 1848–9, consisted of 6236 vehicles of all descriptions, the chief part of which were merchandise wagons, carrying an average load of $2\frac{1}{4}$ tons. We have no direct or accurate means of calculating the mileage of this stock, but I have made an approximate estimate of it by comparing the total receipts with the average tariff per ton per mile.

TABULAR ANALYSIS of the Movement of the Goods-carrying Stock on the Lines worked by the Northwestern Company during the half-year ending Dec. 31, 1848.

Number of vehicles	6,236
Total estimated mileage	31,259,840
Average mileage per vehicle	5,013
Average mileage per vehicle, per day	27·5

The small amount of the daily useful mileage of the goods-carrying stock, is explained by the great length of time which is always consumed in the loading and unloading of the wagons, and in waiting for the formation of complete loads and trains. The goods are not generally dispatched at stated intervals, like the passenger traffic; they are collected in the goods dépôt, sorted according to their destinations, and loaded. The wagons are detained in sidings, until a sufficient quantity is collected to form a complete load. When they have arrived at their several destinations, they have to be discharged, and to wait for a return load, or to be sent back empty.

All these circumstances involve a large consumption of time, and it will be easily understood, when the speed of the transport is considered, how small a proportion the time of transport must be to the time during which the goods-carrying stock is either waiting or undergoing the process of loading or discharge.

Taking the average speed of the goods traffic on the continental line at 14 miles an hour, it would follow that the average time that the carrying stock is actually employed in carrying transport does not much exceed one hour.

If we take the average speed of the goods trains on the English railways at 18 miles an hour, it will follow that each vehicle is worked for an hour and a half daily.

In exhibiting the annual duty of the rolling stock, it is necessary to ascertain the average number of each class of vehicle drawn by each engine, or, in other words, the average composition of each train. This may always be determined by comparing the analysis of the carrying stock, such as above described, with the analysis of the performance of the locomotive stock exhibited in the last chapter.

To ascertain, for example, the average number of *first-class* carriages drawn by each engine, it is only necessary to divide the total mileage of the first-class carriages by the total mileage of the passenger engines; and in the same way may be determined the number of each class of vehicles drawn by each class of engine.

As an example of this calculation, the following computation, from the official reports of the Belgian railways for 1844, is given. The numbers are merely the quotients found by dividing the total mileage of the several classes of vehicles already given by the mileage of the passenger engines on the one hand, and of the goods engines on the other.

Average Number of Vehicles of each Class drawn by each Engine.

In passenger trains:
 Passenger carriages, 1st class .... 1·61
   ,,   2d class .... 1·94
   ,,   3d class .... 2·50
 Baggage-vans .... 0·81
 Parcel-vans .... 1·01
 Horse-boxes .... 0·09
 Carriage-trucks......................... 0·30

In goods trains:
 Goods-wagons........................... 15·41
 Cattle-wagons (beasts)................... 0·25
   ,, (small cattle) .... 0·08

Total number drawn:
 In passenger trains...................... 8·26
 In goods trains .... 15·74

To explain the meaning of the numbers contained in the above table, it is only necessary to state that, when it is said that the average number of vehicles composing a passenger train was 8·26, and the average number of vehicles composing a goods train was 15·74, it is meant that 100 passenger engines drew 826 vehicles, and that 100 goods engines drew 1574 vehicles. In like manner, when it is said that the average number of baggage-vans drawn by the passenger train was 0·81, it is meant that, in 100 passenger trains, there were 81 baggage vans.

On railways where passenger traffic is to any considerable extent combined with goods traffic, it is desirable that a mileage account should be kept of such passenger traffic as is carried with the goods train separate from the general passenger traffic.

The following example, computed from the reported performance of the Paris and Orleans Railway, will further illustrate this.

As the goods trains were frequently drawn by two engines, we shall give separately the computation of the average number of vehicles drawn by such goods engines, and the average number of vehicles composing each train. The one will be found by dividing the mileage of the vehicles respectively by the total mileage of the goods engines; the other will be found by dividing them by the mileage of the trains. The latter will evidently give the average composition of the trains; while the former will give the average composition of the trains, considering each train drawn by two engines as two trains.

In the first column of the following table is given the designation of the vehicles, in the second is given their mileage, and in the third is given the quotients obtained by dividing this mileage by the total mileage of the goods engines, which, in this case, was 153,227 miles; and in the fourth column is given the quotient obtained by dividing the mileage of the vehicles by the total mileage of the trains, which, in this case, was 140,147.

Vehicles drawn.	Mileage.	Average Number of Vehicles per Engine.	Average Number of Vehicles per Train.
Flour-wagons	1,303,298	8·5	9·30
Covered goods-wagons	992,244	6·5	7·08
Platform-wagons	627,614	4·1	4·48
Cattle-wagons	580,108	3·8	4·14
Horse-boxes	22,423	0·15	0·16
Carriage-trucks	21,023	0·14	0·15
Passenger carriages:			
1st class	32,232	0·21	0·23
2d class	140,147	0·91	1·00
3d class	21,023	0·14	0·15
Baggage-wagons	60,725	0·39	0·43
Total	3,800,837	23·13	27·12

The reports of the English railways afford no general data for such estimates of the composition of the trains. Some conclusions respecting the composition of the trains may, however, be deduced from the data given above, in reference to the traffic of the lines worked by the Northwestern Company.

By dividing the estimated mileage of the three classes of passenger-coaches by the mileage of the passenger-engines, of which we have given the return, p. 85, we find that the number of each class of carriage drawn by each engine was, on an average, as follows:

1st class coaches	2·00
2d class ,,	1·48
3d class ,,	0·69
Total	4·17

This result must be interpreted with reference to the manner in which the trains are organized on these and other English railways. Some trains consist of first-class carriages only; others of first and second-class; and others exclusively, or principally, of third-class coaches. The above computation gives the number of coaches of each class which would enter into the composition of each train, if the coaches of each class were uniformly distributed among all the trains. In the practical working of the line the first-class trains have more than 2·00 first-class coaches; and the third-class trains more than 0·69 third-class coaches.

It is necessary also to state, that the data on which these calculations are made, so far as relates to the English lines, are altogether insufficient and unsatisfactory; and the conclusions are only to be received as the best approximation that can be made with the stinted information obtained.

No data are attainable by which either the mileage of the other vehicles composing the passenger trains, such as horse-boxes, carriage-trucks, vans, &c., or the number of these respectively which enter into the average composition of a train, can be ascertained, even approximately.

To ascertain the average number of wagons composing a goods train, we must divide the mileage of the goods wagons by that of the goods engines. This gives, for the lines worked by the Northwestern Company, as quotient, 21·7. Thus it would follow that the average number of goods wagons entering a train was 21·7, which, with brake-vans, &c., would compose a train of 24 to 25 vehicles.

These conclusions, though obtained only on approximate data, are in near accordance with the average magnitudes of the trains, according to the estimate of Captain Huish.

He estimates a passenger train, on the Northwestern lines, at 70 tons, engine and tender included. If the engine and tender, with their complement of water and fuel, be taken at 30 tons, and $5\frac{1}{2}$ tons be allowed for each vehicle with its load, we should have about seven vehicles composing the train. But, from the preceding calculation, it appears that of these, 4·17 are passenger-coaches. There would remain, therefore, about three for horse-boxes, carriage-trucks, luggage and parcel-vans, break-vans, and post-offices.

Captain Huish also estimates the average weight of a goods train at 154 tons. If 34 tons be allowed for the engine and tender, we shall have 120 tons for the wagons, which, at 5 tons per wagon, would give 24 wagons as composing the train. By the preceding computation the number of goods wagons would be nearly 22, which, with brake-vans, would make up the estimated number.

If it be required to exhibit the average extent to which the railway has been used by the rolling stock, it will be sufficient to compare the mileage of each class of vehicle with the length of the line. To prevent erroneous inferences, it will be necessary, however, clearly to explain what meaning ought to be attached to the results of such a process of calculation.

Let us first take the locomotive stock.

If the total mileage of the passenger engines be divided by the total length of the railway upon which they are worked, the quotient will represent the average number of passenger engines which have run over every part of the road. The meaning of this is, that the quotient will express the number of passenger engines which, having run each once over the entire extent of the railway, will have accomplished the same total mileage as have the actual passenger engines. In effect, this is nothing more than diffusing, as it were, the mileage of the engines, which was unequally distributed over different parts of the line, uniformly over the whole line.

The same explanation will apply to the mileage of the goods engines, and to the mileage of every class of vehicles.

If, then, we divide successively the total mileage of each class of engines, and of each class of vehicles composing the carrying stock, by the length of the railway, we shall find a series of quotients which will express the number of engines and of vehicles of each class, each of which being once moved over the entire railway would have accomplished the same total mileage as the entire rolling stock has actually done.

Thus, as already explained, this process consists in diffusing uniformly over the whole line the mileage of the rolling stock.

As an example of this, let us take the Belgian railways for the year 1844.

The entire length of the railways on which the rolling stock was employed was 347 miles. If we divide this into the mileage of the locomotive stock given in table p. 84, and into that of the carrying stock given in table p. 95, we shall obtain a series of quotients which will exhibit the number of engines, and mileage of each kind, which, being distributed uniformly over the whole length of the railway, will represent the actual amount of traffic. This is exhibited in the following table:

TABLE showing the Quantity of locomotive and carrying Stock which, being moved the whole Length of the Belgian Railways, consisting of 347 Miles, would have the same Mileage as the actual Stock.

Engines		4556
Passenger-carrying stock:		
	Passenger carriages, 1st class	4814
	,, 2d class	5802
	,, 3d class	7467
	Baggage-vans	2418
	Parcel-vans	3044
	Horse-boxes	268
	Carriage-trucks	895
Goods-carrying stock:		
	Goods-wagons	2429
	Cattle-wagons (beasts)	402
	,, (small cattle)	134

In the case of a system of railways on which the traffic is tolerably uniform, this average distribution of the traffic over the entire line may be safely adopted as the basis of general reasoning; but it frequently happens, in an extensive system of railways, that different parts of the line are very unequally used by the traffic. An extremely active traffic will prevail on some sections, while others are comparatively deserted. Any average calculation of this kind requires, therefore, in such case, to be applied in a qualified sense; and indeed it is desirable in all cases to obtain, as far as practicable, an estimate of the extent to which every separate section of the railway is used by the rolling stock.

On the continental railways, where records of the services are maintained with more care and accuracy than appears to be customary in England, the amount of traffic on every section of the line can be separately obtained and exhibited. We shall return to this subject in a following chapter.

To ascertain the dead weight drawn by each engine, it is only necessary to know the average weight of each species of empty vehicle. In the case of the Belgian railways, the following were the weights of the different classes of vehicles:

	In Tons.
Passenger carriage, 1st class	3·15
,, 2d class	3·00
,, 3d class	2·75
Baggage-vans	3·50
Parcel-vans	3·25
Horse-box	3·40
Carriage-truck	2·60
Goods-wagon	2·60
Cattle-wagon (beasts)	2·60
,, (small cattle)	2·60

The average amount of dead weight drawn by each engine may be found by comparing the average composition of each train with the average weights of the different classes of carriages composing it. Thus, by comparing the above tables, the one showing the average composition of the passenger and goods trains, and the other the weights of the vehicles composing them respectively, we shall find the following to be the average dead weight drawn by each class of engine:

	Tons.
In passenger trains:	
Passenger carriages, 1st class	5·07
,, 2d class	5·82
,, 3d class	6·88
Baggage-vans	2·84
Parcel-vans	3·28
Horse-boxes	0·30
Carriage-trucks	0·78
In goods trains:	
Goods-wagons	40·07
Cattle-wagons (beasts)	0·65
,, (small cattle)	0·21
Total dead weight drawn by each engine:	
In passenger trains	27·73
In goods trains	40·93

As the carrying business of the railway companies is at present conducted, some practical difficulty may arise in making deductions from the mileage of the carrying stock, as compared with that of the traffic; for, as will be presently explained, the carrying stock of each company runs more or less over the lines of the others. The traffic, therefore, of each company is not, strictly speaking, carried by its own carrying stock exclusively; and, on the other hand, its own carrying stock is not exclusively employed in carrying its own traffic. If, however, it may be assumed, in reference to the operations of a large company like the Northwestern, that the average amount of mileage of the rolling stock of other companies which pass over its lines is equal to the average mileage of its own rolling stock upon other lines, the result of calculations made by comparing the mileage of the rolling stock with the traffic, will still in the main be correct.

To obtain perfectly exact inferences, however, with regard to the use of the carrying stock, we ought to be in possession, on the one hand, of the total mileage of the traffic of each class carried by all the companies, who use their carrying stock in common; and, on the other hand, of an account of the mileage of the total carrying stock they use in common. In effect, the general business should be treated as though it were the business of a single company, and the general carrying stock similarly regarded.

This point naturally leads to the consideration of the subject of the clearing-house, which we shall explain in a subsequent chapter.

To ascertain the proportion of the dead weight to the profitable load on the English railways, we do not possess as full or satisfactory data as in the case of foreign railways, where the official and other reports supply more ample and minute details. It may be stated, however, generally, that the weight of the first-class coaches on the English railways at present varies from $4\frac{1}{2}$ tons to nearly 5 tons; that the weight of the second-class carriages varies from $3\frac{1}{2}$ tons to $4\frac{1}{2}$ tons; and that of the third-class carriages from 3 to 4 tons.

CHAPTER VII.

MAINTENANCE AND REPRODUCTION OF THE ROLLING STOCK.

A QUESTION has lately been raised among railway companies, respecting the wear and tear of the rolling stock, and the proper method of maintaining it in a state of perfect efficiency.

Analogies have been suggested between this and the permanent way, and it has been argued that, as the permanent way, notwithstanding its annual repair, is liable to a gradual deterioration from year to year, and will at length become so worn as to require complete renewal; so the rolling stock, notwithstanding its annual repairs, will be in a like condition, and at a certain epoch, more or less remote, will be brought to a state of decrepitude, so to speak, which will reduce its value to that of old materials; and that at this epoch, whenever it may arrive, a like renewal of the rolling stock, including under this term the drawing stock and the carrying stock, will become necessary.

It was only lately, however, that the question was raised whether the rolling stock was really, in the condition here described, analogous to the permanent way, and whether there is in fact incidental to it the insensible deterioration not made up by the regular annual repairs and replacement of worn-out stock.

Nothing can be more simple and manifest than the economical principles upon which the solution of such a question must be founded. Railway companies have a double character. They are at once proprietors and farmers, landlords and tenants. As owners of the road they are proprietors, as workers of the road they are tenants.

In the one capacity, they are guardians of capital; in the other, they are administrators of revenue: in the one, they have an interest to maintain the permanent way and the floating capital in the highest state of efficiency out of revenue; in the latter, they have an interest not to expend more out of revenue than they are required to do with reference to the stock delivered to them for work.

The first projectors of the improved modern railways contemplated themselves only as proprietors of the lines. They intended to make a road, and to offer it to the public to be run upon, all persons having the means of transport upon it, paying them a toll for its use. The railways, however, had scarcely come into operation, when it became glaringly manifest that this analogy to a common road was altogether destitute of foundation, and that the new instrument of transport must be worked upon principles, and by methods, totally different. It became evident, in a word, that the proprietors of the road must themselves become *carriers* upon it; the unity of management, and the harmony of movement, indispensable to the efficient action of its peculiar mode of transport, rendering this indispensable.

The Liverpool and Manchester Railway Company therefore at once provided, under the force of circumstances, an apparatus for transport between these two great commercial marts. Other railways quickly succeeded, and followed the same course.

Various other exigencies soon pressed upon the railway proprietary. In the first instance, they derived their supply of drawing and carrying stock from the established manufactories of engines and carriages in various parts of the country. The demand, however, for these objects of fabrication multiplied with unparalleled rapidity. A supply was required, not only by companies throughout the United Kingdom, but by companies which sprung into existence in all parts of Europe. The established manufacturers were utterly unable to meet demands so extensive, and, in a short period after the opening of the Liverpool and Manchester Railway, all the steam-engine manufacturers in England had more orders than they could satisfy in several years.

Under these circumstances, the railway companies saw themselves reduced to the alternative, either of suspending their progress, or of fabricating for themselves. They, of course, adopted the latter measure, and proceeded to erect extensive works for the manufacture of engines and carriages, at convenient points upon the principal lines.

Ultimately, this measure was crowned with complete success; and the large companies were soon in a condition, not only to supply all their own wants, but to furnish engine power and vehicles of transport for the smaller companies, whose means did not justify them in erecting similar establishments. Thus, the Northwestern Company have establishments for the fabrication of every part of their rolling stock at Crewe, Wolverton;

Longsight, Liverpool, and London; and the other large companies, though less amply, are still adequately provided. The establishments of the Northwestern Company are of such magnitude as to enable them to supply the stock necessary to work, not only their own lines, consisting of about 450 miles, but also the lines of other companies, extending to about 220 miles more. The three factories at Crewe, Wolverton, and Longsight have absorbed a capital of nearly half a million sterling.

At Wolverton, a station about 50 miles from London, and therefore midway between London and Birmingham, the Northwestern Company have built a factory for the maintenance and repair of the locomotive stock employed upon this section of the railway, with its branches included between London and Birmingham, formerly known as the London and Birmingham Railway, and at present distinguished as the southern division of the Northwestern Railway. The aspect of this establishment would afford to any intelligent observer a striking evidence of the great cost at which the locomotive power of a railway, having so active a traffic as this, is maintained.

The factory itself, of immense extent, is supplied with a large stock of machinery of every kind used in constructing those great engines whose performance has so justly excited the astonishment and admiration of the public. Here are seen two or three dozen lathes driven by steam, as well as planing machines, screw-cutting machines, boring and drilling machines, and, in a word, all the stock of an engine factory on a vast scale. Attached to it is an extensive stable, for the reception of the engines which are under repair, corresponding in form and magnitude with those already described as being erected at chief stations.

The company have built a small village around the works for the habitations of the operatives employed in them, and we there see a population of from 1800 to 2000, with a church, schools, libraries, reading-rooms, and all the conveniences that an opulent and intelligent body like that which presides over this system of railways may be conceived to provide.

The establishment of Crewe is on a still more extensive scale, being erected for the purposes not merely of maintenance and repair, but for the manufacture of engines.

The town of Crewe has sprung up within a few years in connection with these works, and now contains a population of about 8000, of whom about one half are in the employment of the railway company.

The works of Crewe are erected upon a vast scale. Here machinery may be seen of every description, driven by steam-engines of great power, and performing all the operations connected with the construction of the ponderous engines which work the passenger and goods traffic, on nearly 700 miles of railway, spread over the country between Birmingham, Liverpool, Holyhead, and Carlisle; for the Northwestern Company not only provides the power necessary for working its own lines, but also works, by a species of contract, several other adjacent lines of railway.

I have already stated that the stock of engines in actual operation during the twelve months ending the 30th June, 1849, was above 457, besides 47 new engines in store.

In the workshops at Crewe may be seen, engines in every stage of progress, from the unconnected parts, the *disjecta membra*, to the machine in combination and ready for starting on the road.

There is sufficient power there to turn out a complete engine every week, making an annual supply amounting to about 10 per cent. on the total stock.

The following statement of the locomotive stock of the Northwestern Railway on the 1st January, 1848, when it was less in amount than at the epoch above mentioned, is given by Captain Huish in his report to the directors, dated June, 1848:

STATEMENT showing Quantity and estimated actual Value of Articles included in Amount charged to Capital for "Working Stock" of £1,462,901.—January 1st, 1848.

ENGINES.	Goods.	Passengers.	Total.	Value.	
				Per Engine Average.	Total.
	No.	*No.*	*No.*	£. *s.*	£.
Southern Division	71	109	180	1,499 10	269,900
Northern Division	60	126	186	1,321 0	245,706
Manchester and Birmingham	8	25	33	1,400 0	46,200
Engines condemned and used in pumping, ballasting, &c.—Southern Division	..	..	12	750 0	9,000
Engines sold, less amount received for 6—deducted from Capital Account to Dec. 31st, 1847	..	..	15	..	6,775
			426		

CHAP. VII.] REPRODUCTION OF ROLLING STOCK.

ENGINES.	Goods.	Passengers.	Total.	Value.	
				Per Engine Average.	Total.
WORK IN PROGRESS. *Locomotive Department.*	*No.*	*No.*	*No.*	£.	£.
Southern Division	..	..	..	..	3,610
Northern Division (Crewe)	..	..	..	27,410 0	} 32,894
Ditto (L. & M.)	..	..	..	5,484 0	
Ditto (Stores)	..	..	..	..	25,802
			No.	Price.	
TENDERS.					
Southern Division	..	..	187	250 0	46,750
Northern Division	..	..	178	274 0	48,772
Manchester and Birmingham	..	..	31	300 0	9,300
TOOLS, MOVABLE MACHINERY, &c., IN ENGINE SHOPS.					
Southern Division	..	..	..	..	31,800
Northern Division	..	..	..	..	23,687
Manchester and Birmingham	..	..	..	..	3,119
Amount advanced to Sharp, Brothers, on account of undelivered engines	..	..	..	..	5,000
Total for Locomotive Account	..	..	..	..	808,315

A second department of this vast establishment is devoted to the supply of the carrying-stock, that is to say, of the passenger carriages of every description—the horse-boxes, baggage-vans, parcel-vans, brake-vans, carriage-trucks, post-offices, and merchandise wagons of every class.

When it is considered that the company keep in active service about 1100 passenger coaches and above 6000 goods-wagons of various kinds, and that, besides the innumerable passenger trains which run upon the lines, there are 15 regular goods trains daily, it will be easily conceived how vast a power of supply must be necessary for the maintenance of the rolling stock, and what ample employment is supplied for this department of the Crewe establishment, where there are always from 50 to 60 new passenger coaches in progress, besides numberless other vehicles.

Captain Huish has given the following statement of the carrying stock employed upon various railways in England and Scotland on the 1st of January, 1848, an epoch when the rolling stock of the Northwestern was considerably less in extent than at the present time:

Line.	Goods wagons.	Cattle-wagons.	Coal-wagons.	Miscellaneous.	Total.	Remarks.
	No.	No.	No.	No.		
London and Northwestern	4845	612	653	97	6,207	
Midland	3600	300	2500*	..	6,400	* Can
Eastern Counties	1057	639	529	70	2,295	be used
Great Western	890	..	..	30	922	for
York and North Midland	861	..	826	34	1,721	Goods
York, Newcastle, and Berwick	1991	..	9798	..	11,788	also.
Edinburgh and Glasgow	917	..	..	..	917	
Lancashire and Yorkshire	3000	..	..	..	3,000	

The Great Western wagons are of twice the capacity of those on the narrow gauge, and their merchandise traffic is one third of the London and Northwestern Company's.

Before the fabrication of railway vehicles was conducted on the present extensive scale, the cost of a first-class carriage was £420, and that of a second-class carriage £300. By improved processes consequent upon the more enlarged scale of the manufacture, these vehicles are now constructed with greater capacity and accommodation, at lower prices. A first-class carriage, affording ample accommodations for 18 passengers, is now constructed for £380, and a second-class carriage, accommodating 25 passengers, costs £260; horse-boxes about £150, and other passenger vehicles, varying in cost, but averaging about £100. These prices, it must be observed, however, are the actual cost incurred by the company fabricating for themselves, without including any profit to the manufacturer. They are, in fact, the cost prices.

From the actual quantity of carrying stock of each kind employed in working certain railways of which the total amount of the traffic is known, we can obtain a close approximation to the quantity employed on all the railways of the United Kingdom.

For this purpose we may, as in like computations relative to the locomotive power, take the gross receipts as a fair exponent of the amount of the traffic.

To find the number of passenger carriages of each kind, and of other vehicles of transport used on the railways, let us then

CHAP. VII.] REPRODUCTION OF ROLLING STOCK. 113

augment the stock of the Northwestern Company in the ratio by which its traffic of each kind, is exceeded by the total traffic of all the railways of the kingdom taken collectively.

We find, by the official reports, that the relative amount of the receipts for the half-year ending 31st December, 1848, was as follows :

	On all the Railways of the Kingdom.	On the Lines worked by the Northwestern Company.	Ratio.
	£.	£.	
For passengers, 1st class	1,003,516	302,892	3·3
,, 2d class	1,360,468	273,434	5·0
,, 3d class	919,316	141,263	6·5
For goods, &c.	2,461,663	603,228	4·0

The stock of the Northwestern Company for the twelve months ending June 30th, 1849, was as follows:

Passenger coaches, 1st class............... 451
    ,, 2d class............... 416
    ,, 3d class............... 229
Horse-boxes........................... 246
Carriage-trucks........................ 228
Goods-wagons 6395

To find, therefore, the stock necessary to work the railways generally we shall multiply the stock of the Northwestern Company by the numbers given in the last column. Hence we find:

ESTIMATE of the total Carrying Stock used for working the Railway Traffic of the United Kingdom in 1848-9.

	Numbers.	Estimated Value.
		£.
Passenger coaches, 1st class	1,488	665,440
,, 2d class	2,080	540,800
,, 3d class	1,488	223,200
Horse-boxes	820	82,000
Carriage-trucks	760	66,880
Wagons for merchandise, live stock, &c.	24,944	1,621,360
Coal-wagons (uncertain)	25,000	875,000
Totals	56,580	4,074,680

Thus the carrying stock of the railways of the kingdom consists of nearly sixty thousand vehicles, of which about six thousand are passenger coaches; and the aggregate value of this stock is four million sterling, being about two per cent. of the entire capital expended.

It appears, therefore, that the chief railway companies are not merely proprietors of railways and carriers upon them, but they are also engine-builders and carriage and wagon-builders upon a scale of almost unparalleled magnitude.

By such means the rolling stock, in the widest sense of the term, is kept in a state of perfect efficiency, and receives from month to month, and from year to year, such additions as the gradual and inevitable increase of the traffic renders necessary.

As has been already observed, a question has lately been agitated as to the necessity of establishing an annual reserve fund for the future replacement of the rolling stock at a future epoch, when, notwithstanding the current annual repairs, and the infusion of new stock, the whole stock will have been so worn as to be in the mass unfit for future use, and of no other value than old materials.

On the assumption of such a contingency, several of the most considerable railway companies have for many years back put aside a sum calculated upon a conjectural estimate for this purpose. It was only recently that the question was raised, whether such a contingency as that here contemplated is really within the scope of possibility, and whether the rolling stock was, like the permanent way, subject to age? Is there or not a gradual and insensible deterioration of its condition, not made good either by annual repairs, or by the gradual infusion of new stock rendered necessary by circumstances? A practical inquiry has been accordingly instituted on this question, and it has been demonstrated that the natural progress of repairs and renewals in the movable capital of railway companies is such that no such gradual deterioration exists, and that at no future epoch could such an event arrive as that of the movable stock being reduced to such a state of deterioration as to require a complete renewal. In the course of time the stock of engines and vehicles is continually repaired. New wheels are put on at one time, and a new body at another. The different moving parts most subject to wear are gradually renewed; and the engines and vehicles may be conceived even to be subject to such a succession of repairs, that in many of them not a vestige of the original materials remains. But, independently of these repairs, fresh stock is added from year to year, to supply the place of stock which has become unfit for use, either because of its insufficient magnitude, or because of its extreme disrepair. Even in this case, however, the old materials of coaches or engines are more or less worked up into other vehicles or engines, and never totally disappear from the road.

The movable capital, therefore, may be considered to be in a state of continual reproduction; and that which, in the case of the permanent way, must take place altogether at a future epoch, when the entire road will have to be relaid, takes place in the rolling stock gradually from year to year. Its existence is perennial, and it is in a constant state of rejuvenescence.

This point having been conclusively established, the companies very properly discontinued to set aside from revenue any fund for the future reproduction of stock; but they would have been justified, in strict equity, in going further, and in taking back from the capital, and placing to the credit of revenue, all the sums which, in previous years, they had erroneously brought to the credit of capital, to represent a deterioration which did not exist, and to pay for a future want which can never arise.

Connected intimately with this circumstance was the whole question between revenue and capital, which has of late been the subject of so much discussion.

If a railway company had the permanent character of a commercial firm, the interchange of value between revenue and capital would be a matter of less importance, being a subject altogether discretionary with the proprietary. But a railway company is a fluctuating body, consisting of a variety of parties, having various, and, in some respects, opposite interests, and, nevertheless, having each claims and rights entitled to respect and consideration on the part of those to whom the management of the affairs of the company is delegated.

A part of the proprietary consists of persons who have selected the railway as a means of permanent investment. These regard the steadiness, uniformity, and permanence of dividends with quite as much solicitude as their amount. To them these dividends form a permanent current income, on the periodical return of which they lay their account.

Another class use the railway as a temporary investment, and no inconsiderable portion of them resort to it as a means of commercial speculation, purchasing the shares, not with a view to the enjoyment of dividends, but with the prospect of their re-sale at advantageous prices. With these the railway shares are objects of commercial speculation, of purchase and sale, as any other object in the market might be, being bought at a lower and sold at a higher price, and becoming thereby an ordinary source of commercial profit. Whatever may be thought of this traffic, it is an inevitable consequence of the facility with which railway stock may be transferred from hand to hand; and that quality having been conferred upon it by its creators, the consequences can not be rejected.

The rights, therefore, even of speculators in railway stock, not to mention those who in good faith use it as a temporary investment, or a sort of savings-bank, are entitled to respect and consideration.

Now the class of proprietors first mentioned have less regard to the amount of present dividends than to the permanent value of the stock, and they chiefly expect from the directors of the railway a due regard to the efficient maintenance of the permanent way and the movable stock out of revenue, before any surplus be appropriated to dividend. On the other hand, the latter class, and especially the speculators, care nothing for the permanent value of the concern, and look only to the present amount of dividend. Between these two classes of proprietors the directors are called on to do equal justice.

To augment revenue out of capital would be beneficial to the latter class at the expense of the former; and to augment capital out of revenue would be beneficial to the former at the expense of the latter. Both proceedings would be equally unjust, and ought to be avoided.

The public has of late been excited in an extraordinary degree on this question by certain reported malpractices in railway management, by which the value of shares has been raised to a spurious price in the market by unacknowledged drafts of revenue on capital, and, as usual when public excitement operates, a clamor has been raised which would hurry railway directors into the other extreme. They have been even urged on all hands to close the capital account with all practicable expedition; a measure which, it is easy to demonstrate, would be utterly impracticable, unless it were deliberately intended in future to feed capital at the expense of revenue.

It is manifest that the total cost of the permanent way, the stations, workshops, the furniture, tools, and machinery, and the entire amount of rolling stock, must be charged to capital. Now, so long as trade is progressive, so long will the traffic on railways be in a state of gradual increase. It consequently follows that a corresponding increase must annually be made in the movable stock necessary to work this traffic.

To charge such annual increase upon revenue would be to debit revenue with capital, or, what is the same, to make unacknowledged drafts on revenue in favor of capital. Such a proceeding would be unjust to the temporary shareholder.

But the impossibility of closing the capital account does not arise solely from the continual necessity of augmenting the movable stock. To the most superficial observer it must be evident that other exigencies upon capital will continually arise.

The extension of traffic renders necessary the augmentation of workshops, the increase of warehouses and stations, the construction of new wharves and sidings, and, in fine, the addition of short branches, on the one side, and on the other, of the main line. These demands on capital are not such as will recur at distant intervals, and in such a manner as to be met by extraordinary measures. They are of constant recurrence; and it must be expected, in every half-yearly account of the extensive companies, that an addition, more or less, will appear to the capital.

In the conflict that has arisen between those who, on the one hand, are interested in the maintenance of capital, and, on the other, in securing present large dividends, a question has arisen as to the expediency of taking an annual valuation of stock, and charging the revenue with a sum representing its depreciation. The propriety of such a measure may be tested by examining its consequences.

The value of the property which a railway company possesses and uses depends jointly upon the condition of efficiency in which it is maintained, and on the market value of the objects which compose it. Now, it is evident that the duty of the existing proprietors is to maintain the entire property, fixed and movable, of the company in a state of perfect efficiency, its quantity and quality being equal to what they were when the railway commenced its operations. If time has deteriorated some portion, new portions have been infused; so that, on the whole, the value in use remains the same. What depreciation, it may be asked, is the existing company called upon to make good from year to year?

The answer to this must be the *marketable* depreciation; that is to say, the fall in price produced, not by any deterioration of real value in the stock, but by other causes foreign to the business of the company acting on the market.

Now let us consider the consequences of the admission of such a principle.

The fluctuation of the marketable value of various classes of objects constituting the property of a railway company is very considerable. The rolling stock, for example, owing to improvements which have taken place in its manufacture, has undergone a considerable fall in price. Thus, a first-class carriage, which in 1837 cost £420, in 1847 could be obtained for £380. But besides this fall in price, the capacity and value for use of the first-class coach obtained in 1847 for £380 was much greater than that for which £420 was paid in 1837. In short, price and value taken together, the carriage of 1847 was more than 25 per cent. cheaper than the carriage of 1837. The same observation would be applicable to all other classes of vehicle.

It appears, then, that, in the course of ten years, a rolling stock could be obtained for £30,000 which would previously have cost £40,000. The rolling stock, therefore, in this interval, underwent a depreciation of £25 per cent. in marketable value, while it suffered no depreciation whatever in real value. Nevertheless, if the principle of annual valuation and making good depreciation out of revenue be admitted, the existing proprietors could be called upon to pay out of revenue this difference of price.

But, if the principle be good in one way, it can not be bad in another; and those who maintain that revenue must make up to capital for the diminution of marketable value in the property of the railway, can not deny that capital should, on the other hand, supply to revenue the augmentation which such value may receive from like fluctuation in the market. Now, since the establishment of railways, the price of iron rails has been subject to great fluctuations. At one time they were as low as £5 a ton, and at another epoch as high as £15 a ton. Let us suppose this fluctuation, as might easily have happened, to take place in two successive years. On valuing the rails in one year they would be estimated at £10 a ton more than their value the preceding year. Now, as in a double line of railway laid with rails of 75 lbs. per yard there are 235 tons of rails per mile, the existing shareholders would be entitled, in case of a rise in the price of the rails of £10 per ton within the year, to take from capital, in favor of revenue in this case, a credit amounting to £2350 per mile of the entire length of the double line. If the principle of depreciation and annual valuation be adopted at all, this consequence of it can not be rejected.

But, in truth, such a principle can not be maintained. If an annual valuation or survey of stock be made, it must be upon the principle of estimating it by its quantity and efficiency only, and not by its marketable value, which is determined by causes over which the company has no control, and quite independent of the use or abuse of their property.*

CHAPTER VIII.

THE STATIONS.

THE ultimate object of the railway business being the transfer from place to place of persons and goods, and the phenomena attending this operation having been peculiarly imposing and unexpected, it has, not unnaturally, so engrossed public attention, that very large and important branches of the service are almost wholly left out of view.

Nevertheless, the mere operation of change of place or transport, properly so called, constitutes in reality only a part of the great business of this branch of commerce.

To secure the safety and promptitude of dispatch and delivery, many operations are necessary, and numerous agents of a highly responsible character are employed, both before the actual business of transport begins and after it has been completed. Even while the process of locomotion is in progress there are a variety of measures necessary, not immediately connected with transport itself, for the attainment of the ultimate object of the traveler or the expeditor.

The great theatres of these operations, preliminary and subsequent to the transport, as well as at certain epochs in its progress, are the STATIONS.

It is impossible to regard the vast buildings and their dependencies, which constitute a chief terminal station of a great line of railway, without feelings of inexpressible astonishment at the

* These questions have been discussed with much ability by Captain Huish, manager of the Northwestern Railway, in two reports addressed to the directors of that company, on the renewal of the permanent way and stock. I have been indebted to these reports for much valuable information relating to the condition of the lines and the stock.

magnitude of the capital and the boldness of the enterprise, which are manifested in the operations of which they are the stage.

Nothing in the history of the past affords any parallel to such a spectacle.

Such an establishment may be regarded as consisting primarily of four distinct departments:

1st. The passenger station, appropriated to the embarkment and disembarkment of the passengers, and other objects of traffic which are carried by the same trains.

2d. The goods station, which is appropriated to the reception and embarkment, and the disembarkment and discharge, of all descriptions of goods and live stock transmitted by railway.

3d. The dépôt for the locomotive power, where the engines repose, are cleaned, examined, and repaired, and from which they issue prepared for the traction of the trains.

4th. The carriage dépôt, appropriated to the cleaning, maintenance, and repairs of the carrying stock, consisting of passenger-carriages of the various classes, carriage-trucks, and horse-boxes, baggage and parcel-vans, goods-wagons of various forms, cattle-trucks and brake-vans.

The stations for passengers and goods are generally in different and sometimes in distant positions, the place selected for each being that which is most convenient for the approach of the traffic to which they are respectively appropriated. Often, at a point short of the terminus, the line forks into two branches, one leading to the passenger, the other to the goods station.

The former is established at a place as near as can conveniently be obtained to the centre of the population which constitutes the passenger traffic; the other is established in the position found most convenient for the arrival of the goods traffic. Thus at Liverpool the branch leading to the passenger dépôt enters the town by a tunnel carried beneath the streets, and terminates at a point not far from the centre of population. The branch leading to the goods station, likewise conducted through a tunnel under the town, is carried to the docks and quays, where the goods are received directly from the shipping upon the rails, and reciprocally delivered from the rails to the shipping.

To avoid the necessity of taking locomotive engines into the town under such circumstances, and sometimes because the lines are conducted to the terminus by inclined planes, these terminal branches of the railways are sometimes worked by stationary engines and ropes. By means of these the trains of passengers or goods, as the case may be, are drawn from their respective stations to the point where the terminal branches intersect, and where they are delivered over to the locomotive engine.

Thus, from the Euston-square passenger station of the Northwestern Railway, the passenger trains were originally drawn by stationary engines up an incline, by which they were taken to the goods station at Camden Town, where they were delivered over to the locomotive. This was afterward done by the locomotive engines. At Liverpool two stationary engines are appropriated to the goods and passenger trains; one draws the passenger trains from the Lime-street station through the tunnel to the point of junction; the other draws the goods trains from the goods station at the docks to the same point.

THE PASSENGER STATION.

The passenger station consists of two departments, which are separated from each other by the lines of railway and the numerous trains of carriages which always occupy them, so that, except to the privileged agents of the railway, these departments are inaccessible to each other.

They consist of separate buildings, are supplied with separate approaches, and often lead into different lines of streets.

These two departments are appropriated, the one to the passengers about to depart upon the railway, and the other to the passengers who have arrived.

To facilitate the service of the station, the companies enter into arrangement with various public vehicles, which start from various quarters of the capital at such hours that they shall arrive at the railway station about a quarter of an hour before the trains leave.

As the hour of departure approaches, lines of these carriages will be seen rapidly converging toward the entrances of the station of departure. As they arrive, they find agents of the ra way, distinguished by their uniform, ready to aid the traveler. The moment the vehicle arrives, these agents assist him to dismount, and immediately take charge of his luggage. They supply him with the local information which may be necessary. such as the proper fare for his carriage, if he arrive in a hired vehi le. This service is important not only for the convenience of the traveler, but for the expedition of the railway business. A ge number of vehicles must arrive, deliver their fare, and depart within a very brief space of time, and such a process could not be completed without all the aid which the well-organized service of the railways can supply. The passenger, dismounted, finds that his luggage has disappeared, an agent of the railway having taken charge of it. He enters the station, and proceeding directly to the booking-office, where he pays his fare, receives a ticket, which bears marks indicating the train by which he is about to start, the hour of his departure, the class of carriage in which he is entitled to travel, and the place of his destination. Entering the building, he is conducted to a waiting-room, several of which are prepared, furnished, warmed, and lighted, and appropriated to the different classes of passengers. Here he finds, if he have a few minutes to wait, innumerable conveniences, such as guide-books, journals, and periodical publications, of the kind most in demand by travelers, offered for sale.

On passing to the platform, he finds his luggage deposited there on a barrow, in charge of a railway agent. He proceeds to the baggage-office, where it is weighed, labeled, and booked, and where he pays for excess of weight, if any such there be. His baggage is then put in charge of a loading-porter, who wheels it to the baggage-van, unless it be so small in bulk and weight that the passenger can take it in or upon the carriage in which he travels.

It is customary on the English roads to allow passengers a certain amount of luggage without additional charge, that amount being, in fact, included in their fare. The quantity allowed to first-class passengers is about 1 cwt.; to second-class passengers generally $\frac{3}{4}$ cwt.; and to third-class passengers $\frac{1}{2}$ cwt. The charge for additional weight varies on different railways. In some it is at the rate of $\frac{1}{2}d.$ per lb., independent of distance; in others it is at the rate of $\frac{1}{2}d.$ for every 80 miles traveled.

On the continental railways the quantity of luggage allowed to be taken without charge by passengers is incomparably less; but, on the other hand, the personal fares charged to passengers are also less. On some railways on the Continent no luggage is allowed to go free, unless it be small parcels which the passenger takes in his hand.

The question of free luggage is one in the equitable arrangement of which the passenger is as much interested as the railway company; and it may fairly be questioned whether the rigorous rules observed by some of the continental railways, under which all luggage whatever must be regularly weighed booked, paid for, and placed in charge of the railway agents, is not, after all, most convenient, most economical, and most advantageous to the traveler.

If an amount of luggage so considerable as that allowed to railway passengers in England be included in their personal fare, it follows that the portion of the passengers who take no luggage pay for the transport of the luggage of the remainder; for it is clear that the railway company carries nothing gratuitously, and in fixing its tariff of fares, it assumes that each passenger will take a certain average amount of luggage.

The passenger who has no luggage is generally of the class who can least afford extra expense, and the injustice of exacting from him, in the amount of his fare, the price of the transport of the luggage of the wealthier passenger is the more unjust and oppressive.

But there is another inconvenience attending the gratuitous transport of luggage. The railway company is responsible only for such articles of transport as are regularly weighed, booked, put upon the way-bill, and paid for. Gratuitously transported luggage involves, therefore, no responsibility on the part of the company. It is presumed to be in charge of its owner. Hence arise endless disputes respecting lost luggage.

An important branch of the traffic transported by passenger trains is that which in England is called Parcels, and on the Continent, "Articles de Messagerie."

Booking and reception offices for such articles are established at various places in the capitals and the large towns with which the lines of railway communicate.

The parcels thus sent are transmitted to the railway station at a specified time before the starting of the trains.

A distinct department is assigned to this business at the chief stations, supplied with a proper staff of agents, consisting of superintendents, book-keepers, weighing and loading porters, conductors, &c.

This parcel office, like the passenger station itself, is subdivided into two bureaux, one appropriated to the business of delivery, and the other of reception; or one to the parcels which arrive, and which are to be distributed and delivered, and the other to the parcels which are received and which are to be forwarded. These two offices, which are constructed on a scale proportionate to the importance of the station, and the extent of the traffic, are usually separated by the bureau of the superintendent.

On the delivery of a parcel, if its carriage is prepaid, it is first handed over to a weighing porter, who throws it into an index weighing machine, and calls out its weight to the booking clerk; the latter enters it with its destination and cost of transport.

Meanwhile the parcel is handed to another porter, who receives from a clerk a label indicating the price paid for the transport, the place of its departure, and the place of its destination, and in some cases the hour of departure. Another clerk prepares a receipt, and delivers it to the party depositing the parcel, receiving the amount of the transport. The porter who labels the parcel hands it over to the loading porter, who takes it in a barrow, with a mass of others which have been similarly dealt with, and rolls it to the parcel-van.

There an immense heap of these parcels is sorted, according to their places of destination, and delivered succesively to the conductor of the parcel vans, who disposes them in different compartments, according to the places to which they are addressed, in such a manner that he may be able, as the train passes along the road, and arrives at the successive stations, to deliver in a mass, and without delay, the parcels corresponding to each station.

To expedite the business of labeling, printed labels are prepared, completely filled up for all parcels which are what is called *light*, that is to say, under 12 lbs. weight, all such being charged at one uniform rate. The weighing porter calls out, in passing the parcels respectively to the booking clerk, "light" for such parcels, and the printed label is immediately attached to them. But when parcels are overweight and subject to a different charge, he calls out their weight, and the corresponding rate of charge is written into the label by the clerk, and is attached to the parcel.

In the experience of railways, it is found that an immense majority of the parcels thus expedited are light; parcels of the heavier description are generally such as do not require very pressing expedition, and are accordingly sent by the goods trains.

The rate charged for the transport of parcels varies more or less on different railways, and still more in different countries. In England the charge for light parcels is sometimes as low as 6*d*., and this includes delivery at the domicile of the party to whom it is addressed.

For a distance of about 100 miles, as, for instance, between Birmingham and London, the charge is 1*s*., including delivery at any part of Birmingham, and delivery in London within a radius of 3 miles round the General Post Office. The charge for such parcels increases with the distance, in the proportion of about 1s. for every additional 100 miles. Thus the charge between London and Edinburgh or Glasgow is 4s.

The establishment, however, of the uniform penny postage has greatly diminished this branch of parcel traffic, compared with what it would have been but for this system of postage reform. Thus it is clear that no parcel would be sent by railway between London and Edinburgh weighing less than 25 oz., inasmuch as the postage of such a parcel sent through the post-office would not exceed the railway tariff. Indeed, this limit might be fairly stated at a higher amount, because the expeditor can deposit his parcel in any receiving-house; whereas for the railway he is very limited in the places of delivery, and forced to observe more troublesome formalities, especially if the parcel be prepaid.

The business of the parcel department is subject, as may be expected, to great variation at different times.

Thus at seasons like Christmas it has an enormous momentary increase in both directions, so that a corps of supernumeraries is obliged to be employed at the chief stations. The average daily amount of parcels transmitted through some of the London stations is nevertheless surprising. Thus it is estimated that more than 2000 parcels per day are booked at the station of the Northwestern Railway.

On the Belgian railways, in 1847, the number of parcels booked, weighing less than 12 lbs., was at the average rate of 750 per day, and the gross weight of the parcels booked which were above that weight was at the average rate of 120 tons per day. This, however, includes the parcels booked at all the stations for 347 miles of railway.

On the Paris and Orleans Railway the average weight of parcels carried per train, during the year ending 30th June, 1847, was $\frac{3}{4}$ of a ton; and, as there were 8 trains per day, the total weight of parcels booked per day was 6 tons. In this estimate are not included the parcels brought by passengers as part of their luggage, and which were also booked and paid for.

The accuracy with which this part of the business of transport is executed may be estimated from the fact that not above one parcel in 400,000 is lost.*

* As an example of the enormous amount of business of this description occasionally transacted at chief stations, it is stated that, in

The other objects which compose the traffic of a passenger station are horses and private carriages. These are embarked at wharves especially provided for their reception at the station; and arrangements are made so that they can be always loaded, provided they arrive at the station 10 or 15 minutes before the hour of starting the train. Horses travel in a vehicle called a horse-box, which is a sort of locomotive stable, consisting of two or three stalls, so placed that the animal in traveling stands sideways. Private carriages are mounted on flat wagons called carriage-trucks, on which they are secured by wedges, and properly tied.

The owners of private carriages have the option either of traveling in them or in the railway carriages. The latter is always the most desirable course, with a view to safety, as will be explained when we come to consider the causes of accidents on railways, and the rules to be observed as conducive to the safety of the traveler.

The railway porters and agents charged with the formation of the trains arrange the carriages composing each successive train, placing usually in front the baggage-vans, horse-boxes and carriages of the inferior classes; the first-class carriages being generally placed in or near the centre of the train, which is considered the preferable position as respects safety. This will be also explained when we come to treat of railway accidents.

The carriages which form the train are screwed together so as to form a solid and compact column, and so that, upon any change of speed, either in slackening or accelerating, there should be no collision between vehicle and vehicle, as necessarily would be the case with any flexible connexion, such as a chain. But in order to prevent the shock which would necessarily be produced by change of speed in a moving mass so ponderous, the carriages are provided with an elastic apparatus called buffers, which have cushions placed at their points of junction, and are pressed by the force of the screw that unites the carriages face to face. These cushions are attached to strong cylindrical rods of iron, which press against springs having sufficient elasticity and strength to yield without breaking, and to

Christmas week, as many as 5000 barrels of oysters have been sent as parcels from the Euston-square station of the Northwestern Railway within 24 hours, each barrel containing 100 oysters. The number of these fish, therefore, expedited from this station alone to the interior, within the day, was half a million.

receive and moderate the momentum arising from change of speed.

These couplings and other arrangements are strictly attended to by the agents of the station, whose business it is to form the trains at starting.

The wharf or platform from which the passengers take their departure is elevated above the rails of the station to such a level as to be flush with the floors of the carriages, so that the passengers step into the carriages with the same facility as they would pass from one room to another.

In cases where the trains are drawn from the passenger station by a fixed engine, as already explained, this engine is usually erected, not at the passenger station, which would be an inconvenient and objectionable position, but at the most remote point to which the train has to be drawn, so that the engine draws the train toward it from the station. Thus, at the London station of the Northwestern Railway, the passenger station is at Euston-square, and the fixed engine was formerly erected at Camden Town ; and on the Liverpool Railway the fixed engine is at the top of the tunnel, the passenger station being at Lime-street. In such cases, when the train is ready to start, a communication by signal is made from the passenger station to the fixed engine, so that the latter is brought into operation when required. The mode of giving this signal varies in different places. It has in some cases been done by a tube containing compressed air, which, being suddenly opened, a whistle is sounded by the air rushing out of the tube; but it is probable, henceforward, that the agent used for this purpose will be the wires of the electric telegraph.

Having thus explained the proceedings of the stations of departure, let us now pass to the other side of the railway, to the station of arrival.

In cases where the station is approached by a tunnel and inclined plane, such as has been already described, on the Northwestern Railway and at Liverpool, signals are given of the approaching arrival of a train, so that the agents of the station of arrival are prepared for it, and have the rails clear. The train is not allowed to start from the fixed engine station until the signal is replied to from below, and an intimation given that all is prepared. These formalities, however, are unnecessary on lines where the locomotive engine is enabled to arrive with the trains directly at the station. In this case its approach is signified by the whistle of the engine, which is generally heard for more than a mile distance; and as the train always begins to slacken its speed at this distance, there is abundant time for preparation.

Generally, before the entrance of the train into the dépôt, the engine is detached from it, passes off into a siding, and allows the train to proceed by its momentum to the station, where it is brought up by the brake.

Previous to the arrival of the train, the carriages, omnibuses, and vehicles of every description, which wait to convey the passengers to their destinations, are admitted to a convenient place in the dépôt. For the good conduct of the drivers of many of these, the railway company makes itself, to some extent, responsible; its title is inscribed on their panels, and in some cases, as they leave the station, the drivers announce to the gate-porter the places to which they are about to take their fares, which is entered by the gate-porter, with the number of the vehicle, so that in case of any question arising for articles left or misconduct, the number of the vehicle, and the time of its departure from the railway station, can be always ascertained.

On the arrival of the train at the station, the agents and porters of the railway open the carriages for the liberation of the passengers, while others rapidly unload the vans containing the passengers' baggage.

The distribution of this is effected with inconceivable rapidity and regularity. Railway porters are ready with the utmost civility and promptitude to take charge of the baggage of each passenger, and carry it to the vehicle by which he is about to depart. The rules of the companies exclude the payment of gratuities for these services; nevertheless, it is most just to say that nothing can exceed the civility and obliging conduct of all the inferior agents thus employed.

When the train has been evacuated, the agents of the railway take possession of it. One class enters the carriages and carefully searches them for such articles as passengers may have inadvertently left behind them. These, some of which almost invariably are found, are taken to the office specially appropriated to the purpose, called the Lost Luggage Office. The carriages are, in fine, drawn away to the dépôt, where they are examined and cleaned.

The "Lost Luggage Office," though not immediately connected with the active business of transport, is a department which demands notice. Such an office, established in connection with all railway stations both in England and on the Continent, and at chief stations, such as those of London and Paris, is an object of considerable interest.

We have already alluded to the operations of the carriage-searchers, who examine the interior of the passenger coaches immediately after the evacuation of each arriving train. They raise the cushions, search the pockets, take up the carpets, and diligently examine every part of the carriage, and it rarely happens that some articles, more or less, are not found which the passengers inadvertently leave behind them. These are sent by the searchers immediately to the "Lost Luggage Office," where they are delivered into the hands of a clerk, who enters in a register a description of the articles, the number and designation of the carriages in which they were left, the hour of the arrival of the train, and the route which the carriage, in which the articles were found, had followed. A label is attached to the article, numbered in accordance with the entry in this register, so that at any future period it may be compared with such entry and identified. If the article in question is marked with the address of its owner, or if any indication of such address can be discovered from its contents, it is sent without delay to the proprietor; if not, it is deposited in a certain place, according to its magnitude and quality, where it is left for a certain assigned time waiting for an application on the part of its owner. If at the end of such specified time, which varies in different railways, no application be made, if it be a box, trunk, or other similar object, it is broken open and the contents ascertained. From the contents the ownership is frequently discovered, and it is restored; but if no clew to such discovery be thus obtained, then the article is transferred to a permanent place of deposit in the office or store-room, where it remains for a more extended period, such as one or two years. If at the end of this period no claim be made on the part of the owner, then the article, with others kept for a like time, is publicly sold by auction or otherwise, and the proceeds of the sale appropriated as directed by the managers of the railway. Such proceeds are usually applied to some charitable object in connection with the railway business.

It frequently happens that applications are made at the railway stations for lost luggage which is not found in the Lost Luggage Office. In that case a circular is dispatched to all the stations along the line or system of lines at which the passenger sustaining the loss has touched, and where, by any possibility, the lost object might have been left, and answers are rapidly obtained. This useful system of inquiry is greatly extended through the agency of the railway clearing-house, which we shall notice hereafter. By this means such inquiries can be extended not merely to all the stations belonging to the railway in which the inquiry originates, but to all the other railways spread over the chief part of the United Kingdom.

I can not conclude this notice of the Lost Luggage Office better than by quoting a part of the description of it given by a popular author in a recent work.

"In this office are to be seen, in shelves and in compartments, the innumerable articles which have been left in the trains during the last two months, each being ticketed and numbered with a figure corresponding with the entry-book in which the article is defined.

"Without, however, describing in detail this property, we will at once proceed to a large, pitch-dark, subterranean, vaulted chamber, warmed by hot-air iron pipes, in which are deposited the flock of lost sheep, or, without metaphor, the lost luggage of the last two years.

"Suspended from the roof there hangs horizontally in this chamber a gas-pipe about eight feet long, and as soon as the brilliant burners at each end were lighted, the scene was really astounding. It would be infinitely easier to say what there is not, than what there is in the 40 compartments like great wine bins in which all this lost property is arranged.

"One is choke-full of men's hats; another of parasols, umbrellas, and sticks of every possible description; one would think that all the ladies' reticules on earth were deposited in a third. How many little smelling-bottles—how many little embroidered pocket-handkerchiefs—how many little musty eatables and comfortable drinkables—how many little bills, important little notes, and other very small secrets each may have contained, we felt that we would not for the world have ascertained; but when we gazed at the enormous quantity of red cloaks, red shawls, red tartan plaids, and red scarfs, piled up in one corner, it was, we own, impossible to help reflecting that surely English ladies of all ages who wear red cloaks, &c. must, in some mysterious way or other, be powerfully affected by the whine of compressed air, by the sudden ringing of a bell, by the sight of their friends—in short, by the various conflicting emotions that disturb the human heart on arriving at the up-terminus of the Euston station; for else, how, we gravely asked ourselves could we possibly account for the extraordinary red mass before us?

"Of course in this Rolando-looking cave there were plenty of carpet bags, gun-cases, portmanteaus, writing-desks, books, cigar-cases, &c.; but there were a few articles that certainly we were not prepared to meet with, and which but too clearly proved that the extraordinary terminus excitement, which had suddenly caused so many virtuous ladies to elope from their red shawls—in short, to be not only in 'a bustle' behind, but all over —had equally affected men of all sorts and conditions.

"One gentleman had left behind him a pair of leather hunting-breeches! another his boot-jack! A soldier of the 22d regiment had left his knapsack containing his kit. Another soldier of the 10th, poor fellow! had left his scarlet regimental coat! Some cripple, probably overjoyed at the sight of his family, had left behind him his crutches! But what astonished us above all was, that some honest Scotchman, probably in the ecstasy of seeing among the crowd the face of his faithful *Jeannie*, had actually left behind him the best portion of his bagpipes!

"Some little time ago the superintendent, on breaking open, previous to a general sale, a locked leather hat-box, which had lain in this dungeon two years, found in it under the hat £65 in Bank of England notes, with one or two private letters, which enabled him to restore the money to the owner, who, it turned out, had been so positive that he had left his hat-box at a hotel at Birmingham, that he had made no inquiry for it at the railway office."*

THE GOODS STATION.

If the passenger station of a great railway excite an interest by its animation, the goods station scarcely excites less by the enormous magnitude of the property in the transfer of which it is employed. The mere statement of the number of goods-wagons used by different railway companies will itself suggest, to some extent, the immense amount of this department of railway business. One railway company alone, the Northwestern, had in active employment during the twelve months ending the 30th June, 1849, 6236 wagons, and another, the York and Newcastle, 11,788.

* "Stokers and Pokers," by the author of "Bubbles from the Brunnens of Nassau."

The goods engines of the former company performed, within that year, a mileage amounting to 2,882,674 miles, and consumed about 40,000 tons of coke. The Belgian railways employed, during the year 1847, 3309 goods-wagons, which made a total mileage of nearly 9 millions of miles. The North of France railway in the year 1848 employed 3069 wagons, and made a total mileage of nearly 15 millions of miles. These numbers present a lively picture of the prodigious amount of the interchange of the products of industry which takes place through this great agency, and the business of registration, embarkation, and delivery of which are necessarily transacted at the goods stations.

It is calculated that from the London goods station of the Northwestern Railway, situated at Camden Town, the average number of wagons arriving and departing per working day, is nearly 500. Now each of these wagons is capable, when fully loaded, of carrying, on an average, nearly 6 tons, but it is found that their actual average load is only $2\frac{1}{4}$ tons, which would give the weight of goods arriving and departing daily at this station alone, 1125 tons. But even this statement is probably below the truth, since we happen to know that the number of tons received and delivered at the Northwestern Railway within one year by Mr. Pickford alone, on account of the company, was at the average rate of very nearly 900 tons a day.

The goods station, like the passenger station, consists of two distinct departments, one appropriated to the goods about to be dispatched, and the other to the goods which have arrived, and which are to be delivered.

A multitude of carts and vans, which serve as a sort of tenders to this department of the railway business, are employed in radiating through every part of the capital, which they sweep over and collect such parcels of goods as are individually too small to be sent by their expediters by separate wagons. These, with the larger and heavier parcels brought by independent drays and wagons, arrive without interruption during the day and a great part of the night at the station of departure, on the wharves and under the sheds of which they deposit their loads. They are received by the loading porters, and booked and labeled by clerks stationed on the wharves for the purpose. The smaller parcels, which are extremely numerous, are rolled in barrows and trucks, after being sorted and classed according to their destinations and qualities, to the wagons and vans in which they are to be transported. The larger articles are seized by cranes, lifts, capstans, and other machinery, much of which is worked by steam power, and expeditiously laid on their respective wagons, having previously undergone the processes of weighing, booking, and labeling.

In all these busy operations, nothing is more surprising than the interminable multitude of small parcels, especially among those which arrive in London from the chief seats of manufacture. Since the establishment of this great agent of commercial intercourse, the London retail dealers, instead of laying in as formerly, at intervals more or less distant, a large stock, now order the goods as they want them, and these arrive in small detached parcels, some of which often contain only a single article. Thus it is not uncommon for a purchaser in a London shop to order an article of household use: the shopkeeper sells it as though it were lying on one of his shelves ready for delivery. The moment the order is received a communication is dispatched to Sheffield, Birmingham, or Manchester for the article in question, and in the course of the succeeding day, or at the latest within 48 hours, the article is delivered to the purchaser.

It may be asked how the dealer can manage his business subject to the cost which must attend the frequent transmission of such small parcels. The answer is easy.

By the perfect organization of the railway system, and the enormous amount of transport executed by each company, they are enabled to deliver these parcels at a cost which falls but lightly on the retail vendor and consumer. These light parcels, such as objects of hardware from Birmingham or Sheffield, are collected, conveyed, and delivered at the domicile of the retailer in London for 1s., and in the case of shorter distances the entire business of the transport, collecting, conveyance, and delivery in spring-vans in London, is actually executed for 6d.

We have already mentioned the rates at which parcels are delivered by the passenger trains, but the objects we now refer to are different, and for the same or a less cost of transport are greater in weight and bulk. They are, however, forwarded by the goods trains, moving at a slower speed, with greater loads, and less promptitude and frequency of departure.

On the Northwestern Railway, which performs a larger amount of goods business than the other English lines, 9 goods trains start from each terminus every 24 hours, 5 during the night, and 4 during the day.

A goods train leaves Birmingham every evening at 8½ o'clock, and arrives in London by 4 o'clock the following morning, and its contents are distributed over all parts of London in two or three hours. Thus an order sent by a London retail dealer by one of the fast trains in the afternoon to Birmingham will be responded to by the goods train which arrives at an early hour the following morning. The possibility of the commercial operation we have described above will therefore be readily comprehended.

By the goods trains which start from London on the different roads during the day, the products of the London markets which are in demand in the interior of the country are carried down, such as fish, fruit, and groceries, hundreds of tons of which are dispersed over the country, and offered for sale in the markets of Birmingham and other central towns.

London fruit is thus supplied to the markets of Liverpool and Glasgow. As much as 20 tons of this article are frequently carried daily on the Northwestern line alone.

The supply of articles of consumption by these goods trains to London is of enormous amount. Not only cattle and smaller live stock, such as sheep, pigs, and calves, are brought up in immense numbers, but meat ready killed is brought in great quantities to the London markets.

ENGINE STATION.

Connected with all the chief stations of great railways, there is an establishment which is not unaptly called the engine stable. It consists of buildings for the reception of the engines detached from the trains on their arrival, where they are cleaned, put to rights, and prepared to renew their work. In short, these iron horses are cleaned, groomed, fed, and refreshed, so to speak, and prepared to renew their periodical labor. When a train arrives, the engine is detached from it while yet in motion, and running on before leaves its load behind. The "pointsman" dextrously shifts his switches, so as to guide the engine to another line of rails, and before the train arrives he again shifts them back again so as to let the train run to the station.

The engine thus unharnessed proceeds toward its stable. On arriving near it, it stops over a pit of some depth, excavated between the rails. There the fireman, opening the grate-bars, lets the coke which remains unconsumed in the fire-box fall into the pit, where it is extinguished by water. He then proceeds with the engine into the stable, which is variously constructed on different lines, but generally in a circular or polygonal form.

In the centre there is an immense revolving platform, called a turn-table. When the engine arrives upon this it is brought to a stand, and the table is turned until the engine is directed straight toward its stall, into which it is then moved.

Between the rails in this stall there is an excavation of such depth that a man can stand upright in it under the engine, without being incommoded by its machinery. This pit is entered for the purpose of enabling the artificers to examine the works of the engine, to clean them and put them in order, tightening and adjusting all the joints, and oiling all the moving parts. The tubes of the boiler are cleaned, the smoke-box and chimney put to rights, and the interior of the boiler itself washed clean at proper intervals; in fine, the engine being put into fresh working order, is again rolled out on the centre turn-plate, turned in the direction of the gate, from which it again issues forth to its labor.

I have adverted elsewhere to the amount of fuel consumed in heating the water in raising the steam in an engine preparatory to starting. In the larger class of railway establishments, expedients are adopted to obtain further economy and expedition in this process.

Thus the water is heated in large reservoirs, and introduced into the boiler at nearly the boiling temperature.

Coke is already prepared in a state of ignition, and thrown into the fire-box while in vivid combustion. A certain amount of coke is thus saved, inasmuch as coal is or may be used in heating the water previously to its introduction into the boiler.

The same expedient may be adopted at the several water stations on the road where there is a sufficiently active traffic. The water-tanks may be kept constantly heated, so that the feed, when introduced into the boiler, does not lower in the same degree its temperature. When the traffic is so active that the feeding-tanks are kept on constant duty, it may be economical to adopt this expedient.

Many of the larger class of engine-stables which we have adverted to, contain from 25 to 30 stalls.

Attached to this department, in all the chief stations, are extensive work-shops provided with all the means for executing the smaller class of repairs necessary for the engines. Here duplicates are kept of the moving parts, which are most liable to fracture and derangement.

The larger class of repairs, as well as the construction of engines, is, however, conducted in larger establishments, which have been erected at convenient places on some of the principal lines of railway.

CARRIAGE AND WAGON STATION.

The fourth and last department of a chief station which we shall notice, is that which is appropriated to the carrying stock.

The passenger carriages, goods-wagons, and vehicles of every description, are collected in proper sheds, of immense extent, adapted for their shelter and preservation.

Here, after performing their work, they are submitted to the process of cleaning, internally and externally, all of which is executed, with admirable skill and dexterity, by a troop of servants of the company, each of whom is disciplined in his duty. Some are appointed to clean the panels and glasses, and are provided with sponges, chamois-skins, brushes, cloths, and other utensils for the purpose. Others have the duty of washing and mopping the wheels and carriage, properly so called, of examining the grease-boxes, and re-oiling, when necessary, all the moving parts. Another set of agents have the internal duty, and are provided with proper brushes and other implements for cleaning the interior of the first and second class carriages. Another is supplied with oil, blacking, and brushes for putting to rights the leather and straps on the roof and different parts of the vehicles. A distinct set of agents have the duty of oiling the buffer-rods and other moving parts of the vehicles, and of replenishing the grease-boxes by which the axles and journals of the wheels are lubricated.

It may be necessary here to explain that the construction of the wheels in railway carriages differs from that of the wheels of common road vehicles.

In the carriages used on common roads, the axle is attached to and forms part of the carriage, and the wheels turn upon it, a circular box being formed in the centre of the wheel fitted to the axle, and provided with means of lubrication, so that it may turn freely upon the axle. In railway carriages, on the contrary, the axle is permanently attached to and connected with the wheels, both being separate from and independent of the carriage. The axle projects on either side beyond the wheels. When the wheels are placed under the carriage, the bearings are outside the wheels, and are formed into a sort of fork, which rests outside upon that part of the axle which projects beyond the wheel.

THE STATIONS.

The outside bearing, as it is called, is provided with a small box made of brass or gun metal, placed immediately over the axle, called the grease-box, which communicates with the axle by an opening in the bottom. The top opens by a hinged lid, so as to enable it to be replenished from time to time. As the carriage passes along the road, men are prepared at appointed stations with grease cans, and they go round the carriage refilling these grease-boxes.

The grease used for this purpose, known by the name of yellow grease, is composed of tallow, palm-oil, soda, and water, which are combined in different proportions according to the season of the year, and according to the varying usages of different railways.

On some of the English railways the following is the customary proportion of these constituents in 1000 lbs. of grease:

```
Tallow .................................... 253
Palm-oil .................................. 88
Soda ...................................... 25
Water ..................................... 634
                                          ----
                                          1000
```

On the Belgian railways, a much larger proportion of palm-oil is used, the following being the composition:

```
Tallow .................................... 83
Palm-oil .................................. 207
Soda ...................................... 14
Water ..................................... 696
                                          ----
                                          1000
```

This analysis compared with the former shows in the constituents 3 times less tallow, and $2\frac{1}{2}$ times more palm-oil.

The only variation in different seasons of the year is that the proportion of water is augmented with the temperature of the weather.

In the year 1844 the quantity of this grease used on the Belgian railways was 75 tons, the cost of which was £84, being at the rate of 22s. 5d. per ton. The cost, according to the English composition, does not differ materially from this.

The mileage of the trains upon which this grease was consumed was equal to a single train of 14 vehicles running about a million of miles.

At the chief stations sheds of vast extent are provided for the reception of the carriages, in which a great number of parallel lines of railway are laid down, and in which the carriages are received for purposes of cleaning and repair. At such stations, also, workshops and artificers are provided for the smaller class of repairs which may be required by the carriages and other vehicles, and a sufficient supply of duplicates is kept.

These observations are applicable chiefly to principal stations. The intermediate stations which are established along the line of railway vary in magnitude according to the population of the town or district with which they communicate, the smallest class consisting of a single waiting-room, booking-office, and two or three clerks and porters.

The number of stations provided upon a line of railway is necessarily governed by the density of the population and the activity of the commerce and intercourse prevailing in the country through which the railway is carried; and in this respect railways differ very much from each other, especially on the Continent.

On the English railways they are necessarily numerous, the population being dense and busy. On May 1, 1848, the total number of miles of railway under traffic in the United Kingdom was 4253. The number of stations distributed over this length was 1831, being at the rate of a station for every $3\frac{1}{4}$ miles. If the number of stations on the railways now open be in the same proportion, their number is 1553.

The activity of the intercommunication which is maintained throughout the country may be indicated, in connexion with the mileage of the traffic, by the number of stations combined with the number of departures which take place daily from them which are seen in the time-tables.

RAILWAY REFRESHMENT ROOMS.

It would be an unpardonable omission if this exposition of the arrangements made by the railway companies for the convenience of the public in their embarkation and disembarkation, and other accessories of transport, were concluded without some notice of the refreshment-rooms.

The stage-coach traveler, who dates his experience from an epoch anterior to the last fifteen or twenty years, will not forget the miseries of the road incident to coach breakfasts, lunches, dinners, and suppers; and the squabbles about the

THE STATIONS.

bill, the wretchedness of the fare, and the indefinite cravings of the waiters, the watermen, luggage-porters, and other interminable animals of prey, which ever infested the coach taverns.

These are now among the things that were, and are henceforward consigned to the novelist and the historian of the manners of a past age.

The railway traveler finds at those points of his route where the train stops for the purpose of refreshment, magnificent salons, luxuriously furnished, warmed, and illuminated. In these are established buffets and all the appliances necessary for the supply of every variety of refreshment which each class of travelers can possibly desire. These being placed directly or indirectly under the control of the railway authorities, are organized and disciplined in the most admirable manner. A tariff of prices, most moderate in amount, guarantees the traveler from extortion. The attendants being all paid by the company or its subordinates, neither desire nor expect gratuities, and, indeed, the acceptance of such is strictly forbidden.

As the trains which move in opposite directions always keep different sides of the road, and as the practice of crossing the line is attended with much personal danger, as will be shown when we come to consider the causes of accidents on railways, the railway companies have in general, at the refreshment stations, erected two buildings, one on each side of the line, in each of which a series of refreshment-rooms is provided.

The upper part of these buildings is appropriated to lodging-rooms for the superintendents and waiters of the rooms, and the two buildings are usually connected by a bridge crossing the road, so that the attendants can pass with facility from one to the other without incurring the danger of passing over the line.

In these establishments a certain number of the waiters and superintendents sit up during the night by turns to attend on the passengers arriving by the night-trains.

CHAPTER IX.

THE CLEARING-HOUSE.

WHEN some progress had been made in the completion of the vast network of iron roads which now overspreads the United Kingdom, and when railway after railway, to the number of some thirty or forty, had been successively opened for traffic, and had effected junctions with each other, so as, in reality, to form one connected system of internal communication, though under numerous independent administrations, an inconvenience arose which for some time appeared to menace the operations of railway establishments with insurmountable difficulties.

The exigencies of the transport had no relation with the arbitrary limits which separated the domain of one company from that of another. Passengers and goods required to be booked and continuously transported from one point of the kingdom to another. But no company possessed the power to do more than carry the passenger or the goods to the limits of its own line; there they were handed over to another company, who, in like manner, carried them over its territory, and transferred them to a third, and so on. Each company had its own independent machinery of transport, consisting of engines, carriages, wagons, and vehicles of every description. It had its own system of financial operations and accounts, and its own tariff; the consequence of which was, that the traveler was compelled, in passing every boundary between the rails of two adjacent companies, to pass from one carriage to another, with his luggage, no matter what might be the inconvenience attending such an operation, arising from inclemency of weather, or from the hour of night.

Great as was this inconvenience, that which attended the transhipment of goods was infinitely more grave. The wagons had to be unloaded, and their contents discharged upon wharves and platforms; and these had again to be reloaded upon the wagons of the other company.

Such an operation was not only attended with great expense, which must necessarily fall upon the expeditor of the goods, but also with serious delay, damage, and risk of loss. In short, the inconvenience to the public was so enormous, and the clamor which it excited, both among the commercial classes, and those who traveled by the railways, was so irresistible, that it became manifest that some arrangement must be adopted by which the public would be accommodated, and the traffic, both in goods and passengers, expedited over the railways of different companies without being rebooked, repacked, or ranshiped.

The point was practically conceded, and the traffic of all descriptions carried without interruption from the lines of one company to those of another.

But this immediately produced grave inconveniences and difficulties among the companies. A portion of the receipts which was paid into the hands of each company at various stations, had to be paid over to other companies upon whose lines the traffic, whether in goods or passengers, was carried. But besides this, the vehicles of every sort, belonging to one company were unavoidably used to carry traffic upon the lines of other companies.

Hence arose an intolerable chaos of cross accounts, out of which sprung vexatious disputes and much litigation.

The confusion and difficulty were at length removed, and this system of complicated debits and credits was reduced to perfect clearness and order by a happy thought suggested by the operations of the London bankers. The similarity of the reciprocal claims of the railway companies arising out of the operations just explained, to those of the London bankers, arising from the bills and checks drawn upon the others, received by each of them daily, struck the mind of Mr. K. Morison, who suggested the plan of establishing a railway clearing-house, founded on principles identical with those which had been so successfully brought into operation in the Bankers' clearing-house.

It is known that a check drawn upon any London banker may be paid to any other London banker, and placed to the credit of the customer who presents it; the banker receiving it undertaking to obtain its liquidation from the banker on whom it is drawn.

This, however, is effected only in an indirect manner; and, as we shall see, the liquidation is accomplished without the actual presentation of the check, or its payment in cash.

It is now about three quarters of a century since the banking operations of London became so extensive and complicated, that the difficulties arising from the daily settlement of the bills and checks respectively payable by each London banker to the others called into existence the establishment now known by the name of the "Clearing-house," which is located in Lombard-street, in the building formerly occupied by the Post-office. This establishment is placed under the direction of a committee delegated by bankers, who mutually associate for this purpose. Two salaried functionaries, called inspectors, have its immediate management, and are there present for the transaction of business. From time to time during the day, the bankers severally transmit to this office the checks and bills which they receive, and which are payable by other bankers. As fast as they arrive they are sorted, and classed according to the bankers by whom they are payable, so that the checks and bills payable by each banker to the various other bankers are classed together.

The clerks from the several bankers who bring to the clearing-house the bills and checks receivable by them take at the same time an account of the bills and checks which have arrived at the clearing-house, and which are payable by them, and are thus enabled, toward the close of the day, to make up in their private books an account, as well of the checks and bills payable by them, as of those receivable by them.

The reception of bills and checks is continued at the clearing-house until four o'clock, after which it ceases; and the interval from that time till about half-past five is devoted to the adjustment of the accounts, which is accomplished in the following manner:

The clearing-house, by a fiction, makes itself the common debtor and the common creditor of all the bankers. It debits each banker with the amount of the checks and bills payable by him to every other banker, and it credits him with the amounts of all the checks and bills receivable by him from every other banker. This operation is facilitated and expedited by a simple printed form, which occupies a sheet of paper consisting of three columns; the left and right-hand columns being left blank for the debits and credits, and the centre column being printed with the names of the bankers associated in the clearing-house alphabetically arranged.

One of these accounts is filled up after four o'clock, as between the clearing-house and each banker. The amounts of the bills and checks receivable by such banker are written on the right-hand or credit column, opposite to the names respectively of the bankers by whom such bills or checks are payable, and the amounts of the bills or checks payable by such banker are written on the left-hand or debtor column, opposite respectively to the names of the bankers to whom such bills or checks are payable.

These statements, thus filled up, may be considered as a debtor and creditor account between the clearing-house, representing all the bankers collectively, and the single banker with whom such account is formed.

When thus filled up, the statement is examined by the clerk of the banker in question, and each item is by him verified by reference to the clerks of the several other bankers. When thus verified, it is returned to the inspector, who signs it, and either receives or pays the balance which appears at the foot of each account, according as the debits exceed the credits, or the credits exceed the debits.

It is clear that the sum of the balances receivable by the clearing-house must be precisely equal to the sum of the balances payable by it, so that the amount which it receives on the one hand liquidates the amount which it has to pay on the other; and, in reality, as must necessarily have been the case, it becomes the mere agent or channel through which the payments pass from one bank to the other.

In the practical working out of the business, there are numerous details, such as certain mutual settlements between clerk and clerk, with the sanction of the inspector, which, being of no importance to the principle of the institution, need not be noticed here.

To render clearly intelligible the operations effected by the railway clearing-house, which has been established upon principles analogous to those of the bankers', it will be necessary, first, to explain the reciprocal interchange of business which takes place, creating systems of mutual credits and debits between company and company.

The number of companies who have combined their operations in this manner is at present (Nov. 1849) forty-five, comprising all those whose railways lie north of a line passing from Bristol through London to Harwich; in fact, all the railways of the kingdom, except the Great Western, the Southwestern, the London, Brighton, and South-Coast, the Southeastern, and their branches and collateral lines.

These railways possess 887 stations, at any one of which traffic may be booked for any other; the consequence of which is, that there are nearly four hundred thousand different pairs of places within the circle of operations of the united companies, between which traffic may be transmitted. In passing from any one such station to any other, the traffic may pass over part of any or all of the lines of the combined companies with as much continuity of progress as if the whole system were under the government of a single company.

The service of the transport, whether of passengers or goods, consists, first, in the service of embarkation, which includes all the formalities observed at the station of departure, consisting of booking, weighing, loading, packing, &c.; secondly, of the transport, properly so called, which is represented by a mileage; and, thirdly, of the formalities and services of the stations of arrival, where the traffic is unloaded, discharged, and delivered, and frequently sent to the domicile of the party to whom it is addressed.

A certain rate of charge, according to the nature of the traffic, being agreed upon for each of these parts of the service of transport, the sum receivable for each object of transport must be divided among the companies over whose lines it passes, including those at whose stations the traffic is received and delivered. But the sum payable for such transport is received either by the company at whose station the traffic is booked, or by the company at whose station it is delivered, or partly by one and partly by the other.

Two companies must be therefore debited with the sums they thus receive, and they, as well as other companies intermediate between them, over whose lines the traffic may have passed, must be credited in the stipulated proportion according to the mileage.

The first object to be attended to by the railway clearing-house is to adjust these complicated debits and credits, as well for passengers as for every species of goods, with simplicity, clearness, and dispatch, and in such a manner as not to give rise to subsequent disputes.

But besides the interchange of credits for traffic, a most complicated account arises, out of the circumstance already explained, for the use of the rolling stock. The wagons of each of the numerous companies which enter into the union of the clearing-house are driven indifferently over the lines of all the others, carrying traffic for various companies, and sometimes transporting a load no part of which is to be credited to the company owning the vehicle in which it is borne.

By mutual agreement, a certain fixed rate is charged for the use of each class of vehicle, and every company over whose lines the vehicles of other companies pass, being in the first instance credited for the traffic carried by these vehicles, is debited for the use of the vehicles themselves in which such traffic is carried. A mileage account must therefore be kept of all the rolling stock of all the combined companies, so that the course of each vehicle may be traced from day to day and from hour to hour, so that its mileage may be debited to such companies as may have shared its use; and in case of undue delay at the stations of any company, a demurrage may be charged, according to a stipulated condition, proportional to such delay.

To adjust in a satisfactory and equitable manner these accounts for the mutual use of the rolling stock is the second function of the clearing-house.

The passenger traffic being liable to a government duty payable on booking to the company at whose station passengers are embarked, must necessarily pay this duty in advance, and must pay it for the entire trip for which the passenger is booked. This duty, however, is chargeable in the proportion of a mileage to all the companies over whose lines the passenger travels. Hence an account must be kept in which the booking company will be credited for the duty thus paid, and the several companies over whose lines the passenger is carried would be debited in proportion to the mileage for their respective shares of the amount.

When the claims of one company upon another, arising out of these transactions, are not liquidated within a stipulated time, they are subject to interest at a rate agreed upon. An interest account must therefore be kept between company and company.

Luggage, parcels, and other objects of traffic being liable to be lost or unduly delayed, claims and complaints arise between company and company. The settlement of such claims enters into the class of operations to be transacted by the clearing-house.

Such are the principal functions which the institution of the clearing-house is called on to discharge.

Let us now consider the manner in which these operations are effected.

The central clearing-house is established in London, in a building situate near the Euston station of the Northwestern Railway. It is placed under the direction of a body of managers elected by the companies, in which each company is represented.

This central office has agents at all the stations comprised within the circle of the united companies.

In adjusting the mutual debits and credits of the companies, no company is regarded either as the debtor or creditor of any other, but the clearing-house is the common creditor and the common debtor of all. We shall explain successively the mode in which each class of claim is arranged, beginning with the most important.

THE GOODS TRAFFIC AND LIVE STOCK.

From each of the 887 stations goods are, or may be, forwarded daily to any or all of the other 886 stations. An account of such goods so forwarded, with the sums paid and received for each parcel, is kept at each of these stations, and a copy of this account, written in *black ink*, is forwarded daily to the central clearing-house in London.

In like manner, at each of the 887 stations a quantity of goods is, or may be, received daily from any or all of the other stations, an account of which is kept. A copy of this, written in *red ink*, is daily forwarded to the central clearing-house in London.

The central clearing-house thus receives, or may receive, 887 black and 887 red accounts daily; the black reporting all the goods which have been forwarded from all the stations, and the red reporting all the goods which have been received at all the stations.

Now, as it is evident that the goods which are received can neither be more nor less than the goods which are forwarded, the red accounts must correspond exactly with the black accounts, although the items will occur in a different order. A parcel of goods dispatched from one station must have arrived at some other, and a parcel of goods which has arrived at any station must have been dispatched from some other. Thus an entry in the black accounts must have a corresponding entry in the red accounts, and an entry in the red accounts must have a corresponding entry in the black accounts.

This is what ought to take place, supposing no error in the accounts, and no miscarriage in the transport; but in practice it is found that this perfect accordance is never realized, and that there is, upon an average, somewhere about thirty per cent. daily of entries in the one which have no corresponding entries in the other. This discrepancy arises from one of three causes, *first*, from an entry being made of an object dispatched, which object has been accidentally, or, through error, mislaid; *secondly*, from an entry being omitted of an object received, although that object may have been received; and, *thirdly*, from a miscarriage *en route*.

At the central clearing-house, where the two statements of accounts, black and red, are compared, and their discrepancies detected, letters are written to such of the stations where the errors have been committed, giving notice of the omission, and demanding explanation. Rectifications and explanations ensue, and the accounts are finally adjusted.

The central clearing-house having opened an account with each of the companies, credits each with the sums which appear to be receivable by it from the system of accounts explained above, and debits it for the sums with which it appears to be chargeable.

At the close of each month, these several accounts between the clearing-house and the companies respectively are balanced. In some of these the balances are in favor of the clearing-house, in others in favor of the company; but from the nature of the transactions, these sets of balances must be precisely equal; the sum due to the clearing-house by the debtor companies must be equal to the sum owing by the clearing-house to the creditor companies. The debtor companies having liquidated their balances, the clearing-house distributes the sum it receives between the creditor companies, in the proportion of their respective balances.

But if the debtor companies, or any of them fail to liquidate their balances within a specified time, then the clearing-house debits such companies with interest on such balance at the rate of five per cent.; and it credits those creditor companies whose balances it fails to liquidate, in consequence of such delay, with interest at the same rate. Thus the interest credits will be exactly equal to the interest debits.

PASSENGER TRAFFIC.

When passengers are booked at any railway station for any other station, they pay their full fare, and receive a stamped ticket, on which is indicated the place, day, and hour of their departure, and the place of their destination.

On arriving at their destination they deliver up this ticket to the agents of the station of arrival. Carriages and horses booked are represented in like manner by tickets or checks, which are delivered up on their arrival. Parcels and baggage are entered on a way-bill, in which are indicated the places of their destination, and the sums paid, or to be paid, for them.

Each station sends daily to the central clearing-house a statement of the number of passengers of each class which it has booked, with their places of destination, and the sums received. It sends, also, a statement of the horses, carriages, and parcels booked, with like particulars.

Each station likewise sends to the central clearing-house all the tickets which have been delivered by passengers who have arrived there daily, as well as the checks for carriages and horses, and likewise a statement of the parcels and luggage which it has received.

At the central clearing-house the tickets are examined and classed, and their number in the gross of each class compared with the number in the gross of the passengers who have been booked. These two ought to correspond, and any discrepancies are notified, and ultimately explained and adjusted. This operation is facilitated by a course observed in all the booking-offices, in consequence of which the passenger tickets of each class are issued in numerical order, each ticket being stamped with a separate number, and the numbers following each other consecutively for each class daily from 1 to 10,000.

The account for parcels is dealt with in a manner precisely similar to that which has been already explained in the case of merchandise.

The clearing-house debits the companies respectively for the sums they have received for all these objects, and it credits them according to the stipulated rate for the mileage, embarkation, or delivery of such as have passed over their lines, for such as they have booked and embarked, and such as they have discharged and delivered.

These accounts are balanced monthly, and dealt with in the same manner, exactly, as has been already explained in the case of goods.

The passenger tickets, after having been duly examined and classed, so as to regulate the clearing-house accounts, are returned to the companies respectively.

A separate account is kept of the government duty payable for passengers, and which, as has been observed, is exacted from the company with whom the passenger is booked, though chargeable to all the companies over whose lines the passenger is carried, in proportion to their respective mileage. The clearing-house credits the company which books for the entire amount of the duty it has paid, and then debits all the companies over whose lines the passengers are carried, including the booking company itself, with their respective proportions of the duty according to the portion of the lines over which the passengers have been carried.

Although the clearing-house accounts are only furnished monthly to the several companies, yet a weekly abstract of the account for the traffic in passengers and goods is sent to them respectively, to enable them to make up, as is customary, their weekly returns of traffic.

CARRYING STOCK.

The clearing-house has agents posted at all the points of junction of the lines of different companies at which traffic is liable to pass from one to another. The duty of these agents is to register the number and quality of each vehicle, which passes from one line to another, indicating its owner. They also register the number of the tarpaulins by which wagons are covered, and which do not necessarily constitute a part of the wagon, nor always belong to the same owners.

The clearing-house agents at all the stations keep a similar register. A comparison of all these registers, copies of which are sent up to the central clearing-house, enables the authorities there to trace the course of every wagon over the network of lines, and to ascertain its daily mileage on each line, and the time it has been detained at the stations respectively. The clearing-house by these means is enabled to debit the companies respectively at a stipulated rate of mileage for the use of the wagons or of the tarpaulins, as the case may be, and to credit the companies who own the same for like sums. A statement of accounts representing the use of the rolling stock is thus opened between the clearing-house and the companies respectively. In each of these accounts there appears on the credit side the sums due to the company for the use of its wagons and tenders by other companies, and on the debit side the sums due by it for the use of the wagons and tenders of other companies upon its lines. The balances of these accounts are settled monthly, and are subject to precisely the same observations as the balance of the traffic.

Finally, all questions and claims respecting lost luggage or parcels are made and arranged through the agency of the clearing-house. When any parcel or other object has failed to arrive at its destination, or when any passenger misses a portion of his luggage, notice is sent to the Lost Luggage Office and the clearing-house, with an indication of the route over which the passenger traveled, or the station at which the lost object was booked. A communication is immediately sent to all the stations along the line indicated, with a description of the object lost, and answers are duly received. In general the object is recovered if lost upon the road.

The enormous extent of the transactions in the settlement of which the agency of the clearing-house is employed may be imagined from the following circumstances:

The number of communications made daily from the central clearing house to the provincial stations respecting errors and omissions in the reports of traffic are estimated at two hundred and fifty. The number of distinct accounts settled and balanced monthly for the goods traffic alone is estimated at about five thousand.

The monthly account furnished to each of the companies who are united in the establishment of the clearing-house contains for each station of each company a statement of the weights of each object of traffic, the distances on the respective lines over which it is carried, the expenses of its embarkation and disembarkation, and the balance on the total traffic at each station.

These monthly accounts are considered final so far as respects their settlement, and in case the companies fail to liquidate them they are chargeable with interest; but any errors or omissions which may be detected in them are corrected and allowed for in the accounts of the subsequent month.

As an example of the complexity of the accounts settled by this establishment, it may be mentioned that in the parcel department alone the majority of parcels booked are under twelve pounds weight, and the total charge for their embarkation, transmission, and delivery, frequently does not exceed four shillings. Thus, from any part of Birmingham to any part of London the charge, including cartage and delivery, is only one shilling, and the charge between London and the remotest part of Scotland is only four shillings. These charges have to be debited among all the companies over whose lines and in whose wagons the objects may have been conveyed. In this way one shilling has sometimes to be credited to three companies.

I am indebted to Mr. K. Morison, the manager of the clearing-house, for the following return of the present statistics of the establishment:

Clearing-house Statistics for Year ending June 30, 1849.

Number of railway companies associated in the clearing system	45
Length of associated lines	3,633 miles.
Average length	$80\tfrac{3}{4}$,,
Number of stations supplying returns	887
Amount of accounts passed through clearing-house	1,691,720*l*. 12*s*.
Tons of goods included in these accounts	2,215,407
Number of passengers, do	696,407
Their total mileage	103,240,304
Average mileage per passenger	148
Number of wagons on which the clearing-house charged mileage	487,304
Number of passenger-coaches, do	79,260
Average number of junctions crossed per passenger	1·85

The principle which has been brought into successful operation in the clearing-house admits of still more extensive application, which doubtless it will receive.

The practical effect of the arrangement, even so far as it is hitherto developed, is to facilitate such an interchange of the use of the rolling-stock, and the service of the stations between company and company, as to render their benefits in a great degree common to all. Each company by this expedient maintains a stock not only for its own traffic, but to some extent for the traffic of other companies, and in exchange receives the benefit of the stock and the stations of other companies.

The perfection to which this system tends would be, that a common rolling stock should be kept for all the companies, in the support of which they should as it were club, each contributing a share to its maintenance, in proportion to the quantity of traffic transported by it.

At present the interchange is limited to the vehicles of transport, the engines of each company being confined in their movements to the lines of the company to which they belong; but there is nothing which should prevent, under proper arrangements, the same interchange of locomotive power as now takes place with so much advantage in the carrying stock.

In fine, the clearing-house may ultimately grow into an establishment for the maintenance of a general locomotive and carrying stock for the use of all the railways, to be supported by the railways in common, and charged to them in the proportion in which they use it.

So far as regards the management of the traffic, there is nothing which should limit the operation of the clearing-house to the railways of the United Kingdom.

By proper arrangements, the same reciprocal conveniences now obtained by the railway companies in reference to the traffic booked through, as it is technically called, might be extended to the entire continent of Europe, so that passengers or goods might be booked at any station on any English railway for any station on any continental railway. The fare might be received on booking either wholly or partially, and might be distributed between the various lines over which the traffic should pass, in the same manner as it at present is among the railways which are united under the clearing system.

CHAPTER X.

PASSENGER TRAFFIC.

THE movement of the passenger traffic, like that of the drawing and carrying stock, is expressed by its mileage.

If the distance in miles over which the passengers are individually transported be added together, the aggregate will be their total mileage, and will express the number of passengers, each of whom being carried one mile would give a mileage equal to the actual traffic.

The mileage of the different classes of passengers is a matter of easy calculation from the records of the booking office. The ticket delivered to each passenger expresses the stations of departure and arrival, from which the distance traveled can be at once ascertained. In the following table is exhibited the total number of passengers of each class carried on the English railways during a period of $6\frac{1}{2}$ years, ending the 31st Dec. 1848, together with the total mileage of each class.

PASSENGER TRAFFIC.

TABULAR ANALYSIS of the Movement of Passengers on the Railways of the United Kingdom during the Six Years and a Half terminating Dec. 31, 1848.

	Number booked.	Total Mileage.
For twelve months ending June 30, 1843.		
1st class	4,576,540	118,990,040
2d class	11,998,512	172,778,573
3d class	6,891,844	86,148,050
Totals	23,466,896	377,916,663
For twelve months ending June 30, 1844.		
1st class	5,393,332	140,226,632
2d class	13,269,686	191,083,478
3d class	9,100,584	113,757,300
Totals	27,763,602	445,067,410
For twelve months ending June 30, 1845.		
1st class	5,644,163	146,748,238
2d class	14,665,825	211,187,880
3d class	13,481,266	168,515,812
Totals	33,791,254	526,451,930
For twelve months ending June 30, 1846.		
1st class	6,525,876	192,513,342
2d class	17,905,788	328,272,780
3d class	19,359,320	277,483,586
Totals	43,790,984	798,269,708
For twelve months ending June 30, 1847.		
1st class	7,110,940	173,702,839
2d class	20,313,966	310,974,797
3d class, &c.	23,927,256	320,327,929
Totals	51,352,162	805,005,565
For twelve months ending June 30, 1848.		
1st class	7,190,779	180,380,695
2d class	21,690,510	348,467,044
3d class, &c.	29,083,782	378,167,196
Totals	57,965,071	907,014,935
For six months ending December 31, 1848.		
1st class	3,743,602	100,982,787
2d class	12,191,549	201,550,815
3d class	15,695,141	220,636,080
Totals	31,630,292	523,169,682

From the data supplied from this table we are enabled to collect the average daily amount of transport in passengers executed by the railways.

To do this it is only necessary to divide the mileage in each of the above periods by the number of days. In like manner, to ascertain the average distance traveled by each passenger booked in the successive periods, it is necessary to divide the numbers given in the second column by the corresponding numbers in the first column.

Finally, to determine the average number of passengers booked per day, it is only necessary to divide the numbers in the first column respectively by the number of days.

The following will be the results:

TABULAR ANALYSIS of the daily Mileage, average Distance traveled by Passengers, and average Numbers booked on the Railways of the United Kingdom.

	Average daily Mileage	Average Distance traveled by each Passenger.	Average Number of Passengers booked daily.
For twelve months ending June 30, 1843.			
1st class	326,000	26·00	12,538
2d class	473,366	14·40	32,873
3d class	236,022	12·50	18,882
Totals and averages	1,035,388	16·10	64,293
For twelve months ending June 30, 1844.			
1st class	384,182	26·00	14,776
2d class	523,516	14·40	36,355
3d class	311,664	12·50	24,933
Totals and averages	1,219,362	16·03	76,064
For twelve months ending June 30, 1845.			
1st class	402,050	26·00	15,464
2d class	578,597	14·40	40,180
3d class	461,687	12·50	36,935
Totals and averages	1,442,334	15·57	92,579
For twelve months ending June 30, 1846.			
1st class	527,434	29·50	17,879
2d class	896,637	18·33	49,057
3d class	760,229	14·33	53,039
Totals and averages	2,184,300	18·22	119,975

PASSENGER TRAFFIC.

	Average daily Mileage.	Average Distance traveled by each Passenger.	Average Number of Passengers booked daily.
For twelve months ending June 30, 1847.			
1st class	475,898	24·40	19,504
2d class	851,985	14·70	57,958
3d class	877,611	14·16	61,978
Totals and averages	2,205,494	15·74	139,440
For twelve months ending June 30, 1848.			
1st class	494,166	25·00	19,767
2d class	954,704	16·00	59,669
3d class	1,036,074	13·00	79,698
Totals and averages	2,484,944	15·65	159,134
For six months ending Dec. 31, 1848.			
1st class	553,330	27·00	20,493
2d class	1,104,388	16·50	66,932
3d class	1,208,964	14·00	86,354
Totals and averages	2,866,682	16·54	173,779

The results of this table are remarkable, and with many will be unexpected. The average distances traveled by the different classes of passengers which are exhibited in the second column are much smaller than might have been supposed. Thus the first-class passengers booked, taken one with another, traveled only 27 miles even in the last half-year, when the distance was increased comparatively with previous results.

The average distance traveled by second and third-class passengers are 16 and 14 miles respectively.

It may be objected to the average distances obtained in this way, that although they are correct for any system of railways conducted under single management, yet that as passengers who start from a station on one railway, pass successively during the same trip over the lines of one or more other companies, they will figure in the returns as so many different passengers booked; that they will therefore unduly augment the divisor by which the mean distances are calculated, and therefore give average distances under the truth.

To ascertain to what extent this objection prevails, we shall take advantage of some returns of the traffic which passes from railway to railway, given by Mr. Morison, the manager of the railway clearing-house.

According to these returns, the total number of passengers who went from one railway to another in the year 1845 was 517,888, and the total mileage of these passengers was 75,783,149. The average distance traveled per passenger was therefore 146 miles. The average length of the railways severally was 41 miles, therefore the average number of junctions crossed by each passenger was in that year 3·61. It follows, therefore, that each of these passengers counted in the total booked as 3·61 passengers, and we shall obtain the true number booked by subtracting from the total the above number of *through* passengers multiplied by 2·61. Thus we have,

Total number booked in 1845,6..............43,790,984
Deduct for passengers booked more than once,
517,888 × 2·61.......................... 1,351,688
                                          ─────────
                                          42,439,296

Dividing then the total mileage, 798,269,708, in 1805,6, by this, we find for the average distance actually traveled by each passenger booked 18·8 miles instead of 18·2.

Since 1845, owing to the amalgamations, the average length of the independent lines is less, and therefore the correction would produce still less effect on the computed average distance.

The number of the passengers recorded in the clearing-house for the twelve months ending June 30, 1849, was (see p. 151)

696,407,

and their total mileage was

103,240,160.

Taking the halves of these numbers as approximately representing the through passenger traffic for the half-year ending December 31, 1848, we have the number of through passengers for that half-year,

348,203,

and their mileage

51,620,080.

The average distance traveled by each through passenger was **therefore**

148·2.

But the total length of the associated railways was

$$3633,$$

and their number was 45. Their average length was therefore 80·7 miles.

Dividing 148·2 by 80·7, we obtain 1·83 as the average number of junctions crossed by each through passenger.

To find, therefore, the true number of through passengers booked, we must subtract

$$348{,}203 \times 0{\cdot}83 = 289{,}008,$$

from the total number of passengers for the half-year:

From	31,630,292
Subtract	289,008
Remains	31,341,284,

which is therefore the actual number of passengers booked.

Dividing the total mileage,

$$523{,}169{,}682,$$

by this, we obtain

$$16{\cdot}7,$$

instead of 16·5, as the average distance traveled by each passenger.

It is evident, therefore, that the through traffic produces no effect worthy of attention on the average distances.

I find that similar results are obtained on foreign railways; so that it may be assumed as a principle of high generality in the commercial phenomena of railways, that the great mass of the passengers consists of those who travel short distances.

The second and third columns of the preceding table taken together, exhibit in the most complete manner the actual daily traffic in passengers on the railways. In the third column we have the actual average number of passengers of each class which were booked, and in the second column we give the average distances which they traveled.

It may be observed that the results above obtained for the year 1846 are exceptional, that year appearing to have been one in which the movement of the population was characterized by extraordinary activity as compared with preceding years. While the total mileage of 1845, as compared with 1844, was only increased about 20 per cent., the total mileage of 1846, as compared with 1845, was increased 50 per cent. We find that the average distance traveled by all classes was augmented from 26 to 29 miles for the first class, from 14 to 18 for the second, and from 12 to 14 for the third, after having been stationary for the three preceding years, and that they returned to their former amount in the following years.

As might be expected, however, on different lines and in different localities, the average distances traveled by the different classes vary within considerably wide limits. In order to exhibit this interesting statistical fact, I have computed separately the average distance traveled by the several classes of passengers on eleven of the principal systems of railways in England, and also upon all the remaining lines collectively, and give the results of this calculation in the following table:

TABULAR ANALYSIS of the average Distances traveled by Passengers on the under-mentioned Railways during the Twelve Months which terminated on June 30, 1847.

Names of Railways.	Average Distance traveled by each Passenger.			General average Distance traveled per Passenger, of all Classes.
	1st Class.	2d Class.	3d Class.	
	Miles.	*Miles.*	*Miles.*	*Miles.*
London and Northwestern	50·50	32·00	25·00	40·19
Great Western	44·33	23·00	44·00	29·66
Midland	33·00	21·00	13·00	16·85
London, Brighton, and South Coast	26·60	22·00	12·00	17·00
London and Cambridge	39·00	32·00	18·00	26·22
London and Colchester	32·50	25·00	21·00	23·68
Bristol and Birmingham	33·60	29·00	35·00	29·18
London and Southwestern	28·20	20·00	29·00	23·92
York and Newcastle	26·50	10·00	16·00	15·60
York and North Midland	27·00	23·00	18·00	21·04
Lancashire and Yorkshire	20·00	16·00	11·00	12·75
All the remaining lines	10·60	7·10	9·20	8·55
General averages	24·40	14·70	14·16	15·74

To ascertain the proportion in which each class of passengers contributed to the business of the railways, it will be necessary to compare, 1st, the numbers booked of the respective classes with the total number; and, 2d, the quantity of mileage they respectively employed, with the total amount of mileage executed. I have accordingly made such a calculation, and the following are the results.

CHAP. X.] PASSENGER TRAFFIC. 159

TABULAR ANALYSIS of the Proportion of Business supplied to the Railways of the United Kingdom by the several Classes of Passengers respectively, during the Seven Years ending June 30, 1849.

	Number of each Class in every 100 booked.	Share of each Class in every 100 Miles traveled.
For twelve months ending June 30, 1843.		
1st class	19·5	31·5
2d class	51·1	45·7
3d class	29·4	22·8
Totals	100·0	100·0
For twelve months ending June 30, 1844.		
1st class	19·4	31·5
2d class	47·7	42·9
3d class	32·9	25·6
Totals	100·0	100·0
For twelve months ending June 30, 1845.		
1st class	16·7	27·9
2d class	43·4	40·1
3d class	39·9	32·0
Totals	100·0	100·0
For twelve months ending June 30, 1846.		
1st class	14·9	24·1
2d class	40·9	41·1
3d class	44·2	34·8
Totals	100·0	100·0
For twelve months ending June 30, 1847.		
1st class	13·8	21·5
2d class	39·5	38·6
3d class	46·7	39·9
Totals	100·0	100·0
For twelve months ending June 30, 1848.		
1st class	12·4	19·8
2d class	37·4	38·4
3d class	50·2	41·8
Totals	100·0	100·0
For six months ending Dec. 31, 1848.		
1st class	19·3	11·8
2d class	38·5	38·6
3d class	42·2	49·6
Totals	100·0	100·0

Hence it appears that in every point of view in which the business of a railway can be considered, the two inferior class passengers form its chief source.

The business consists conjointly, as has been already shown, in that of the stations and that of the road: in the reception, registration, and embarkation, and in the discharge and disembarkation, which constitute the business of the stations; and in the transport, properly so called, which constitutes the business of the road. The former is in the ratio of the number of passengers booked, irrespective of the distances they are carried; the latter, on the contrary, is in the direct ratio of their average mileage, or the distance they are carried, irrespective of their number. Accordingly, it follows that the numbers in the first column of the above table, are the *moduli* of the business transacted in the stations, and those in the second column the *moduli* of the business transacted on the road.

Taking the average of all the results, it may be stated that the business supplied to the stations by the three classes of passengers, first, second, and third, is in the ratio of the numbers, 1, 3, and 4; and, consequently, that the second and third-class passengers collectively supply seven-eighths of the entire business.

It appears also from the second column, that the same predominance prevails with the inferior classes in supplying the business of the road. The mileage employed by the second class is double that of the first, and the mileage employed by the third class is two and a quarter times that of the first; the relative proportion of transport among the three classes being as the numbers 4, 8, and 9, very nearly. The second and third classes collectively, therefore, employ more than four-fifths of the mileage.

It will be observed that the relative proportion of third-class passengers to the other classes underwent a considerable augmentation from 1845 to 1847. The causes of this are easily explained. Previously to 1846, the carriages provided for third-class passengers were frequently without roofs or windows. The third-class trains were started at inconvenient hours, and were transported at a comparatively slow rate. In fact, the companies appeared to study the means which were most likely to discourage the use of these cheap trains, prompted apparently by the apprehension that, the more affluent classes resorting to them, the revenue and the profits from the other trains would be diminished. By these means the laboring classes were in a great measure deprived of the benefits of this mode of transport.

The attention of the legislature was called to this in 1845, when an act was passed with a view to secure to the poorer classes the means of traveling by railway at moderate fares, and in carriages in which they might be protected from the weather It is incumbent upon all railway companies to whom the act extends, to provide, by one train, at the least, on every weekday, and also on Sundays (if they work on that day), a conveyance for third-class passengers to and from the terminal, and other ordinary passenger stations of the railway.

The hour at which this train starts is regulated by the commissioners.

The train must travel at an average rate of speed not less than twelve miles an hour for the whole distance traveled, including stoppages. It must take up and set down passengers at every passenger station.

The carriages must be provided with seats, and protected from the weather in a manner satisfactory to the commissioners.

The charge is not to exceed a penny a mile.

There are provisions as to luggage, and children under three years of age are to be taken without charge, and above three years and under twelve, at half the charge for an adult passenger.

The carriages that have been approved of by the commissioners for the conveyance of third-class passengers are generally commodious, protected from the weather, lighted and ventilated, and in many instances provided with lights at night, although this is not required by the act.

The fares in no case have been allowed to exceed $1d.$ per mile (and some companies are in the habit of charging less). The regulations of the act in reference to the weight of luggage allowed to passengers, and the fares to be charged for children, have been enforced, and are, in most cases, in conformity with the suggestions of the commissioners, stated in the printed time-tables of the railway companies.

These regulations were immediately followed by the great increase of the relative proportion of third-class passengers, exhibited in the above table.

It would be highly interesting and instructive to investigate the proportion in which the business of the railways is supplied by passengers, classified according to the distances they travel. To accomplish this, it would be necessary to possess returns of the average mileage of the passengers, classed according to certain given limits of the distances for which they are booked. I have not obtained such a return for the English railways, nor am I aware whether such data have been recorded; but I have procured some from foreign railways, which will elucidate this point, and which will be found in subsequent chapters.

On comparing together the results of successive years, there appears a tendency to augmentation in the relative numbers of the lower classes booked, as well as of the mileage they employ.

It appears from the table, p. 154, 5, that the daily passenger service of the railways has gradually augmented for the last two years, but in a different ratio for different classes of passengers.

In the following table (see page 163) I have exhibited the rate at which the average daily passenger traffic has increased since 1843.

We perceive in these results the same tendency which is uniformly manifested in the progress of the traffic, to vastly greater increase in the inferior than in the superior class of passenger traffic.

It will not be without interest to compare the prodigious extent of locomotive service rendered by steam power on railways, with the amount of horse power by which the same service would be executed. The experience of stage-coach proprietors, in business conducted on a large scale, establishes the general fact that a fast coach, traveling between any two distant places both ways daily, requires to work it as many horses as there are miles. The average load of such a coach is found to be about two-thirds of what it is capable of carrying. Thus, supposing it to be capable of carrying 15 persons inside and out, its average load would be 10.

These ten passengers would be carried both ways one mile per day per horse. The daily locomotive service of a horse thus working is therefore represented by twenty passengers carried one mile.

If we would then ascertain the number of horses which would be necessary to execute the service of the railways, it is only necessary to divide their daily mileage by 20; the quotient will be the number of horses required.

Let us take, for example, the six months ending Dec. 31, 1848. The daily mileage of the passengers generally during these six months was 2,866,682. This, divided by 20, gives 143,334, which would therefore be the number of horses work-

PASSENGER TRAFFIC.

TABLE showing the Rate at which the average Daily Passenger Traffic has augmented on the Railways of the United Kingdom, during the Six Years and a Half ending December 31, 1848.

	Total increase on the average Traffic of 1842,3.		Increase per cent. on the average daily Traffic of 1842,3.	
	Total Increase of Mileage	Total Increase of Number booked.	Increased Percentage of Mileage.	Increased Percentage of Number booked
Twelve months ending June 30, 1844.				
1st class	58,182	2,238	11·8	11·8
2d class	50,150	3,482	11·1	11·1
3d class	75,642	6,051	13·2	13·2
Totals and averages	183,974	11,771	11·8	11·8
Twelve months ending June 30, 1845.				
1st class	76,050	2,936	12·3	12·3
2d class	105,231	7,307	12·3	12·2
3d class	225,665	18,043	19·6	19·6
Totals and averages	406,946	27,286	14·0	14·4
Twelve months ending June 30, 1846.				
1st class	201,434	5,341	16·2	14·3
2d class	423,271	16,184	19·0	14·9
3d class	524,207	34,157	32·3	28·0
Totals and averages	1,148,912	55,682	21·1	18·7
Twelve months ending June 30, 1847.				
1st class	149,898	6,966	14·6	15·6
2d class	378,619	25,085	18·0	17·7
3d class	641,589	43,096	37·2	32·8
Totals and averages	1,170,106	75,147	21·3	21·7
Twelve months ending June 30, 1848.				
1st class	168,166	7,229	15·2	15·8
2d class	481,338	26,796	20·2	18·2
3d class	800,052	60,816	43·8	42·2
Totals and averages	1,449,556	94,841	24·0	24·8
Six months ending December 31, 1848.				
1st class	227,330	7,955	16·9	16·3
2d class	631,022	34,059	23·3	20·4
3d class	972,942	67,472	51·0	45·6
Totals and averages	1,831,294	109,486	27·7	27·0

ing daily in stage-coaches, which would execute the passenger traffic of the railways which took place during this half year.

It is worth while to compare the cost at which this amount of public service has been performed, with that at which it would have been effected by stage-coaches. In making such a comparison, it must be observed, that railway transport presents three sources of relative economy; 1st, the saving of fare; 2dly, the saving of time; and 3dly, the saving of tavern expenses on the road.

Before the establishment of railways on their present scale, the average fares of mail and stage-coaches, including the allowance to guards and coachmen, which are not chargeable to railway passengers, were as follows

	Per 100 Miles.
	s. d.
Mail (inside)	52 0
" (outside)	30 0
Fast coach (inside)	48 0
" (outside)	26 0

The average railway fares for the same distance at present would be as follows:

	Per 100 Miles.
	s. d.
Per mail, express, and first-class trains, corresponding with inside coach places	20 0
For second and third class	11 0

Hence it follows, that for every 100 miles traveled by first-class passengers there is a saving in the fare amounting to 30s., and for every passenger of the inferior classes there is a saving amounting to 17s.

The fast stage-coaches would travel, stoppages included, at $7\frac{1}{2}$ miles an hour, and consequently would require 13 hours and twenty minutes to travel 100 miles. This distance would be traveled on the railway, by slow passenger trains, in less than 5 hours, by the faster trains in 3 hours, and by express trains in a still less time. But let us take it at 4 hours. Then there will be 9 hours and 20 minutes time saved to each passenger on a 100 miles trip. Now, if we take the value of the time of the class who travel at the average value of 6s. per working day of 12 hours, this will be 6d. an hour, which will make a saving of 4s. 8d. for every 100 miles traveled.

Finally, every traveler who is detained long upon the road, must resort to taverns for refreshment. If he is 13 hours on the road, he will at least take one meal; many will take two. A traveler, however, who is detained only 3 or 4 hours on the road, will take none. Let us put down the cost thus incurred at 6d. per 100 miles for each passenger—a very low estimate; we shall then have the following account of the amount saved to the public, in the two years ending June 30, 1848, by the railways in passenger traffic, as compared with stage-coaches, supposing that such an amount of traffic by such means were practicable:

	£.
Fares saved by 354,083,534 first-class passengers carried one mile at 3½d. per head..............	5,163,718
Do. by 1,357,936,966 second and third-class passengers carried one mile at 2d. per head	11,316,141
Value of time saved by 1,712,020 passengers traveling 100 miles, at 4s. 8d. per head..............	399,417
Tavern expenses on 1,712,020 passengers traveling 100 miles, at 6d. a head.....................	42,800
Total saving in the two years ending June 30, 1848	16,922,076

It will be shown in a subsequent chapter, that the total sum expended by the public upon the passenger traffic on the railways, in the two years ending June 30, 1848, was £10,868,385. It appears, from the above estimate, that the same amount of traffic, if executed by stage-coaches, including all the additional expense incidental to that mode of conveyance, would have cost £27,890,461. The saving, therefore, by the new mode of transport, as compared with the old, is about sixty per cent. of the latter: or, in other words, about seventy per cent. more than the total sum at present expended.

During the seven years terminating on the 30th June, 1849, the railways were in a state of rapid development; each year added largely to the total length of railway open for traffic. The augmentation of the amount of traffic, exhibited annually in the preceding tables, was therefore to be ascribed partly to the increased length of the railway, and partly to the increased demand of the public for railway transport.

Let us, then, compare the progress of the traffic with the progress of the development of railways.

To accomplish this, we must obtain an estimate of the average amount of railways which were under traffic during each successive year. This may be obtained by taking the length of railways open on the last day of each year as equal to the average length under traffic during each twelve months terminating on the 30th June.

In the following table I have given, in the second column, therefore, the length of railway which was in operation on the 1st January in each of the years specified in the first column; and in the third column I have given the average number of passengers per day which would have been carried over each mile of the entire system of railways under operation, if the actual passenger traffic were uniformly diffused over the whole.

This calculation is made by dividing the total average daily mileage of every class of passengers carried within the year, as given in the table, p. 154,5, by the numbers given in the second column of the following table.

TABULAR ANALYSIS of the progressive Development of the Railways of the United Kingdom, and of the Movement of Passengers upon them during the Seven Years ending June 30, 1849.

	Miles open.	Number of Passengers carried per Mile.
Twelve months ending June 30, 1843	1857	558
,, ,, 1844	1952	625
,, ,, 1845	2148	672
,, ,, 1846	2441	895
,, ,, 1847	3036	726
,, ,, 1848	3816	654
,, ,, 1849	5007	..

The numbers given in the above table, while they present an astonishing example of the movement of the population, indicate nevertheless the fact, that the increase of the passenger traffic has not kept pace since 1846 with the increase of the railways. While the absolute quantity of passenger traffic increased, as appears from the table, p. 163, in a rapid proportion, the daily numbers transported per mile of railway open has undergone a regular diminution.

The last column of the above table shows the number of passengers which would have been carried over each mile of the railways open, if the entire passenger business had been uniformly distributed over the whole extent of railways under traffic. Independently of this average result, it would have been desirable to exhibit the manner in which the actual traffic is distributed, and how it varies from section to section of the several lines. No data, however, by which this can be ascertained, are extant among the records of the English railways

CHAP. X.] PASSENGER TRAFFIC. 167

In succeeding chapters will be found some interesting results of this kind, obtained on foreign lines. Meanwhile, in the absence of more detailed and satisfactory information, I have calculated the following table of the comparative traffic per mile on certain lines during the year 1846,7.

TABULAR ANALYSIS showing the average Number of Passengers carried daily on each Mile of the under-mentioned Railways of the United Kingdom during the Twelve Months ending June 30, 1847.

	Number of Miles open.	Average Number of Passengers carried daily per Mile.			
		1st Class.	2d Class.	3d Class.	Total.
London and Northwestern.................	428	360	478	345	1183
Great Western	245	228	518	206	952
Midland................................	283	103	192	305	600
London, Brighton, and South Coast	135	230	313	358	901
London and Cambridge } Eastern Counties.. London and Colchester	182	161	330	305	796
Bristol and Birmingham..................	85	133	310	176	619
London and Southwestern.................	190	162	326	190	678
York and Newcastle	229	48	114	126	288
York and North Midland.................	175	69	114	213	396
Lancashire and Yorkshire	108	93	198	535	836
All the remaining Lines	976	104	212	321	637
Total and averages......	3036	157	281	289	727

In the following table I have given the rates at which the total passenger traffic, estimated by its mileage, has augmented from year to year; the rate at which the total length of the railways in operation has augmented; and the rate at which the average passenger traffic upon them per mile has varied.

TABULAR COMPARISON of the Annual Rates of Increase of the Railways in operation, the total Traffic in Passengers, and the corresponding Variation of the average Traffic per mile of Railway.

	Increased Length of Railway per Cent.	Increased Passenger Traffic per Cent.	Increased Traffic per Mile per Cent.	Decreased Traffic per Mile per Cent.
Year ending June 1844 compared with year ending June 1843	5·12	18·00	12·00	..
Year ending June 1845 compared with year ending June 1844	10·05	18·28	7·52	..
Year ending June 1846 compared with year ending June 1845	13·64	51·44	33·20	..
Year ending June 1847 compared with year ending June 1846	24·33	0·97	..	19·00
Year ending June 1848 compared with year ending June 1847	25·69	12·70	..	10·00
Year ending June 1849 compared with year ending June 1848	33·10			

These results are curious and interesting. The total passenger traffic, increasing at the uniform rate of 18 per cent. per annum until 1845,6, underwent in that year a sudden and enormous increase of above 50 per cent.; it then stopped short and suffered no change for 12 months, after which it again began to increase, but at a slower rate than that at which it progressed previously to 1845,6; notwithstanding the length of railway in operation in 1847,8 increased about 100 per cent., compared with its length previously to 1845,6.

It further appears that, in 1845,6, notwithstanding the length of railway in operation was increased nearly 14 per cent., the average traffic per mile was increased upward of 33 per cent.; but in the succeeding year the length of railway in operation being increased 24 per cent., the average traffic per mile was diminished 19 per cent.

The reason of the decreased traffic per mile is evident. The first railways constructed were naturally those which were conducted through the districts of most active traffic; the latest were subsidiary lines of comparatively less importance, and having considerably less traffic. While, therefore, during the two years 1846,8 the total amount of daily passenger traffic was augmented 13 per cent., the traffic per mile of railway was diminished 30 per cent.

Meanwhile, however, the average daily traffic per mile on railways, during the twelve months ending 30th June, 1848, was 654 passengers; the meaning of which is, that if the total number of passengers daily carried on the railways of the United Kingdom were uniformly diffused over the whole extent of these railways, 654 passengers would be carried over every mile of their entire length per day.

By comparing the mileage of the passengers with the mileage of the carriages by which they are transported, we may ascertain the average number of passengers borne by each carriage.

It happens, however, as has been already stated, that no direct mileage account is kept for the carriages on the English railways. Captain Huish, who has had under his superintendence the traffic of between 600 and 700 miles of railway, being nearly one-seventh part of all the railways of the United Kingdom, gives the following estimate of the average load carried by each class of passenger carriage:

PASSENGER TRAFFIC.

	Full Load.	Average Load carried.	Proportion of average Load to full Load per Cent.
First class	18	7	39
Second class	25	13	52
Third class	32	21	66

On the foreign railways, where the mileage account of the carriages is generally kept, we find the results to correspond very nearly with this. Thus, on the North of France Railway, the number of passengers borne by first-class carriages in 1848 was 7: they are built to accommodate 24. The proportion in this case is even less than that which obtains in England, being under 29 per cent. In the second-class carriages, on the same railway, the average number of passengers was $10\frac{1}{2}$, and in the third-class carriages 19, the proportion in all cases being less than that which prevails on the English railways.

On the Belgian railways the average number of passengers carried by the first-class carriages is $8\frac{1}{2}$, by the second-class 12, and by the third-class $16\frac{1}{2}$.

On the Orleans Railway, similar computations show that the number of passengers in each first-class carriage is $7\frac{7}{10}$, and in the second and third-class carriages $21\frac{3}{4}$.

We may therefore take generally, as a good practical estimate, not only for England but for foreign traffic, the loads given by Captain Huish, and assume that, in the practical working of railways, 39 per cent. of the capacity of the first-class carriages, 52 per cent. of the second-class, and 66 per cent. of the third-class, constitute the average profitable load.

Having determined the average loads of the respective classes of carriages, and their average mileage, we can compute the number of carriages employed daily in executing the traffic of the English railways.

It has been shown (p. 98) that, on an average, each first-class carriage travels 59 miles a day, and carries 7 passengers; it therefore executes a portion of the average daily mileage of the first-class passengers, expressed by the number $7 \times 59 = 413$.

In like manner, it appears that every second-class carriage carries, on the average, 13 passengers, and travels on an average 45 miles; it therefore executes a portion of the average daily mileage of the second-class passengers, expressed by the number $13 \times 45 = 585$.

It further appears, that the third-class carriages carry an average load of 21 passengers, and travel an average distance of 38 miles;

they execute, therefore, a portion of the average daily mileage of the third-class passengers, expressed by 38 × 21 = 798.

We shall find, therefore, approximately, the number of the several classes of carriages employed in working the traffic of the English railways by dividing the average daily mileage of the several classes of passengers, as already given, by the numbers here calculated.

To obtain the number of the first-class carriages, divide 553,330 (table, p. 155), the average daily mileage of the first-class passengers, by 413, and we find 1340. In the same way, to find the number of second-class carriages, divide 1,104,388, the daily mileage of the second-class passengers, by 585, and the quotient is 1888, the number of second-class carriages; and, to find the number of the third-class, divide 1,208,964, their average daily mileage, by 798, and the quotient, 1515, gives the number of third-class carriages.

These approximate results, compared with those already obtained by a different process (p. 111), will show that they can not be far from the truth.

	By present Process.	By former Process.
Passenger coaches, 1st class	1340	1488
" 2d class	1888	2080
" 3d class	1515	1488

In general, if the passenger traffic of a railway be given or estimated, and it be required to determine the necessary carriage stock to work it, supposing the capacity of the carriages and the nature of the traffic the same as those which prevail on the English lines, the requisite number may be found as follows:

To determine the requisite number of first-class carriages, divide the estimated daily mileage of the first-class passengers by 413, that of the second-class passengers by 585, and that of the third-class passengers by 798; the quotients will respectively give the necessary number of carriages of each class.

In this calculation I have assumed that the carriages are similar to those which prevail generally on the English railways; the first class being built to accommodate 18, the second class 25, and the third class 32. On railways constructed with a wide gauge this calculation will not be applicable. I have not been able to ascertain the average loads carried on these latter roads, which would require a separate computation.

By comparing the mileage of the passenger traffic with that of the passenger engines, the number of passengers of each class drawn by each engine or carried by each train can be ascertained

As an example of this computation, I give the following results of computations derived from the official reports of the railways therein mentioned. The number of passengers carried is in each case ascertained by dividing the total mileage of the passengers by the total mileage of the engines.

Table showing the average Number of Passengers of each Class carried by each Passenger Train on the under-mentioned Railways.

	Average daily Mileage of Passenger Engines.	Average daily Mileage of Passengers	Number of Passengers per Train.
Belgian railways, 1844.			
1st class	2843	39,079	13·78
2d class	..	68,274	24·00
3d class	..	116,493	41·00
		223,846	78·78
Belgian lines, 1845.			
1st class	2575	38,583	15·00
2d class	..	68,167	26·50
3d class	..	100,666	39·00
		207,416	80·50
North of France, 1848.			
1st class	3473	29,566	8·51
2d class	..	66,643	19·18
3d class	..	114,139	32·86
		210,348	60·55

The results which appear above for the North of France in 1848 afford a curious illustration of the local effect of the political convulsions of that year in France, the number of passengers carried being considerably below its normal amount.

The reports published by the directors of the English railways, and by the Government Commissioners, supply no data from which general conclusions of this kind can be deduced. In a few instances, the half-yearly reports presented to the shareholders have given the mileage of the engines, and that of the passengers can be approximately obtained from a comparison of the receipts with the average tariff. I have by these means calculated the following table, exhibiting the relation of the movement of the passenger traffic to that of the engines on the railways worked by the Northwestern, Great Western, and Brighton companies. The mileage of the engines of the Northwestern Company during the twelve months ending the 30th June, 1849, was 4,649,556, according to a return I have obtained from Captain Huish. Not having any distinct return for the half-year ending 31st December, 1848, I have taken half this number as representing the mileage, which can not vary much from the truth.

TABULAR ANALYSIS showing the Relation between the Movement of the Engines and the Movement of the Passengers on the under-mentioned Railways.

	Total Mileage of Passenger Engines.	Number of Passengers.	Total Mileage of Passengers.	Average No. of Passengers per Engine.	Average Distance traveled by each Passenger.
Northwestern, including the Chester and Holyhead, Lancaster and Carlisle, Kendal and Windemere, and North Union lines.					
For half-year ending December 31, 1848	2,324,778				
Passengers, 1st class..	..	586,332	33,840,267	14·5	57·6
,, 2d class ..	..	1,437,833	44,827,743	19·3	31·3
,, 3d class ..	..	1,477,411	33,941,960	14·6	23·0
Totals and averages	..	3,501,576	112,619,970	48·4	32·2
Great Western, including Bristol and Exeter, and South Devon.					
For twelve months ending June 30, 1847	2,004,814				
Passengers, 1st class..	..	546,862	21,339,187	10·7	39·0
,, 2d class ..	..	2,224,721	48,939,269	24·5	22·0
,, 3d class ..	..	530,569	19,713,692	9·8	37·2
Totals and averages	..	3,302,152	89,992,148	45·0	27·3
For twelve months ending June 30, 1848	2,229,958				
Passengers, 1st class..	..	567,878	20,931,842	9·4	37·0
,, 2d class ..	..	2,490,246	50,324,011	22·5	20·2
,, 3d class ..	..	649,777	22,952,910	10·3	35·3
Totals and averages	..	3,707,901	94,208,763	42·2	25·5
For half-year ending December 31, 1848	1,263,956				
Passengers, 1st class..	..	267,583	10,750,878	8·5	40·2
,, 2d class ..	..	1,253,060	27,301.727	21·6	21·8
,, 3d class ..	..	422,763	14,733,120	11·7	34·9
Totals and averages	..	1,943,406	52,785,725	41·8	27·2
London, Brighton, and South Coast.					
For half-year ending June 30, 1849	398,139				
Passengers, 1st class..	..	232,807	5,632,488	14·2	24·1
,, 2d class ..	..	483,502	8,494,080	21·4	17·6
,, 3d class ..	..	417,189	7,334,160	18·4	18·8
Totals and averages	..	1,133,498	21,460,728	54·0	19·0

On comparing the average distances traveled with those found in the table (p. 158), it will be observed that some slight discordance prevails. This may be explained partly by the circumstance of the two tables referring to different epochs, and partly by their including different lines of railway.*

If the average number of passengers carried by each class of passenger coaches were taken, the average composition of the trains, so far as relates to the passenger coaches, could be determined from the above results. Captain Huish, in his return already quoted, estimates, that on the Northwestern Railway, the number of first-class passengers carried by each coach is 7; the number of second-class passengers, 13; and the number of third-class passengers, 21. If the same estimate be taken as applicable to the Brighton Railway, in which the carriages are of the same magnitude, we shall obtain the following as the numbers of each class of carriages composing an average train:

	Northwestern Railway.	Brighton Railway.
Average number of passenger coaches contained in each train.		
1st class	2·07	2·00
2d class	1·46	1·61
3d class	0·70	0·88

It must be observed that the actual composition of the trains, both as regards passengers and passenger coaches, differs from this average, inasmuch as third-class passengers and third-class coaches are excluded from first-class trains; so that the actual number of first-class passengers taken in first-class trains, and of third-class passengers taken in third-class trains, will be greater than the above average estimates; and the same will be true of the coaches.

It must be further observed, that these conclusions rest upon the estimate of the average loads of the passenger coaches made by Captain Huish. This estimate has been made, I believe, from general observation, and not from any exact statistical record of the mileage: but it is, nevertheless, supposed to be tolerably correct.

It has been already observed, that horses and carriages are usually carried by passenger trains.

* The Great Western, as given in the table, p. 158, does not include the South Devon.

To complete the analysis, therefore, of the passenger traffic, we ought to show how the proportion of these objects of transport respectively is estimated and compared with the movement of the carrying and drawing-stock.

The mileage of the horses and carriages transported is recorded in the booking-office in the same manner as that of the passengers. By comparing the mileage of the horses with the mileage of the horse-boxes, we are enabled to calculate the average load transported by each horse-box; and, in the same way, by comparing the mileage of the carriage-trucks with the mileage of the carriages, we are enabled to determine the average load taken by each carriage-truck.

I have given, as an example of this, the transport of horses and carriages on the Belgian railways in 1844:

ANALYSIS of Transport of Horses on the Belgian Railways in 1844.

Number of horses........................	1,434
Mileage of horses........................	156,079
Mileage of horse-boxes...................	93,208
Average number carried per horse-box......	1·67
Average distance traveled per horse........	109·00

ANALYSIS of Transport of Carriages on the same Railways in 1844.

Number of carriages.....................	2,546
Mileage of carriages.....................	229,161
Mileage of carriage-trucks................	310,700
Number of carriages per truck.............	0·22
Average distance traveled per carriage......	90·00

To estimate justly the degree of accommodation afforded to the public by the railways, it is necessary to consider the frequency of departures, and the speed of transit. How often per day a man of business has an opportunity of starting for a given place, and within what time he can be taken there, are the first questions which every one will ask whose time is of value. The traveler for pleasure can choose his hour of departure; the man of business must depart at those times which are most compatible with his engagements; and in reference to that class the frequency of departure is, perhaps, even more important than the speed of transport.

The railways, accordingly, afford greater advantages, as compared with the former means of transport by stage-coaches, by frequency of departure, than even by their increased speed. If we take the common table of arrivals and departures on any of the great lines of railway, we shall easily obtain proof of this.

PASSENGER TRAFFIC.

We find that from the London stations of the principal railways there are departures daily as follows: Great Western, 15; Southwestern, 17; Brighton, 8; Southeastern, 7; and Northwestern, 20.

The actual time requisite to travel between any two points of a line of railway, does not depend so much on the speed of the train when in motion as is generally supposed; nor is there so much difference between the velocity of the first-class trains and that of the slowest, when in full speed, as may be imagined. The comparative celerity with which the traveling is executed depends more upon the number of stations at which the train stops, than on its actual speed when in motion.

A railway passenger train having a gross weight of 70 tons, when in full speed at 40 miles an hour, can not be stopped, as may easily be understood, very suddenly. It must be deprived of its enormous momentum by slow degrees. In proportion as it is suddenly stopped will there be damage done both to the rolling stock and the permanent way.

From the moment that the steam is cut off, and that the speed begins to be slackened, either by the ordinary friction and resistance of the air, or by the aid of brakes, the momentum which is lost is spent upon the permanent way; and the shorter the space over which it is expended, the more severe will be the action upon the rails. It is therefore a matter of economy, with regard to the wear of the permanent way, not to attempt to stop the trains within too short a distance. In all cases, stoppage produces a considerable wear and tear of the rails; and hence it arises, that the rails which are adjacent to stations, and especially to chief stations where trains of all classes stop, are subject to much more rapid wear than are the rails elsewhere upon the road.

The distance within which a train can be conveniently stopped without acting injuriously on the rails will depend on the velocity of the train and its weight. In any case, its average velocity over that part of the line along which it passes, after cutting off the steam until it comes to rest, will be only half its full speed.

Thus, if a train moving at 40 miles an hour cut off its steam at half a mile from a station, that half mile will be run over at the rate of only 20 miles an hour; and the same will be true of the space run by every train after its steam is cut off, whatever may have been its speed.

It is calculated that, in this manner, a train loses upon an average about $1\frac{1}{4}$ minutes in coming to rest at each stoppage;

and since an equal time is lost in getting up the speed at starting, it may be stated generally that there is a loss of $2\frac{1}{2}$ minutes in stopping and starting; and, if an equal time be allowed for standing, we shall have an average of five minutes' delay for each station at which a train stops.

The celerity of the fastest trains on the railways is accordingly obtained by causing them to stop only at a few principal stations; and other trains of varying speed are accordingly so regulated, that the slower trains alone stop at all the stations.

In respect to their average speed, the railway trains may be resolved into four classes :

        1st. The express trains.
        2d. The mail trains.
        3d. The first and second-class trains.
        4th. The third-class trains.

As an example of the progress of these different classes of trains, we have exhibited, in the following table (see page 177), the distances they travel on some of the principal main lines of railway diverging from London; the total time they take to complete the trip; the number of their stoppages; their average speed, stoppages included; and their average speed when in motion.

The subject of passenger traffic ought not to be dismissed without some notice of the extraordinary speed at which it is conducted, and the consequences of this expedition. The public has become so familiar with the announcement of such or such a trip being performed with a speed of 50 or 60 miles an hour, that people have ceased to reflect upon what the locomotive phenomenon really is, which they so flippantly advert to.

The average speeds from station to station, given in the above table, are taken from the published time-tables of the companies, and are estimated on certain average conditions; but the actual speed which is frequently attained by the express trains in motion, often greatly exceeds even the highest given in these tables. Thus, a speed of 60 miles an hour is far from being uncommon when in full motion, and I have myself not unfrequently been carried, in experimental trips, at the rate of above 70 miles an hour.

Let us endeavor to convey to the unpracticed reader some definite idea of this enormous speed of locomotion.

Seventy miles an hour is, in round numbers, 105 feet per second; that is to say, a motion in virtue of which the passen-

PASSENGER TRAFFIC.

TABULAR ANALYSIS of the Movement of the Passenger Traffic on the principal Lines of Railway diverging from London, showing the average Speed, Stoppages, &c. of each Class of Trains.—N.B. An average Loss of Five Minutes is allowed for each Stoppage, except in particular Cases, where a greater Delay is fixed by the Programme. This is intended to include the Time lost in coming to Rest and getting up Speed.

Name of Railway.	Train.	Distance traveled.	Time.	No. of Stoppages	Average Speed, including Stoppages.	Actual Speed in Motion, excluding Stoppages.
		Miles.	h. m.		Miles per Hour.	Miles per Hour.
London to Liverpool	Express	201	5 45	5	35·00	37·75
,, ,,	Express Mail	201	6 45	15	29·75	36·60
,, ,,	Mail	201	7 57	15	25·25	31·00
,, ,,	1st and 2d cl.	201	8 0	20	25·10	31·70
,, ,,	3d class	201	14 45	45	13·65	18·25
London to Exeter	Express	193¼	4 30	7	43·00	51·60
,, ,,	Mail	193¼	7 10	21	27·00	36·80
,, ,,	1st and 2d cl.	193¼	7 15	25	26·65	38·60
,, ,,	3d class	193¼	13 5	37	14·75	19·32
London to Southampton	Express	80	2 15	6	35·60	45·80
,, ,,	Mail	80	3 0	11	26·65	38·25
,, ,,	1st and 2d cl.	80	3 20	13	24·10	35·50
,, ,,	3d class	80	4 45	18	16·85	24·65
London to Dover	Express	88	2 30	8	35·20	48·50
,, ,,	Mail	88	2 30	5	35·20	42·10
,, ,,	1st and 2d cl.	88	3 45	15	23·45	29·35
,, ,,	3d class	88	4 0	17	22·00	30·40
London and Brighton	Express	50½	1 30	1	33·80	35·85
,, ,,	Mail	50½	1 30	3	33·80	40·50
,, ,,	1st and 2d cl.	50½	2 0	3	25·25	28·90
,, ,,	3d class	50½	2 25	11	20·65	33·80
Totals and averages		2652	108 42	301	24·45	32·00

ger is carried over 35 yards between two beats of a common clock. Two objects near him, a yard asunder, pass by his eye in the thirty-fifth part of a second; and, if 35 stakes were erected at the side of the road, a yard asunder, these 35 would pass his eye between two beats of a common clock, and it is scarcely necessary to say that they would not be distinguishable, the retina not being capable of receiving distinct successive impressions in so minute a fraction of time. If the stakes had any strong color, such as red, they would have the appearance of a continuous flash of red color. At such a speed, therefore, the objects on the side of the road are undistinguishable.

When two trains having this speed pass each other, the relative velocity will be double that, or 70 yards per second; and if one of the trains were 70 yards long, it would flash by in a single second.

It will be somewhat curious to investigate the movement of the mechanism of the engine, which produces this extraordinary speed.

Let us suppose that the driving-wheels of the engine are about 7 feet in diameter, and, consequently, that they measure a little more than 21 feet, or 7 yards, in circumference. These wheels would revolve five times in passing over 35 yards of the rails; and as this space is, on the supposition we have made, passed over in one second, these driving-wheels must, necessarily, at such a speed, revolve five times per second. Now, to produce one revolution of the driving-wheels, each piston must once pass backward and forward in the cylinder, and its motion, therefore, must divide a second into ten equal parts. On arriving at each end of the cylinder, at the moment it is about to change the direction of its motion, and to return, a valve must be shifted by which steam may be admitted on one side of the piston and withdrawn from the other side. This valve must therefore also be moved ten times per second, and must complete its motion so rapidly as to form but a small fraction of the entire stroke of the piston, and therefore its motion must be computed by a small fraction of the tenth part of a second, and this must be done with the utmost punctuality and uniformity, otherwise the action of the piston could not be continued. The cylinder discharges its contents through the escape valve every time that the piston changes its direction, and consequently this discharge must take place, under the circumstances here supposed, ten times per second.

But there are two cylinders, and the mechanism is so regulated that the discharge from the one is intermediate between two successive discharges from the other. There are therefore 20 discharges of steam per second, at equal intervals; and thus these 20 puffs divide a second into 20 equal parts, each puff having the twentieth of a second between it and that which precedes or follows it. The steam which thus puffs from the cylinders is conveyed by a pipe to the chimney, where it escapes upward in a succession of blasts, by which the draft through the fire-place is maintained. It is these blasts of steam in the chimney which produce the coughing noise heard when a locomotive engine is moving slowly. As the rapidity augments, these coughs become more rapid, and when the speed attains the amount which we have supposed above, there will be 20 coughs per second. The ear, like the eye, is limited in the rapidity of the sensations of which it is susceptible, and, active and sensitive as that organ is, it is not capable of distinguishing sounds which succeed each other at intervals of the twentieth part of a second; therefore, when the engine moves at such a rate, the puffing in the chimney ceases to be appreciated by the ear, although, as a mechanical effect, it continues to be produced as accurately and regularly as when the engine is moving slowly.

According to the experiments of Dr. Hutton, it appeared that the time of flight of a cannon-ball, having a range of 6,700 feet, is one quarter of a minute.

The velocity was therefore 26,800 feet per minute, which is equal to 5 miles per minute, or 300 miles per hour.

It follows, therefore, that a railway train, moving at 75 miles an hour, not an uncommon speed for express trains to attain, would have a velocity only 4 times less than a cannon-ball.

The momentum of such a mass, moving at such a speed, is difficult to conceive. It would amount to a force equivalent to the aggregate force of a number of cannon-balls equal to one fourth of its own weight.

The consideration of the great damage done to the railway, as well as to the rolling stock, by these extreme speeds, is a serious drawback to the gratification which such wondrous performances naturally excite. The fracture and wear of rails is augmented in a very high ratio with the speed; so likewise is the wear of all parts of the vehicles most affected, such as wheels, axles, &c.

I have shown that, at the speed we have here considered, a driving-wheel, 7 feet in diameter, revolves 5 times per second; but the bearing-wheels of carriages, wagons, and vans are in general only 3 feet in diameter, and sometimes even less. Now, if a wheel of 7 feet in diameter revolve 5 times per second, a wheel 3 feet in diameter, proceeding at the same speed, must revolve very nearly 12 miles per second.

This, therefore, is the action which must take place upon all the wheels of the vehicles composing each express train.

The expense attending such extreme speed is not, however, limited to the cost which attends the trains themselves to which this motion is imparted. The whole traffic of the road is more or less affected by it. All other trains must be hurried forward to get out of the way of the express train, or detained in sidings to wait for its passage.

From these causes goods trains, which need not and ought not to move at a speed of more than 16 or 18, are frequently compelled to be driven at 30 miles an hour and upward.

Their average speed is made up by undue speed when in motion, for the time lost waiting in sidings for the progress of express trains.

The damage done to the road by these causes is not merely that which arises from the undue speed which must occasionally be given to heavy goods trains; great damage is also done by the frequent stoppages of such trains. When they are stopped, their momentum must be spent upon the rails; and when they are put in motion afterward, and momentum imparted to them, the reaction produced by their driving-wheels on the rails is another cause of most injurious wear and tear.

Railway directors and managers are deeply sensible of the great damage sustained by the property under their care in consequence of these circumstances, and frequent murmurs and remonstrances are heard upon the subject. The public, however, appear to be too exigent to be successfully resisted. I have no doubt, from long and careful practical investigations into the effects produced by the action of engines and carriages on railways, that the damage sustained directly and indirectly by railway proprietors in consequence of express trains moving at this extraordinary speed, is far greater than any profits derivable from such trains can cover; and I have no hesitation in saying, that, considered in a commercial point of view, railway proprietors would be fully justified, either in laying a much higher rate of fare upon express trains, or, which would be much more advisable and more consistent with their own interests, suppressing them altogether.

The injurious effects proceeding from these causes would have been considerably less, if in the original construction of railways sufficient width had been left in the bridges, tunnels, and other works of art, for an additional line of rails. If this additional line of rails had been reserved for the exclusive use of the merchandise traffic, and the third-class passenger trains, with proper sidings, the main line, which now performs the entire work of the railway, being reserved for the fast passenger traffic, less inconvenience and injury would have arisen to the railway property, and much more expedition, punctuality, and safety have been insured to the traveling public.

We must not dismiss the subject of express trains without noticing the danger of which they are productive. In railway traffic the entire stream of transport ought to proceed as much as possible with an uniform speed, so that one part should be not liable to overtake another. The greater the difference of velocity of the different objects of transport, moving in the same direction, and on the same rails, the greater is the danger of collision; and the consequences of collision are dangerous in the exact proportion of the difference of velocities of the bodies which strike each other. These causes of danger and injury are augmented to the highest conceivable degree by the express trains. These trains move with an enormous and exceptional speed. Collision becomes inevitable unless a warning be sent along the line to clear the way. Nor is it always practicable, even with the warning, to avert it.

An engine attached to a goods train, for example, becomes lamed between two stations. It is necessary to send on to the adjacent station for help, and notice must be sent back to stop the following train. This notice may in general be rendered effectual to trains moving at ordinary speeds, but an express train, moving at the usual rate of such trains, can not safely pull up except within a considerable distance. The chances, therefore, of an express train running into a disabled train upon the road are very considerable.

The use of the electric telegraph diminishes this danger; but to give notice by the telegraph a message must be sent to the nearest station, which may be at a considerable distance.

It is not without regret that one would discourage the ardor for improvement produced by wholesome competition; but it is indispensably necessary to regulate our progress with discretion, and it must not be forgotten that the safety of the public is not less to be considered than expedition of traveling.

The public, in general, concerns itself very little with the question of safety. The traveler who desires to reach a distant point with speed, is seldom so well informed as to be enabled to appreciate the degree of danger which must attend the attainment of his object; and it is necessary that those who have the control and management of railways, and who alone are competent to appreciate the danger, should resist this tendency in the public, which would impel the conductors of railways into a course attended with serious damage and loss to railway proprietors, and with no small danger to the traveling public.

CHAPTER XI.

GOODS TRAFFIC.

The transport of merchandise is the branch of railway business on the due improvement and cultivation of which the ultimate and durable success of these vast enterprises, and the extent of their public utility, will mainly depend: yet it is a branch which has been hitherto comparatively neglected. The brilliant and unexpected results of the business in passenger traffic have not unnaturally dazzled the public, and engrossed the attention of proprietors, directors, and managers. Nothing has been neglected which could contribute to the extension of this branch of transport, and it may even be questioned whether the great expenses which have been entailed on railway establishments in affording the unexampled accommodation of extreme speed and frequency of departure have been or can be adequately repaid by any practicable extension of the traffic.

The transport of goods, though presenting less striking phenomena, is attended with not less benefit to the country, and may soon, if duly cultivated, become the source of even more permanent and extensive profits to the railway establishments. But to realize these, it will be necessary that this branch of the business should receive a more profound study on the part of railway managers than has hitherto been bestowed upon it. The transport of goods is subject to more various and difficult conditions than that of passengers. If frequency of departure and extreme speed are not so imperatively demanded for it, the accommodation of the tariff, so as to render the transport compatible with the commercial conditions of the local markets, is a subject out of which arise numerous and difficult questions for solution; and on the solution of these questions, and on the due regulation and graduation of the goods tariff, will depend altogether the extent and the success of this important branch of railway business.

The official reports of the railway commissioners and directors, meagre and unsatisfactory as they are with reference to the passenger traffic, are much more so relative to the traffic in merchandise. If we have not all the necessary details of the passenger traffic, we are at least informed of the number of each class booked, the gross receipts, and the average tariff, supplying data by which we have been enabled to approximate to those statistical details relating to the transport which ought to have been supplied by direct and accurate records. We are not able, however, to do even this with reference to the goods traffic. The reports in general supply no information relative to this branch of railway business, except the receipts, and even these are given in a lumped sum, in which is included the revenue which proceeds from a variety of objects not properly included under the head of merchandise, such as mails, parcels, private carriages, &c.

To supply a complete analysis of the goods business, it would be necessary to possess the following data.

1st. The quantity of each class of goods booked, T.

2dly. Their mileage, t.

3dly. The number and description of vehicles employed in their transport, W.

4th. The mileage of these vehicles, w.

By comparing the first and second, we should obtain the average distance which each unit of each class of traffic is carried. This would be done by dividing the number expressed by t, or the mileage, by the number expressed by $T := -\left(\dfrac{t}{T}\right)$.

By comparing the second with the fourth we should obtain the average load carried by each vehicle. This would be done by dividing the number expressed by t by the number expressed by $w := -\left(\dfrac{t}{w}\right)$.

By comparing the third and fourth, we should obtain the average distance run by each vehicle of transport. This would be done by dividing the number expressed by w by the number expressed by $W := -\left(\dfrac{w}{W}\right)$.

In this way, all the circumstances attending the movement of each class of goods traffic could be inferred from simple and clear data, which might be easily recorded.

It would be necessary to classify the merchandise, first, according to the description of vehicle in which it is transported; and, secondly, according to its tariff.

Special vehicles are appropriated to different descriptions of goods, as has been already explained; and, in order to ascertain the cost of the transport of each class of goods, it would be necessary to keep a second mileage account not only of each class of traffic, but of each class of vehicle appropriated to its transport. The average load carried by each vehicle would be determined by a comparison of these mileages; and upon this average load would depend, as will be explained hereafter, the cost of the transport.

No general data of this kind, or any other data from which they can be inferred, are supplied in the railway reports. Reports somewhat more detailed, however, appeared in the returns published by the railway commissioners for the two years ending June 30, 1846, and June 30, 1847; but, owing to the discrepancies which appear in the returns of different companies, and to the different senses in which they use the same terms, it is extremely difficult to deduce any general inferences from them. I have, however, computed from these returns the quantity of goods and live stock, and their total mileage, for the twelve months ending June 30, 1847, which are exhibited in the follwing table :

TABULAR ANALYSIS of the Quantity of Goods and Live Stock Traffic on the Railways of the United Kingdom for Twelve Months ending June 30, 1847.

	Denomination.	Quantity or Number.	Mileage.
Merchandise	Tons.	16,460,599	370,138,271
Cattle	Number.	584,287	17,692,210
Sheep	Do.	2,509,529	82,096,451
Pigs and Calves	Do.	615,214	34,242,281

From this we can infer the average daily mileage, the average distance over which each unit of transport was carried, and the average number of such units daily booked. These are exhibited in the following table :

TABULAR ANALYSIS of the daily Traffic in Goods, and of the Distance carried on the Railways of the United Kingdom for Twelve Months ending June 30, 1847.

	Average Number of Units booked daily.	Average daily Mileage.	Average Distance traveled per Unit booked.
			Miles.
Merchandise ....tons	45,097	1,014,077	22·5
Cattle ....number	1,600	48,471	30·3
Sheep .... ,,	6,875	224,922	32·7
Pigs and calves... ,,	1,685	93,813	55·7

The result of this table will be as unexpected as were those obtained by analogous calculations with respect to the passenger traffic. The average distance through which merchandise was transported, $22\frac{1}{2}$ miles, is much less than might have been expected, or than would have taken place under the operation of a properly graduated tariff. It is evident from this, that the tariff is prohibitory for a greater average distance than about 20 miles. It would be interesting, if we possessed the requisite data, to apply a like investigation to the various classes of merchandise, so as to ascertain what classes are transported to the greatest distances; but the reports supply us with no data for this purpose.

It is curious, also, that the pigs and calves are transported to an average distance so much greater than the cattle and sheep.

As we have already observed with respect to the traffic in passengers, the average distances which the goods were transported is found to vary, within very wide limits, on different lines of railway. I give, in the following table, the results of a calculation made upon the returns for eleven different railways, for the twelve months ending June 30, 1847, showing the average distances which each ton of goods was transported on the several lines therein mentioned in that year.

TABULAR ANALYSIS of the average Distances which each Ton of Goods was transported on the under-mentioned Railways, during the Twelve Months ending June 30, 1847.

Name of Railway.	Tons of Goods.	Total Mileage.	Average Distance carried per Ton.
London and Northwestern	1,411,080	98,428,462	69·75
Great Western	371,327	19,007,395	51·18
Midland	1,195,177	37,626,074	31·48
London, Brighton, and South Coast	156,930	3,354,325	21·37
London and Cambridge	236,463	12,493,632	52·9
London and Colchester	83,364	3,172,898	38·10
Bristol and Birmingham	254,038	8,809,052	34·69
London and Southwestern	148,415	7,023,005	47·39
York and Newcastle	1,847,689	29,436,800	15·97
York and North Midland	446,181	12,134,231	27·19
Lancashire and Yorkshire	597,262	17,974,432	30·09
All the remaining lines	9,712,673	120,687,965	12·32
Totals and averages	16,460,599	370,138,271	22·50

Although we possess no data by which we can ascertain the quantity of goods booked for any period of long duration, nor even any direct record of the mileage of the goods traffic, we can nevertheless approximate to the latter by combining an approximate estimate of the receipts with the average tariff per ton per mile. By subducting the estimated revenue proceeding from mails, parcels, carriages, and horses, from the gross totals given in the official returns for them and the goods, we obtain approximate estimates of the revenue proceeding from goods. It appears also that, the average tariff being taken at $1\cdot67d$. per ton per mile, the annual and average daily mileage of the goods for the six years and a half ending Dec., 1848, was as follows:

TABULAR ANALYSIS of the Goods Traffic on the Railways of the United Kingdom during the Six Years and a Half ending Dec. 31, 1848.

	Total Mileage.	Average daily Mileage.
Twelve months ending June 30, 1843	161,865,276	443,466
,, ,, 1844	185,239,340	507,477
,, ,, 1845	262,600,039	719,452
,, ,, 1846	338,674,622	927,876
,, ,, 1847	409,392,412	1,121,623
,, ,, 1848	530,983,310	1,454,749
Six months ending December 30, 1848	309,118,238	1,693,798

Not possessing any return of the quantity of goods booked, we are unable to ascertain the average distances over which each ton was transported in each successive year.

The comparative rates of increase of the passenger and goods traffic for the last six years and a half are exhibited in the following table:

TABLE showing the comparative Rates at which the average daily Traffic in Passengers and Goods has augmented on the Railways of the United Kingdom during the Six Years and a Half ending December 31, 1848.

	Total Increase on the average daily Mileage of 1842,3.		Increased Percentage on the average daily Mileage of 1842,3.	
	Passengers.	*Goods.*	*Passengers.*	*Goods.*
Twelve months ending June 30, 1844	183,974	64,011	11·8	14·4
,, ,, 1845	406,946	275,986	14·0	62·3
,, ,, 1846	1,148,912	484,410	21·1	109·1
,, ,, 1847	1,170,106	678,057	21·3	153·0
,, ,, 1848	1,449,556	1,011,283	24·0	228·0
Six months ending December 31, 1848	1,831,294	1,250,332	27·7	282·0

The results of this table are perhaps more striking than any of the various calculations which we have hitherto deduced from the statistical data of railways. It appears from these, that while the passenger traffic, during the period of six years and a half previous to Dec. 31, 1848, increased scarcely 28 per cent., the goods traffic was augmented 282 per cent., the increase in the traffic of merchandise being thus tenfold that of passengers.

It will be also observed, that in the year 1847, compared with 1846, while no increase took place on the passenger traffic, there was an increase of 44 per cent. on the goods traffic.

If a proper record had been kept of the mileage of the various classes of the goods-carrying stock, we should have been able, by a comparison of this with the mileage of the goods themselves, to infer with accuracy the average amount of useful load carried by each class of vehicle; but no such mileage having been observed or recorded, we are forced to accept the best estimates, rough and approximate as they are, which can be obtained.

It has been already observed that Capt. Huish, by extensive observations made on the goods traffic of the Northwestern Railway, has found that the average loads of the goods wagons which arrive at and depart from the chief station of that railway is $2\frac{1}{4}$ tons. If, in the absence of more accurate returns, we adopt this as the general estimate of the average loads of the goods wagons, we can deduce their average mileage by dividing the mileage of the goods themselves by $2\frac{1}{4}$.

It appears also, as we have shown in Chap. VI., from the report of Capt. Huish, that the average number of wagons forming a goods train on the Northwestern lines of railway is 26. But it is probable, from the very active traffic of these lines, that this is above the general average. We shall therefore take the average number of wagons composing a goods train, upon the average of all the English railways, at 22.

In the following table I have exhibited the mileage of the goods-carrying stock and that of the goods engines, calculating each approximately in this manner:

TABULAR ANALYSIS showing the Total daily Mileage of the Goods Wagons and of the Goods Engines on the English Railways for Six Years and a Half ending December 31, 1848.

	Total daily Mileage of Goods Wagons.	Total daily Mileage of Goods Engines.
Twelve months ending The 30, 1843	197,096	8,959
,, ,, 1844	255,544	11,615
,, ,, 1845	319,756	14,535
,, ,, 1846	412,388	18,745
,, ,, 1847	498,500	22,659
,, ,, 1848	646,556	29,389
Six months ending December 31, 1848	752,796	34,218

Thus it appears that the distances traveled daily by the goods trains on the English railways during the last six months of 1848, amounted to nearly once and a half the circumference of the globe.

It will be interesting to compare this enormous amount of transport of merchandise, as executed by steam on railways, with the amount of horse power which would be necessary to perform the same service, were it practicable, by wagons and common roads.

The experience of carriers shows that in wagon transport, a horse must be allowed for each ton of goods transported, and that with this power a wagon may travel about 20 miles a day. The number of horses, therefore, requisite to execute a given traffic, will be found by dividing the daily mileage of the tons of goods by 20. Taking, therefore, the daily mileage of the goods for the six months ending 31st December, 1848, we find that to execute it by horse power in wagons, with a speed of about 3 miles an hour, would require the employment of 84,689 horses.

Let us now compare the progressive increase of the goods traffic with the progressive development of the railways during the last seven years, in the same manner as we have done with relation to the passenger traffic in the last chapter.

In the following table I have given, in the second column, as before, the length of railway which was under traffic in each successive year; and, in the third column, the average number of tons of goods per mile transported upon it, the numbers in this column being obtained by dividing the total mileage of the goods by the number of miles of railway open.

TABULAR COMPARISON of the progressive Development of the Railways of the United Kingdom and of the Movement of Goods upon them during the Six Years and a Half ending December 31, 1848.

	Miles open.	Number of Tons carried per Mile.	Increase per Cent.	Decrease per Cent.
Twelve months ending June 30, 1843	1857	238	..	..
,, ,, 1844	1952	260	9·25	..
,, ,, 1845	2148	335	28·80	..
,, ,, 1846	2441	381	13·75	..
,, ,, 1847	3036	370	..	2·90
,, ,, 1848	3816	382	3·25	..
Six months ending December 31, 1848	5007	338	..	11·50

GOODS TRAFFIC.

The goods traffic, therefore, in common with the passenger traffic, has failed to keep pace with the development of the railways. It appears by table p. 167, that the passenger traffic per mile continued to increase until June, 1846, but a decrease was manifested in the year ending June, 1847. The same result is obtained on the goods. In the case of the goods, however, there was again a relative increase in the twelve months ending June, 1848, while there was a considerable decrease in the same year in the relative amount of passenger traffic.

On the whole, then, it follows that neither the traffic in passengers nor goods has kept pace with the development of the railways, but that the relative falling off in the passenger business has been greater than that of the goods; while the absolute increase of the amount of goods business, without reference to the length of railway open, has been tenfold that of passenger business.

To give a complete analysis of the traffic, whether in passengers or in goods, on any system of railways, it is not enough, however useful it may be in itself, to give general averages, either in reference to a given period of time, as a year, or in reference to the entire extent of the line or lines. The traffic is not only distributed unequally with relation to time, but also with relation to space. The quantity executed in different months is different, and the quantity carried on different sections of the line still more so. Complete returns would supply us with data by which we could exhibit the variation in the quantity of traffic at different epochs, and on different sections of the line; but none of the returns published by the English railways, which are accessible to us, supply the means of doing this. As I have often had occasion to observe, the reports of foreign railways are much more ample and explicit; and illustrations of the variation to which the traffic is subject, in passengers and goods, in the different months of the year, and upon the different sections of the lines on some foreign railways, will be found in succeeding chapters.

The statistical reports of the railway commissioners for 1847 are, however, sufficiently ample to enable us to deduce from them the average daily mileage of the goods traffic on several of the principal railways, so as to afford some degree of comparison of the relative prevalence of the traffic in merchandise on different parts of the network of railways which overspread the country. In the following table I have given, in the first column, the length of the railways open, therein named; in the second, the average daily mileage of the tons of goods carried upon them; and in the third, the average quantity per mile on each line of railway.

TABULAR ANALYSIS showing the average daily Mileage of Tons of Goods, and the average Number of Tons carried daily per Mile, on the under-mentioned Railways during the Twelve Months ending June 30, 1847.

	Number of Miles open.	Average daily Mileage.	Average Number of Tons carried daily per Mile.
London and Northwestern	428	269,639	631
Great Western	245	52,075	212
Midland	283	103,085	364
London, Brighton, and South Coast	135	9,187	68
London and Cambridge ⎱ Eastern Counties London and Colchester ⎰	182	42,919	235
Bristol and Birmingham	85	24,132	283
London and Southwestern	190	19,241	101
York and Newcastle	229	80,651	352
York and North Midland	175	33,244	190
Lancashire and Yorkshire	108	49,240	456
All the remaining lines	976	330,650	338

From this table it follows, as might have been expected, that the proportion of traffic in goods to the length of the lines open is extremely variable; on the London and Brighton the traffic being at the rate of only 68 tons per mile, while on the London and Northwestern it is 631.

The immense activity of the traffic on the English railways, and the extent to which it affords employment to industry, may be in some degree calculated from the following statement of the number and class of persons in the employment of one company alone, the Northwestern:

Secretaries	2
General manager	1
Superintendents	3
Resident engineers	2
Clerks	966
Police constables	701
Engineers and stokers	738
Porters	3,054
Artificers	3,347
Laborers	1,452
	10,266

The number of horses employed in the local delivery of goods is 612, and the number of vans 256.

This, however, is independent of the goods establishments of Messrs. Pickford and Chaplin, the former of whom employed nearly 800 clerks and porters, 400 horses, and upward of 150 vehicles.

This company possesses 438 miles of railway, and supplies the locomotive power for about 200 miles more. It therefore employs about 23 persons per mile of its own lines.

CHAPTER XII.

THE EXPENSES.

THE tendency of the progress of the arts is to render the cost of production more and more independent of the quantity of the article produced. In the infancy of industry the application of labor is simple, and the quantity of production is always in the exact ratio of the labor itself. The knitter who produces in ten hours a pair of stockings, with the consumption of a certain weight of thread, will produce two pair of stockings in twenty hours, with the consumption of double the quantity of thread; three pair in thirty hours, with the consumption of three times the quantity of thread, and so on; and the cost of the stockings produced, representing the wages of the labor and the cost of the raw material, will be in the exact proportion of these, and will, consequently, be in the direct ratio of the number of pairs which have been made. Thus three pairs will cost precisely three times, ten pairs ten times, and one hundred pairs one hundred times as much as one pair, and so on.

But as the art improves, and the demand for stockings becomes more extensive, invention is stimulated, and a machine is contrived and constructed, by which the labor of the knitter is exchanged for that of the weaver, and the number of pairs of stockings which can be produced by the same expenditure of labor is largely multiplied. Their cost, therefore, so far as depends on the consumption of labor, is proportionally diminished. But this advantage is purchased by a large expenditure, preparatory to the fabrication, in the construction and purchase of the stocking-loom. By this loom many hundreds of thousands of pairs of stockings will be fabricated; and the cost of the loom, being divided among so enormous a number of articles, almost vanishes from the price of any single one.

Another step in the progress of invention supersedes the weaver himself. A power-loom is invented, by which the process of weaving is completed, independently of manual labor, by an engine deriving its motion directly from some physical agent, such as steam or water.

As another striking example of this principle, we may refer to the book now in the hand of the reader.

In the infancy of literature books were multiplied by copyists, and their cost was in the exact proportion of their number. One hundred copies of a book like this would have cost precisely one hundred times the price at which a single copy could be procured. Movable types were invented, and now a larger amount of preparatory labor and machinery is employed, before the production of even a single copy can take place; but when the types are set and the printing-press ready to work, five hundred or one thousand copies can be produced at a less expense than would previously have been incurred in the production of a single copy.

The ultimate point of perfection to which this progress tends, is to render the cost of production of each individual article precisely in the inverse proportion of the quantity produced. This is, however, a limit to which it is probable improvement can never actually attain; and the cost of production of the objects of industry, at present, may always be regarded as consisting of two parts, one of which is quite independent of the number of articles produced, and being, therefore, equally divided among them, will render one element of their price precisely in the inverse ratio of the number; but still there will be another component, which, depending on the direct application of manual or other labor, and on the immediate consumption of raw material, will be in the direct ratio of the number of articles produced. The greater the perfection to which art attains, the greater will be the former and the less the latter part of the cost. In the case of the power-loom above mentioned, the second element of price is reduced to the cost of the raw material, labor being very nearly if not altogether superseded.

These principles are illustrated in a striking manner by the improvements which have taken place in transport within the last century.

Before the construction of roads, the transport of persons and goods on pack-horses was a simple application of labor, and the cost of transport was in the direct ratio of the quantity. Roads

CHAP. XII.] THE EXPENSES.

were then constructed, and wheel-carriages employed. By the preparatory cost thus incurred, transport was so facilitated, that the same labor was enabled to accomplish a multiplied quantity of it. The cost of the roads and the improved carriages being divided among the increased quantity of transport, gave an element of its cost, which was inversely as its quantity; but still the labor of traction remained simple, and was in the direct ratio of the quantity of locomotion effected.

A further improvement produced the railway and the locomotive engine. Here an expense of an immense amount is incurred before a single object can be transported. Extensive lines of road, attended by works of art of prodigious magnitude and cost, are formed. Large buildings are provided for stations, and, in fine, a stock of engines and carriages is fabricated. All these expenses are incurred preparatory to locomotion, and must be divided among the quantity of transport executed. Indeed, the mere labor or expenditure of mechanical power necessary to transport the objects of traffic from point to point along the road forms the most insignificant item of the entire cost; and this item alone is in the direct proportion of the quantity of transport.

We should not, therefore, be far from the truth, if we stated that this great improvement in the art has reduced the cost of transport in a ratio which is very nearly the inverse of the quantity of transport executed.

When the question was agitated which led to the establishment of the uniform system of postage, the public was startled by the paradox that the transmission of a letter or dispatch was attended with the same cost, whether it were expedited ten miles or five hundred.

Nevertheless it was demonstrated, by the plainest principles of arithmetic, that the difference of expense was a sum so utterly evanescent in amount, as to confer practical truth on the principle on which the establishment of a uniform rate of postage was claimed. In a word, it was made manifest that the cost of transmission of letters was practically independent of the distance to which they were conveyed.

If any one should maintain that the same principle equally prevails in railway transport, he would certainly commit an error; but any one who should affirm that such a principle had no application at all in this case, would commit a scarcely less grave one.

The transmission of letters and dispatches differs from the transmission of persons and goods only in the weight of the objects carried. In the one case and in the other there is a part of the cost attending the transmission, which is quite independent of the expenses of transport properly so called, limiting the term transport to the mere locomotion or translation of the person or object from place to place.

Now, in the case of letters, the part of the expense which is independent of the mere cost of conveyance, bears so immense a proportion to the whole, that the latter may be wholly disregarded.

In the case of the transport of persons and goods this is not so, but nevertheless, even in this case, there is an item of the expenses which has no reference to the cost of locomotion, and which is therefore the same whether the person or thing transported be carried ten miles or five hundred miles. This item of expense, to whatever it may be related, is therefore independent of the distance, and is chargeable equally on objects transmitted to great or small distances.

An analysis of the past expenses of a railway may have two objects—retrospective and prospective.

Considered retrospectively, its purpose can only be the adjustment of accounts, an object which has no relation to our present purpose.

Considered prospectively, such an analysis has the most important purposes.

1st. It supplies the grounds of an estimate of future expenses.
2d. It supplies the basis of a future tariff.

To obtain an estimate of the future expenses of a railway is easy, provided the expenses of past years, properly classified, be known. If the circumstances of the traffic remain the same, the expenses must necessarily also remain unaltered; and the actual amount expended in the past year may be transferred unchanged into the estimate of the coming year.

But if the circumstances of the traffic, or the extent of line to be worked, be changed, then modifications must be made in the estimates for each branch of the service, in accordance with the anticipated change in the traffic.

But the analysis required for the second purpose above mentioned, to supply the basis of a tariff, must be one of a much more elaborate and a very different sort. For this purpose it will not be sufficient to be informed of the gross sums expended under the usual heads of expenditure, such as direction and management, way and works, locomotive power, &c. It will be necessary to ascertain, with some degree of precision, the expense which has attended in past years the transport of each class of traffic, such expenses being obviously the first condition upon which a tariff can be based.

It is easy to understand that a tariff may be constructed so as to produce a gross amount of receipts greater than the gross amount of expenses, and thus on the whole to yield an annual profit to the enterprise; and yet that such tariff may be one most unjust toward those who employ the railway, and most disadvantageous to those who own it. It is not enough that the tariff produce, on the whole, an annual balance in favor of the railway. It is indispensable that such a balance should be produced independently on each class of objects transported. Thus it is quite conceivable that the total receipts may exceed the expenses, while the receipts arising from any one or two classes of objects of transport may fall considerably short of the expenses attending these branches. In such a case the profit realized by the railway would result from a balance of profit and loss, of the profit on one class of transport more than obliterating the loss on another.

Such a result would arise either from the exaction of a tariff, in which some objects would be overtaxed, while others would be underrated, or by the railway undertaking to transport objects incapable of bearing the expenses of carriage.

It is clear, therefore, that, to obtain from the investigation of the past expenses the conditions which ought to determine a future tariff, it is necessary, not only to classify the expenses under the usual heads already mentioned, but to dissect each branch of expenditure, so as to ascertain the share which each class of traffic has had in producing it.

Although it may be true that, in the formation of a tariff, it may not be expedient in all cases to exact from the various objects of traffic the same proportion of profit, yet it may be affirmed, that it never can be right, as a permanent measure, to transport any object of traffic at a loss. Now, how can it be known whether a railway transport this or that class of traffic at a loss, or not, unless the proportion of expenses caused by such class of traffic is known?

Again, the gross profits of a railway, like all other commercial enterprises, being made up of a large aggregate of small profits, it will happen that the amount of the gross profits may be increased by the diminution of the small profits. Thus, for example, the total profits derivable from passengers may be greatly augmented by diminishing the profit derivable on each single passenger. There is a certain point at which the profit per passenger may be fixed, so as to afford a maximum of aggregate profit. Above that point, though the profit per passenger will be augmented, the aggregate profit will be diminished, because the number of passengers carried will be diminished in a greater ratio than the profit per passenger is augmented. Below that point, on the other hand, the profit per passenger will be diminished in a greater ratio than the number of passengers carried is augmented, and there will be again a diminution of the aggregate profits. The skill of the administration is evinced by so adjusting the tariff as to hit this nice point; but how can such an adjustment be effected, unless it be previously known what the transport of each passenger costs?

Like observations will be applicable to every other class of objects transported; and it is evidently indispensable to the good management of a railway establishment that those who direct it should be in possession of a clear knowledge of the actual cost of the transport of each class of traffic.

But it may be objected, that this knowledge can only be possessed for past years, and that for these it is a matter of difficult and intricate calculation. It may be further objected, that, even when obtained, it does not follow that the cost of such transport for coming years will be the same as for past years, since the change in the quantity and proportion of the various classes of traffic may change the cost of their respective transport.

This is true; but it is also certain that the knowledge derived from an accurate analysis of the past experience of railway traffic supplies means of approximation more or less close to the cost of the future transport. In short, such data enable the managers of a railway to make an estimate of the cost of the traffic for each successive year sufficiently accurate for practical guidance, and certainly accurate enough to prevent the establishment of a tariff which would produce the irregularities and inequalities above referred to.

But these, important as they are, form but a small part of the advantages resulting from an accurate analysis of the expenses. Such an analysis alone will supply the data necessary for all ameliorations in the organization of the management of the traffic. For example, if it be desired to ascertain whether it be advantageous to attract increased traffic to the railway, by multiplying the departures or increasing the number of trains, a question of a delicate and difficult nature arises. By multiplying the departures, though the traffic will be augmented, the load drawn by each engine will diminish as well as the load borne by each vehicle. The proportion of the profitable to the dead weight will be diminished, not only as regards the engine, but also as regards the vehicles of transport.

By diminishing, on the other hand, the number of departures, the quantity of traffic carried will be diminished; but the quantity drawn by each engine, and borne by each vehicle of transport, will be augmented. On the one side, a gain is obtained by the increased amount of traffic; on the other, a gain is obtained by the increased ratio of the profitable load to the dead weight. Between these two a balance must be ascertained. The point must be established at which the multiplication or the diminution of the trains ought to stop. Now this can not be accomplished unless those who have the control of the railway are in a condition to say what the cost of each object of traffic is when the trains are multiplied, and what the reduced cost is when they are diminished. In one case, the gain will be found by subducting the increased cost of the diminished loads of the more numerous trains from the augmented results of the increased traffic. In the other case, the profit will be estimated by subducting the diminished cost of the increased loads of the less multiplied trains from the diminished results of the lesser traffic.

Such instances might be multiplied without end.

The reader who has not been intimately conversant with railway affairs, will probably be startled at being told that, important as such an investigation is, it has never been attempted by the managers of English railways. We are indebted, however, to some foreign engineers and economists for inquiries on this subject.

The Belgian railways, more especially, being organized and worked by the government of that country, and the most minute details of their expenditure being made public, have supplied valuable data for such inquiry. M. Belpaire, one of the engineers connected with the department of public works, has made an investigation of this kind, based upon the detailed accounts of the Belgian railways for 1844. This inquiry, which is full of valuable suggestions, has been published by order of the Belgian government.

M. Jullien, of the Paris and Orleans Railway, has also published a series of papers on the distribution of the expenses of a railway in the "Annales des Ponts et Chaussées," and other periodicals.

M. Teisserenc, central commissary of government in the

French railway department; M. Prestat, railway commissary of the French government; and M. Legoyt, of the statistical bureau of the Minister of the Interior of France, have severally contributed, in various essays, to this investigation; but, so far as I am informed, nothing has been done or written in England on this subject.

I have therefore thought it would be useful to devote a large space to the present analysis.

The problem which I propose, then, for solution, is to ascertain the connection between the expenses incurred by a railway establishment and the services which such railway establishment performs for the public; in other words, how much of such sum expended by the company ought to be debited to this or that object of traffic.

The remoteness of several of the expenses from the services to which they are ultimately conducive, renders such an inquiry difficult, and the distribution of the expenses may be in some cases more or less arbitrary; but still the problem admits of a solution sufficiently definite for practical purposes.

If only one sort of objects were transported upon a railway, and all the units of that sort were transported over the same distance, and carried with the same speed, then the distribution of the expenses among the traffic would have no difficulty, however complicated these expenses might be; for we should only have to take them in the gross, and to divide their aggregate by the number of units of traffic transported. Such a division would be strictly and evidently applicable, inasmuch as precisely the same service would have been performed toward each unit transported.

But suppose that the objects transported, though all of the same kind, are carried over different distances, some being carried only one mile, and some a hundred, we will immediately have a serious cause of difference of cost. It will presently appear that the cost of transporting an object a hundred miles is by no means one hundred times the cost of transporting an object one mile. In apportioning the expenses, therefore, it would be necessary to classify the objects according to the distances to which they are transported, and to charge the expenses upon them in a ratio to be determined by the influence which difference of distance produces in the expenses of executing the transport.

But let us next suppose that the objects transported, though of the same kind, require to be carried with different speeds.

In this case they must be again divided into classes, inasmuch as the cost of transport for the same distance augments with the speed.

Let us further suppose that the objects transported are not of the same kind, and, consequently, that they require different sorts of vehicles. Thus, suppose they consist of passengers and merchandise, all the merchandise, however, being still of the same kind, and all the passengers demanding the same accommodation. It will then be necessary to provide two separate descriptions of carriage; one adapted to the passengers, the other to the goods. The loads transported by these carriages will necessarily be different, and their transport will be attended with different expenses.

In fine, let us imagine that the passengers to be transported consist of different classes, requiring different accommodation: some demanding a luxurious carriage and a superabundance of room, a few only being carried in each vehicle; another class requiring less accommodation and less luxury, and being content to be stowed in greater number in each carriage; and a third class being contented to be crowded together in a sort of covered van; and even a fourth class demanding still less accommodation.

Add to this, that these various classes may demand different speeds, and require to be transported to very different average distances, and it will become apparent how very different will be the expense which their transport will necessarily occasion to the enterprise of the railway.

The same observations are applicable to the merchandise, some species of goods requiring to be carefully arranged in covered vans, others promiscuously packed together, while others again, such as minerals and the like, may be thrown into open wagons; different species of merchandise requiring very different vehicles, different care of transport, and producing different expenses.

Live stock presents another variety of transport, requiring another form of vehicle, and attended with another class and degree of expense.

The problem, then, which is presented for solution, is to determine the proportion according to which the complicated expenses of a railway establishment, many of which are so remote from these several services, that it is extremely difficult to institute any relation or connection between them, can be charged respectively upon the various objects of transport.

The first step toward the solution of this problem will obviously be to make a classification of the expenses. The basis of such a classification is supplied by the analysis of railway business which has been developed in the preceding chapters. The expenses may then be classed as follows:

1st. The general direction and management of the establishment.
2d. The maintenance of the ways and works.
3d. The maintenance of the locomotive power.
4th. The carrying expenses.
5th. The station expenses.

Let us then consider successively how these several classes of expenses are related to the service of transport.

But first, it may be observed in general, that the most immediate relation between the operation of transport and the machinery of a railway, is that which exists between the object transported and the vehicle which carries it. For each class of traffic there is a special vehicle. Thus there is a special class of vehicle appropriated to the first-class passengers, another to the second-class passengers, a third to the third-class passengers. Again, there is a special vehicle appropriated to the transport of horses; another to the transport of private carriages. Vans are built, and internally constructed in a manner to be suitable for the transport of passengers' baggage; others are appropriated to the transport of parcels.

In the goods department, in like manner, there are also vehicles of various forms, adapted to different kinds of goods, and to live stock.

The relation, then, between the object transported and the vehicle which carries it, being obvious and fixed, the connection of the expenses with the objects transported, may, in the first instance, be determined by investigating the share of the general expenses which is produced by the transport of these different classes of vehicles; and when the cost of transporting any of such vehicles per mile is ascertained, this cost can be easily distributed, by a simple arithmetical proportion, between the average amount of the load it carries.

Thus, if we know the cost of transporting a first-class carriage a mile, and if we also know the average number of passengers carried by such carriage, then the charge per passenger per mile is the result of an operation of common arithmetic.

We shall therefore consider, in the first instance, how and in what proportion each class of expenses is chargeable upon the different classes of vehicles.

THE EXPENSES.

DIRECTION AND MANAGEMENT.

The department of the direction and management in the organization of a railway is the executive government of the enterprise, and has a common relation with all the branches of the service. Its special expenses, therefore, might very properly be charged primarily upon those several branches in proportion to the gross amounts of their respective expenses; but it will be a more simple process, and in its ultimate effects not less equitable, to distribute these general expenses immediately among the traffic, by the means already explained, of the vehicles in which the traffic is transported. If, then, we express the general expenses of direction by D, and the total mileage of all the vehicles of transport of every kind by m, then

$$\frac{D}{m}$$

will express the share of the expenses of direction and management which will fall per mile on each vehicle.

This share, as has already been explained, must be subsequently divided among the average load of profitable traffic which each vehicle carries.

The details of the expenses, which are understood to be included under the direction and management, and expressed by D, are as follow:

Maintenance and repair of the offices and furniture of the general direction.

Salaries of directors, managers, secretaries, clerks, and superintendents, and wages of all inferior agents and servants employed in the office of the general direction.

Printing and advertising, stationery, and subscription to journals for the use of the offices.

Warming and lighting.

Traveling expenses of directors, managers, secretaries, and, in general, of all the agents of the general direction.

In the year 1844 these expenses, on the Belgian railways, were £30,477,* and the total mileage of all the vehicles of transport upon them was 17,193,658 miles.

---

* It may be necessary to state here that the share of the expenses assigned to the several heads will not be found to correspond precisely with those given in the report of the Minister of Public Works, the items being appropriated, in the present analysis, according to a different principle.

The charge per mile upon each vehicle for direction and management is, therefore

$$\frac{D}{m} = \overset{d.}{0\cdot 426}.$$

It is desirable, but very difficult, to derive practical illustrations of this calculation from the reports of the English railways, the meagre character of such documents never supplying, with any degree of accuracy, the necessary data.

By the published report of the Northwestern Railway, it appears that the annual expenses for direction and management have been about £32,000. No account of the mileage of the carrying stock having been published, we can only estimate it by combining the mileage of the traffic, as given in Chapters X. and XI., with the estimated average loads of the several classes of vehicles.

Captain Huish estimates the average loads of the passenger-coaches at 7 passengers for each first-class carriage, 13 for each second-class carriage, 21 for each third-class carriage, and $2\frac{1}{4}$ tons of goods per wagon. Assuming these estimates, and comparing them with the total mileage of these several classes of traffic, we obtain the following as the mileage of the carrying stock on the Northwestern Railway for the twelve months ending 30th June, 1847:

1st class passenger coaches	8,033,049
2d class passenger coaches	5,725,411
3d class passenger coaches	2,568,925
Goods-wagons	43,745,983
Total mileage of all the vehicles of transport	60,073,368

If the expenses of direction and management be taken at £32,000, we shall have

$$\frac{D}{m} = \frac{\overset{\pounds.}{32,000}}{60,073,369} = \overset{\pounds.}{0\cdot 000,533} = \overset{d.}{0\cdot 128}.$$

By comparing this result with that obtained from the Belgian railways, we have a striking example of the effects of a great amount of traffic on the cost of transport. In the case of the Belgian railways, the mileage of the vehicles of transport was only a little more than 17 millions; while on the Northwestern Railway this mileage was 60 millions.

While the proportion of the mileage of the vehicles of transport was, therefore, greater on the Northwestern Railway, in the ratio of 60 to 17, the expenses of direction and management were greater only in the proportion of 32 to 30; and we find, accordingly, that while the share of these expenses chargeable per mile on each vehicle on the Belgian lines was nearly $\frac{1}{2}d.$, the share chargeable on vehicles per mile on the Northwestern lines was less than $\frac{1}{8}d.$

In order to be enabled to form an estimate of the cost of direction and management of a projected railway, it would be necessary to determine some relation between this class of expenses and some determinate element of the railway establishment. It has been proposed to express the expenses of direction and management by reference to the length of the line worked, by stating it at so much per mile. Such a mode of estimation implies that every augmentation made in the length of the line worked would cause a proportionate increase in the expenses of direction and management. Thus, if the annual expenses of management of a railway 150 miles in length be £30,000, it would be implied that the same railway, having doubled its length, would require twice the number of superintending functionaries, with equal salaries, increasing the annual expense to £60,000.

This is evidently a fallacy. The increased length will add but little to the expense of management, certainly infinitely less than the proportion of the increase.

It would be desirable, by comparing the expenses of management of the various railways in operation with their respective lengths, the mileage upon them, and other elements of their expenses, to ascertain with which of these the expenses of direction have a determinate relation; but, unfortunately, the discrepancy which prevails in the manner in which the published accounts of the different railways are made up, precludes the possibility of such a comparison. The same general terms, used in different accounts, have different meanings, and as no details are given it is impossible to discover what items are understood to be included under the same nominal heads.

Thus direction and management, in the accounts of one railway, will include certain items of expense which, in the accounts of other railways, are transferred to other heads.

This is one of the many reasons for introducing uniformity into railway accounts. Without such uniformity it will be impossible to compare, with any degree of precision, the working of any one railway with the working of any other railway, or to draw general conclusions entitled to any degree of confidence.

I find that not only the different statements of different railways vary from each other in the signification attached to the same terms, but even in successive half-yearly reports of the same railway, the same heads of expense do not include the same items.

For all purposes of a general nature, such reports are utterly useless.

The expenses of direction and management are probably determined by the total amount of traffic, rather than by any other element in the working of a railway. They vary with the prosperity of the enterprise. When large dividends are declared, proprietors are disposed to be liberal to the superior class of functionaries; the higher officers are more munificently paid, and their number less restricted. However, this branch of the expenses depends so much on local circumstances, and on conditions so peculiar to each individual enterprise, that no general or constant relation between it and the other elements of their organization probably exists.

THE WAY AND WORKS.

The expenses of the maintenance of the way and works consist of two parts, distinct from each other, and depending on different causes.

- 1st. Those which are appropriated to the repair of the wear and damage produced by time and the vicissitudes of weather, independently of all action of the traffic or use of the road, properly speaking.
- 2dly. Those which are appropriated to the repairs of the wear and damage produced by the action of the rolling stock and the traffic upon the road, independently of any effects of time or the vicissitudes of weather.

In railway accounts generally, the stations, the dépôts for carriages and engines, as well as workshops for the repair of the rolling stock, are included under this head of the maintenance of the way. It must, however, be clearly understood that they are here excluded, being assigned to other heads. The maintenance of the stations, properly so called, is carried to the account of the expenses of the stations; the maintenance of workshops for the repair of the vehicles of transport is brought to the account of the carrying department; and the maintenance of the engine stables and shops is brought to the account of the locomotive department.

The maintenance of the way, therefore, must be here understood to be limited to the repairs of the road, and the works of art upon it and accessory to it exclusively.

That portion of the expenses which is appropriated to the repairs of the class of damage and wear produced by time and weather, independently of the action of the traffic, includes the repairs of the slopes, of cuttings and embankments, of the substructure of the road, consisting of ballasting and drains, of the renewal of the sleepers, which perish only by time and weather, and are not affected by the rolling stock; also the repairs of bridges, tunnels, and viaducts; the repairs of gates and fences, and, in a word, of all the appendages and accessories of the road.

The second head of expenses of the maintenance of the way, which is altogether independent of time and weather, and depending exclusively on the traffic, includes the iron work of the road, comprising the rails, chairs, and fastenings. These owe their wear and deterioration entirely to the mechanical effect of the rolling stock upon them.

The first class of these expenses consists of the following particulars:

1st. Repairs of the substructure of the road, and works of art.
2dly. Salaries and wages of superintendents and the police of the road.
3dly. Materials consumed in such repairs and superintendence.

These expenses being independent of the traffic, are, like those of the direction and management, related in common to all branches of the business of a railway, and may be, for the same reasons, primarily distributed among the vehicles of transport, in proportion to their mileage, and subsequently among the traffic which they carry.

Let the total amount of these expenses be expressed by W; we shall then have, in the same manner as in the case of the expenses of direction and management, the share chargeable per mile on each vehicle of transport, which will be expressed by

$$\frac{W}{m}.$$

On the Belgian railways the expenses designated by W

amounted in 1844 to £68,348. The share of these charges per mile on each vehicle was therefore

$$\frac{W}{m} = \frac{£.\ 68,348}{17,193,658} = £.\ 0\cdot 003975 = d.\ 0\cdot 954$$

being very nearly 1*d.* per mile on each vehicle.

An examination of the annual expenses for the maintenance of the way on some of the railways, might create an impression that the expenses which we have here affirmed to be independent of the traffic, have nevertheless some dependence upon it; inasmuch as it would be found, by comparing these expenses for several years after a railway has been opened, that they go on augmenting while the traffic also increases. We should, however, in this case be wrong in ascribing the one increase to the other, as will be made manifest by comparing the expenses of maintenance with the traffic, after the road has been a sufficient length of time in operation. It has been already explained, in Chap. III., that for a certain time after any railway has commenced work, the embankments are in a state of progressive consolidation, which is accelerated under the pressure of the rolling stock. This produces a constant source of expense from the readjustment of the rails, and ballasting which it occasions. The slopes, also, until they are carpeted with vegetation, are more apt to slip, and all accidental defects in the road and works are developed.

These expenses, however, which are naturally enough brought to the current account of the maintenance of the road, must, strictly speaking, be regarded as a part of the expenses of constructing the road.

A correct estimate of the current expenses of maintenance can only be obtained after the road has been a sufficient length of time in operation to have become permanently consolidated.

From a comparison of half-yearly accounts of the Northwestern Railway, the annual expenses of the maintenance of the way appear to have been in round numbers £75,000.

Taking the mileage of the vehicles of transport as already given, we have then

$$\frac{W}{m} = \frac{£.\ 75,000}{60,073,368} = £.\ 0\cdot 00125 = d.\ 0\cdot 3.$$

We find here again an example of the diminished charge produced by the circumstance of the traffic being increased in a much larger ratio than the expenses.

While the expenses of maintenance on the Northwestern Railway exceed those of the Belgian in the ratio of 75 to 68, the traffic estimated by the mileage of the vehicles on the Northwestern is greater than on the Belgian lines, in the ratio of 60 to 17. We accordingly find that while a charge of $1d.$ per mile must be exacted from each vehicle, to pay the expenses of maintenance on the Belgian lines, $\frac{3}{10}d.$ are sufficient on the Northwestern lines.

Let us now consider the second class of expenses of maintenance above mentioned, which depend on the action of the traffic.

These consist of the wear of the rails, chairs, and sleepers, and may again be subdivided into two classes, in reference to the periods at which the necessity for expenditure arises.

The action of the traffic produces from time to time fracture and displacement of the rails, chairs, and fastenings.

These repairs are made from year to year; but besides these, as has been already explained, in Chap. III., the action of the traffic produces a gradual abrasion of the rails, by which they lose weight slowly from year to year, and in consequence of which, at certain distant intervals, the entire iron-work of the road must be reconstructed. The expenses of this reconstruction are provided for, as has been already explained, by an annual reserve fund, which constitutes, therefore, a part of the current expenses of the maintenance of the way.

The total expenses arising from the wear of the iron-work of the road by the rolling stock may be ascribed to the operation of three distinct agents:

1st. The engines and tenders.
2dly. The vehicles of transport.
3dly. The load carried by each vehicle.

An elaborate investigation, based upon an extensive series of experiments, has been made on the Belgian railways, with a view to ascertain the share which each of these agents has in producing the wear of the road. The result of this inquiry, which has been already referred to, in Chap. IV., is, that for every myriamètre of distance run by the rolling stock, a wear was produced, occasioning expenses at the following rates:

$9\frac{1}{3}$ centimes for each engine and tender.
$1\frac{1}{6}$ centime for each vehicle of transport.
$\frac{1}{3}$ centime for each ton of load.

It seems to have escaped the notice of the Belgian engineers that these figures are almost exactly proportional to the weights of the objects which produced the wear.

Thus, an engine and tender, with its complement of fuel and water, would weigh nearly 30 tons, and the average weight of a vehicle of transport would be about 3 tons. The above figures are in the ratio of 30, 3, and 1. If, then, a ton weight, placed in a vehicle of transport, produce a certain expense for wear and tear of rails, the vehicle itself weighing 3 tons will produce three times such expense, and the engine and tender, weighing about 30 tons, will produce thirty times the same expense.

The distribution, therefore, of these expenses, which has occasioned so elaborate an investigation, is, as might naturally have been expected, determined by the proportionate weights of the objects producing the wear.

It was found by the result of the Belgian experiments, that about one-sixth of the total annual expense for the maintenance and repair of the road represented that portion which was due to the fracture of rails, chairs, and pins.

Let the share of the expenses of the maintenance of the iron-work of the road due to the operation of the engine and tender, taken collectively, be expressed by W'.

Let the share of these expenses due to the vehicles of transport, taken collectively, be expressed by W''.

Let the remainder of these expenses, which is due to the operation of the loads carried by the vehicles of transport, taken collectively, be expressed by W'''.

Let the average weight of the engine and tender, with their water and fuel, be expressed by a.

Let the average weight of a vehicle of transport, without its load, be expressed by a'.

Let the expenses of repairing the wear and tear of the rails produced by one ton weight rolled upon them be expressed by x.

It will follow then, from what has been stated, that if we multiply the average weight of an engine and tender, a, by the total mileage of the engines, which has been already expressed by e for the passenger engines, and e' for the goods engines, we shall obtain the number of tons carried one mile, which are equivalent to the weight and mileage of the engine taken together. If this, then, be multiplied by x, the expense of the repairs of the wear produced by one ton rolled one mile, we shall have

$$W' = x\,a\,(e + e');$$

that is to say, the total expenses of the repairs due to the action

CHAP. XII.]   THE EXPENSES.   209

of the engines and tenders will be equivalent to the cost of the wear of one ton rolled one mile, multiplied by the product of the average weight of the engine and tender by their mileage.

In the same manner, and for the same reasons, if the product of the average weight a' of a vehicle of transport, and the total mileage m of such vehicle, be multiplied by x, we shall obtain a product which will be equal to W''; so that

$$W'' = x \times a' \times m.$$

Finally, if t express the total mileage of the tons of load carried by the vehicles of transport, we shall have

$$W''' = x \times t:$$

in other words, the expenses of repairing the wear produced by one ton carried one mile, multiplied by the total mileage of the load, will be equal to the total share of the expenses due to the loads.

By adding together the formulæ obtained above for the three parts of the expense of the repairs of rails due to the engines, carriages, and loads, we obtain the following:

$$W' + W'' + W''' = x \times a \times (e + e') + x \times a' \times m + x \times t.$$

Now, by this formula it appears that if the total cost of the repairs be known, and also the weights and mileage of the engines, vehicles of transport, and load, we can, by a simple arithmetical calculation, obtain the expense, x, representing the wear produced by one ton passing over one mile of the road. This is obtained by dividing the sum of the expenses, W', W'', and W''', by the three products obtained above, which are combined with x as a common multiplier.

This process gives the following formula:

$$x = \frac{W' + W'' + W'''}{a \times (e + e') + a' \times m + t}.$$

As a practical illustration of such a calculation we will take, as before, the reports of the Belgian railways for 1844. In that year the total estimated wear of the rails was £3966; so that we have

$$W' + W'' + W''' = 3966.$$

It has been already shown that

$$\begin{aligned}
e + e' &= 1{,}584{,}532, \\
m &= 17{,}193{,}658, \\
t &= 33{,}105{,}141, \\
a &= 30, \\
a' &= 3.
\end{aligned}$$

By substituting these numbers for the corresponding letters, we obtain

$$x = \underset{£.}{0.00003} = \underset{d.}{0.0072}.$$

This is therefore the expense of repair per mile produced by a ton weight of load.

The expense per mile produced by an empty vehicle of transport will therefore be

$$a' = 3 \times 0.0000 = \underset{£.}{0.00009} = \underset{d.}{0.0216}.$$

In like manner, the expenses per mile, representing the wear produced by an engine and tender will be

$$a = \underset{£.}{30} \times \underset{£.}{0.00003} = 0.0009 = \underset{d.}{0.216}.$$

By substituting the above values of x, a, a', e, e', m, and t, in the above formulæ, we find

$$
\begin{array}{rr}
 & £. \\
W = & 68,348 \\
W' = & 1,426 \\
W'' = & 1,547 \\
W''' = & 993 \\
\hline
W + W' + W'' + W''' = & 72,314
\end{array}
$$

Thus we see that the entire expenses of the maintenance of the road under the regular operation of the transport is resolved into four items, expressed respectively by

$$W, W', W'', W''';$$

the first, W, being that which includes the expenses of the entire staff of engineers, artisans, and laborers employed in maintaining the way and works, in repairing the slopes, embankments, and cuttings, and the wear produced by time and the vicissitudes of weather, on the works of art and on the substructure of the road; the second, W', being that portion of the expenses produced by the locomotive engines and their tenders alone, not including that part of the action of these machines which is caused by the load which they draw; the third, W'', that which is produced by the vehicles of transport, including the increased wear of the locomotive engine, which is the consequence of drawing them; and, finally, W''', being the increased expense due to the wear of the rails produced by the weight of the traffic itself, added to that of the carriages, augmenting also the action of the engine on the road.

The first of these, W, is obviously common to all the traffic, and equally chargeable upon all the vehicles in which it is borne, according to their mileage. Expressing, therefore, the total mileage of all the vehicles of transport by m, the charge per mile on each vehicle for this part of the maintenance of the way and works, will be $\frac{W}{m}$.

The second, W', must be brought to the account of the locomotive power, and charged in common with it upon the traffic.

The third, W'', must be brought to the account of carrying stock, and distributed with the expenses of these upon the traffic.

The fourth, W''', is a direct charge upon the traffic in the ratio of its weight and mileage.

We shall revert to these severally hereafter.

THE LOCOMOTIVE POWER.

The expenses of the locomotive power may be classed as follows:
1. The repairs of the locomotive engines and tenders.
2. Salaries and wages of engine-drivers, stokers, and other agents, employed in cleaning and tending the locomotive engines and tenders.
3. Materials consumed, such as grease, oil, coke, water.
4. That part of the maintenance of the way which has been expressed by W'.

Let us suppose that all the engines and tenders used in the service of the railway are moved over the road through the same distance as that through which they are moved in actually working the traffic, but that they are so moved unaccompanied by any vehicle or object of transport; and let the expense of this movement be estimated. Let this expense, with all the other charges of the locomotive stock enumerated above, be expressed by L.

Let us now suppose that the various vehicles in which the transport is carried are attached to the locomotives, but that they are empty; and let the locomotives be imagined to draw these empty vehicles over the same length of the line as that over which they are drawn in actually conveying the traffic. An increased expense of locomotive power will thus be produced, arising from the increased power exerted by the locomotives in consequence of the resistance of the vehicles which they draw. This increased power will be represented by the augmented consumption of fuel, oil, and grease, and the augmented wear and tear of those parts of the engines which are immediately affected by the resistance. Let this addition to the expense of the locomotive power be expressed by L'.

Finally, let us suppose that the various objects of transport carried upon the road are placed in their respective vehicles and drawn by the engines. A further expenditure of locomotive power will now take place, caused by the increased resistance to the tractive power produced by the increased weight drawn, and this increased resistance will cause an increased consumption of fuel, grease, and oil, and an increased wear and tear of those parts of the engine which react against the resistance. Let this increase of the expenditure of the locomotive power be expressed by L''.

Thus we see that the total amount of the expenses of the locomotive power consists of three items, which we have expressed by

$$L, L', \text{ and } L''.$$

The part of the expenses expressed by L' is to be brought to the account of the carrying expenses.

The part expressed by L'' is to be charged directly on the objects of transport.

The expenses expressed by L are primarily chargeable on the mileage of all the engines. Let, therefore, the total mileage of the engines be found. We have expressed this in former chapters by e for the passenger engines, and e' for the goods engines. Thus $e + e'$ will express this total mileage; and if the expenses, L, be divided by this total mileage, we shall have

$$\frac{L}{e + e'},$$

expressing the share of the expenses chargeable per mile upon each engine.

This charge is now to be transferred to and distributed among the vehicles drawn by such engine; and here a further classification becomes necessary, inasmuch as the average number of vehicles drawn by the passenger engines is different from the average number of vehicles drawn by the goods engines.

We must then find first the portion of the expenses expressed by L, which is chargeable to each class of engines, and then we must distribute these charges respectively among the mileage of the vehicles which these engines draw.

Since $\dfrac{L}{e+e'}$, is the expense per mile of each engine, we shall find the total expense of the passenger engines by multiplying this by their mileage e, and the total expense of the goods engines by multiplying the same by the mileage of the latter, e'. The total charge, therefore, upon the passenger engines will be expressed by

$$\frac{L \times e}{e + e'};$$

and the total expenses chargeable upon the goods engines will be expressed by

$$\frac{L \times e'}{e + e'}.$$

Let us now express the total mileage of all the vehicles drawn by passenger engines by m', and the total mileage of all the vehicles drawn by goods engines by m''. We shall find the charge per mile on each vehicle drawn by passenger engines by dividing the total expense of the passenger engines by m', and the total expense chargeable per mile on each vehicle drawn by the goods engines by dividing the total expenses of these latter engines by m''.

It therefore follows that the expenses chargeable per mile on the vehicles drawn by passenger engines is

$$\frac{L\, e}{m'\, (e + e')};$$

and that the expenses per mile chargeable upon each vehicle drawn by goods engines is

$$\frac{L\, e'}{m''\, (e + e')}.$$

This charge must be divided among the traffic carried by these vehicles respectively, in a manner and proportion which will be explained hereafter.

There is another mode by which the cost of the locomotive

power may be distributed among the vehicles of transport, which will, in some cases, be more conveniently applicable than that which has just been explained.

Let us suppose that the average number of vehicles which is drawn by each class of engine is ascertained, and let the average number drawn by passenger engines be expressed by n', and the average number drawn by goods engines be expressed by n''.

Now it is evident that we shall distribute the expenses of the passenger engines among the vehicles they draw simply by dividing the expense of the engines per mile by the number of vehicles they draw. Thus it follows that the charge per mile for locomotive power on each vehicle composing a passenger train would be.

$$\frac{L}{n'\,(e+e')}.$$

And, in the same manner, the charge for locomotive power on each vehicle drawn by the goods engine,

$$\frac{L}{n''\,(e+e')}.$$

It is necessary, however, to observe here, that in general the number of vehicles drawn by the engines respectively, here expressed by n' and n'', can only be obtained with accuracy by first taking the mileage of the engines, and then the mileage of the vehicles they draw, and dividing the latter by the former.

In estimating the performance of a projected railway, however, it sometimes happens that the probable average number of carriages to be drawn by each engine may be obtained without previously estimating the mileage of the vehicles of transport. In such case the latter method of calculation may be used, and will be the most simple.

The expenses expressed by L consist of three items, which it is important to consider separately.

1st. The actual cost of working the engines, when moving on the road; which cost is in the direct proportion of their mileage.

2d. The expenses of cleaning, lighting, and raising the steam of the engine preparatory to its work.

3d. The cost of keeping the engine standing with its steam up, either waiting for its work, or being maintained in reserve to meet the contingencies of the road.

CHAP. XII.] THE EXPENSES. 215

Let us call the expense of working an engine per mile l. Then the total expenses of working the engines will be found by multiplying this expense, l, by the total mileage of the engines. The total expense of the engines while actually working will therefore be expressed by

$$l\,(e + e').$$

Let us express the expense of cleaning, lighting, and raising the steam of an engine preparatory to work by l', and let the number of engines cleaned and lighted be expressed by E'', as in Chap. V.

The total expense of cleaning, lighting, and steaming will then be expressed by

$$l'\,E''.$$

Finally, let the cost per hour of keeping an engine standing with its steam up without work be expressed by l'', and let the number of hours which engines have been kept standing be expressed by S. The total expenses of the engines while standing will therefore be expressed by

$$l''\,S.$$

Hence it follows that the total expenses, expressed in the preceding paragraph by L, will be equal to the aggregate of the three expenses which have been just explained. In other words, we shall have

$$L = l\,(e + e') + l'\,E'' + l''\,S.$$

The expenses chargeable per mile for each engine will then be found by dividing the above total by the mileage, $e + e'$, which will give

$$\frac{L}{e + e'} = l + \frac{l'\,E''}{e + e'} + \frac{l''\,S}{e + e'}.$$

It appears from this that the cost per mile for driving a train consists of three parts, two of which are in the inverse proportion of the total mileage of the engines, and, consequently, that the greater the proportion which this total mileage shall bear to the cost of cleaning, lighting, and steaming the engines, and to the cost of keeping them standing, the less will be these two parts of the expense.

As an example of the practical application of this, we shall take the Belgian railways for 1844. In that year the expenses of the locomotive power, which we have expressed by L, amounted to £63,454, and consisted of the following items:

	£.
Cost of working locomotive engines	50,044
Cost of lighting, raising steam, and putting them in train	9,688
Cost while standing with steam up	3,722
	63,454

Hence we have $l \times (e + e') = 50,044l$.; and since $e + e = 1,584,532$, we shall obtain the cost per mile of working each engine: thus,

$$l = \frac{\overset{£.}{50,044}}{1,584,532} = \overset{d.}{7 \cdot 58}.$$

In like manner we have $l' \times E'' = 9,688l$.

By dividing this, therefore, by the number of engines which were lighted and steamed, and which was 23,021, we shall obtain the cost of lighting, steaming, and putting in train each engine. This gives

$$l' = \frac{\overset{£.}{9,688}}{23,021} = \overset{s.\ d.}{8\ \ 5}.$$

In the same way we have $l'' \times S = 3722$. By dividing this third item by the number of hours which the engines were kept standing, and which was 178,637, we shall find the cost per hour for each engine standing. This gives

$$l'' = \frac{\overset{£.}{3,722}}{178,637} = \overset{d.}{5 \cdot 00}.$$

To find the share of the expenses expressed by L, which falls on each engine, we have to divide the expenses, L, by the total mileage of the engines. This gives

$$\frac{L}{e + e'} = \frac{\overset{£.}{63,454}}{1,584,532} = \overset{£.}{0 \cdot 04} = \overset{d.}{9 \cdot 6}.$$

The average number of vehicles drawn in that year by passenger engines was, as we have already shown, 8·26. Hence the charge per mile upon each vehicle will be

$$\frac{L}{n'\ (e + e')} = \frac{\overset{d.}{9 \cdot 6}}{8 \cdot 26} = \overset{d.}{1 \cdot 16}.$$

The average number of vehicles drawn by each goods engine was 15·74. Hence we find the charge per mile on each vehicle as follows:

$$\frac{L}{n''(e+e')} = \frac{9\cdot6\ d.}{15.74} = 0\cdot61\ d.$$

Thus, it appears that the charge per mile on each vehicle forming the passenger trains was 1·16$d.$; and upon each vehicle composing the goods trains, was only $\frac{6}{10}d.$

The share of the expenses of the locomotive power, chargeable upon the vehicles of transport in the same year, and which we have expressed by L′, was £11,348.

This being divided by the total mileage of all the vehicles, will give the charge per mile on each vehicle. Thus we have

$$\frac{L'}{m} = 0\cdot00066\ £. = 0\cdot158\ d.$$

In like manner the share of the expenses of the locomotive power which we have expressed by L″, produced by the weight of the traffic, was £4,453; and the proportion of this chargeable per mile on each ton of load carried, will be found by dividing this sum by the total mileage of the tons of load which gives

$$\frac{L''}{t} = \frac{4,453}{33,105,141} = 0\cdot0001345\ £. = 0\cdot032\ d.$$

Thus it appears that the respective amounts of the parts of the locomotive expenses which we have expressed by L, L′, and L″, were

$$
\begin{aligned}
&\ £.\\
&L\ = 63,454,\\
&L'\ = 11,348,\\
&L''= 4,453,\qquad £.\\
&L + L' + L'' = 72,255.
\end{aligned}
$$

The published reports of the expenditure of the English railways do not afford the data necessary to enable us to subdivide the total expense of the locomotive power in the manner and proportions here explained; but it will be observed that the parts expressed by L′ and L″ are only about 20 per cent. of the total amount. We shall therefore not commit any considerable error, if, in taking a practical example from the English railway reports, we divide the entire amount of the locomotive expenses among the vehicles of transport, according to their mileage, as we have done with the general expenses of direction and maintenance of the way.

More strict accuracy could certainly be obtained if we possessed accounts as clear and full as those of the Belgian railways; but in the absence of these we must approximate to the truth as nearly as the data will permit us.

On the London and Brighton railways, during the twelve months ending 31st December, 1848, the expenses for locomotive power amounted to £56,381, and the total mileage of the engines to 1,360,168. Hence we have

$$L = 56,381l.,$$
$$e + e' = 1,360,168,$$
$$\frac{L}{e + e'} = 9{\cdot}96 \; d.$$

Thus the working cost of each engine was 10d. a mile. To compare the results obtained upon the Belgian railways with this, it is necessary to observe that the expense expressed here by L is the whole expense of the locomotive power, and includes, therefore, all the expenses expressed by L, L′, and L″ in the case of the Belgian lines. It will therefore be necessary to divide the expense L + L′ + L″ for the Belgian lines, by $e + e'$, for the same lines, in order to compare the two results. This gives,

$$\frac{L + L' + L''}{e + e'} = \frac{79,255}{1,584,532} = 0{\cdot}05 = 12 \; d.$$

It appears, therefore, that the working expense of the engines on the London and Brighton Railway, was $16\frac{6}{10}$ per cent. less than on the Belgian lines.

The reports do not supply us with the data necessary to ascertain the average number of vehicles of each kind drawn by each engine on the Brighton line, and we can not, therefore, subdivide this among the vehicles.

On the Great Western Railway, during the twelve months ending 30th June, 1849, the expenses for locomotive power, according to the published reports, were £96,462; and the total mileage was 2,737,928. Hence we have,

$$L = 96,462l.,$$
$$e + e' = 2,737,928,$$
$$\frac{L}{e+e'} = 8\cdot 45,\ d.$$

which was the working cost of each engine per mile.

It is necessary to observe, that the reported mileage of the engines in the case of the Great Western Railway includes, as indeed it ought to do, the mileage of the assisting engines on inclined planes, of empty engines, and of the engines used in forming the train at the stations. In the case of the London and Brighton, these do not appear to be included. On the Great Western, the mileage of the engines while actually drawing trains amounted to 2,603,934.

If the expenses be divided by this mileage, the quotient would be $8\cdot 88d.$, or very nearly $9d.$ a mile, corresponding with the results already obtained on the Brighton Railway.

But still it would appear that a greater economy is obtained on the Great Western Railway, when the superior magnitude and power of its engines are considered; unless, indeed, the average loads they draw are proportionally less.

We are unable to ascertain the amount of the loads drawn by the engines from the data supplied by the published reports of this railway.

Documents which I have obtained from the manager of the Northwestern Railway enable me to give another striking example of this item of expense.

The Northwestern Railway Company, besides working the traffic of its own lines and branches, consisting of 438 miles, also supplies locomotive power for working the Chester and Holyhead, Lancashire and Carlisle, Kendal and Windermere, Shropshire Union,* and North Union railways, making a total of 670 miles; being about the eighth part of the entire railways of the United Kingdom in operation.

The traffic of this extensive system of railways was worked, during the twelve months ending the 30th June, 1849, by 457 locomotive engines, which performed a total mileage, in

---

* The Shropshire Union (30 miles), connecting Shrewsbury with Stafford, was not opened for traffic till June, 1849.

working such traffic, amounting to 7,532,230. The total cost of this power was £306,668. We have therefore,

$$L = 306,668l.,$$
$$e + e' = 7,532,230,$$
$$\frac{L}{e + e'} = 9\cdot 8. \overset{d.}{}$$

This example is entitled to the more weight, because of the extensive system of lines from which it is deduced; and we may, therefore, safely assume that the average cost for locomotive power in working the trains on the English railways, taken one with another, including both goods and passenger trains, is, in round numbers, $10d.$ a mile.

If the average number of vehicles drawn by passenger engines be eight, as it would appear to be from the estimate of Captain Huish, already referred to, then it will follow that the average cost for locomotive power, for each vehicle, is $1\frac{1}{4}d.$ per mile.

THE CARRYING EXPENSES.

Under this head are comprised all the expenses, direct and indirect, which arise from the maintenance of the vehicles of transport of every class.

These expenses may be classed under the following heads:

1st. The repairs of that portion of the wear of the rails produced by the action of the weight of the vehicles of transport, independently of the load they carry. This we have already explained and designated by W''.

2dly. That part of the wear of the locomotive engines and the additional expense of fuel consumed in consequence of the exertion of the tractive force in drawing the vehicles of transport, independently of the load they carry. This has been already designated by L'.

3dly. The maintenance and repairs of the carrying-stock itself, including the necessary renewals, and the general expenses of the coach-houses, or dépôts.

These expenses might be taken in the aggregate, and shared among the vehicles of transport according to their mileage, in the same manner as we have proceeded with the expenses of direction and the maintenance of the way.

By such a distribution, however, the expenses would not be shared among the carrying stock, in accordance with the causes which produced them. For example, the expenses produced by the passenger carriages are greater in proportion than those produced by the goods-wagons, horse-boxes, carriage-trucks, &c.; and among the goods-wagons themselves the expenses will obviously differ to some extent according to their magnitude and weight. In the analysis of the expenses already referred to on the Belgian railways, M. Belpaire divides the vehicles of transport into three classes, the passenger carriages: the covered wagons, including horse-boxes, baggage-vans, &c.; and the flat, uncovered goods-wagons. The expenses of the coaching department are distributed among the passenger carriages; and the expenses of the wagon department distributed between the two classes of wagons, according to their weights.

The result of this calculation, however, gives differences so extremely small, between the expenses of the passenger carriages and the heavier class of goods-wagons, that it is scarcely necessary to complicate the calculation by distinguishing them. Thus the share of the expenses per 1000 miles run, which falls on passenger carriages and covered goods-wagons, is in the proportion of 40 to 39. A somewhat greater difference prevails between the expenses of passenger-carriages, and those of the flat and uncovered wagons, being in the ratio of 40 to 33.

It will nevertheless be more simple, and productive of scarcely any sensible error in the distribution of the expenses, to take the entire expenses, direct and indirect, of the carrying stock, and divide it among the vehicles of transport, as we have already done with the expenses of direction and the maintenance of the way, according to their mileage.

If the coaching expenses be kept sufficiently independent of, and distinct from the wagon expenses, then it will be easy, and more strictly equitable, to divide each by their mileages respectively, and thus obtain the charges on each vehicle of the passenger trains distinct from the goods trains.

As a practical example of such calculation, we will take, as before, the Belgian railways. Let V express the total expenses of all the vehicles of transport, independent of the loads they carry; and let V' express the additional expense produced by the load. We find that,

$$\begin{align}
& \pounds. \\
V &= 24{,}900 \\
V' &= 5{,}084 \\
V + V' &= 29{,}984; \\
m &= 17{,}193{,}658;
\end{align}$$

$$\frac{V}{m} = 0.35$$
$$\frac{V'}{m} = 0.072$$
$$\frac{V+V'}{m} = 0.42.$$

The last is therefore the charge per mile on each vehicle for the entire expense, including the load.

In the preceding analysis, the expenses arising directly and indirectly from the load borne by the vehicles of transport, have been kept apart and reserved for separate consideration, and the expenses which have been enumerated are those which would be produced if the trains of every description which actually carry the traffic were drawn upon the railway empty. The addition of the load produces augmented expenses, which have been already indicated, and which were reserved to be separately chargeable upon the traffic. These expenses are as follow:

1st. The increased wear and tear of the rails produced by the weight of the traffic, and which has been expressed by W'''.
2dly. The increased wear and tear of the locomotive engines, and the increased consumption of fuel in them produced by the weight of the traffic, and which has been expressed by L''.
3dly. The increased wear and tear of the vehicles of transport produced by the increased weight of the traffic.

Now, in fact, these charges constitute the entire share of the expenses of transport, properly so called, which is directly chargeable upon the traffic. They are the difference between what the expenses of the railway would be if the trains were carried upon it empty, and the expenses which are actually incurred in conducting the trains loaded as they are.

It may be contended, that the process would be more simple, and equally effectual for all practical purposes, if the expenses which have been just enumerated were at once included under the several heads of maintenance of the way, locomotive power, and carrying expenses, already indicated.

To this it may be replied, that if the sole end of such an analysis as the present is to ascertain the actual expenses produced by each object of traffic, such purpose will be defeated if the expenses occasioned by certain objects be charged upon others, even though the aggregate result of such account should be correct; since such correctness would only be produced by a compensation of errors. In analyzing the expenses of an enterprise so complicated as a railway establishment, some compensation of errors is inevitable. It is quite impracticable to assign precisely to each article of transport the share of the expenses which it produces. The weight, therefore, of the objection will altogether depend on the extent to which the principle of compensation of errors in such a case is carried. We are enabled to ascertain this extent by the reports and accounts of the Belgian railways, and the consequences which we have deduced from them.

By taking the special expenses chargeable upon each object of traffic. independently of the general expense, which we have designated in the preceding analysis by D, W, L, and V, and by combining such special expenses with the average load which each class of vehicles carries, we can ascertain the increased expenses per mile produced on each vehicle by the addition of its load. We have done this with respect to the Belgian railways in the following table, in the first column of which appear the expenses per mile produced by each object of traffic; in the second column the average number of such objects of traffic carried by each vehicle respectively; and in the third column the product of these two numbers, representing the expenses per mile on each vehicle, produced by its load.

Object of Traffic.	Expense per Mile.	Average Number per Vehicle.	Expense per Vehicle per Mile.
	d.		
1st class passenger	0·042	8·5	0·357
2d and 3d class passengers	0·006	14·4	0·0864
A ton of baggage	0·07	0·56	0·0392
A ton of parcels	0·07	1·85	0·1295
A horse	0·05	1·67	0·0835
A private carriage	0·07	0·75	0·0525
A ton of goods	0·07	2·5	0·1750
A head of cattle	0·03	4·19	0·1257
A head of small cattle	0·007	34·9	0·2443

To ascertain to what extent this differs from the charges which would fall on the objects of traffic respectively by dividing the total amount of the special expenses among the vehicles of transport indifferently, in the ratio of their mileage, we divide the total amount of the special expenses, £10,849, by the total mileage, 17,193,658, of the vehicles, and the quotient, 0·1514d., is the share per mile which falls on each vehicle. Dividing this by the average quantity of the objects of transport which each vehicle carries, and comparing these with the actual share of the expenses chargeable to each object, we obtain the following results:

	Actual Share of Expenses.	Share by equal Division of Expenses among Vehicles.	Difference.	
			Over-charge.	Under-charge.
	d.	d.	d.	d.
Passenger, 1st class	0·042	0·0178	..	0·0242
„ 2d and 3d class	0·006	0·0105	0·0045	..
A ton of baggage	0·070	0·2704	0·2004	..
„ parcels	0·070	0·0818	0·0118	..
A horse	0·050	0·0907	0·0407	..
A private carriage	0·070	0·2018	0·1318	..
A ton of goods	0·070	0·0605	..	0·0095
A head of cattle	0·030	0·0361	0·0061	..
„ small cattle	0·007	0·0043	..	0·0037

Such, then, is the compensation of errors by overcharge and undercharge which would be produced if the expenses properly chargeable in various proportions on the traffic were distributed uniformly among the mileage of the vehicles of transport. But to estimate the importance of this departure from strict accuracy, it will be necessary to compare these deviations from the truth with the total amount of expenses chargeable upon each object of traffic. I have accordingly done this in the following table, in the first column of which is exhibited the actual share of the total expenses per mile which was produced by each object of traffic; and, in the second and third columns, the amount per cent. of the overcharge or undercharge, which would be committed by the adoption of the principle of uniform distribution among the vehicles.

	Total Expense of Transport per Mile.	Percentage of Total Expenses.	
		Overcharge.	Undercharge.
	d.		
Passengers, 1st class	0·37	..	6·50
„ 2d class	0·25	1·80	..
„ 3d class	0·20	2·20	..
Baggage per ton	7·05	2·80	..
Parcels per ton	2·50	0·50	..
Horses per head	1·70	2·40	..
Private carriage	3·80	3·40	..
Goods per ton	1·11	..	0·90
Cattle per head	0·66	0·93	..
Small cattle per head	0·09	..	3·00

CHAP. XII.]   THE EXPENSES.   225

It appears that these errors form but a small percentage of the whole expenses, and would form a much smaller percentage of the fares which would be charged upon the several articles. We may therefore conclude, that the simplicity of calculation gained by dividing the entire expenses among the mileage of the vehicles, and then among the objects they carry, more than compensates for the minute errors which would be produced by the distribution of this part of the expenses.

We may, then, recapitulate the various heads of expenses explained above, including, however, under them respectively, the entire expenses of the maintenance of the way and works, the locomotive power, and the carrying expenses produced by the traffic, as follows:

Total expenses of direction and management........	D
Total mileage of carrying stock..................	m
Share of expenses of direction chargeable per mile on each vehicle of carrying stock................	$\dfrac{D}{m}$
Expenses of maintenance of way and works.......	W
Share of these expenses chargeable per mile on each vehicle of carrying stock......................	$\dfrac{W}{m}$
Expenses of locomotive power..................	L
Total mileage of passenger engines..............	e
Total mileage of goods engines.................	e'
Share of expenses L chargeable per mile on each engine....................................	$\dfrac{L}{e+e'}$
Share of expenses L chargeable upon the passenger engines collectively..........................	$\dfrac{L'e}{e+e'}$
Share of expenses L chargeable upon the goods engines collectively...........................	$\dfrac{L\,e'}{e+e'}$
Total mileage of the vehicles composing the passenger trains.................................	m'
Total mileage of the vehicles composing the goods trains......................................	m''
Share of the expenses of passenger engines chargeable per mile on each vehicle drawn by them....	$\dfrac{L\,e}{m'\,(e+e')}$
Share of expenses of goods engines chargeable per mile on each vehicle drawn by them............	$\dfrac{L\,e'}{m''\,(e+e')}$
Share of expenses of carrying stock chargeable on the vehicles composing the passenger trains.....	V
Share of expenses of passenger stock per mile chargeable upon each vehicle composing the passenger trains	$\dfrac{V}{m}$

Share of expenses of carrying stock chargeable to the vehicles composing the goods trains............ V'

Share of expenses of goods stock per mile chargeable upon each vehicle composing the goods trains $\dfrac{V'}{m'}$

Hence it appears that the total amount of the expense chargeable per mile upon each vehicle composing a passenger train is as follows:

$$\frac{D}{m} + \frac{W}{m} + \frac{L \times e}{m' \times (e + e')} + \frac{V}{m'}.$$

And the total amount of the expenses chargeable upon each vehicle composing a goods train is

$$\frac{D}{m} + \frac{W}{m} + \frac{L \times e}{m'' (e + e')} + \frac{V'}{m''}.$$

THE STATIONS.

In what precedes, I have explained the manner of distributing among the traffic all those expenses which are chargeable upon it in the form of a mileage.

It now remains to notice a class of expenses which, being independent of locomotion, are chargeable upon the traffic in a proportion depending conjointly on its quantity and quality, without any reference whatever to the distance to which it may be transported.

The expenses of the stations consist principally of the following items:

- 1st. The maintenance and repair of the buildings and furniture of the various stations for the reception and embarkation and disembarkation and discharge of passengers and goods.
- 2d. The salaries of all classes of agents, from the superintendents down to the lowest porter employed in the service of the embarkation, booking, disembarkation, discharging, and delivery of the objects of transport, including those agents who accompany the trains for the purpose of delivering the various articles of transport at the stations, and of receiving and discharging the passengers.
- 3d. The cost of all articles consumed in the stations, including all the machinery and stock requisite for the embarkation, disembarkation, and delivery of goods.

THE EXPENSES.

Under these heads are, of course, included a multitude of miscellaneous expenses connected with the ordinary business of the stations, such as lighting and warming them, attendance in the waiting-rooms on the passsengers, all the details of the booking offices, the necessary attendance in the offices for the reception of passengers' baggage and parcels, and the labor and materials consumed in loading the same, the necessary attendance for the embarkation of carriages and horses, of live stock, and of every species of goods; and, in some cases, the means for delivering the goods, as they arrive, at the domicile of the party to whom they are addressed, and of collecting the goods which are about to be dispatched.

From the nature of this service it will be evident that the expenses attendant upon it have no reference to the distance to which the traffic is transported. Two bales of goods delivered at a railway station are received, weighed, booked, entered on the way-bill, labeled, and loaded. On arriving at their respective destination they are unloaded, discharged, delivered, and the charge upon them, if any, collected.

All these various services will be precisely the same for these two bales of goods, if one be carried 500 miles, and the other only 5 miles.

Such expenses must therefore be debited to the traffic, without any reference to its mileage.

But these expenses will evidently vary within very wide limits, according to the nature of the objects which are embarked and delivered.

Passengers, on arriving, must be provided with proper booking-offices, a staff of clerks, a waiting-room properly illuminated, warmed, and furnished, and a convenient wharf for embarkation, with suitable attendants for their guidance, and for the disposition of their baggage. On arriving at their destination, similar services are required.

Live stock require particular attendance and labor for their safe embarkation and discharge. Goods of various qualities require various degrees of care and labor for their secure embarkation and discharge.

Now it will be evident that the distribution of the total expenses of the establishment of the stations between these various objects must be a process attended with much difficulty, and, to some extent, arbitrary. If only one species of traffic were embarked and delivered, then it would be sufficient to divide the total expenses of the stations between this quantity, expressed in weight or number, as the case might be; but the traffic consisting of a great variety of different classes of objects, the distribution of the expenses among them requires that some common measure be selected, by which the proportional expenses of each class of traffic may be determined. Estimates of this kind have been made in different foreign railway establishments.

M. Teisserenc, who has devoted much attention to the statistics of railways, and has been practically connected with the French lines, proposes that the average expenses of the embarkation and delivery of a ton of merchandise, which he estimates, on the French lines, at about 1s. 6d., should be taken as the unit or common measure for the expenses of the embarkation and delivery of the traffic in general, and that the expenses of the stations shall be divided among the traffic in the following proportions relatively to the cost of a ton of goods.

Let A express the cost of the embarkation and delivery of a ton of goods. Then we may adopt, according to M. Teisserenc, the following scale for other objects of transport:

A ton of parcels	3 A
„ of baggage	10 A
A carriage	2 A
A horse	$1\frac{1}{4}$ A
A head of cattle	$\frac{3}{4}$ A
A pig	$\frac{1}{6}$ A
A calf	$\frac{1}{8}$ A
A sheep	$\frac{1}{20}$ A

The same authority gives the following scale as applicable to the Belgian railways, where he estimates the cost of the embarkation and delivery of a ton of goods at the same amount as above:

A ton of parcels	$3\frac{1}{2}$ A
„ of baggage	10 A
A carriage	$1\frac{1}{2}$ A
A horse	A
A head of cattle	$\frac{2}{3}$ A
A pig	$\frac{1}{5}$ A
A calf	$\frac{1}{6}$ A
A sheep	$\frac{1}{7}$ A
A passenger	$\frac{1}{4}$ A

According to M. Belpaire, who has given a very elaborate distribution of the expenses of the Belgian railways among the traffic, the following are, or were (in 1844), the proportional expenses of embarkation and discharge, the unit being, as before,

THE EXPENSES.

the average cost of embarkation and discharge of a ton of merchandise:

A ton of baggage	8	A
,, of parcels	$3\frac{1}{2}$	A
A carriage		A
A horse	$\frac{9}{10}$	A
A passenger	$\frac{1}{12}$	A

M. Belpaire gives no estimate of the embarkation of live stock, as this process was then conducted at the charge of the expeditor.

The difference between the amount of the expenses assigned to the embarkation and discharge of these different classes of objects, admits of easy explanation.

The embarkation of a ton of merchandise, consisting of a bale dispatched by one individual and consigned to another, is limited to a single entry in the books and way-bill, the labeling and loading, unloading and delivery, of a single bale.

But a ton of parcels, consisting of a great multitude of detached packets of different weights, dispatched by a great number of different persons, requiring as many different entries on the books and way-bills, and followed by as many different operations for their discharge and delivery, obviously involves a vastly increased expense.

It will not, therefore, be surprising, that the average expenses for a ton of such objects is much greater than for a ton of goods.

The expenses of embarkation and delivery of passengers' baggage is still greater than that of parcels, because the baggage arrives at the last moment, is weighed, booked, and loaded with precipitation, and requires the attention of numerous agents. The parcels, on the other hand, are received, booked weighed, and loaded with more deliberation and order, and therefore employ a less number of agents in proportion to their number and weight.

The distribution of the expenses of the service of the stations among the traffic depends on circumstances, which vary so much, not only in one railway compared with another, but with the changes incidental to the traffic itself and its management, that it is impossible to state any general principles relative to it, and each case must be arranged according to the peculiar circumstances attending it. The expenses of a ton of merchandise, which is taken as the common modulus or unit, vary within very wide limits. Iron in bars, cast iron, or lead in pigs, coals, and minerals, do not cost half the expense per ton which attends merchandise which requires more careful loading.

The following are the estimated expenses of the stations on the Belgian railways:

	s.	d.
A passenger	0	0·8
A ton of baggage	10	0
,, parcels	4	3
A private carriage	1	5
A ton of merchandise (average)	1	5

We shall conclude this analysis of the expenses by a general practical example of its application in the case of the Belgian railways, showing the proportion chargeable to each object of traffic.

It has been already shown (p. 97), that the average number of vehicles composing a passenger train was 8·26, and the average number composing a goods train was 15·74.

	Total Expenses.	Per Vehicle per Mile.	
		Passenger Trains.	Goods Trains.
	£.	d.	d.
Direction and management	30,477	0·426	0·426
Maintenance of way	72,314	0·954	0·954
Locomotive power	79,255	1·453	0·762
Carrying service	29,984	0·422	0·422
Totals	212,030	3·255	2·564

The comparative expenses per mile of the passenger and goods trains arise, as will be seen, from the charge for the locomotive power per vehicle in the one being double the other; and this proceeds from the circumstance of the goods trains consisting of fuller loads, or a greater number of vehicles. The charge for the locomotive power, therefore, has a greater divisor, and the share falling on each vehicle of transport is proportionally less. Although it be true that the increased magnitude of the trains produces some increased expense in the locomotive power, this expense is comparatively trifling, consisting only of the small cost of the traction of each additional vehicle.

This will illustrate the economy to be derived from working in general with full trains. An additional vehicle drawn by

CHAP. XII.]   THE EXPENSES.   231

the engine, produces an increase of the divisor, by which the expenses of the moving power is distributed among the traffic.

These expenses, chargeable respectively on the vehicles composing the trains, are now to be distributed between the units composing the average loads of these vehicles. It has been shown that, on the Belgian railways, the average loads of the several denominations of vehicles were as follows:

Description of Vehicle.	Average Load.
Passenger carriage, 1st class, number of passengers	8·54
,, 2d class ,,	12·38
,, 3d class ,,	16·41
Baggage-van, tons	0·56
Parcel-van, tons	1·85
Horse-box, number of horses	1·67
Carriage-truck, number of carriages	0·74
Goods-wagons, tons	2·46
Large cattle-wagons, head of cattle	4·19
Small cattle-wagons ,,	34·90

By dividing the expenses chargeable per mile on each vehicle by the number of units of load as here given, we shall find the share of the expenses per mile chargeable to each unit. If this be multiplied by the average distance over which each unit of load was carried, we shall obtain the average total mileage expenses of each unit; and if to this be added the share of the expenses of the stations chargeable to the objects of traffic, irrespective of distance, we shall obtain the entire average expenses of each object. These results are given in the following table:

	I. Expense of Stations.	II. Expense of Transport per Mile.	III. Average Distance carried.	IV. Total Expense of Transport.	V. Total Expense of Transport and Stations.
	s. d.	d.	Miles.	s. d.	s. d.
Passengers, 1st class	0 0·82	0·38	43·20	1 4·41	1 5·23
,, 2d class	0 0·82	0·26	28·50	0 7·41	0 8·23
,, 3d class	0 0·82	0·20	21·50	0 4·30	0 5·12
Ton of baggage	10 0·00	5·80	52·10	25 2·18	35 2·18
,, parcels	4 3·00	1·77	54·40	8 0·29	12 3·29
A horse	1 5·00	1·95	109·00	17 8·55	19 1·55
A carriage	1 5·00	4·40	90·00	33 0·00	34 5·00
Ton of goods	1 5·00	1·04	44·80	3 10·60	5 3·60
A head of cattle	0 9·00	0·61	57·00	2 10·77	3 7·77
,, small cattle	0 1·00	0·07	42·70	0 3·00	0 4·00

The arithmetical process by which the above table has been

computed will easily suggest means whereby the economy of transport may be promoted. The numbers in the second column, expressing the cost per mile for the transport properly so called, of each unit of traffic, have been found by dividing the cost per mile by the number of units in the average load of each vehicle. Now it has been shown that the increased expense arising from any increase of the load of each vehicle, produces an insignificant effect on the total expense of transport; and it therefore follows that the share of the expenses of transporting such vehicles which falls on each unit of its load, will be in the inverse proportion of the magnitude of such load. It may, therefore, be inferred that the cost of transport, properly so called, of each unit of load will be inversely as the magnitude of the load transported by each vehicle.

It would be desirable, if sufficiently precise data could be obtained for the purpose, to ascertain the average proportion in which the working expenses of the English railways are distributed under the different heads. The want of uniformity, however, in the published accounts of the different companies, where we find different expenses frequently classed under the same denominations, and the same expenses under different denominations, and where, from the want of clearness, it is often difficult, and sometimes impossible, to determine the head to which certain disbursements should be assigned, renders it impracticable to obtain any general and exact estimate of this kind.

I have, however, extracted from the mass of published reports thirteen half-yearly statements of five of the principal companies, from which I have formed the following tabular analysis. I repeat, however, that it must be received only as the best that can be obtained, in the absence of more precise and satisfactory data.

The numbers which appear in the columns of the following table (see page 233) express the proportion of every £100 of the total working expenses, which were appropriated to the different heads specified in the table.

From all that has been explained in the present and preceding chapters, it may be inferred, that, among the principal measures tending toward an increased economy of expenses in the working of railways, the following are the most prominent:

    1st. So to manage the traffic, that the various classes of vehicles of transport should carry more complete loads; because the share of the expenses falling on each unit of

THE EXPENSES.

Analysis of the approximate Proportion in which the working Expenses of the under-mentioned Railways were distributed under the several specified Heads.

	Direction and Management.	Way and Works.	Locomotive Power.	Carrying Department.	Office and Sundries.	Total.
Northwestern. Half-year ending						
Dec. 31, 1847	4·34	11·68	32·86	49·12	2·00	100·00
June 30, 1848	4·17	11·31	34·03	48·53	1·96	100·00
Dec. 31, 1848	3·80	11·40	33·39	47·79	3·62	100·00
June 30, 1849	4·32	11·06	32·73	48·64	3·25	100·00
Great Western. Half-year ending						
Dec. 31, 1848	11·10	22·80	29·60	34·50	2·00	100·00
June 30, 1849	12·90	26·16	26·35	32·45	2·14	100·00
Brighton. Half-year ending						
June 30, 1848	5·62	15·90	42·01	34·80	1·67	100·00
Dec. 31, 1848	7·30	18·20	39·41	34·11	0·98	100·00
June 30, 1849	5·31	16·90	33·50	41·89	2·40	100·00
Southeastern. Half-year ending						
June 30, 1848	4·85	8·31	53·71	32·71	0·42	100·00
Dec. 31, 1848	5·40	8·94	43·00	41·80	0·86	100·00
Southwestern. Half-year ending						
June 30, 1848	11·70	19·30	28·30	25·30	15·40	100·00
Dec. 31, 1848	7·97	23·01	28·01	30·71	10·30	100·00
Mean	6·83	15·76	35·15	38·64	3·69	100·00

load, diminishes very nearly in the same ratio as the load of such vehicles increases.

2dly. So to manage the traffic as to encourage transport to increased distances, because those expenses which are independent of distance will thereby be spread over a greater mileage; that part of the cost per mile of each object of transport diminishing in the same ratio as the distance transported increases.

3dly. So to manage the traffic, that the number of vehicles drawn by each engine shall be increased, because the cost of traction will thus be divided among a greater number of vehicles. This cost is but slightly increased by the increase of the number of vehicles drawn by each engine; while the expenses falling on each vehicle are diminished in a much larger proportion.

4thly. So to manage the business of transport, that the distance run by each engine lighted shall be increased; because, in this case, those charges on the engine power which are independent of distance are divided among a greater extent of mileage; and the share of those charges falling on each vehicle drawn will be diminished, *cæteris paribus*, in the same proportion as the engine mileage is increased.

5thly. In cases where the traffic prevails chiefly in one direction, and, consequently, where "empties" are drawn in great quantities in the other direction, to study the local products, and modify the tariff so as to attract loads for the empty vehicles at a tariff which may be productive under such circumstances, though unproductive under ordinary conditions. By these means, the average load of the vehicles of transport will be augmented.

6thly. Not to multiply the trains beyond that point which the reasonable accommodation of the public renders indispensable. The more the trains are multiplied, the less complete will be the loads of every description of traffic, and the greater will be the share of the expenses which will fall on each unit carried.

7thly. To sort the loads of each description of traffic as far as possible, according to its destination; and for the passenger traffic to provide mixed carriages, which may take up in the same vehicle the complements of load composed of different classes. By this expedient, a single carriage in a passenger train may perform the office of three.

8thly. To diminish, as far as possible, the number of express trains, if it be not practicable to abolish them altogether. Express trains are a source of vast expense, directly and indirectly, which can never be repaid by any practicable tariff to be levied upon them. They are a source of expense directly by their extreme speed, which produces a rapid deterioration of the rails, and shakes to pieces the engine and the vehicles of transport. They are a still greater source of expense indirectly, by the effect they produce on the ordinary traffic of the line. Regular trains are either urged forward at undue speed to get out of their way, and thereby the wear of the line, the engines, and the carrying stock, is increased, or they are compelled, as in the case of goods trains, to stop in sidings to let the express pass.

By multiplying the stoppages of heavy goods trains, the wear of the rails, engines, and vehicles of transport themselves is seriously increased by the effects of the absorption of the momentum of so great a mass in stopping, and the action of the engines in producing the momentum in starting; both of which, by the common laws of motion, must be expended on the rails, the axles, and other parts of the mechanism upon which the strain is thrown.

CHAPTER XIII.

RECEIPTS.—TARIFFS.—PROFITS.

None of the difficulties which have been encountered in the nvestigation of the services of railways are presented in the analysis of their receipts. The relation of the expenses to the services ultimately rendered, is most uncertain and arbitrary. The relation of the receipts to these services is immediate and obvious. The reports of the railway commissioners, moreover, although scanty and obscure so far as relates to the expenses, are sufficiently ample as respects the receipts. It is only when we come to compare the receipts with the expenses, for the purpose of investigating and dissecting the profits, that we encounter difficulties, and these difficulties arise exclusively from the uncertainty and obscurity of the accounts of expenses.

In the following table is exhibited the receipts proceeding from the transport of passengers on the English railways during the six years and a half ending Dec. 31, 1848; showing also the average receipts per day, the average sum contributed by each person booked, and the sum paid per passenger per mile.

Tabular Analysis of the Revenue arising from the Passenger Traffic on the Railways of the United Kingdom during the Six Years and a Half ending December 31, 1848.

	Total Receipts.	Average Receipts per Day.	Average Receipts per Passenger booked.	Average Receipts per Passenger per Mile.
	£.	£.	s. d.	d.
Twelve months ending June 30, 1843.				
1st class	1,386,942	3,799	6 0·75	2·51
2d class	1,300,758	3,564	2 2·25	1·80
3d class	422,557	1,158	1 2·50	1·17
Totals and averages	3,110,257	8,521	2 8·00	1·98

	Total Receipts.	Average Receipts per day.	Average Receipts per Passenger booked.	Average Receipts per Passenger per Mile.
	£.	£.	s. d.	d.
Twelve months ending June 30, 1844.				
1st class	1,499,688	4,108	5 7·00	2·56
2d class	1,436,537	3,936	2 2·00	1·80
3d class	503,069	1,378	1 1·75	1·05
Totals and averages	3,439,294	9,422	2 5·75	1·85
Twelve months ending June 30, 1845.				
1st class	1,610,805	4,413	5 7·50	2·63
2d class	1,683,633	4,613	2 3·75	1·92
3d class	681,903	1,868	1 0·75	0·97
Totals and averages	3,976,341	10,894	2 4·25	1·82
Twelve months ending June 30, 1846.				
1st class	1,691,724	4,635	5 2·75	2·11
2d class	1,967,773	5,391	2 2·25	1·44
3d class	1,065,719	2,919	1 1·75	0·92
Totals and averages	4,725,216	12,945	2 2·00	1·44
Twelve months ending June 30, 1847.				
1st class	1,725,759	4,729	4 10·50	2·38
2d class	2,098,080	5,748	2 0·75	1·62
3d class	1,324,163	3,628	1 1·75	0·99
Totals and averages	5,148,002	14,105	2 0·00	1·54
Twelve months ending June 30, 1848.				
1st class	1,796,033	4,920	4 11·00	2·39
2d class	2,355,653	6,454	2 1·75	1·63
3d class	1,568,696	4,297	1 1·75	1·00
Totals and averages	5,720,382	15,671	1 11·75	1·51
Six months ending December 31, 1848.				
1st class	1,003,516	5,498	5 5·00	2·38
2d class	1,360,468	7,454	2 2·75	1·62
3d class	919,317	5,028	1 2·50	1·00
Totals and averages	3,283,301	17,980	2 0·75	1·51

In the following table is exhibited the proportion per cent. of these receipts contributed by each of the three classes of passengers:

TABULAR ANALYSIS of the Proportions in which each class of Passengers contributed to every £100 of Gross Revenue in the Six Years and a Half ending December 31, 1848.

	1st Class.	2d Class.	3d Class.
For Twelve months ending June 30, 1843	44·58	41·83	13·59
,, ,, 1844	43·60	41·77	14·63
,, ,, 1845	40·51	42·34	17·15
,, ,, 1846	35·80	41·65	22·55
,, ,, 1847	33·52	40·76	25·72
,, ,, 1848	31·39	41·18	27·43
For Half-Year ending December 31, 1848	30·57	41·45	27·98

This table exhibits in a remarkable manner the progressively increased use of the railway made by the inferior classes of passengers. It will be observed that the proportion of the entire revenue contributed by the second-class passengers was sensibly the same during the entire period included in the above table, being about $41\frac{1}{2}$ per cent.; but while the proportion contributed by the first-class passengers fell from $44\frac{1}{2}$ to $30\frac{1}{2}$ per cent., the proportion contributed by the third and inferior classes rose from $13\frac{1}{2}$ to 28 per cent.

It must be observed that the actual amount contributed by all classes of passengers gradually augmented throughout the period referred to; the daily receipts in 1843 being £8500, while in the last six months of 1848 they were nearly £18,000. The general receipts were therefore more than doubled in this interval.

It is also worthy of observation, that while the average receipts proceeding from each first-class passenger booked gradually diminished from 6s. to 5s. 5d., the receipts proceeding from those of the other classes of passengers remained nearly stationary.

The relative diminution of the receipts proceeding from the first-class passengers is to be attributed, therefore, not merely to the comparatively smaller number of these, but also to the prevalence of their traveling shorter distances.

In order to exhibit the operation of the causes of local variation in the railway revenues, I have exhibited in the following table an analysis of the receipts from the passenger traffic for eleven of the principal lines of railway.

TABULAR ANALYSIS of the Revenue proceeding from the Passenger Traffic of the Railways of the United Kingdom during the Twelve Months ending June 30, 1847.

	Receipts.	Average Receipts per Day.	Average Receipts per Passenger.	Average Receipts per Passenger per Mile.
First Class.	£.	£.	s. d.	d.
London and Northwestern	513,796	1,407	9 2·75	2·193
Great Western	232,855	638	10 1·50	2·744
Midland	133,388	364	8 3·25	3·000
London, Brighton, and South Coast	124,220	340	5 10	2·630
London and Cambridge	66,109	181	6 4	1·944
London and Colchester	24,622	67	7 3	2·328
Bristol and Birmingham	45,237	124	7 4·70	2·625
London and Southwestern	95,822	263	4 9·60	2·029
York and Newcastle	45,040	123	5 11	2·484
York and North Midland	44,011	120	5 4·40	2·399
Lancashire and Yorkshire	34,239	94	3 8·25	2·220
All the remaining lines	366,420	1,004	2 1·25	2·385
Totals and averages	1,725,729	4,725	4 10·20	2·385
Second Class.				
London and Northwestern	450,113	1,233	3 10·30	1·450
Great Western	364,257	998	3 7·80	1·878
Midland	165,168	452	3 6·50	2·000
London, Brighton, and South Coast	105,883	290	3 0·25	1·645
London and Cambridge	83,620	229	3 6·70	1·339
London and Colchester	45,133	123	3 3·70	1·505
Bristol and Birmingham	69,978	192	4 2·75	1·750
London and Southwestern	133,084	364	2 5·16	1·413
York and Newcastle	59,956	164	1 3·80	1·495
York and North Midland	55,916	154	3 7·30	1·838
Lancashire and Yorkshire	53,186	146	2 1·50	1·630
All the remaining lines	511,786	1,403	0 11·50	1·620
Totals and averages	2,098,080	5,748	2 0·80	1·620
Third Class, &c.				
London and Northwestern	213,133	584	1 11·40	0·948
Great Western	77,130	211	3 8·00	1·000
Midland	131,235	359	1 1·30	1·000
London, Brighton, and South Coast	84,390	231	1 1·60	1·130
London and Cambridge	41,598	114	1 3·75	0·844
London and Colchester	32,638	89	1 8·00	0·963
Bristol and Birmingham	22,120	60	2 1·90	0·750
London and Southwestern	55,499	152	2 4·70	1·012
York and Newcastle	42,257	116	1 3·60	0·959
York and North Midland	65,407	179	1 9·50	1·150
Lancashire and Yorkshire	83,704	229	0 10·75	0·954
All the remaining lines	475,052	1,303	0 9·10	0·992
Totals and averages	1,324,163	3,627	1 2·00	0·992
Recapitulation.				
First Class	1,725,759	4,725	4 10·20	2·385
Second Class	2,098,080	5,748	2 0·80	1·620
Third Class, &c.	1,324,163	3,627	1 2·00	0·992
Grand totals and averages	5,148,002	14,100	2 0·06	1·535

The sums contributed per passenger would be subject to a correction, owing to the circumstance of passengers traveling from one railway to another without interruption. Such a passenger figures twice in the estimated number booked, once in the return of each railway over which he passes.

It has been already observed, however, in reference to the average distances traveled per passenger, that this correction would have so slight an effect on the results, that it may be neglected without sensible error. The returns of the clearing-house, in which the through passenger traffic is given, demonstrate this.

In the following table I have exhibited an analysis of the receipts proceeding from the traffic in goods during the six years and a half ending December 31, 1848. The returns do not supply the quantity of goods booked, or their mileage, and I have therefore been compelled to limit the present analysis to the statement of the gross receipts:

STATEMENT of the Gross Receipts proceeding from Merchandise, Cattle, Carriages, Parcels, Mails, &c., on the Railways of the United Kingdom during the Six Years and a Half ending Dec. 31, 1848.

	Total Receipts.	Average daily Receipts.
	£.	£.
Twelve months ending June 30, 1843	1,424,932	3,903
„ „ 1844	1,635,380	4,481
„ „ 1845	2,233,373	6,120
„ „ 1846	2,840,354	7,781
„ „ 1847	3,362,884	9,213
„ „ 1848	4,213,170	11,543
Half-year ending December 31, 1848	2,461,663	13,488

In order to exhibit the local variation in the merchandise traffic, I have given in the following table (see page 240) an analysis of the receipts on eleven of the principal railways for the twelve months ending June 30, 1847:

I have already observed that the first projectors of the modern railways contemplated chiefly, if not exclusively, a traffic in merchandise. The event proved to be the reverse. The traffic in merchandise was comparatively little, nearly the whole revenue proceeding from the traffic in passengers. As the railways, however, have become more extensively developed, and improvements have been made in the machinery of locomotion, the goods traffic has been more and more extended, so as to bear a con-

TABULAR ANALYSIS of the Receipts produced from the Traffic in Merchandise on the Railways of the United Kingdom during the Twelve Months ending June 30, 1847.

	Total Receipts.	Average daily Receipts.	Receipts per Ton booked.	Receipts per Ton per Mile.		
				Average.	Highest.	Lowest.
	£.	£.	s. d.	d.	d.	d.
London and Northwestern..	595,957	1632	8 5·28	1·533	2·451	0·783
Great Western	201,320	551	10 10·08	2·542	..	..
Midland	262,630	719	4 4·68	1·675	..	..
London, Brighton, and South Coast	49,216	135	6 3·84	3·560	10·000	2·000
London and Cambridge	100,415	275	8 5·88	1·903	3·700	1·000
Bristol and Colchester	31,760	87	7 7·44	1·903	4·750	1·708
Bristol and Birmingham	67,726	186	5 4·00	1·845	..	1·140
London and Southwestern	68,635	188	9 3·00	2·344	7·260	1·520
York and Newcastle	152,874	418	1 7·80	1·240	3·250	1·250
York and North Midland	58,971	164	2 7·68	1·166	3·000	0.750
Lancashire and Yorkshire	174,087	479	5 9·96	2·325	12·090	1·000
All the remaining Lines	842,402	2308	1 6·36	1·675	..	..
Total and averages	2,606,393	7142	3 2·20	1·675		

tinually increasing proportion to the traffic in passengers. In order to demonstrate this, I have exhibited in the following table an analysis of the relative amounts of revenue proceeding from passengers and goods for the six years and a half ending December 31, 1848.

TABLE showing the Total Receipts for Passengers and Goods on the British Railways during Six Years and a Half ending Dec. 31, 1848.

Year ending.	Total Receipts from Passengers.	Received for Goods, Cattle, Carriages, Parcels, Mails, &c.	Total Receipts.	Per Cent. of Total Receipts contributed by	
				Passengers.	Goods, &c.
	£.	£.	£.		
June 30, 1843	3,110,257	1,424,932	4,535,189	68·5	31·5
,, 1844	3,439,294	1,635,380	5,074,674	67·5	32·5
,, 1845	3,976,341	2,233,373	6,209,714	64·0	36·0
,, 1846	4,725,216	2,840,354	7,565,569	62·4	37·6
,, 1847	5,148,002	3,362,884	8,510,886	60·4	39·6
,, 1848	5,702,382	4,213,170	9,933,552	57·3	42·7
Dec. 31, 1848	3,283,302	2,461,663	5,744,965	57·4	42·6

It appears from this, that while, in 1843, thirteen years after the opening of the Liverpool and Manchester Railway, the goods contributed only 30 per cent. of the gross revenue of the railways, they contributed, in the eighteen months terminating December 30, 1848, more than 42½ per cent.

CHAP. XIII.] RECEIPTS.—TARIFFS.—PROFITS.

It would be interesting to ascertain the proportion of the gross revenue of railways which proceeds from the different classes of traffic. The more recent railway returns, however, supply no data for such a computation.

Until 1847 the railway commissioners published annually reports of the traffic, containing some useful details, but since that year nothing appears in the reports except a general summary of the traffic, which for statistical purposes is almost useless. I have taken from the returns for 1847 data which have enabled me to calculate approximately the proportion of the receipts arising from certain objects of traffic. This is exhibited in the following table :

TABULAR ANALYSIS showing the Proportion in which the Gross Revenue proceeding from the Railways of the United Kingdom arose from certain Classes of Traffic during the Twelve Months ending June 30, 1847.

	Receipts.	Per Cent. of Total Receipts.
	£.	
Passengers, 1st class	1,725,759	20·3
,, 2d class	2,098,080	24·6
,, 3d class	1,324,163	15·5
Merchandise	2,606,393	30·8
Cattle	71,482	0·8
Sheep	53,091	0·6
Pigs	23,718	0·3
Horses	78,549	0·9
Private carriages	52,521	0·6
Baggage, parcels, and mails	377,290	4·4
Sundries not classed	99,840	1·2
Grand total	8,510,886	100·0

It appears from this table, that in the year referred to, the passenger traffic constituted 60 per cent. of the gross revenue, the goods traffic nearly 31 per cent., the remainder arising from baggage, parcels, &c. It also appears that the live stock and carriages constitute but an insignificant fraction of the revenue, not exceeding 3 per cent.

A most instructive and interesting light might be thrown on the circumstances which determine the phenomena of railway traffic, by exhibiting the relations developed from year to year between the receipts, expenses, and profits, and the length of the railways, the movement upon them, and the capital involved in them. But, unfortunately, I have not been able to obtain any authentic or exact data of a general nature for this purpose. The receipts alone are ascertainable with precision; the expenses and profits are left to conjecture. The movement on the railways might be exhibited by the mileage of the trains: but we have these only for particular periods and particular railways. It happens, however, that, in all the cases where this mileage is given, there is a remarkable accordance in its ratio to the receipts. By dividing the one by the other, we find an almost invariable quotient; the conclusion from which is, that the average receipts per mile run on the railways for which authentic returns are given of the running of the trains are uniform. In the absence, therefore, of exact data, we may assume, as a means of approximation which can not widely err, that on the railways, taken collectively, the receipts bear this proportion to the mileage of the trains. On this hypothesis I shall therefore calculate the receipts per mile run by the trains on all the railways.

To find the proportion of the receipts to the capital expended, I shall assume that the average cost of the railways open at each successive period was at the rate of £40,000 per mile. (See page 69.)

I have therefore calculated the following table (see page 243) on these hypotheses, in the successive columns of which are given the average receipts per day, per mile of the lines open, per mile of the trains run, and per cent. of the capital expended.

It appears, from the result of this computation, that the daily receipts per mile were £6 14s. in 1843; that they augmented until 1846, when they amounted to £8 10s.; and that since that date they have regularly diminished, having fallen to £6 2s. in the last six months of 1848.

It also appears, that the gross receipts on all the railways collectively have never amounted to eight per cent. of the capital expended. In 1846, when they bore the highest proportion to the capital, they amounted only to £7 14s. 7d. per cent. Until that year the proportion had increased, having been £6 1s. 9d. in 1843. Since that epoch the proportion has constantly diminished, being only £5 12s. 9d. per cent. in the last six months of 1848.

In a former chapter I have shown that the increase of the transport has not kept pace with the extension of the railways. This conclusion may be further illustrated by comparing the receipts from the different classes of traffic with the extent of

CHAP. XIII.]   RECEIPTS.—TARIFFS.—PROFITS.   243

TABLE showing the Proportion of the Receipts on the Railways of the United Kingdom to their Length, to the Movement of the Traffic upon them, and to the Capital expended on them.

Year ending.	Total average Receipts per Day.	Average Receipts per Mile of Railway.	Average Receipts per Mile run by Trains.	Average Receipts per Cent. of Capital.
	£.	£.	s.	
June 30, 1843.				
Passengers	8,521	4·6	7·0	4·18
Goods	3,903	2·1	7·0	1·91
Total	12,424	6·7	7·0	6·09
June 30, 1844.				
Passengers	9,422	4·8	7·0	4·39
Goods	4,481	2·3	7·0	2·09
Total	13,903	7·1	7·0	6·48
June 30, 1845.				
Passengers	10,894	5·1	7·0	4·60
Goods	6,120	2·8	7·0	2·59
Total	17,014	7·9	7·0	7·19
June 30, 1846.				
Passengers	12,945	5·3	7·0	4·83
Goods	7,781	3·2	7·0	2·90
Total	20,726	8·5	7·0	7·73
June 30, 1847.				
Passengers	14,105	4·6	7·0	4·25
Goods	9,213	3·0	7·0	2·77
Total	23,318	7·6	7·0	7·02
June 30, 1849.				
Passengers	15,671	4·1	7·0	3·74
Goods	11,543	3·0	7·0	2·75
Total	27,214	7·1	7·0	6·49
Six months ending Dec. 31, 1848.				
Passengers	17,980	3·5	7·0	3·23
Goods	13,488	2·6	7·0	2·41
Total	31,468	6·1	7·0	5·64

244 RAILWAY ECONOMY. [Chap. XIII.

the railways on which this traffic was carried. I have done this in the following table:

TABULAR ANALYSIS showing the Proportion which the Increase of Receipts has borne to the Increase of Railways open during the Six Years and a Half ending December 31, 1848.

	Railway open Miles.	Daily Receipts per Mile.	Increase per Cent.	Decrease per Cent.
Twelve months ending June 30, 1843.		£.		
Passengers, 1st class		2·04		
2d class		1·92		
3d class		0·62		
Total	1857	4·58		
Goods		2·13		
Grand Total		6·67		
Twelve months ending June 30, 1844.				
Passengers, 1st class		2·11	3·50	
2d class		2·01	4·75	
3d class		0·71	14·75	
Total	1952	4·83	5·30	
Goods		2·30	8·00	
Grand Total		7·13	6·60	
Twelve months ending June 30, 1845.				
Passengers, 1st class		2·05	---	3·00
2d class		2·14	6·50	
3d class		0·86	21·00	
Total	2148	5·05	4·50	
Goods		2·85	24·00	
Grand Total		7·90	10·70	
Twelve months ending June 30, 1846.				
Passengers, 1st class		1·90	---	8·00
2d class		2·20	3·00	
3d class		1·20	39·50	
Total	2441	5·30	5·00	
Goods		3·18	11·75	
Grand Total		8·48	7·20	
Twelve months ending June 30, 1847.				
Passengers, 1st class		1·56	---	22·00
2d class		1·89	---	16·25
3d class		1·20	---	0·00
Total	3036	4·65	---	14·00
Goods		3·04	---	4·70
Grand Total		7·69	---	11·20

RECEIPTS.—TARIFFS.—PROFITS.

	Railway open Miles.	Daily Receipts per Mile.	Increase per Cent.	Decrease per Cent.
		£.		
Twelve months ending June 30, 1848.				
Passengers, 1st class	} 3816	1·29	---	21·00
2d class		1·70	---	11·00
3d class		1·13	---	6·00
Total		4·12	---	12·80
Goods		3·02	---	0·66
Grand Total		7·14	---	7·75
Six months ending Dec. 31, 1848.				
Passengers, 1st class	} 5007	1·10	---	17·00
2d class		1·49	---	14·00
3d class		1·00	---	13·00
Total		3·59	---	14·75
Goods		2·70	---	11·75
Grand Total		6·29	---	13·50

It appears from this table that after 1846, when 2600 miles of railway were brought into operation, every species of traffic began to decrease in proportion to the length of the railway worked. The receipts per mile from first-class passengers commenced first to decrease in 1845, as compared with 1844, and the decrease of revenue from this class per mile of railway rapidly augmented from year to year, being in 1846 8 per cent., and in 1847 and 1848 22 per cent. It is observable also that the proportionate increase of receipts from third-class passengers was considerably more rapid than the other classes until 1846, when it was nearly 40 per cent. more than in the preceding year; and in accordance with this, the decrease of revenue per mile from this class was less than the decrease upon the other classes in the succeeding years.

The revenue proceeding from goods per mile of railway underwent considerable change, increasing until 1846, and decreasing afterward. Its augmentation was more rapid, and its decrease slower, than the revenue from passengers.

Thus it appears that goods and third-class passengers supply a more steady revenue in general, in proportion to the length of the lines worked, than the other classes.

It would be highly important, if we possessed the necessary data for the purpose, to exhibit a classified analysis of the receipts, expenses, and profits on the English railways, showing the amounts of these respectively for each class of traffic and for every distance; but, as we have more than once observed, the scanty and insufficient reports issued by the directors of English railways supply no means of forming such an analysis.

As an example, however, of this I have obtained from the official reports of the Belgian railways the necessary data for this purpose. I have therefore given in the following tables the receipts, expenses, and profits, total and per mile, on the Belgian railways for the year 1844.

TABULAR CLASSIFICATION of the Receipts, Expenses, and Profits of the Belgian Railways during the Year 1844.

Classified Traffic.	Denomination.	Total Receipts.	Receipts per Unit booked.	Receipts per Unit per Mile carried.
RECEIPTS.		£.	s. d.	d.
Passengers, 1st class	Number	63,645	4 0·00	1·12
„ 2d class	„	88,742	2 1·25	0·90
„ 3d class	„	92,853	0 11·75	0·55
Baggage	Tons	15,789	36 7·00	8·35
Parcels	„	37,526	21 8·00	4·82
Horses	Number	1,680	24 5·00	2·70
Carriages	„	8,253	67 6·00	9·00
Goods	Tons	130,645	5 10·00	1·57
Cattle (large)	Number	2,557	5 2·00	1·10
„ (small)	„	737	0 4·75	0·11
Total Receipts		442,427		
EXPENSES.				
Passengers, 1st class	Number	22,534	1 4·50	0·38
„ 2d class	„	25,898	0 7·10	0·25
„ 3d class	„	36,938	0 4·50	0·19
Baggage	Tons	13,862	30 9·00	7·10
Parcels	„	20,015	11 1·00	2·50
Horses	Number	1,106	15 5·00	1·70
Carriages	„	3,576	28 1·00	3·75
Goods	Tons	95,723	4 1·00	1·10
Cattle (large)	Number	1,609	3 2·20	0·65
„ (small)	„	627	0 0·40	0·09
Total Expenses		221,888		
PROFITS.				
Passengers, 1st class	Number	41,111	2 7·50	0·74
„ 2d class	„	62,844	1 6·15	0·65
„ 3d class	„	55,915	0 7·25	0·36
Baggage	Tons	1,927	5 10·00	1·25
Parcels	„	17,511	10 7·00	2·32
Horses	Number	574	9 0·00	1·00
Carriages	„	4,677	39 5·00	5·25
Goods	Tons	34,922	1 9·00	0·47
Cattle (large)	Number	948	1 9·80	0·45
„ (small)	„	110	0 3·35	0·02
Total Profits		220,539		

It must be observed, however, that in estimating the expenses per head, or per ton per mile, expenses which are chargeable upon the traffic independent of distance, such as the expenses of the stations, are shared among the traffic according to the average distance traveled by each class.

The chief financial object to which the vigilance and skill of those who direct the affairs of the railways ought to be directed, must be to render the render the ratio of the gross receipts to the gross expenses as great as possible; and this economical problem is of a complex and difficult character, involving all the points of railway management which require the greatest sagacity and experience.

Let us consider the elements upon which the amount of the gross receipts depends, and the circumstances which govern its variation.

The gross receipts depend on,

1. The average tariff of transport per mile imposed on each unit carried.
2. The average number of miles over which such unit is transported.
3. The total number of such units which are carried.

It is evident that the gross receipts may be augmented by the increase of any one or more of these quantities, the others remaining unchanged.

But over the second and third the managers of the railway have no direct control. They can not compel the traffic to come, nor when it does come can they prescribe the distance which it may require to be transported. These two elements, then, can only be indirectly influenced by that element of the traffic over which the managers have the most direct and absolute control, viz., the average *tariff per mile exacted for the transport.*

The problem, therefore, which presents itself for solution, is to investigate the manner in which the quantity of traffic offered to the railway, and the average distance to which it is transported, can be influenced by the charge per unit per mile, or the tariff to which it is subjected. Let us consider the effects and limits of this influence.

It is evident that, by lowering the tariff, the quantity of traffic, as well as the average distances, will be augmented, and this increase will go on even if we were to carry the diminution of the tariff to the extreme length of extinguishing it altogether, and transporting the traffic gratuitously. But at this imaginary limit the receipts would be nothing.

On the contrary, if the tariff be augmented continually, the quantity of traffic, as well as the average distance it is to be carried, will be continually diminished; the magnitude of the charge being such as a less and less quantity of traffic is capable of bearing. A limit will at length be attained, at which the traffic will altogether vanish, the tariff becoming so great, that no objects can bear it. Here, again, the receipts become nothing

Thus it appears that, at the two limits of a vanishing tariff and a prohibitory tariff, the receipts are nothing. Between these, the gross receipts vary, augmenting as the tariff is diminished from its prohibitory amount to a certain point, and, after passing that point, diminishing until they vanish altogether with the tariff.

With a vanishing tariff, the traffic is a maximum, but the receipts altogether vanish; with a prohibitory tariff, both the traffic and receipts vanish.

The relation between the variations of the tariff, and that of the receipts, may be illustrated by a simple diagram.

Let distances be taken along the horizontal line O X, representing the successive values of the tariff, and let perpendiculars, corresponding to these distances, be taken representing the corresponding amounts of the gross receipts. These perpendiculars will terminate in a curve, which will indicate the variation of the amount of the gross receipts.

Let us take O X to represent the prohibitory tariff, which would cause the traffic and receipts to vanish together. Let O m be any other value assigned to the tariff, and let mp represent the corresponding amount of the gross receipts.

If we assign to the tariff any value, such as Om''', less than the prohibitory value, there will be a certain amount of traffic and a certain amount of receipts. Let the amount of receipts be expressed by the perpendicular, $m'''p'''$.

Now, if a less value still be assigned to the tariff, such as Om'', the receipts will be augmented, because the influence of the increased number of objects booked, and the increased distances to which they are carried, owing to the diminution of the tariff, will have a greater effect in increasing the gross receipts than the reduction of the tariff has in diminishing them. By thus gradually diminishing the tariff, the traffic will increase both in quantity and distance, and the gross receipts will be placed under the operation of two contrary causes, one tending to increase, and the other to diminish them. So long as the influence of the former predominates, the gross receipts will increase; but when the effect of the reduction of the tariff counterpoises exactly the effect of the increase of traffic in quantity and distance, then the increase of the gross receipts will cease. After that, the influence of the reduction of the tariff in diminishing the receipts will predominate over the influence of the increased traffic in augmenting them, and the consequence will be their diminution.

This effect is illustrated by the diagram.

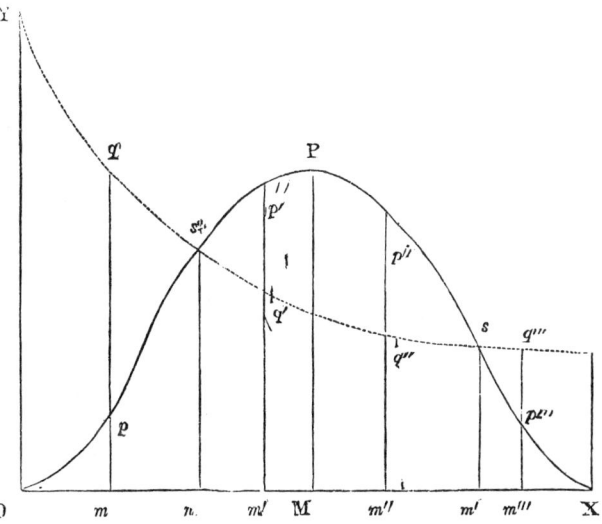

While the distances Om''', Om'', &c., are gradually diminished, the perpendiculars $m''' \, p'''$ and $m'' \, p'$ &c. gradually increase, and the curve rises; but when the distance from O, representing the tariff, is reduced to OM, then the perpendicular ceases to increase, and has attained its *maximum*, which is MP. At this point the curve ceases to rise, and when the distance representing the tariff is further diminished, as at Om', then the perpendicular $m' \, p'$ is diminished, and the curve descends, for in this case the influence of the diminished tariff predominates over that of the increased traffic and produces diminished receipts. This goes on as the tariff is further diminished, and the curve descends toward O. The perpendiculars representing the receipts continually diminish, and when the tariff vanishes, that is, when m arrives at O, the perpendicular itself vanishes, the receipts disappear, and the curve descends to O.

Thus it appears that, while the tariff is gradually augmented from its vanishing to its prohibitory point, the gross receipts gradually increase, arrive at a maximum, and then gradually diminish, and finally vanish.

The problem which the railway manager has to solve, for each description of traffic, is the discovery of the point at which the gross receipts are a maximum. It is to adjust the tariff so nicely, that the influence of its gradual increase in diminishing the receipts shall be precisely balanced by the influence of the traffic in augmenting them.

But it is not enough to consider the influence of these circumstances on the receipts. It is necessary, also, to have regard to the expenses; for it is on the excess of the receipts above the expenses that the commercial prosperity of the enterprise will depend.

The gross expenses may be considered as consisting of two parts:

1. The expenses which are independent of the distances to which the objects of traffic are carried. These are, the expenses of direction and management, the maintenance of the way and works (except the small part of this expense which relates to the wear of the iron-work of the road), and the expenses of the stations.

2. The expenses which are in the direct ratio of the distances to which the objects of traffic are transported. These are the expenses of the locomotive power and the carrying stock.

The former being independent of the transport, properly so called, will be the same, however the average distance to which the objects of traffic are transported may vary; and even though that distance were reduced to nothing, as would be the case with a prohibitory tariff, this class of expenses would still remain unaltered. Every increase of traffic produced by a diminishing tariff will produce an increased expense; and this will continue until we attain the imaginary limit of a vanishing tariff, when the expense will become a maximum because the traffic becomes a maximum.

To illustrate further, by the aid of the diagram, the relation of the receipts and expenses, let us take the imaginary limit of

CHAP. XIII.] RECEIPTS.—TARIFFS.—PROFITS. 251

a vanishing tariff, and suppose that the traffic is carried gratuitously. Even in this case, however, the amount of the traffic will not be unlimited.

A railway which should offer transport for nothing, would still find only a limited number of passengers and a limited amount of goods demanding the change of place which it offers. Let us suppose that the expense of this gratuitous traffic is represented by the perpendicular O Y.

Even when the traffic altogether vanishes by reason of the prohibitory tariff represented by O X, there is still an amount of expense. Let that amount of expense be represented in the diagram by X y. Thus we have represented the two extreme limits of the expenses, O Y representing the expenses which would correspond to gratuitous transport, and X y representing the expenses which would correspond to a prohibitory tariff. The curve, representing the expenses in a manner analogous to that which has been already explained in reference to the receipts, is here represented by a dotted line extending from Y to y. The expense attending the traffic, which would correspond to the tariff represented by O m, will thus be represented by $m\,q$; the expenses of the traffic corresponding to the tariff O m' will be represented by $m'\,q'$, &c.

Now, so long as the dotted curve lies above the continuous curve, mq will be greater than mp; or, what is the same, the expenses will be greater than the receipts, and the railway will be worked at a loss; but wherever the dotted curve lies below the continuous curve, then the perpendiculars representing the receipts will be greater than those representing the expenses, and there will be a profit.

The curve of expenses intersects the curve of receipts at two points, s and s', which lie on opposite sides of the point P of maximum receipts, and which correspond to the tariffs represented by O n and O n'. At these points of intersection the same perpendicular which represents the receipts also represents the expenses, and the expenses are therefore equal to the receipts; so that there is neither profit nor loss.

From O to s, that is, from a vanishing tariff to a tariff O n which renders the receipts and expenses equal, the curve of expenses is above the curve of receipts, the expenses are greater than the receipts, and the railway is worked at a loss. From s to P, the curve of receipts lies above the curve of expenses, and the perpendicular representing the receipts is continually increasing, while the perpendicular representing the expenses is continually diminishing; consequently the difference of the two, which represents the profits, is continually increasing.

In passing from P toward s', the perpendicular representing the receipts diminishes, but the perpendicular representing the expenses also diminishes. A question therefore arises, as to whether the profit, represented by the difference of these perpendiculars, both diminishing, will increase, diminish, or remain stationary. It may be easily shown that in starting from P, the perpendicular representing the expenses will diminish more rapidly than that which represents the receipts; and, therefore, the difference of the two perpendiculars which represents the profits will increase. It consequently follows, that the point of maximum receipts is not the point of maximum profit, but that this latter point will be found somewhere between P and s', at a point to be determined by the condition that the two perpendiculars, one representing the receipts and the other representing the expenses, shall decrease at the same rate.

This may be geometrically expressed by stating it to be the point at which the two curves become parallel to each other. After passing this point, the perpendicular representing the receipts will diminish faster than that which represents the expenses, and the profits will diminish.

It is therefore demonstrable that the point of maximum receipts is not the point of maximum profits; but that this latter point lies between the point of maximum receipts and a prohibitory tariff.

To determine this point of maximum profits rigorously, it would be necessary to express the strict arithmetical relation between the tariff and the traffic. Now this relation will be different for every different railway, and for every different class of traffic on the same railway; and therefore it admits of no general expression. It is a point which only can be determined by tentative means; and in adjusting the tariff so as to correspond to it, the highest managerial skill will be shown.

Although the strict arithmetical connection between the tariff and the traffic does not admit of any general expression, we may nevertheless trace some particular relations which will supply practical illustrations of the principles we have adverted to. We shall take as an example the goods traffic.

Let r express the tariff imposed per mile on each ton of goods carried.

Let D express in miles the average distance to which each ton of goods is carried.

Let N express the number of tons of goods booked.

Let R express the gross receipts proceeding from the transport of goods.

The average receipts produced by each ton of goods carried will then be expressed by

$$D \times r,$$

and the total receipts will be

$$R = N \times D \times r.$$

In like manner, let the actual cost of transport for goods, properly so called, per ton per mile be expressed by e, this being understood to include locomotive power and the expenses of the carrying stock.

The cost of carrying each ton booked will then be

$$D \times e,$$

and the cost of carrying all the merchandise booked will be

$$N \times D \times e.$$

Let the expenses which are independent of the movement of the traffic, and which consist of the share of direction and management, the way and works, and the stations, chargeable to the goods traffic, be expressed by E', and let the total expenses chargeable to the same traffic be E. We have then

$$E = E' + N \times D \times e.$$

The expense chargeable to each ton of goods booked will be

$$\frac{E}{N} = \frac{E'}{N} + D \times e.$$

If the profit be expressed by P, we shall have

$$P = R - E = N D (r - e) - E',$$

and the profits on each ton booked will be

$$\frac{P}{N} = D (r - e) - \frac{E'}{N}$$

This is equivalent to stating that the profit realized on each ton booked is found by multiplying the difference between the tariff and the expenses of transport per mile by the average distance to which the ton is carried, and subtracting from the product the expenses which are independent of the distance.

The several quantities which enter the preceding formula reciprocally influence each other in a manner which it is important to notice.

Any diminution of r (the tariff) must produce an increase either of D (the distance to which the traffic is carried), or of N (the quantity of traffic), or of both of these.

The increase of D will produce a decrease of e, the average expense of transport per mile; for, in general, the greater the quantity of locomotion, the less will be the rate per mile at which it can be executed.

The increase of N will produce a proportionate decrease of $\frac{E'}{N}$, and a corresponding increase of the profits per ton booked.

If the decrease of $(r-e)$ be in a less ratio than the consequent increase of D, then an increase of D $(r-e)$ must take place; and since the same cause produces a decrease of $\frac{E'}{N}$, an increase of the profits per ton booked must ensue.

But even though the increase of D should not be in a ratio greater than the decrease of $(r-e)$, an increase of the profits per ton must ensue in consequence of the decrease of $\frac{E'}{N}$.

In each of these cases, therefore, a diminution of the tariff would be productive of augmented profits.

To illustrate this, let us take the case of the Belgian railways, on which each ton of goods was carried the average distance of 45 miles, and produced an average receipt of 70d.

The expenses chargeable upon it were 51d., of which 34d. were independent of the distance, and 17d. dependent on it.

Hence we have in this case $D = 45$ and $\frac{R}{N} = 70d$.

Hence it follows that

$$r = \frac{R}{ND} = \frac{70d.}{45} = 1{\cdot}55.$$

We have also $D \times e = 17d.$, and therefore

$$e = \frac{17d.}{45} = 0{\cdot}377d.;$$

and since $\frac{E'}{N} = 34d.$, we have

CHAP. XIII.] RECEIPTS.—TARIFFS.—PROFITS. 255

$$\frac{P}{N} = 45 \times (1{\cdot}55 - 0{\cdot}377) - 34 = \overset{d.}{18{\cdot}65}.$$

The net profit per ton booked was therefore $\overset{d.}{18{\cdot}65}$.

The manner in which any proposed reduction in the tariff would augment the traffic, either as to quantity or distance, can not be determined in a definite manner by the preceding formula; nor could it be by any formula whatever, inasmuch as the solution of the question would depend on conditions peculiar to each railway and each class of traffic.

If we assume, however, that it be required to reduce the tariff (r) so that, producing the same net profits $\left(\dfrac{P}{N}\right)$ per ton carried, the average distance (D) to which each ton is transported be augmented in any assigned proportion, we may approximate to the required tariff by taking the expenses per ton $\left(\dfrac{E'}{N}\right)$, which are independent of the distance, at the same amount as at present. This will not be strictly true, because the reduction of the tariff would necessarily augment the amount of the traffic, unless counteracted by some other condition, and therefore the tariffs which we shall obtain will be a little higher than those which would give the same profits per ton.

Let us suppose that the average distance to which each ton is carried is augmented from D to D', and that the tariff is reduced from r to r', the profits remaining unchanged; we shall then have

$$\frac{P}{N} = D(r - e) - \frac{E'}{N},$$

$$\frac{P}{N} = D'(r' - e) - \frac{E'}{N},$$

and therefore

$$D(r - e) = D'(r' - e).$$

From what has been stated, we have on the Belgian railways

$$D = 45,$$
$$r = 1{\cdot}55,$$
$$e = 0{\cdot}377.$$

Hence we have

$$52{\cdot}78 = D'(r' - 0{\cdot}377);$$

and therefore

$$r' = \frac{52\cdot 78}{D'} + 0\cdot 377.$$

By this formula we can compute the value of the tariffs, r', which correspond to any increased distances, D'.

In the following table such a computation is exhibited. In the fourth column a series of increasing distances are given. In the third column are exhibited the corresponding values of the tariff. In the fifth column is given the total receipts which would be obtained for each ton booked; and in the sixth column the total expenses. In the seventh column are given the expenses per ton per mile.

By this last column is rendered apparent the increased saving per mile on the expenses of transport produced by the augmented average distance.

Cost of Transport per Mile.	Expenses per Ton booked independent of Distance.	Tariff per Ton per Mile.	Average Distance carried.	Total Receipts per Ton booked.	Total Expenses per Ton booked.	Total Expenses per Ton per Mile.
e	$\dfrac{E'}{N}$	r	D	$\dfrac{R}{N}$	$\dfrac{E}{N}$	
		1·55	45	69·7	50·9	1·13
		1·43	50	71·5	52·8	1·05
		1·33	55	73·2	54·7	0·99
		1·25	60	75·0	56·6	0·94
		1·19	65	77·5	58·5	0·90
0·377	34·0	1·13	70	79·1	60·4	0·86
		1·08	75	81·0	62·3	0·83
		1·04	80	83·2	64·2	0·80
		1·00	85	85·0	66·1	0·78
		0·96	90	86·4	68·9	0·76
		0·93	95	88·3	69·8	0·74
		0·92	100	92·0	71·7	0·71

From this table it appears that if the average distance to which each ton of goods is transported were doubled, a tariff 50 per cent. less than the present would yield the same amount of profit per ton carried as is now obtained; and if a less reduction of the tariff would produce this augmented distance, an increased profit would arise both from the increased quantity of goods carried, and from the increased average distance.

It may be useful here to repeat that it is assumed in the second column that the constant expenses remain the same, notwithstanding the gradual reduction of the tariff.

It is evident, however, that these expenses must be diminished,

CHAP. XIII.]   RECEIPTS.—TARIFFS.—PROFITS.   257

inasmuch as the divisor by which they are obtained, being the number of tons booked, must be augmented by the reduced tariff.

We have used in the preceding investigation the letter r, to express the *average* tariff, implying thereby that the rate of charge per mile upon the same class of traffic is liable to variation. This variation forms a question of capital importance in railway economy, and one which is too often overlooked.

It has been more than once demonstrated in the preceding chapters, that the cost of railway transport, of any class of traffic, is not in the ratio of the distance to which it is transported. A portion of the expenses is independent of the distance, and, consequently, it follows that the expenses chargeable per mile upon any object of transport will be less as the distance to which it is transported increases. It is evident, therefore, that, consistently with realizing the same proportion of profits upon the business executed, a railway company can always afford to reduce the charge per mile in a greater or less proportion as the distance increases.

The distance to which any class of merchandise admits of being transported, will depend on the charge which such object will bear in the market, in addition to its cost of production. This is a limit which can not be surpassed, and this limit, combined with the rate per mile charged for the transport, will determine the radius which limits the market of the producer.

Thus, if we suppose that a certain description of merchandise will bear, in addition to the cost of production, a charge of 10s. per ton, then such article will bear to be transported from the place of production a number of miles, determined by dividing 10s. by the tariff per mile. If the tariff, for example, be 1d. per mile, such an object would bear to be carried 120 miles, without surpassing the limit of price which would become prohibitory in the market.

It is clear, therefore, that every reduction which can be made on the tariff, affecting the larger class of distances, will have the effect of increasing the area over which the producer can carry on a profitable business, and will proportionally increase the available traffic of the railway. For lesser distances, the reduction of the tariff will only have the effect of augmenting the quantity of the articles transmitted, and this can only be effected in the proportion which the reduction of the tariff can effect a diminution of price in the market.

A due consideration of these circumstances will easily demonstrate the advantage which must result to the railways from such a graduated tariff as would favor transport to greater distances. Let us suppose an article transported to a distance of 20 miles, at the rate of $2d.$ per ton per mile. The total cost of transport of this article would be $40d.$ Let us suppose its price in the market to be $100s.$ The cost of transport would then amount to $3\frac{1}{3}$ per cent. of the market price. Now let us suppose that on the transport of such an article a reduction of 10 per. cent. were made. This would reduce the cost of transport to $36d.$, or 3 per cent. of the market price. The difference to the consumer would, therefore, be only $\frac{1}{3}$ per cent., while the difference to the carrier would be 10 per cent. The loss, therefore, to the railway, would be thirty times the amount of the gain to the consumer. It is clear that such a reduction would be inexpedient.

But suppose the same article to be transported 120 miles, the cost of its transport would then be $240d.$, or $20s.$; and suppose that it is sold in the market for $120s.$, paying the producer $100s.$ and the carrier $20s.$; and suppose this $20s.$ to be the utmost increase of price which the article will bear: a radius of 120 miles would therefore be the limit of the market which the railway can supply to the producer.

Let us again suppose that a reduction of 10 per cent. be made on the transport, and that the rate per mile be reduced from $2d.$ to $1·8d.$ An addition of 20 per cent., or $20s.$, to the cost of production, will now carry the article to a distance of 132 miles instead of 120 miles, because the radius which determines the market of the producer will thereby be increased by 12 additional miles, or in the ratio of 10 per cent.

Although, therefore, a reduction of 10 per cent. on the market price, which in this case would amount to only $2s.$ upon an article costing $120s.$, would have an inappreciable effect on the quantity consumed, yet the extension of the market by the additional distance to which the object can be conveyed would have a very important effect, especially if within such increased radius there existed centres of population where a demand might exist.

But if we suppose these circumstances to prevail in a country, such as certain districts of England, closely reticulated by railways, the increase of the market would be not in the simple ratio of the increased radius of transport, but in the ratio of its square, as has been explained generally in the first chapter of this volume.

The effect which the increase of the average distance to which the traffic is transported has in reducing the cost of transport per mile, is strikingly illustrated in the fourth and seventh columns of the preceding table. By comparing numbers in these columns, we find that the following are the rates at which the expenses of transport per mile are decreased, corresponding to the rates of increase of the distances, upon the actual average distance of 45 miles on the Belgian railways:

Increased Percentage of the present average Distance.	Corresponding Decrease per Cent. of the present Cost of Transport per Mile.
11·1	7·0
22·2	12·4
33·3	16·8
44·4	20·4
55·5	23·9
66·7	26·6
77·8	29·2
88·9	31·0
100·0	32·7
111·1	34·5
122·2	37·2

It follows, therefore, that for traffic generally, but more especially for every description of merchandise and of live stock, a tariff graduated upon the principle of diminishing as the distance transported increases, must be the source of largely augmented profits, and by these means the gross receipts of a railway may be increased, while the *average* amount of the tariff may remain unaltered.

Recurring to the arithmetical symbols which we have adopted to express the gross receipts,

$$R = r \times D \times N,$$

it will be apparent that the tariff may be so regulated that the average value of r shall remain the same, while the tariff imposed on objects carried to considerable distances is diminished, that which is imposed on objects carried to lesser distances being proportionally increased. By such means the number expressed by D, which is the average distance to which the objects of traffic are carried, will be augmented: and if this modification of the tariff be managed with such skill that the multiplier N, expressing the total number of objects booked, shall not be diminished, then the gross receipts, R, will be augmented in the same ratio as the average distance, D, *although no change has taken place in the average amount of the tariff, r.*

It may be contended that the increase which must, in this case, take place in the tariff imposed on short distances, will have the effect of diminishing the number of objects booked for such distances, and that the diminution of tariff which favors objects carried to great distances will not altogether counteract this effect. This may be admitted to be true in some cases, or even generally; but with skillful management the diminution of the multiplier N will not be so great as the increase of the multiplier D, so that the effect of the latter will prevail over the former, and therefore there will still be on the whole an increase.

But even in this case, in which the diminution produced on the multiplier N, or the number of objects booked, will balance the effect of the augmented distance, and therefore the gross receipts will not be increased, the gross profits nevertheless will be augmented; for it has been demonstrated that greater profit is made, other things being the same, on long than on short traffic.

It is not alone by reference to distance, however, that the regulation of the tariff may be rendered conducive to the increase of the gross receipts and profits. A field for the exercise of managerial skill is presented by the prevalence on the railways of a large amount of *empty transport* and incomplete loads. It is well known that traffic has a tendency to prevail more in certain directions than in others; the consequence of which is, that vehicles of transport which travel with complete or considerable loads in one direction, return either empty or with very imperfect loads in the other. In this case it is clear that any objects of transport which might be attached to the empty or incompletely loaded vehicles thus returning, would yield a profit equal to nearly their entire receipts, for in this case the cost of their transport would not exceed the additional fuel, oil, and grease which their weight would cause to be consumed in the engine, and the additional wear and tear which it would produce in the engine, the carriages, and the rails. It has been already shown how infinitely minute and insignificant this expense would be, and therefore any tariff, however trivial, which could be obtained from traffic attached to such vehicles, would be profitable.

The same observations will be applicable, more or less, to the traffic which may form the complement of the incomplete loads.

It has been already explained that, in the case of merchandise-wagons capable of carrying five tons, the actual average load carried by them is only two tons and a quarter. Now the cost which would attend the remaining two tons and three quarters necessary to complete their load would be quite insignificant. A modification of the tariff, therefore, which would have a tendency to accomplish this, must produce a favorable effect in augmenting the gross receipts.

On the Belgian railways great encouragement has, for this reason, been offered to secure complete loads of the goods trains. A liberal reduction of the tariff is offered to all expeditors who will engage wagons for full loads; and this has been attended with most favorable results.

In the case of passenger traffic, great difficulties exist in the solution of the problem to obtain complete loads.

It has been shown that first-class carriages, built to accommodate eighteen passengers, carry on the average only seven; that second-class carriages, capable of accommodating twenty-four passengers, carry only thirteen; and that third-class carriages, having capacity for thirty-two, carry only twenty-one passengers.

The great expense entailed on the railways by this large proportion of empty or imperfectly loaded vehicles, demands serious attention. Although it is evidently impracticable to avoid the evil, its magnitude may be diminished by judicious management.

Something may be accomplished in mitigation of it by a careful classification of the passengers in carriages according to the distances they have to travel; passengers having the same destination being as far as possible placed in the same vehicle. This, combined with a proper distribution of the carrying stock among the stations, and facilities for attaching and detaching the carriages there, without objectionable delay, may do much toward its mitigation.

A part of this evil arises from the passenger coaches of different classes being always independent of each other. Thus, if a single first-class passenger presents himself, no room being available in a first-class carriage composing the train, it will be necessary to attach a first-class carriage, having accommodation for eighteen passengers, and weighing four tons or upward, for his individual accommodation.

Nor is this an extreme or imaginary case, but one which I have frequently witnessed. This evil has been mitigated on some of the continental railways by providing mixed carriages, composed of divisions appropriated to different classes of passengers, one of these being placed in each train for the purpose of receiving the surplus passengers of each class, without the necessity of attaching complete vehicles of the several classes.

Another means of augmenting the receipts, and diminishing the expenses, consists in contriving measures to secure for the engines full loads and long trips. An engine loaded under its power, or working for a less portion of time than is consistent with its capability, wasting fuel and wages, by standing with steam up without work, and in lighting and cleaning more frequently than is indispensable, is another source of expense needlessly increased.

A good system of management will direct its affairs so as to diminish such sources of wasteful expense.

In relation to this, it may be useful here to investigate, so far as there are available data for the purpose, the relation between the mileage of the engines and the receipts, so as to exhibit the average amount of receipts obtained for each mile run. I have exhibited this in the following table, for all the cases of the English railways in which I have been able to obtain the engine mileage; to which I have added some of the foreign railways, to show the comparative results:

	Total Mileage of Engines.	Gross Receipts.	Average Receipts per Mile run by Engines.
	Miles.	*£.*	*s.*
Northwestern Railway, including the Chester and Holyhead, Lancashire and Carlisle, Kendal and Windermere, and North Union.			
For six months ending December 31, 1848..	3,766,115*	1,324,227	7·0
London, Brighton, and South Coast.			
For twelve months ending June 30, 1848...	1,189,295	426,512	7·2
For six months ending December 31, 1848..	691,383	255,303	7·3
,, ,, June 30, 1849.......	593,844	214,062	7·2
Great Western, including Bristol and Exeter, and South Devon.			
For twelve months ending June 30, 1847 ...	2,664,539	979,754	7·4
,, ,, June 30, 1848 ...	2,876,108	1,052,399	7·3
For six months ending December 31, 1848..	1,582,672	571,799	7·2
Belgian Railways.			
For twelve months, 1844.................	1,584,532	442,427	5·6
,, ,, 1845.................	1,694,203	496,128	5·9
,, ,, 1846.................	2,027,014	546,236	5·4
,, ,, 1847.................	2,366,885	593,444	5·0
North of France Railway.			
For twelve months, 1847.................	1,789,152	606,428	6·8
,, ,, 1848.................	1,917,855	592,682	6·2

* This is one-half the engine mileage for the twelve months ending June 30, 1849, which I have assumed here, as in former instances, as the nearest approximation I can obtain to the mileage for the half-year ending December 31, 1848.

The accordance which prevails in the receipts exhibited in the third column of the above table, is most striking and satisfactory. It appears that the average receipts per mile for the distance run by the engines on the English railways is a little more than 7s. per mile.

It will also be observed, that, notwithstanding the increased gauge, and consequently augmented power, of the engines, and capacity of the carriages used upon the Great Western Railway, the receipts per mile are not greater on that line than on the London and Brighton.

The inferior amounts obtained per mile on the Belgian and French railways, may be ascribed partly to the inferior tariff, and partly to the less active traffic.

In the case of an active traffic in goods, these causes of increased expense may be, to a great extent, mitigated. More frequent departures from the chief termini, than are consistent with securing full loads, are not necessary; but the full loads which are thus dispatched consist of wagons having various destinations along the line, at which they are severally detached, and where other wagons are not prepared to be substituted for them. Although, therefore, the goods-wains may start full, they will arrive, and perform a great portion of their trip, very incomplete.

In the case of passenger trains, frequent departures are indispensable for the public accommodation; and it becomes a problem of much difficulty to fix such quantity of departures as, on the whole, will produce the greatest amount of profit to the railway, with all reasonable accommodation to the public. It is clear that the more frequent the departures are, the less complete will be the load, not only of the engines, but of the carriages. But, on the other hand, if the departures were so few as to secure nearly complete loads, then a considerable amount of the traffic would be lost to the railway.

We can not advance a step in investigations of this kind, without being rendered sensible of the disadvantage under which we labor in regard to the English railways. We are left absolutely destitute of all statistical data which could afford the slightest aid in such inquiries.

On foreign railways, however, observations have been made, which indicate some of the laws which govern the circulation both of passengers and goods.

Thus it is found, generally, that the stream of passenger traffic sets in toward all great centres of population, from a certain distance around them, in the early part of the day, and prevails in the contrary direction in the latter part; produced by the necessity of the surrounding population visiting such centres during the day for the purposes of business, and returning to their homes in the afternoon.

This effect is frequently augmented at certain seasons of the year. In great cities, where a considerable portion of the population who are in a condition to use the railway reside, during the summer, in the environs, places of residence are selected adjacent to the different lines of railway; and such persons, being generally engaged in business, arrive by the railway in the cities in the morning, and leave in the afternoon.

It would be desirable to compare the receipts and profits obtained from year to year by the railway traffic, with the capital absorbed by the establishments and stock. We possess no returns by which we are enabled with precision to assign the amount of capital expended on the railways in operation from year to year, as distinguished from those which were merely in progress but unopened. A general average estimate of the cost per mile, however, of the entire length of railway under traffic has been already obtained.

In the following table I have in this manner exhibited the proportion which the receipts have borne to the capital during the six years and a half ending December 31, 1848.

Assuming the working expenses not to be less than 40 per cent. of the receipts, the major limits of the profits from year to year are given in the last column.

	Length of Railway open.	Capital Expended.	Total Receipts.	Per Cent. on Capital.		
				Receipts.	Minor Limit of Expenses.	Major Limit of Profits.
Twelve months ending June 30, 1843.......	*Miles.* 1857	£. 74,280,000	£. 4,535,189	6·1	2·4	3·7
,, 1844.......	1952	78,080,000	5,074,674	6·5	2·6	3·9
,, 1845.......	2148	85,920,000	6,209,714	7·2	2·9	4·3
,, 1846	2441	97,640,000	7,565,569	7·8	3·1	4·7
,, 1847.......	3036	121,440,000	8,510,886	7·0	2·8	4·2
,, 1848.......	3816	152,640,000	9,933,552	6·5	2·6	3·9
Six months ending Dec. 31, 1848	5079	205,160,000	5,744,965	5·6	2·2	3·4

These figures show, that, whatever may be the advantages of particular railways as investments, the aggregate of the whole presents no signal advantages over other enterprises; and that they have been, since 1846, not much more productive to the capitalist than the public funds. It is probable, however, that the depression shown in the results of the last two years may be only temporary; nevertheless, it is evident that the railways, taken in the aggregate, have never yet produced a net profit of 5 per cent.

CHAPTER XIV.

ACCIDENTS ON RAILWAYS.

THE advantages of increased expedition, economy, certainty, and regularity of traveling presented by railways have been regarded by a large part of the public as subject to a serious drawback, in consequence of the terrible character of the accidents which from time to time occur. These disasters have been occasionally attended by circumstances which must naturally operate in a very forcible degree on the imagination of all persons, and powerfully excite the alarm of the timid. To reduce these fears within reasonable limits, it will be only necessary to investigate the actual amount of the risk in railway traveling; and to diminish as much as practicable the amount of that risk it will be necessary to investigate the causes of accidents, and to deduce from these causes such rules for avoiding them as the circumstances of the case shall suggest.

I shall therefore in the present chapter investigate successively,

1. The chances of accident attended with loss of life or bodily injury.
2. The prevailing causes of such accidents.
3. And shall state some plain rules for the greater security of the traveler.

SECT. I.—*The Chances of Accident.*

The accidents which are incidental to railway traveling may be reduced to two classes:

1. Those which arise from causes beyond the control of the sufferer.

2. Those which arise from his own imprudence or want of ordinary caution

The chances of the former admit of calculation as accurate as those by which the average duration of life is ascertained, and which form the basis of the operations of life insurance.

The chances of the latter vary in each individual case, depending on the vigilance, the personal temperament and character, and often on the degree of sobriety and state of mind of the persons exposed to them. Although the occurrence of even these, when considered in the mass, admits of calculation on the general principles of the doctrine of chances,* our present object will be attained by indicating the manner in which individual imprudence and neglect of proper precautions contribute to them, so as to suggest to the unwary traveler what he should do and abstain from doing to avoid accidents which depend solely on himself, and to lessen the chances and degree of suffering from those which are beyond his control.

The frequency, as well as the gravity of each of these classes of accident, depends also on the individuals who suffer. The agents and servants of the railway, who are employed directly and indirectly in the conduct and management of the trains, including those whose duties detain them on the road, as well as those who travel on the trains, are more exposed to danger than the traveler, and it is found that the proportion of fatal accidents is larger with respect to this class than in the case of passengers.

It will therefore, in classifying the accidents, be necessary to distinguish not only those which arise from causes beyond the control of the sufferer from those produced by want of prudence, but also those from which the passenger suffers from those which occur to the agents and servants of the railway.

In the following table (see page 267) the accidents which occurred on the English railways in the years 1847, 8 are thus classified.

Hence it appears that in this period of two years 243 passengers suffered more or less from railway accidents from which

* Some curious investigations and calculations on this subject have been made by M. Quetelet of Brussels, who has even shown that the frequency of murders admits of being reduced to a numerical law, and that the ratio of the number of murders committed with particular weapons is constant. Thus the proportion of homicides by the pistol to homicides by the sword is invariable.

they had no power of protecting themselves, and that of this number 28 were either immediately killed, or died soon afterward in consequence of their wounds.

It further appears, that in the same period 87 agents of the railway were more or less injured by accidents from which it was not in their power to protect themselves, of whom 30 were killed.

The proportion of deaths to the total number injured is therefore much greater among the servants of the company than among the passengers.

While only $11\frac{1}{2}$ per cent. of the passengers injured lost their lives, $34\frac{1}{2}$ per cent. of the servants injured were killed. The cause of this difference of proportion is signally obvious from the fact of the greater exposure of the railway agents, more specially of the engineers and firemen, to the more dangerous effects of accidents.

ANALYSIS of the Railway Accidents for the Two Years ending December 31, 1848.		
	Killed.	Injured.
Passengers suffering from causes beyond their own control	28	215
Passengers suffering from causes which they might have prevented	23	13
Railway servants suffering from causes beyond their own control	30	57
Railway servants suffering from causes which they might have prevented	232	85
Trespassers and strangers suffering from crossing or standing on the railway	96	22
Persons suffering from misconduct of railway servants	2	1
Suicides	2	--
	413	393

But to estimate duly the actual degree of danger incurred in this mode of traveling, the mere numerical amount of the killed and injured is not sufficient.

To estimate the risk of suffering from accident, it will be necessary to compare the number of sufferers with the total amount of railway traveling. In the official reports, the number of accidents has hitherto been compared with the total number of passengers booked; but it is easy to show that such a comparison does not afford a true measure of the risk. By adopting such a measure we should assume that there is the same risk of accident to the passenger who travels ten miles, as to him who travels five hundred miles, which would be an obvious error. The risk of accident to any passenger is, *cæteris paribus*, in the exact proportion of the distance he travels, or, to use a term already adopted, of his mileage.

To calculate the risk, therefore, the number of accidents must be compared, not with the total *number* of passengers booked, but with the total *mileage* of the passengers.

If we find, for example, that in a given time the distance traveled by passengers was equivalent to 500,000 passengers traveling one mile, and that in such period there occurred only one accident attended with loss of life, it will follow that, when a passenger travels one mile, the chances are 500,000 to 1 against encountering a fatal accident. If he travel ten miles, the chances are 50,000 to one against such an accident; and, in general, the probability of such an accident will be augmented in the exact ratio in which the distance traveled is increased.*

In the two years ending the 31st of December, 1848, the total mileage of the passengers on the railways of the United Kingdom, was

$$1,830,184,617 \text{ miles.}$$

The number of accidents to passengers attended with loss of life, arising from causes beyond their own control, in the same period, was 28. Dividing the mileage, therefore by 28, we obtain the quotient,

$$65,363,736.$$

Hence it appears that if a passenger travel one mile, the chances against his suffering an accident fatal to life are

$$65,363,735 \text{ to } 1.$$

---

* More strictly, the chances in these cases would be 499,999 and 49,999 to 1. Of 500,000 balls contained in an urn, 1 is black. Supposing balls to be successively drawn, and returned to the urn after each drawing, the chance of *no* black ball in ten drawings would be $\left(\frac{499,999}{500,000}\right)^{10}$. The chance of one or more black balls is,

$$1 - \left(\frac{499,999}{500,000}\right)^{10} = 1 - \left(1 - \frac{1}{500,000}\right)^{10} = \frac{10}{500,000} = \frac{1}{50,000},$$

very nearly.

I have, in this and like cases, taken the round numbers, as practically exact and more convenient.

CHAP XIV.]   ACCIDENTS ON RAILWAYS.   269

In the same period the number of accidents attended with bodily injury to passengers, arising from causes beyond their own control, was 215. Dividing this in the same manner into the total mileage, we find that the chances against such an accident in traveling one mile are

8,512,486 to 1.

In each case we find the chances for greater distances by dividing these numbers by the distances respectively.

In the subjoined table I have given in the second and third columns the chances against such accidents for all distances under 10,000 miles.

It must be here observed that in this calculation every accident productive of the slightest bodily injury, even the smallest bruise or scratch, is included.

While the numbers registered in these columns will reassure the timid, the solicitude of the humane passenger will be extended to the agents and servants who are employed in conducting the train and in guarding and watching the railway, on whose vigilance and skill depends in a great degree the extremely small amount of risk of the passenger, and to whom, in fact, is transferred a part of that danger to which the passenger himself would otherwise be exposed. It will therefore be satisfactory to calculate the amount of the risk to which each railway passenger exposes the agents by whom the business of transport is conducted.

It appears, by the results given in table, p. 267, that in the two years ending 31st Dec. 1848, the number of accidents fatal to life occurring to railway servants, from causes beyond their own control, was 30, and the number resulting in personal injury was 57. These accidents occurred in conducting both the passenger and the goods business, and ought, therefore, to be shared between them in the ratio of the mileage of the passenger and goods trains.

I have no general data by which this can be ascertained, and it varies very much on different railways. If, however, we take as a mean the business done on the extensive lines of railway worked by the Northwestern Company, I find that the mileage of the passenger engines bears to that of the goods engines the ratio of 5 to 3.

From this it would follow that three-eighths of the accidents ought to be assigned to the goods business. But as the relative frequency of accidents is greater with passenger than with goods trains, we shall assume that five-sixths of all the accidents to railway servants are produced, directly or indirectly, by passenger trains.

It follows, then, that in the two years above mentioned, 25 fatal accidents, and 50 accidents resulting in personal injuries, occurred to railway servants from passenger trains.

During that period, as has been shown, the total passenger transport was equivalent to 1,830,184,617 passengers carried a mile. If we divide this total mileage of the passengers by 25, we obtain the quotient,

$$732,073,847,$$

which is the number of passengers who must travel one mile to cause the death of a railway servant; and if we divide the same mileage by 50, we obtain

$$366,036,923,$$

which is the number who must travel one mile o cause the injury of a railway servant.

But whenever one passenger travels a mile, as many others also travel a mile as make up the average load of a passenger train. There are no general data recorded from which this average load can be accurately deduced, but it may be estimated at about 50 for all the railways, taken one with another.

Hence, wherever one individual travels a mile by railway, 50 passengers travel a mile, and the mileage 50 is performed. To calculate the corresponding number of accidents to railway servants we must, therefore, divide the preceding numbers respectively by 50.

Hence it appears that when a passenger travels a mile, the chances against such a fatal accident are

$$14,641,477 \text{ to } 1;$$

and the chances against an accident producing personal injury are

$$7,320,738 \text{ to } 1.$$

The chances corresponding to greater distances are found by dividing these numbers by the distance traveled.

CHAP. XIV.]   ACCIDENTS ON RAILWAYS.   271

TABLE showing the Number of Chances to One against Accidents producing Loss of Life or bodily Injury to a Railway Passenger in traveling Distances from 10 Miles to 10,000 Miles; and also the Chances against his being the Cause of Loss of Life or bodily Injury to a Railway Servant in such a Journey.*

Distance traveled.	Passenger.		Railway Servant.	
	Loss of Life.	Bodily Injury.	Loss of Life.	Bodily Injury.
Miles.				
10	6,536,374	851,249	1,464,148	732,074
20	3,268,187	525,624	732,074	366,037
30	2,178,791	283,749	488,049	244,024
40	1,634,093	212,812	366,037	183,018
50	1,307,275	170,250	292,829	146,415
60	1,089,396	141,875	244,024	122,012
70	933,768	121,607	209,164	104,582
80	817,047	106,406	183,018	91,509
90	726,264	94,582	162,683	81,341
100	653,637	85,125	146,415	73,207
120	544,698	70,937	122,012	61,006
140	466,884	60,303	104,582	52,291
160	408,523	53,203	91,509	45,754
180	363,132	47,291	81,341	40,670
200	326,819	42,562	73,207	36,604
250	261,455	35,050	58,566	29,283
300	217,879	28,375	48,805	24,402
350	186,754	24,321	41,833	20,916
400	163,409	21,281	36,604	18,302
450	145,253	18,916	32,536	16,268
500	130,727	17,025	29,283	14,641
550	118,843	15,477	26,621	13,310
600	108,939	14,187	24,402	12,201
650	100,559	13,096	22,525	11,263
700	93,377	12,161	20,916	10,458
750	87,152	11,350	19,522	9,761
800	81,705	10,641	18,302	9,151
850	76,898	10,015	17,225	8,613
900	72,626	9,458	16,268	8,134
950	68,804	8,961	15,412	7,706
1,000	65,363	8,513	14,641	7,320
1,500	43,575	5,675	9,761	4,880
2,000	32,682	4,256	7,321	3,660
2,500	26,145	3,405	5,856	2,928
3,000	21,788	2,837	4,880	2,440
3,500	18,675	2,432	4,183	2,092
4,000	16,340	2,128	3,660	1,830
4,500	14,525	1,892	3,254	1,627
5,000	13,073	1,702	2,928	1,464
5,500	11,884	1,548	2,662	1,331
6,000	10,894	1,419	2,440	220
6,500	10,056	1,310	2,252	126
7,000	9,338	1,216	2,092	045
7,500	8,715	1,135	1,952	976
8,000	8,170	1,064	1,830	915
8,500	7,689	1,002	1,722	861
9,000	7,262	946	1,627	813
9,500	6,880	896	1,541	771
10,000	6,536	851	1,464	732

* The numbers given in this table are only approximative, but sufficiently exact for all practical purposes.

To illustrate the application of this table, let us suppose it to be required to ascertain the risk of life or bodily injury to a passenger, and also the chances against his being the cause of death or injury to a railway servant in traveling 250 miles. On finding 250 in the first column, we find that the chances against loss of life are

>   For passenger,   261,455 to 1 ;
>   For railway servant,   58,566 to 1 ;

and against any bodily injury not resulting in death,

>   For passenger,   34,050 to 1 ;
>   For railway servant, 29,283 to 1.

On the foreign railways, the ratio of accidents to the quantity of traffic is still less, owing to the less crowded state of the lines. On the Belgian railways, during the three years ending 1st Dec., 1846, there were but three fatal accidents to passengers arising from causes beyond their own control, and the total passenger mileage in these three years was,

> 239,629,541 miles.

The chances against loss of life in traveling a mile were, therefore,

> 79,876,383 to 1.

On the railways of the United Kingdom the chances are,

> 65,363,735 to 1.

The Belgian railways are, therefore, subject to less risk than the English, in the ratio of 65 to 79.

On the French railways accidents have been still more rare. One fatal accident occurred many years ago on the Paris and Versailles Railway, on which occasion a train took fire, and appalling consequences followed. Another serious accident occurred on the Fampoux embankment of the Northern Railway, in 1846. These, however, stand almost alone.

In the two years ending 31st Dec., 1848, there was not a single fatal accident to a passenger reported on any French railway.

It may not be uninteresting to put in juxtaposition with this the returns of accidents produced by ordinary horse-coaches, traveling in Paris and its environs:

Year.	Killed	Wounded.
1834	4	134
1835	12	214
1836	5	220
1837	11	361
1838	19	366
1839	9	384
1840	14	394
Total	74	2073

SECT. II.—*The Causes of Accidents.*

However insignificant may be the proportion of the number of persons injured to the total amount of passenger traffic, it may not be without interest or utility to inquire into the causes which produced these accidents.

The causes which are not dependent on the imprudence of the sufferers are, generally, either collision of the passenger train with some other carriages or wagons, or the escape of the train, or some part of it, from the rails.

The English railways are in general constructed with double lines, the train observing the common rule of the road, and keeping always on the left-hand line. The consequence of this is, that, in regular work, all trains upon the same line move in the same direction. The collision of one train with another, therefore, can only take place by a faster train overtaking a slower, or a train running into one which is at rest.

It is evident, therefore, that, if all trains moved with the same speed, and all stopped at the same stations, no collisions could ever happen, except when a train should be retarded or stopped by accident, or in the case of a vehicle being improperly left standing on the line.

The probabilities of collision will therefore depend on the differences between the speed with which the several trains travel, and the differences between the number of stations at which they stop.

But, on railways as worked at present, it is impracticable to maintain uniformity of speed. Passenger and goods traffic being necessarily worked on the same line of rails, and the latter being carried at less speed than the former, a source of danger is produced. If the present enormous amount of transport had been foreseen when railways were in an early stage of their progress, it might have been a question for consideration whether it would not have been advantageous to construct the trunk railways with three lines of rails, reserving one line exclusively for the goods traffic. This would have been infinitely more politic than augmenting the capacity of the railway by increasing the width of the rails, and, consequently, the magnitude and weight of the engines and vehicles of transport. But the railways being constructed, it is now too late, and nothing remains to be done but to adopt the most efficient precautions against those collisions, the probability of which is augmented with the frequency of the trains, and the differences of their average speed.

The accommodation of the public requires frequent departures, great expedition, and means of arriving at numerous intermediate points of the lines. These demands can not be satisfied without calling into existence all the conditions which are productive of the danger of collision.

To satisfy the urgent call for great expedition, express trains are dispatched at extraordinary speed, stopping only at chief stations. To satisfy the want of intercommunication with the intermediate stations, trains are dispatched which stop at all the stations; and as the stations, in the average, are not four miles asunder, these trains must be in a state either of retarded or accelerated motion. They scarcely get up their speed after starting from one station, before they are obliged to slacken their pace, in order to stop at the next. The average speed of such trains is therefore comparatively small.

Between these and the express trains, which present the extremes of speed, there are several which move at intermediate average rates, stopping less frequently than the one, and more so than the other, and, when at full speed, proceeding with a less velocity than the express trains.

When all these circumstances are taken into account, and when it is also considered that, on some of the great trunk lines, such as the Northwestern, as many as fifty trains pass over the same rails every twenty-four hours, more than the half of which are worked during the day, and therefore succeed each other at very short intervals, the wonder is, not that collisions occasionally occur, but that a movement so crowded and complicated can be conducted at all, without most imminent danger.

The most frequent source of accidents from collision, arises from single wagons or trucks being left standing upon the rails.

When express trains have to be stopped, the steam must be cut off, and the brakes applied at a considerable distance from the place where they come to rest. Hence arises the greater liability of accidents by collision with these trains If an obstacle is observed upon the railway by the engine-driver, it must be noticed at a distance so great as to render it possible to stop the train, otherwise collision must take place.

Next in frequency to accidents from collision, are those which arise from the engine or the vehicles escaping from the rails. The causes which produce this class of accidents are very various.

The most frequent are impediments left on the rails, such as blocks of wood, bars of iron, spare sleepers or rails. The engine encountering obstacles of this kind is generally thrown off, dragging with it one or more of the carriages.

Cattle from adjacent fields, through deficient fences, have sometimes got upon the road, and the engine encountering them has run over them and been thrown off.

A wheel or axle of the engine, tender, or any of the carriages breaking, is sometimes the cause of escape from the rails. A defect in the rails themselves is not unfrequently the cause of this class of accidents. This is especially liable to occur at a joint chair, that is to say, a chair where the ends of two successive rails are united. It frequently happens that one of these rails is considerably above or below the other, or that the rails are not sufficiently fastened in the chair. The impact of the wheel of the engine on such a defective joint, may either immediately break the rail, or so weaken it that one of the succeeding carriage-wheels will break it, and the carriages thus escape from the rails.

Another not unfrequent cause of accidents is the neglect of the points and switches, a name given to a part of the mechanism by which trains are enabled to pass from one line of rails to another, or from either line into the sidings.

When such passage is intended, a certain change is made in the position of the points and switches by a person employed for this purpose on the line, and after the train passes from the line the switches are restored to their usual position. If any neglect take place in this operation, considerable danger will ensue to the trains which next pass.

In order to ascertain the proportion in which these causes of accident respectively operate, I have taken indiscriminately, from the returns of accidents, 100 cases of which the following is the analysis:

Accidents	from collision	56
,,	broken wheel or axle	18
,,	defective rail	14
,,	by switches	5
,,	impediments lying on the road	3
,,	off rails by cattle on line	3
,,	bursting boiler	1
		100

Hence it appears that 56 per cent. of these accidents arise from collision. Next to these comes the escape from the rails by the breaking of a wheel or axle, or by defective rails, which together make up 32 per cent., the remaining causes operating in small proportions.

Since more than half the total number of fatal accidents which occur upon railways arise from collision, it is important that the attention of railway companies be more specially directed to precautions against this source of danger.

Before a collision takes place, the engine-driver and others in management of the following train, have, or ought to have, the means of observing the object in advance of them, with which the collision is about to take place. If it be possible to bring the train to rest before it can pass over the length of road between the point where the obstacle has been observed, and the point where such obstacle would be overtaken, the collision will be prevented. This possibility will depend upon the proportion which the number of brakes and brakesmen upon the train bears to its weight and speed. It is clear, therefore, that in all cases the number of brakes provided should have reference to the magnitude and speed of the train.

It is found by experience that the distance within which a train of given weight can be brought to rest by a given number of brakes, will be in proportion to the square of its speed, that is to say, with a double speed it will require four times the number of brakes; with a treble speed, nine times the number of brakes; and so on.

In the case of an accident which occurred near Wolverton, on the 5th of June, 1847, it was found impossible to bring a train of 19 carriages to rest within a distance of 540 yards, the speed of the train being about 25 miles an hour. In this case a collision took place, by which seven persons were killed : on an inquiry it was found that this train was provided with three brakes, one upon the tender and two upon the carriages.

Inquiries suggested by this and other similar accidents, induced the Board of Trade to propose a rule to be observed by railway companies, that a brake should be attached to every fourth carriage.

A similar rule was imposed by the French government, in February, 1848, on the trains working on the railways of that country.

Since, however, the brake power necessary to stop a train is increased in so large a ratio with the speed, a still greater number of brakes would be necessary with a fast train, such as the express trains, each carriage of which ought to be provided with an independent brake and brakesman. This would certainly cause a considerable increase in the working expenses of the faster class of trains, but the public safety is a matter of too great importance to be postponed to considerations of this kind.

In attempting to avoid one source of danger another is often produced. When an obstacle is seen on the rails before a train moving with great speed, all means must of course be used to bring the train suddenly to rest. But if this be not done with great caution and skill, danger may be produced even more serious than that from which it is attempted to escape. The means of stopping a train are, the brake on the the tender, the brakes on the vehicles composing it, and, in fine, *reversing the action of the engine.* This process consists in so changing the motion of the slides, that the steam shall obstruct instead of accelerating the pistons. In this way the whole force of the steam is suddenly made to resist the progressive motion of the engine.

This is a dangerous process. The progress of the engine is arrested by an agent which does not act on the vehicles which follow it. They are consequently urged against the engine and against each other with all the force of which the engine is deprived by the back action of the steam. The effect is nearly the same as if an engine acting behind the train suddenly pushed the train against the engine in front. The effect of this is an obvious tendency to drive the intermediate carriages off the rails by *doubling up the train.*

Before reversing the engine, or even applying the brake to the tender, it is therefore always advisable to warn the brakesmen to apply the brakes to the vehicles composing the train. This being done, and the brake being then applied to the tender, there is less danger in reversing the steam on the engine.

But it unfortunately happens that in the emergencies in which these extreme measures are demanded, there is rarely time to observe these precautions. The prudence of providing a signal on the tender which shall be within view of the brakesmen, and seats for the latter from which they can always see such signal, is so obvious that it need not here be enlarged on.

We must not dismiss this subject without noticing the ingenious application of detonating substances, now called *fog-signals*.

These are detonating balls, which on being crushed explode with the report of a pistol. When a train is stopped on the line by an accident, or in general when an obstacle is found upon the railway from any unexpected cause, and which can not be immediately removed, if there be a fog at the time, or any other cause which may prevent the driver of a following train from seeing the obstacle, the guard or policeman runs back along the line and places these balls on the rails at certain distances, so that when a train approaches it causes them successively to explode in rolling over them, and the driver thus receives warning to stop.

The evil consequences resulting from collision are frequently aggravated by the manner in which the carriages or wagons composing the trains are connected with or adapted to each other. The mode of connecting the successive carriages forming a train is as follows. From the end of the frame supporting each carriage project two strong iron rods, which rest against spiral springs, and which are terminated by circular cushions about a foot in diameter, called buffers. When two successive coaches are brought into contact, these buffers ought to meet each other so that their centres should coincide. This requires that the buffers of all the carriages should have the same gauge, that is to say, that there should be the same distance between their centres; and, secondly, that they should be at the same height above the rails. If this be not the case, a collision would have the effect of causing one carriage to push the other either aside or upward, as the case might be; aside if the centre of the buffer deviated horizontally, and upward if it deviated vertically.

In any case there would be a tendency of the coaches to throw each other off the rails.

The successive coaches forming a train were originally held together by a chain, which was necessarily always a little slack, so that when the power of the engine was driving the train, the buffers were not in close contact, and whenever the train stopped, or even slackened its speed, the hinder carriages ran against the foremost one with a collision, the force of which was proportional to the difference of their speeds.

This mode of connection was replaced by a coupling screw, by means of which the carriages are drawn together, so that the buffers are pressed into close contact, and their springs a little compressed.

In this manner the train is formed into one complete column, and the change of speed to which it is subject does not produce the partial collision just mentioned.

One of the means, therefore, of diminishing the chances of injuries resulting from collision is to provide against the occurrence of eccentric buffers, and to insure the proper coupling of the trains.

Although, in most cases of derailment,* it is the engine which escapes from the rails, yet it occasionally happens that, while the engine maintains its position, one or more of the carriages forming the train escape.

This happens frequently when an axle or wheel breaks, but it sometimes happens that a defect of the rail throws a carriage off after the engine and preceding carriages have passed over it.

On the 16th September, 1847, on the Manchester and Liverpool Railway, the last carriage of the express train, having two passengers in it, was derailed, the other carriages being undisturbed. and was dragged a considerable distance before the engine-driver was made aware of the accident. The two passengers it contained were killed.

This accident was ascribed to a defect in the rails. It was supposed that the weight of the engine being too great for the strength of the road, it had deranged the rails in passing over them, and that the succeeding carriages increasing the injury, the displacement only became great enough to derail the wheels on the arrival of the last coach at the point.

* I have adopted this word from the French: it expresses an effect which is so often necessary to mention, but for which we have not yet had any term in our railway nomenclature. By *déraillement* is meant the escape of the wheels of the engine or carriage from the rails; and the verb *to derail* or *to be derailed* may be used in a corresponding sense

This and some other accidents have suggested to the railway authorities the expediency of adopting some method by which a communication can be made between the several carriages forming the train and the engine-driver. If, in the above instance, the engine-driver had been made aware of the accident at the moment of the derailment, it is probable that such fatal results might not have occurred.

A case will be mentioned hereafter, in which a private carriage caught fire by a cinder projected from the funnel of the engine falling on its roof. The carriage continued to burn until the arrival of the train at the next station, the engine-driver and conductor being ignorant of the accident.

Previously to this, the necessity of some means of watching a train, and of notifying promptly to the engine-driver the occurrence of any accident, had attracted the attention of the government commissioners, and they consulted some of the principal railway companies on the most desirable means of remedying the evil.

The Great Western Company proposed to fix at the back of the tender a seat for a conductor, in a sufficiently high position to see along the roofs of the carriages, so as to have a perfect view of the entire side length of the train, and a means of passing from side to side of the tender, so as to get a view of each side of the train. Such a conductor, from his proximity to the engine, could immediately communicate with the driver, and each guard upon the coaches of the train could communicate with such conductor by signals.

The Northwestern Company proposed that the under guard should always stand in his van next to the engine, with his face to the train, so as to observe any signal of distress, irregularity, or derangement among the carriages which the chief guard, stationed at the rear of the train, might make. A communication between the under guard and the engineman was only necessary to complete this arrangement, and the company accordingly ordered that means should be provided by which the under guard should be enabled at pleasure to open the whistle of the engine.

The late Colonel Brandreth had interviews with some of the most eminent railway engineers, with a view to obtain some additional protection for the traveling public, by contriving a method, not only for securing the constant watching of the trains while on their journey, but also to provide the passengers with means, in case of accident or sudden illness, of communicating with a guard, and of enabling the guard to communicate with the engineman, for the purpose, when necessary, of stopping the train.

There could be no difficulty in providing means by which any passenger could at his pleasure sound the whistle of the engine, so as to give the engine-driver notice to stop; but the government commissioners considered that it would be objectionable to give a passenger a power to stop the train at will, though it was admitted that it would be extremely desirable to establish a practicable and sure communication between the passengers in each coach with a guard, and to provide the latter with means of communicating with the engine-driver. This subject is still under consideration of the commissioners and the companies.

While noticing the subject of railway accidents arising from causes beyond the control of the passengers, or those who have the management of the trains, it would be an injustice to a most meritorious and generally intelligent class of persons not to acknowledge the zeal, courage, skill, and good conduct of the engine-drivers, conductors, and stokers, as a body. All who have had opportunities of experience in railway transport will feel the justice of such a tribute in the exact proportion of the extent of their experience. Innumerable instances might be offered of admirable judgment and presence of mind exhibited by this class of men in the emergencies which arise in railway traveling.

An incident which occurred on the Chester and Holyhead Railway may be mentioned as one among numbers in attestation of this, and in which, although the promptness and presence of mind of the engineer were not successful in effecting the safety of the passengers, they were not the less admirable.

On the 24th of May, 1847, a fatal accident occurred to a train in crossing the bridge over the river Dee. The train consisted of the engine and tender, weighing 30 tons, followed by three passenger carriages, a luggage van, and another passenger carriage, containing in all 25 passengers, the gross weight of the train being 60 tons.

The train proceeded safely over the first and second arches, and the engine reached the middle of the third arch to a point about 50 feet from the abutments of the bridge. At that point the engine-driver felt the railway sinking under him. With admirable promptitude he instantly opened the steam valve to the fullest extent of its power, giving to the train a sudden pull, so as to endeavor to clear the bridge before the catastrophe, of the imminence of which he was instantly conscious, should occur.

His purpose was but partially successful. The engine cleared the bridge as the railway sunk under it, and dragged the tender with it. The fireman, who was upon the tender, was thrown off upon the side of the railway beyond the end of the bridge, and killed. The passenger coaches had not cleared the bridge when it sunk under them, and their connection with the tender was broken. The carriages which had the passengers were precipitated into the river from a height of 36 feet above the surface of the water, the depth of which was 10 feet.

It appeared afterward that the tender in following the engine had been derailed, and was dragged along, rubbing hard against the parapet wall at the end of the bridge. It was left standing apart at 50 feet from the water's edge and 3 feet off the rails, the engine having broken away from it, and proceeded with the driver, the only individual who escaped, to the adjacent station.

Having investigated the circumstances which produce that class of accidents against which the sufferer can not effectually protect himself by measures of precaution, it remains now to notice those which arise from imprudence, or from the want of that vigilance and care on the part of the traveler, which the very nature of railway transport renders necessary.

The railway commissioners publish periodically reports of all accidents attended with personal injury which take place on railways. The most certain method of ascertaining the manner in which imprudence or negligence operates in the production of these disasters, will be to take from the reports those accidents which have occurred to passengers, and to classify them according to their causes. I have accordingly taken indiscriminately a hundred such occurrences, and have classified them in the following table:

ANALYSIS of 100 Accidents produced by Imprudence of Passengers.

Causes.	Results.		
	Killed.	Injured.	Total.
Sitting or standing in improper place, attitude, or position	17	11	28
Getting out of carriage while train in motion	17	7	24
Getting into carriage while train in motion	10	6	16
Jumping out to recover hat blown off, or parcel dropped	8	5	13
Crossing the railway incautiously	11	1	2
Getting out on wrong side	3	3	6
Handing an article into a train in motion	1	0	1
	67	33	100

Sect. III.—*Precautions against Accidents.*

From what has been stated and explained it will be evident that of all the means of locomotion which human invention has as yet devised, railway traveling is the safest in an almost infinite degree. Indeed, the risk to life and limb, when reduced to a numerical statement, seems to be evanescent. Nevertheless the apprehension of danger in this mode of traveling entertained by timid persons, and even by some who scarcely merit that appellation, is not inconsiderable.

This may arise partly from the circumstance of the public not being generally aware of the smallness of the amount of the danger which has been here described, but in a greater degree from the terrific results of some of the rare accidents which have occurred.

In the modes of traveling used before the prevalence of railways, accidents to life and limb were frequent, but in general they were individually so unimportant as not to attract notice, or to find a place in the public journals. In the case of railways, however, where large numbers are carried in the same train, and simultaneously exposed to danger, accidents, though more rare, are sometimes attended with appalling results. Much notice is therefore drawn to them. They are commented on in the journals, and public alarm is excited.

Notwithstanding the smallness of the amount of risk, yet, as in many cases the danger of accident beyond the control of the passenger may be diminished by the adoption of proper precautions, and in all cases the causes of danger arising from his own ignorance or neglect may be wholly removed, it may be beneficial to give in a succinct form short rules, by the observance of which the traveler will render still less the amount of that risk already so small.

With this view I have put together the following series of plain, intelligible rules, founded partly upon rather a large personal experience in railway traveling in every quarter of the globe where this species of locomotion has been adopted; and in order to render these rules the less arbitrary, and illustrate the utility of their observance, I have annexed to each of them examples of the injurious consequences resulting from their neglect, such examples being accompanied by the date, time, and place of their occurrence.

PLAIN RULES

FOR

RAILWAY TRAVELERS

RULE I.

NEVER ATTEMPT TO GET OUT OF A RAILWAY CARRIAGE WHILE IT IS MOVING, NO MATTER HOW SLOWLY.

Illustration.

It is a peculiarity of railway locomotion that the speed, when not very rapid, always appears to the unpracticed passenger much less than it is. A railway train moving at the rate of a fast stage-coach seems to go scarcely as fast as a person might walk. To this circumstance (which is explained by the extreme smoothness of the motion) is to be ascribed the great frequency of accidents arising from passengers attempting to descend from trains while still in motion. This is the most common cause of that class of accidents on railways, which are owing to want of due caution on the part of the passenger. I have witnessed many accidents of this class, and the reports of the Railway Board abound with them.

Examples.

Dublin and Drogheda........	July 4, 1844.	Jumping out before the train stopped, fell with his hand on the rail, over which the carriage-wheels passed.
Grand Junction..............	July 25, 1844.	Jumping out while in motion, broke his leg.
Liverpool and Manchester....	August 26, 1844.	Jumping off before train had stopped. Killed.
Manchester and Birmingham.	Sept. 9, 1844.	Ditto.
Manchester and Leeds.......	Oct. 10, 1844.	Ditto.
Glasgow, Garnkirk, and Coat-Bridge....................	Oct. 30, 1844.	Ditto, injured.
North Union	Aug. 23, 1846.	Ditto, broke his leg.
Grand Junction..............	August 7, 1846.	Ditto, killed.
Great Western	Aug. 17, 1846.	Ditto, ditto.
Midland	Oct. 31, 1846.	Ditto, ditto.
Sheffield, Ashton, and Manchester	Jan. 21, 1846.	Ditto, ditto

ACCIDENTS ON RAILWAYS.

Dundee and Arbroath	July 22, 1846.	Ditto, severely injured.
Edinburgh and Glasgow	Feb. 16, 1846.	Ditto, killed.
Northwestern	June, 1847.	Ditto, arm crushed by wheels.
London and Southwestern	Jan. 9, 1847.	Ditto, killed.
East Lancaster	April 14, 1847.	Ditto, both legs broken.
Ditto	May 29, 1847.	Ditto, killed.
Northwestern	Feb. 19, 1848.	Ditto, ditto.
Newcastle and Carlisle	April 5, 1847.	Ditto, leg crushed.
Northwestern	Feb. 1, 1847.	Ditto, killed.
Great North of England	Feb. 17, 1845.	Ditto, ditto.
Manchester and Birmingham	Feb. 18, 1845.	Ditto, injured.
Midland	Oct. 27, 1845.	Ditto, killed.
Ditto	Oct. 31, 1845.	Ditto, ditto.
Stockton and Darlington	Feb. 18, 1845.	Ditto, ditto.
Northwestern	Feb. 1, 1847.	Ditto, ditto.
Dublin and Kingstown	Nov. 6, 1847.	Ditto, ditto

RULE II.

NEVER ATTEMPT TO GET INTO A RAILWAY CARRIAGE WHEN IT IS IN MOTION, NO MATTER HOW SLOW THE MOTION MAY SEEM TO BE.

Examples.

London and Blackwall	July 13, 1846.	Attempting to get upon a train after it had started. Killed.
London and Birmingham	April 17, 1846.	Ditto, ditto.
Newcastle and Berwick (including Newcastle and North Shields)	Feb. 14, 1847.	Ditto, ditto.
London and Brighton	Sept. 17, 1848.	Ditto, arm broken.
Newcastle and Carlisle	June 23, 1846.	Ditto, foot crushed.
London and Blackwall	July 18, 1846.	Ditto, killed.
Manchester and Leeds	Feb. 8, 1847.	Ditto, broke his leg.
Dublin and Kingstown	March 4, 1846.	Ditto, leg fractured.
London and Birmingham	August 3. 1844.	Ditto, killed.
Southwestern	Nov. 3, 1848.	Ditto, ditto.
Bolton and Preston	April 23, 1844.	Ditto, broke his leg.
Midland	Feb. 5, 1848.	Ditto, killed.
North Union	Aug. 23, 1846.	Ditto, ditto.
Dublin and Kingstown	Dec. 26, 1845.	Ditto, injured.
Edinburgh and Glasgow	May 16, 1845.	Ditto, ditto.
London and Brighton	July 15, 1845.	Ditto, killed.
Midland	July 15, 1845.	Ditto, ditto.
Manchester and Leeds	Feb. 8, 1847.	Ditto, leg fractured.
Lancashire and Yorkshire	Nov. 20, 1847.	Ditto, killed.

RULE III.

NEVER SIT IN ANY UNUSUAL PLACE OR POSTURE.

Illustration.

On some lines of railway seats are provided on the roofs of the carriages. These are to be avoided. Those who occupy them sometimes inadvertently stand up, and when the train passes under a bridge they are struck by the arch. Guards and brakesmen, whose duty brings them to these positions, and who are disciplined to exercise caution, are nevertheless frequent sufferers from this.

Examples.

Newcastle and Carlisle	Sept. 2, 1846	Sitting on top, stood up as the train was approaching an archway, was struck by it. Killed.
Manchester and Sheffield	March 5, 1847.	Struck by a bridge. Killed
North Union	Jan. 6, 1847.	Ditto, ditto.
Southeastern	Jan. 30, 1846.	Ditto, ditto.
Bristol and Birmingham	July 11, 1846.	Ditto, ditto.
Glasgow and Ayr	May 16, 1844.	Ditto, ditto.
Manchester and Birmingham.	May 31, 1844.	Ditto, injured.

Illustration.

Passengers should beware of leaning out of the carriage window, or of putting out their arm, or if a second-class carriage, as sometimes happens, has no door, they should take care not to put out their leg.

Examples.

Preston and Wyre	April 18, 1844.	Leaning out of carriage, struck by signal board. Wounded.
Manchester, Bolton, and Bury	July 26, 1846.	Leaning out of second-class carriage, struck by iron column supporting a bridge. Killed.
Grand Junction	July 20, 1846.	Sitting improperly upon the side rail, fell off. Killed.
Hull and Selby	April 17, 1846.	Fell off, while reaching over to get his coat. Arm broken.
Edinburgh and Glasgow	June 9, 1847.	Climbing from one compartment of a carriage to another, fell. Killed.
Manchester and Leeds	Sept. 1, 1846.	Attempting to get over the side of the carriage, instead of by the doorway. Leg broken.
Bodmin and Wadebridge	Aug. 3, 1844.	Jumping from one carriage to another, fell between. Killed.
Midland	July 15, 1846.	Two passengers, imprudently standing on the seat, thrown off. Both killed.
Liverpool and Manchester	June 15, 1845.	Fell, attempting to pass from one carriage to another. Injured.
Grand Junction	August 8, 1845.	Fell off the buffer of a wagon. Injured.
Preston and Wyre	Aug. 8, 1845.	Improperly sitting on the side of a carriage, fell off. Killed.
York and North Midland	Nov. 2, 1845.	Fell from the foot-board of a carriage in motion. Killed.
Dublin and Kingstown	Nov. 25, 1845.	Over-reaching herself, fell from a train in motion. Injured.
Eastern Counties	March 1, 1845.	Struck head against a signal post while leaning over. Killed.
Stockton and Darlington	April 14, 1845.	Leaning over, struck a wagon. Injured.
Dundee and Perth	July 24, 1847.	Struck by a bridge, on the roof. Killed.
Northwestern	Dec. 26, 1847.	Upon step of tender, after the train got into motion, jumping off. Killed.
Newcastle and Carlisle	Aug. 22, 1847.	Got upon step of carriage, before train stopped, fell. Injured.
Lancashire and Yorkshire	June 19, 1848.	Riding on top, contrary to orders, came in contact with a bridge. Killed.
South Staffordshire	July 8, 1848.	Sitting on the bar of window, fell out, fracturing leg and head.
York and North Midland	Aug. 28, 1848.	Seated on the edge of an open carriage, lost his balance, and fell between the carriages. Arm broken

CHAP. XIV.   ACCIDENTS ON RAILWAYS.   287

RULE IV.

IT IS AN EXCELLENT GENERAL MAXIM IN RAILWAY TRAVELING TO REMAIN IN YOUR PLACE WITHOUT GOING OUT AT ALL UNTIL YOU ARRIVE AT YOUR DESTINATION. WHEN THIS CAN NOT BE DONE, GO OUT AS SELDOM AS POSSIBLE.

RULE V.

NEVER GET OUT AT THE WRONG SIDE OF A RAILWAY CARRIAGE.

Illustration.

All who are accustomed to railway traveling know that the English railways in general consist of two lines of rails, one commonly called the *up line*, and the other the *down line*. The rule of the road is the same as on common roads. The trains always keep the line of rails on the left of the engine-driver as he looks forward. The consequence of this is, that trains moving in opposite directions are never on the same line, and between these there can never be a collision.

The doors of the carriages which are on your right as you look toward the engine open upon the space in the middle of the railway between the two lines of rails. The passenger should never attempt to leave the carriage by these doors; if he do, he is liable to be struck down or run over by trains passing on the adjacent line of rails. If he leave the carriage by the left-hand door, he descends on the side of the railway out of danger.

On quitting a train under such circumstances, immediately retire to the distance of several feet from the edge of the line, so as to avoid being struck by the steps or other projecting parts of carriages passing.

Example.

Northwestern	Jan. 12, 1847.	Got out of the train on the wrong side, was run over by another train which was passing at the time. Killed.
Southeastern	June 6, 1848.	Ditto, leg broken.
Manchester and Leeds	Jan. 23, 1845.	Ditto, injured.
Southeastern	June 6, 1848.	Ditto, leg broken.
Ditto	Dec. 25, 1848.	Ditto, killed.

RULE VI.

NEVER PASS FROM ONE SIDE OF THE RAILWAY TO THE OTHER, EXCEPT WHEN IT IS INDISPENSABLY NECESSARY TO DO SO, AND THEN NOT WITHOUT THE UTMOST PRECAUTION.

Illustration.

Care should be taken before crossing the line to look *both ways*, to see that no train is approaching. The risk is not merely that of a train coming upon you before you can pass to the other side. You slip or trip, or otherwise accidentally fall, and a train may be upon you before you can raise yourself and get out of its way.

Precaution in this case is especially necessary at a point where the line is curved, and where you can not command a view to any considerable distance. It is true that the noise of the train generally gives notice of its approach, but this can not always be depended on, as the wind sometimes renders it inaudible.

In crossing a railway at a place where there are sidings and numerous points (which is always the case at and near stations), the feet are liable to be caught between the rails and points, and in such cases it has happened very frequently that the person thus impeded is run over by a train before he is able to disengage himself.

Passengers waiting at stations for the arrival of a train, or having descended from a train which has stopped and waiting to remount, stand in need of the greatest caution. The refreshment-room is sometimes on the side of the road opposite to that on which the train stops, in which case it can only be arrived at by crossing the line.

Examples.

Northwestern	Jan. 6, 1848.	Standing on the line at a station, was run over, and killed.
Manchester and Leeds	Feb. 27, 1847.	Attempted to cross in front of an approaching engine, and was run over; he had been previously warned not to make the attempt. Killed.
Midland	Jan. 26, 1847.	While incautiously crossing the line, knocked down by an engine. Leg broken.
Ulster	March 31, 1847.	Standing on the line at a station, run over by a passing train. One leg had to be amputated, and otherwise severely injured.
London and Brighton	June 29, 1846.	Waiting for a train, was crossing the railway, and fell, it is supposed with fright, on seeing the train approaching. The station-clerk, on perceiving her situation, hurried to her assistance, and while endeavoring to remove her, the train went over and killed both.
Manchester and Birmingham.	Oct. 31, 1846.	Waiting at station, was run over while crossing the rails. Killed.
Newcastle and Darlington	June 15, 1846.	Waiting at a station for a train, fell asleep on the edge of the platform, and was struck by a passing goods train. Killed.

CHAP. XIV.]   ACCIDENTS ON RAILWAYS.   289

York and Newcastle......... March 26, 1847. Foot caught in the points, which held him fast until the engine went over him. Killed.
Eastern Counties........... May 8, 1846. Attempting to cross the line, in order to prevent one of her children getting upon it from the opposite side was run over and killed.

Illustration.

It frequently happens that while the attention of a person crossing a line is directed to a train approaching from one direction, which he thinks there is time to avoid, he is run over by a train, from which his attention has been withdrawn, coming from the opposite direction.

Examples.

Caledonian (Glasgow, Garnkirk, and Coatbridge line) March 15, 1847. Run over by a train while his attention was directed to another train coming from the opposite direction. Killed.
North Union .... Oct. 2, 1846. Ditto, ditto.
Leeds and Thirsk .. .. Feb. 14, 1848. Ditto, ditto.
Manchester and Leeds .... Oct. 29, 1846. Two, ditto, ditto.
East Lancaster .... Oct. 19, 1846. Ditto, ditto.
Midland .... Dec 30, 1847 Having left the train, attempted to cross the line, and was crushed by the step of the break-van against the platform. Killed.
Northwestern .... Sept. 11, 1845. Attempting to cross the line in front of an approaching train, although warned not to do so, was killed.

RULE VII.

EXPRESS TRAINS ARE ATTENDED WITH MORE DANGER THAN ORDINARY TRAINS. THOSE WHO DESIRE THE GREATEST DEGREE OF SECURITY SHOULD USE THEM ONLY WHEN GREAT SPEED IS REQUIRED.

Illustration.

The principal source of danger from express trains arises not so much from their extreme speed as from their rate of progress being *different* from that of the general traffic of the line. If all trains, without exception, moved with exactly the same speed, no collision by one overtaking another could occur. The more they depart from this uniformity the more likely are collisions. Now the speed of express trains is both exceptional and extreme. Inasmuch as it is exceptional, they are likely to overtake the slower and regular trains, if these be retarded even in the least degree by any accidental cause; and inasmuch as it is extreme, they are more difficult to be stopped in time to prevent a collision in such a contingency. If a collision occur, the effects are disastrous, in the direct ratio of the relative speed of the trains, one of which overtakes the other. The momentum of the shock, other things being the same, will be proportional to the excess of the speed of the faster over that of the slower train.

The probability of a collision will also be increased in the same ratio.

To work express trains with safety, an additional line of rails should be laid down and appropriated to them.

Their number per day being necessarily small, and the duration of their trips short, the same line of rails might, without inconvenience or danger, serve for the traffic in both directions as on single lines of railway.

Examples.

Northwestern	Jan. 22, 1847.	Passenger had his leg broken. Express train ran into a siding, and came in contact with a wagon.
Bristol and Birmingham	May 23, 1848.	Engine-driver, stoker, and guard killed, and two passengers slightly injured, in consequence of the train getting off the line.
Great Western	May 10, 1848.	Six passengers killed, and thirteen injured, in consequence of a train coming in collision with a horse-box at the Shrivenham station.
Lancaster and Preston	Aug. 21, 1848.	One passenger killed, and two seriously injured, in consequence of a collision at the Bay Horse station between a Lancaster and Carlisle Company's express train, and a local train belonging to Lancaster and Preston Company.
London and Brighton	Sept. 22, 1848.	Guard injured. Several carriages of an express train thrown off the rails, in consequence of the tire of one of the engine-wheels breaking.
Northwestern	Sept. 2, 1848.	Express train ran off the rails near the Newton Road station, causing severe injury to two passengers, Mr. Shuard and Colonel Baird, both of whom died afterward.
Ditto	Oct. 31, 1848.	The engine and five carriages of the express train to Edinburgh ran off the rails near Weedon, causing injury to one passenger and to the driver.
Southwestern	Nov. 17, 1848.	Express train ran into a ballast-engine on the Richmond line, causing death to one servant of the company and injury to four others, all of whom were riding on the engine; also injury to eight passengers in the express train.

RULE VIII.

SPECIAL TRAINS, EXCURSION TRAINS, AND ALL OTHER EXCEPTIONAL TRAINS ON RAILWAYS ARE TO BE AVOIDED, BEING MORE UNSAFE THAN THE ORDINARY AND REGULAR TRAINS.

Illustration.

There is always more or less danger of collision when any

object on a railway is out of its customary place. The engine-drivers of the regular trains are always informed of the course of other regular trains, and except in cases of accidental stoppage or delay, they know where they are liable to be encountered. Special trains are supplied on sudden and unforeseen occasions, and although their drivers are informed of the movement of the regular trains, and may therefore provide against collision, this information is not reciprocal.

Excursion trains are exceptional but not unforeseen, and are not, therefore, as unsafe as special trains. They are, nevertheless, to be avoided by those who scrupulously consult their safety. An examination of the statistics of accidents would conclusively prove the prudence of such a course.

Example.

Maryport and Carlisle .... Nov. 10, 1846. Collision between a special train and a coal train, in consequence of neglect on the part of the signal man at the Wigton station, and of the agent and superintendent of locomotives at Carlisle, in not informing the driver of the coal-train that a special train was expected, and that he was not to start until it arrived. Engine-driver and sole passenger injured.

Illustration.

The danger of collision with special trains may be diminished by the use of the electric telegraph.

Example.

Edinburgh and Glasgow...... May 19, 1845. Special train from Glasgow, containing only one passenger, lost speed by the way, and was overtaken and run into by a passenger train that started an hour and a half after it, the engine of which crushed the carriage of the special train, and killed the occupant.

RULE IX.

IF THE TRAIN IN WHICH YOU TRAVEL MEET WITH AN ACCIDENT, BY WHICH IT IS STOPPED AT A PART OF THE LINE, OR AT A TIME WHERE SUCH STOPPAGE IS NOT REGULAR, IT IS MORE ADVISABLE TO QUIT THE CARRIAGE THAN TO STAY IN IT, BUT IN QUITTING IT REMEMBER RULES I., V., AND VI.

Illustration.

It may be affirmed generally, that there is always more or less danger on a railway when carriages or wagons are found at a place where, in the regular working of the line, they ought not to be. In such cases, a train following them, not expecting to find them there, is likely to run upon them, and produce a collision. I have personally witnessed more than one example of this, and the reports of the railway commissioners supply several. I should therefore recommend the above rule for general observance; but in leaving the train passengers should beware of crossing the line, or standing on it, or of getting out of the carriages at the wrong side.

Examples.

Southwestern	Jan. 14, 1848.	The engine of a passenger train having been partially disabled, the engine-driver got under it to repair the damage. While thus employed, a goods train overtook and ran into the passenger train, causing the instant death of the driver, and injury to the fireman and eleven passengers; also injury to one of the guards of the goods train.
Manchester and Leeds	March 9, 1847.	Passenger train stopped by broken axle; another train belonging to the Manchester and Leeds Railway Company, notwithstanding signals were made, ran into and injured the two hindmost carriages.
Midland	Oct. 20, 1845.	Pilot engine, sent after a disabled passenger train to assist it, overtook and ran into it. Two passengers killed.

RULE X.

BEWARE OF YIELDING TO THE SUDDEN IMPULSE TO SPRING FROM THE CARRIAGE TO RECOVER YOUR HAT WHICH HAS BLOWN OFF, OR A PARCEL DROPPED.

Illustration.

It would appear that there is an instinctive impulse, which in some individuals is almost irresistible, to leap from a train to recover their hats when blown off or accidentally dropped. The reports of railway accidents supply numerous examples of this.

Examples.

North Midland	April 1, 1844.	Passenger jumped out after his hat. Arm broken by fall.
Great Western	July 23, 1844.	Passenger jumped out of a carriage after his hat while the train was in motion. Killed.
Edinburgh and Glasgow	Dec. 2, 1846.	Falling between carriages in motion, while attempting to recover his cap, which had been blown off into the next carriage. Killed.
Eastern Counties	March 4, 1846.	Jumping out after hat, hip-dislocated.

CHAP. XIV.] ACCIDENTS ON RAILWAYS. 293

Northwestern	June 26, 1847.	Jumping out after hat, injured.
Ditto	May 10, 1847.	Ditto, killed.
Manchester and Birmingham.	Oct. 16, 1845.	Struck by a bridge while getting on the roof of one of the carriages to recover his hat which had been blown off. Killed.
Edinburgh and Glasgow	Feb. 22, 1845.	Jumping out after his hat. Injured.
Dublin and Kingstown	Dec. 10, 1845.	Jumped from a train after a parcel which had fallen. Injured.
Manchester and Leeds	Jan. 23, 1845.	Attempting to recover his hat, fell off the train. Killed.
Northwestern	June 26, 1847.	Jumping after his hat from a train in motion. Killed.
Ditto	May 10, 1847.	Jumping after his hat from a train in motion, fell upon a block of stone, and was killed on the spot.
Barham Union	April 12, 1848.	Trespasser run over while seeking to recover his hat, which had been blown across the line. Killed.

RULE XI.

WHEN YOU START ON YOUR JOURNEY, SELECT, IF YOU CAN, A CARRIAGE AT OR AS NEAR AS POSSIBLE TO THE CENTRE OF THE TRAIN.

Illustration.

In case of collision, the first and the last carriages of a train are the most liable to damage. If the train run into another, the foremost carriages suffer. If it be run into by a train overtaking it, the hindmost carriages suffer. Almost every case of collision affords an example illustrating this rule.

In case of the engine running off the rails, the carriages most likely to suffer are the foremost.

Examples.

Eastern Counties	July 25, 1845.	Pilot engine, which was to assist a passenger and goods train up the Brentwood incline, ran into it too rapidly, through want of care on the part of the engineman. Two passengers injured.
Southeastern	July 28, 1845.	A passenger train having left the Tonbridge station at 6·30, P.M., without tail lamps, a pilot engine was sent after it with lamps. Owing to the reckless conduct of the driver, the pilot engine ran into the train at the Penhurst station. Twenty-two passengers injured.
London and Brighton	June 14, 1847.	An engine having been sent to assist a passenger train up an incline, ran into it, injuring four passengers.

RULE XII.

DO NOT ATTEMPT TO HAND AN ARTICLE INTO A TRAIN IN MOTION.

Example.

London and Brighton .... Feb. 15, 1847.   While handing a basket to the guard of a passing train, had his coat caught by one of the carriages, and was dragged under the wheels. Killed.

RULE XIII.

IF YOU TRAVEL WITH YOUR PRIVATE CARRIAGE, DO NOT SIT IN IT ON THE RAILWAY. TAKE YOUR PLACE BY PREFERENCE IN ONE OF THE REGULAR RAILWAY CARRIAGES.

Illustration.

The regular railway carriages are safer in case of accident than a private carriage placed on a truck. They are stronger and heavier. They are less liable to be thrown off the rails, or to be crushed or overthrown in case of a collision. The cinders ejected from the smoke funnel of the engine are generally in a state of vivid ignition, and if they happen to fall on any combustible object, are liable to set fire to it. The railway carriages are constructed so as to be secured from such an accident, but private carriages are not so, and, moreover, from their greater elevation when placed on a truck, are more exposed. Serious accidents have sometimes occurred from this cause.

The trucks which carry private carriages are also often placed at the end of the train, the least safe position. (See RULE XI.)

Example.

On the 8th Dec., 1847, an accident happened to the Countess of Zetland, while traveling in her private carriage, on the Midland Railway, of which Lady Zetland herself gave the following narrative. The accident occurred about 5 o'clock in the afternoon, as the train was approaching Rugby from Derby, en route to London, and at about six miles from Rugby.

"Aske, Richmond, Yorkshire.

"On the 8th of December, I left Darlington by the 9h. 25m. train for London. I traveled in my chariot with my maid. The carriage was strapped on to a truck, and placed with its back to the engine, about the centre of the train, which was a long one. Soon after leaving Leicester, I thought I smelt something burning, and told my maid to look out of the window on her side to see if any thing was on fire. She let down the window, and so many lumps of red-hot coal or coke were showering down that she put it up again immediately. I still thought I smelt something burning; she put down the window again, and exclaimed that the carriage was on fire. We then put down the side-windows, and waved our handkerchiefs, screaming 'fire' as loud as we could. No one took any notice of us. I then pulled up the windows, lest the current of air through the carriage should cause the fire to burn more rapidly into the carriage, and determined to sit in it as long as possible. After some time seeing that no assistance was likely to be afforded us, my maid became terrified, and, without telling me her intention, opened the door, let down the step, and scrambled out on to the truck. I followed her, but having unluckily let myself down toward the back part of the carriage, which was on fire, was obliged to put up the step and close the door as well as I could to enable me to pass to the front part of the carriage, furthest from the fire, and where my maid was standing. We clung on by the front springs of the carriage, screaming 'fire incessantly, and waving our handkerchiefs. We passed several policemen on the road, none of whom took any notice of us. No guard appeared. A gentleman in the carriage behind mine saw us, but could render no assistance. My maid seemed in an agony of terror, and I saw her sit down on the side of the truck and gather her cloak tightly about her. I think I told her to hold fast to the carriage. I turned away for a moment to wave my handkerchief, and when I looked round again my poor maid was gone. The train went on, the fire of course increasing, and the wind blowing it toward me. A man (a passenger) crept along the ledge of the railway carriages, and came as near as possible to the truck on which I stood, but it was impossible for him to help me. At last the train stopped at the Rugby station. An engine was sent back to find my maid. She was found on the road and taken to the Leicester Hospital, where she now lies in an almost hopeless state: her skull fractured; three of her fingers have been amputated. I am told the train was going at the rate of 50 miles an hour.

(Signed)   "S. Y. ZETLAND."

The train, consisting of seven passenger carriages, two brake-vans, and four private carriages on trucks—altogether thirteen separate carriages—was drawn by an engine with driver and fireman, and was under the charge of one guard, who was placed in the rear of the entire train, and within a luggage-van, from which it was impossible for him to see the burning carriage, which was the eighth from the engine.

RULE XIV.

BEWARE OF PROCEEDING ON A COACH ROAD ACROSS A RAILWAY AT A LEVEL CROSSING. NEVER DO SO WITHOUT THE EXPRESS SANCTION OF THE GATEKEEPER.

Illustration.

On the English railways, common roads are usually carried over or under the railway, which is crossed by or crosses them, by bridges. This, however, is not invariable, and the greatest caution should be observed in passing such level crossings. A restive horse has frequently produced injurious or fatal accidents in such cases.

RULE XV.

WHEN YOU CAN CHOOSE YOUR TIME, TRAVEL BY DAY RATHER THAN BY NIGHT; AND IF NOT URGENTLY PRESSED, DO NOT TRAVEL IN FOGGY WEATHER.

Accidents from collision and from encountering impediments accidentally placed on the road happen more frequently at night and in foggy weather, than by day and in clear weather.

Persons on or near railways appear to be seized with a delirium or fascination which determines their will by an irresistible impulse to throw themselves under an approaching train. Cases of this kind occur so frequently, and under such circumstances as can not be adequately explained by predisposition to suicide.

Examples.

Midland	June 20, 1845.	Plate-layer, jumped suddenly in front of a train in motion; no cause can be assigned.
Ditto	June 25, 1845.	Trespasser, ran from behind a bridge, and laid himself across the rails in front of an approaching train.
Ditto	Sept. 18, 1845.	Trespasser, laid his neck on the rail in front of an approaching train; supposed to be insane.
Southwestern	June 9, 1847.	Francis Arney threw himself under the wheels of train. Killed.
Glasgow and Paisley	Nov. 19, 1847.	A woman of dissipated habits rushed from the side of the railway, and throwing herself in front of an approaching train, was run over. Killed.
Southwestern	Feb. 19, 1848.	Person committed suicide by placing himself before an approaching train.
Sheffield and Manchester	May 4, 1846.	Person committed suicide by laying himself across the rails in front of an approaching train.

CHAPTER XV.

ELECTRIC TELEGRAPH.

ALTHOUGH the subject of the present volume is limited to the economy of railways, and therefore a notice of the adaptation of the electric telegraph to railway purposes might, strictly speaking, be considered as sufficient, yet, probably, from the great interest attached to this curious application of physical science to commercial and social objects, some brief exposition of its origin and the mode of producing its effects may not be unacceptable.

The discovery of electricity as a science dates within a century, and the discovery of those phenomena which have been rendered subservient to telegraphic purposes dates within a much more brief period, having been for the most part made within the last 25 years.

The leading phenomena of electricity had not long engaged the attention of the scientific world before the idea of conveying intelligence by them to a distance was suggested, and many ingenious persons employed themselves in contriving telegraphs by which this might be accomplished.

Several of these had been suggested, and actually tested by

ELECTRIC TELEGRAPH.

experiment on a considerable scale, in the early part of the present century.

It was not, however, until within the last 15 or 16 years that the invention, which has now been reduced to such extensive practice, actually assumed a form in which it might be regarded as practically useful.

The means whereby electricity has become useful as a telegraphic agent are easily explained.

The electric influence admits of being propagated to a distance from the place of its production, in virtue of a quality by which it passes by preference over certain substances rather than others.

These substances are called for distinction *Conductors*, while the other class of substances upon which the influence refuses to pass are called *Non-conductors*.

The most conspicuous examples of the one class are the metals; the most conspicuous examples of the other are the resins, wax, silk, &c. The rate at which the electric influence passes along a conducting substance, such as a metallic wire or rod, is not accurately ascertained, but it appears tolerably certain that it is not less than the speed at which light is propagated, that is to say, at the rate of about 200,000 miles per second.

The second quality by which electricity subserves to telegraphic purposes is its power of producing sensible or mechanical effects of various kinds after having passed over any length of a conducting substance.

These effects, which may be used as signals, are very various. Among them are the production of a visible spark, the decomposition of water, the deflexion of a magnetic needle from its position of rest, and the power to convert iron suddenly into a magnet, and as suddenly to divest it of the magnetic virtue.

The first two of these effects were suggested at an early period in the history of this invention, but the two latter were ultimately found to be the most available, and are now the only effects used as signals.

To explain the deflexion, let us suppose a copper wire extended over the magnetic needle of a common compass so that the direction of the wire shall be parallel to the needle without touching it. In this state of things the needle will remain undisturbed; but if we send a galvanic current along the wire, which may be done by connecting the extremities of the wire with a common galvanic trough, the needle will instantly throw itself at right angles to the wire, and will remain in that position so long as the galvanic current is maintained; but if that current be discontinued, by withdrawing either end of the wire from the trough, the needle will instantly resume its position of rest.

It is found, also, that the north pole of the needle will turn, in this case, in the one direction or in the other, according to the direction given to the galvanic current. If this current flow in one direction, the north pole will throw itself to the east, and the south to the west; if it flow in the contrary direction, the north pole will be thrown to the west, and the south pole to the east.

To explain the last-mentioned effect of the sudden conversion of iron into a magnet, and the sudden destruction of the magnetic virtue thus imparted, let us suppose a copper wire to be coiled round a piece of soft iron spirally, so that the successive coils shall not touch each other or touch the iron, which may be done by coating the wire with silk, or any resinous or non-conducting substance. This being done, let us suppose that an electric current is transmitted through the wire, so that it shall flow spirally round the rod of soft iron, which may be effected by placing, as before, the ends of the wire in a galvanic trough. If steel filings, a needle, or any light piece of iron, be brought near the iron thus circumstanced, they will instantly be attracted by it, showing that it has acquired the magnetic virtue; and this effect will continue to be produced so long as the galvanic current shall be maintained along the spiral wire; but the instant the end of the wire is withdrawn from the galvanic trough, the magnetic virtue deserts the iron, and it will no longer attract.

To render intelligible the means by which these properties have been made instrumental to the transmission of intelligence to a distance, let us suppose a quantity of copper wire to be coated with a substance which is at once a non-conductor of electricity, which is impenetrable by moisture, and is capable of withstanding the vicissitudes of weather. The wire thus inclosed still retains its power of transmitting the electric influence, while the non-conducting coating in which it is enveloped effectually prevents the escape of the subtle fluid. The electric fluid flowing along such a wire may be regarded as in all respects similar to water or gas flowing through a tube, being as effectually confined within the tube of non-conducting substance which surrounds the wire as the water or gas in the iron tube provided to conduct it, but being infinitely more free to move within this tube than is either the water or the gas; indeed, the power of numbers can scarcely express the superior freedom of motion which the one fluid has, compared with the others. In passing along the wire, in this case, the electric fluid loses none of its virtue; however extended the wire may be, on arriving at its extremity, it will be capable of producing the same sensible or mechanical effects. It will still deflect the magnetic needle, or impart the attractive power to soft iron.

Now let us imagine the globe of the earth to be surrounded by such a wire as we have here described, the extremities being brought to the right and left hand of the operator. The moment the galvanic current is transmitted through it at one end, a magnetic needle will be deflected at the other end, or a piece of soft iron, arranged as above described, will receive the attractive power, and this after the electric fluid has made the circuit of the globe. The interval of time which will elapse between the moment at which the electric fluid starts on its trip and the moment when it arrives at and deflects the needle, or imparts the attractive power to the iron, will not be so much as the eighth part of the interval between two beats of a common clock; yet in this interval the fluid will have made the entire circuit of the globe.

It will now be easily understood how, by carrying this wire coated by non-conductors, as just described, to comparatively short distances along the sides of roads, and supported on non-conducting rollers, signals may be made instantaneously at distances which, however great, are incomparably less than that which we have here supposed.

It now only remains to explain in what manner the signals may be multiplied and varied so as to indicate letters, figures, and words.

I have explained that a magnetic needle will be deflected either to the right or to the left, according to the direction given to the current. Now it is always easy to give the current one direction or the other by merely changing the ends of the galvanic trough with which the wire is connected. A person, therefore, in London, having command over the end of a wire which extends to Edinburgh, and is there connected with a magnetic needle, can deflect this needle to the right or to the left at will.

Thus a single wire and a magnetic needle are capable of making at least two signals.

But signals, whatever may be the form of telegraph used, may be multiplied by repetition. Thus the operator at London may make the needle at Edinburgh move twice successively to the left, and this may be conventionally settled as a sign, independent of that which is produced by a single movement to the left. In like manner, two successive movements to the right will supply another signal, and thus we have four independent signals.

But from these four signals we may immediately produce four more, as we may combine one movement to the right with two to the left, one to the left with two to the right, or one to the right with one to the left, or two to the right with two to the left; and thus we have eight independent signals.

We may carry this method further, and so arrange the system that three successive movements to the right and three successive movements to the left shall have independent significations; and these again may be combined with each of the eight signals already explained; and, in short, we may carry this system to an extent which shall be limited only by the inconvenience of the delay which would take place in making the repetitions necessary for such signals.

Apart from this delay, however, it is clear that with a single wire and a single needle we may easily obtain expressions for all the letters of the alphabet and the ten numerals.

But to obviate the inconvenience which would attend multiplied repetitions in the movements of a single needle, we may provide two independent wires which shall act upon two independent needles.

Each of these needles primarily will afford two independent signals by their movements right and left. These four signals may be combined in pairs, so as to afford four other signals producible by a single movement. Thus, simultaneously with the right-hand movement of one needle we may produce the right-hand movement of the other. In the same way we may simultaneously produce the left-hand movement of both, or the right-hand of either combined with the left-hand movement of the other, which would give eight independent signals, the production of each of which would occupy no more time than that of a single movement. We may then adapt the signals by double movement of each needle, which, combined with each other, and with the single movements, will afford another set of combinations; and by combining these systems, we may obviously obtain all the signals requisite to express the letters and numerals.

Such is, in general, the nature of the signals adopted in the electric telegraphs in ordinary use in England, and in some other parts of Europe.

It may aid the conception of the mode of operation and communication if we assimilate the apparatus to the dial of a clock with its two hands. Let us suppose that a dial, instead of carrying hands, carried two needles, and that their north poles, when quiescent, both pointed to 12 o'clock. When the galvanic current is conducted under either of them, the north pole will turn either to 3 o'clock or to 9 o'clock, according to the direction given to the current.

Now, it is easy to imagine a person in London governing the hands of such a clock erected in Edinburgh, where their indications might be interpreted according to a way previously agreed upon. Thus, we may suppose that when the needle No. 1 turns to 9, the letter A is expressed; if it turn to 3, the letter B is expressed. If the needle No. 2 turn to 9 o'clock, the letter C is expressed; if it turn to 3, the letter D. If both needles are turned to 9, the letter E is expressed; if both to 3, the letter F. If No. 1 be turned to 9, and No. 2 to 3, the letter G is expressed; if No. 2 be turned to 9; and No. 1 to 3, the letter H, and so forth.

It may be presumed that there can be but little difficulty in conceiving how, by practice, two persons may communicate with each other by such means, almost, if not altogether, as rapidly as they could write and read.

But a difficulty will doubtless suggest itself to the intelligent and inquisitive reader. It will be asked whether a sentinel must be kept ever on the watch to observe when a message is coming; for as the hands of our clock do not speak, notice could only be received of a coming message by the incessant vigilance of an observer.

Would it not, however, be admirable if we could attach to this clock a striking apparatus which should address the ear the moment a message is about to be sent, and which should, as it were, awaken the attention of the person on duty?

Such an expedient has, in fact, been contrived. The person in London who desires to communicate a message to the telegraphic agent at Edinburgh can actually make the clock strike at his will, and thus command attention.

The manner in which this is accomplished is as admirable by its simplicity and efficiency as that which we have just described.

The quality resorted to in this case is the last of those we have mentioned above, namely, the power to impart the magnetic virtue at will to soft iron.

One of the wires conducted from London passes into the chamber of the telegraphic apparatus at Edinburgh, where it is connected with a coil of wire which envelops a rod of soft iron. The ends of this rod, which has the form of a horse-shoe, are placed in contiguity, but not in contact, with the detent of a striking apparatus like an alarm-bell. When a message is about to be sent from London this bell-wire is put in communication with the galvanic trough in London. Immediately the subtle fluid flows along the wire and converts the horse-shoe rod at Edinburgh into a powerful magnet.

The attractive power which it thus suddenly receives irresistibly draws toward it the detent of the alarum, and lets go the bell, which continues to ring until the agent of the telegraph at Edinburgh answers the demand of the messenger from London, and tells him he is attentive. Then the London communicator withdraws the galvanic current from the bell-wire, the horse-shoe at Edinburgh is instantly deprived of its magnetic virtue, the detent flies back to its place by the action of a spring, and silences the bell.

I do not pretend, nor is it necessary here, to go into the practical details of the electric telegraph. My object is merely to render its principle and mode of communication generally intelligible, which I trust will be effected by the preceding observations.

While the observer stands reading the indications of the dial plate, the amanuensis sits beside him, committing to paper from dictation the message, which is speedily transmitted to those to whom it is addressed.

This is generally the mode in which the electric telegraphs in Europe are constructed and worked.

In the United States, where the electric telegraph is extensively used, a different, and in some respects a more efficient, mode of operation has been adopted. There the signal by magnetic needle is not used, and the entire operation of the telegraph is effected in virtue of the power to make and unmake a magnet by coiling the electric current round soft iron. The paramount advantage of the American system is that it not only transmits the message, but writes it.

Incidental to this there is a further advantage, that it is possible to keep the message secret even from the agents of the telegraph.

The principle of the American telegraph is easily explained.

Let us suppose a small lever formed of steel and balanced on a point. At one end of this lever let a point be formed, so as to constitute a pencil or style. Under the other end let a horseshoe of soft iron be placed, at such a distance that, when the latter shall receive the magnetic virtue from the electric current, the lever will be drawn to the horse-shoe; and let it be so arranged, by means of a spring or otherwise, that, when the horse-shoe shall lose its magnetic virtue, the lever shall detach itself from the magnet, and the end bearing the pencil or style shall fall.

By such an arrangement, whenever the soft iron is rendered magnetic, the pencil will be raised to a certain definite position, and will be maintained in that position so long as the horse-shoe continues to be magnetic; but the moment the horse-shoe loses its magnetic power, then the pencil will fall.

Now, suppose that immediately above the pencil is placed a small roller or cylinder, under which a band or ribbon of paper passes, and that this paper receives a slow and regular progressive motion from the cylinder.

Whenever the pencil is raised by the magnet, its point presses upon the paper, and if it is kept pressed against the paper, which moves over it, a line will be traced by the pencil. If the pencil be only momentarily brought into contact with the paper, a dot will be produced; if it be kept in contact with the paper only twice the length of time necessary to produce a dot, a line will be produced, the length of which will be twice the magnitude of the dot; if it be kept in contact with the paper three times as long as is necessary to make a dot, a line will be produced of three times the length, and so on.

It is clear, then, that if we have the power of keeping the pencil any determinate time in contact with the paper, or of making it only momentarily touch the paper, the paper being understood, as before mentioned, to be kept moving uniformly and progressively over the pencil, we can at pleasure make dots and lines of various determinate lengths, and also combinations of dots and lines of different lengths.

We can further, by leaving the pencil at intervals of more or less length out of contact with the paper, leave between these lines and dots spaces of more or less width.

It is easy to imagine that a conventional alphabet may be formed by these lines and dots, and their combinations, and that words may be thus formed. The spaces left while the pencil is not in contact with the paper might indicate the separation of the letters, words, and sentences. Small spaces might indicate the separation of letters, greater spaces the separation of words, and greater still the separation of sentences.

As the formation of an alphabet by such signs is evidently arbitrary, and as infinitely various alphabets may be formed by the endless combinations which such a system offers, no particular signs need be indicated here, it being sufficient for our present purpose to show the principle.

To explain the operation of this system, let us suppose a person at New York desirous of sending a message to New Orleans. A wire of the usual kind connects the two places.

The end at New Orleans is coiled round a horse-shoe magnet, as above described. The end at New York can be put in communication with the galvanic trough at the will of the person sending the message. The instant the communication is established, the horse-shoe of soft iron at New Orleans becomes magnetic, it attracts the small lever, and presses the pencil against the paper.

The moment the operator at New York detaches the wire from the trough, the horse-shoe at New Orleans loses its magnetic power, and the pencil drops from the paper. It is clear, then, that the operator at New York, by putting the wire in contact with the trough, and detaching it, and by maintaining the contact for longer or shorter intervals, can make the pencil at New Orleans act upon the paper, as already described, so as to make upon it dots and lines of determinate length, combined in any manner he may desire, and separated by any desired intervals.

In a word, the operator at New York can write a letter with a pencil and paper which are at New Orleans.

Provisions in such an arrangement are made so that the motion of the paper does not begin until the message is about to be commenced, and ceases when the message is written. This is easily accomplished by the same principle as has been already described in the case of the bell, which gives notice to the attendant in the European telegraph. The cylinders which conduct the band of paper are moved by wheel-work, and a weight properly regulated. Their motion is imparted by a detent, which detent is detached by the action of the magnet, and returns to its position, and stops the motion when the magnet loses its virtue.

Without going into detail on this point, it is evident that the object may be accomplished by various expedients.

Such is the principle of the electric telegraph as used in

the United States. A black-lead pencil was first adopted, and afterward a sort of fountain-pen, but ultimately it was found most convenient to use a style consisting of a steel point, which forms a trace upon the paper, and produces marks in relief like those with which blind persons are enabled to read.

When the message is completed, the strip of paper on which it is written is cut off, and inclosed in an envelope addressed to the person for whom it is intended.

It is possible by this system for two correspondents to have a language, of which they alone have the key, and even the operator who communicates the message may be unable to interpret what he himself writes. The address alone, in this case, is rendered intelligible to the agent of the telegraph.

Another advantage of this system is that it supersedes the necessity of an amanuensis, and prevents the possibility of error in taking down a message.

In the needle telegraph one person interprets and reads, and another writes, and the signals, as fast as they are made, are, as it were, effaced and obliterated. In the American telegraph the signals themselves are rendered permanent.

While I am writing these pages, projects are in progress for electric communication on a scale still more extensive, and having objects the importance of which it is difficult to estimate. It is proposed to establish electric wires between London and the Continent, across the Straits of Dover, by sinking them in the bottom of the Channel. If this be realized, intelligence may be instantaneously transmitted from the English capital to any part of Europe to which the telegraphic arrangements extend.

But this project, startling as it is, sinks into insignificance in comparison with another which has been still more recently announced.

It is said that at New York a proposition has been made to establish electric wires between New York and England, by sinking them to the bottom of the Atlantic. The estimate of the expenses of realizing this project is said to be about £600,000; and by the expenditure of this sum thirty-six wires, protected by a coating of gutta percha, and guaranteed to last for ten years, can be carried through the Atlantic from New York to London. The projectors are reported to have offered to guarantee the completion of the arrangements in less than two years. The total length of the wires to be employed would be about 120,000 miles.

In England the electric telegraphs are in the hands of a private company, which has a practical monopoly of them; and, as is invariably the case with all monopolies, complaints and remonstrances, well or ill founded, are constantly brought against the establishment.

A central station is established in London, in Lothbury, near the Bank of England. The lower part of the building is appropriated to the reception of orders and messages. A person desiring to forward a message to any part of England connected with London by the wires writes his message on a sheet of letter-paper, provided for the purpose, and prepared according to a printed form, having the names and address of the writer, and of the party to whom the message is communicated, in blank spaces assigned to them, together with the date and hour at which the message is dispatched. The answer is received, accompanied by the date and hour at which the message arrived, and at which the answer was dispatched.

The tariff of charges for transmission of telegraphic messages differs very much, according to the destination of the message, and is not strictly regulated by distance.

The charge, for example, from London to Dover is, or was lately, about $6d.$ a word; while the charge between Birmingham and Stafford, a greater distance, was something less than $4d$, a word. The charge between London and York is $5·4d.$ per word, between London and Edinburgh $7·8d.$ per word, and between London and Glasgow $8·4d.$ per word.

The room containing the telegraphic instruments is in the upper part of the building, to which communications by wires are made from a cellar in the lower part, where the galvanic apparatus is deposited. This apparatus consists of a collection of galvanic batteries, having different powers, to be used according to the distance to which the message is to be transmitted. The wires which communicate between this establishment and the termini of the several railways are inclosed in leaden pipes, which are carried under the streets. There they are connected with the wires supported on poles, with which every railway traveler is familiar, and by which the communication is maintained with different parts of the country.

It is found that by practice the operators of the telegraphic instruments are able to communicate about 20 words per minute, being nearly at the same rate as ordinary writing.

In the chief telegraphic stations in different parts of the country, besides the transmission of private messages, a sort of subscription intelligence rooms have been opened, where the subscribers can daily and hourly obtain in common the general commercial information which is most in request; such as the state of the stock and share market, and of the money market; the state of the wind and weather at different ports of the kingdom; shipping and sporting intelligence; the rates of the markets of every description; and the general political news of most importance. These subscription-rooms are supplied by the establishment in London, at which a sort of telegraphic editor prepares from the morning papers at an early hour a short abstract of the most important news—the stock market, &c., &c.

This, when prepared and written out, is sent up to the instrument room, from whence it is dispatched to the various subscription rooms in different parts of the country. It arrives there by 8 o'clock in the morning, and is immediately accessible to the subscribers. All news of adequate importance is thus diffused over the kingdom literally with the speed of lightning. Thus the public in Edinburgh are informed by 8 o'clock in the morning of all interesting facts which appear in the London morning journals, which are not issued in the metropolis until 6 o'clock.

The provincial journals also profit by these means of obtaining intelligence, and are enabled to supply in their columns all important news as early as it can be supplied by the London journals.

Whatever be the nature of signal used, the wires which convey the electric current over the country may be constructed in either of two ways, the one by being supported on poles, as is usual in this country; the other by being sunk under ground like gas or water-pipes. The latter method has some advantage in security, being less liable to be disturbed by ill-disposed persons or by accident. It has been found that the flight of birds has sometimes accidentally broken the communication, the birds striking the wire, and breaking or deranging it; violent storms also have occasionally blown down the posts and broken the wires.

In Prussia, where there are about 1400 miles of electric telegraph in operation, the wire is buried, being protected with a covering of gutta percha. It is said that in the late political disturbances a small portion of the electric telegraph, which was erected above ground on posts in that country, was destroyed by the populace, while all that portion which was buried remained undisturbed.

An improvement on the American method has lately been projected, though, so far as I am informed, not yet actually realized. Instead of making arbitrary signs by a style on paper, consisting of lines and dots, it is proposed to make the magnet actually bring types to act upon the paper, so as to print the words in the ordinary language.

Whatever be the nature of the sign employed by this method, it is estimated that 1000 words an hour can be printed by it.

The extent of electric telegraph in operation in England is at present about 2000 miles. The extent in operation in America is said to be 10,000 miles. The East India Company have adopted a project for establishing a line of telegraphic communication through a portion of their territory, which will consist of 10,000 miles in length, and will be laid under ground.

The cost of constructing the electric telegraph varies extremely in different countries, according to the conditions of the population, and the cost of labor, land, and materials. In England the electric telegraph is said to have cost at the rate of £150 a mile, while in America its cost has not exceeded £30. Considerable sacrifices, however, have been made to facilitate the construction of the telegraph in that country. The farmers and settlers residing along the line are allowed the use of the telegraph for their own purposes, as a compensation to them for watching the wires and repairing them when necessary, for which purpose they are furnished with the requisite tools and instructions. In this way an entire population, among whom the telegraph passes, are interested in its preservation.

CHAPTER XVI.

INLAND TRANSPORT IN THE UNITED STATES.

No quarter of the globe presents a natural apparatus of internal communication so stupendous as that which the European settlers found at their disposal on the North American continent.

This immense tract, included between the Atlantic and the Rocky Mountains on the east and west, the great chain of lakes extending from Lake Superior to Lake Ontario on the north, and the Gulf of Mexico on the south, is divided into two districts by the ridge of the Alleghanies, which traverses it in a direction north and south. The western division consists of the vast valley drained by the Mississippi and its tributaries, a territory greater in superficial extent than Western Europe. The eastern district consists of that portion between the Alleghany ridge and the

Atlantic, falling toward the ocean and drained by innumerable rivers, navigable for vessels of greater or less burden, and running generally eastward. Provided with such means of water communication, it might have been expected that a population thinly scattered over an area so extensive, and engrossed by the exigencies of incipient agriculture, would hāve continued for ages contented with means of transport afforded them on so vast a scale, without having recourse to the resources of art.

It is, however, the character of man, and more especially of Anglo-Saxon man, never to rest satisfied until he renders the gifts of nature, however munificent, ten times more fruitful by his industry and skill; and it will be presently seen to what a prodigious extent the enterprise of the population of the United States has improved these means of inland transport.

CANAL NAVIGATION.

The spectacle of a machinery of commerce so imposing in magnitude and power, and so remarkably co-extensive with the vastness, the fertility, and the mineral wealth of the territory of which this emigrant people found themselves possessors, only provoked their ambition to rival the enterprise of the parent country, and to import and naturalize its improvements and its arts. Their independence was scarcely established before the same resources of arts and science which ages had not been more than sufficient to develop in Britain were invoked; and a system of artificial communication was undertaken, and finally executed, on the new continent, for which, all things considered, there is no parallel in the history of civilization.

Immediately after the acknowledgment of the independence of the American colonies by England, in 1783, several companies were formed in the two principal states of the Union, those of New York and Pennsylvania, for the purpose of constructing a system of canals. These enterprises were accordingly commenced, but on a scale too limited for the attainment of the ultimate objects; and as the United States advanced in commercial prosperity, more extensive plans were adopted. In 1807 the senate charged the Secretary of State, Mr. Gallatin, to prepare a project for a general system of intercommunication by canals, based upon the geographical character of the territory of the Union.

A system of artificial water communication was accordingly

projected, which, with some modifications was at a later period adopted and carried into execution.

These projects, however, suffered an interruption from the renewal of the war in 1812; and it was not until five years later that the vast works were commenced, the result of which has been a system of inland navigation which is without a rival in any country in the world.

On the anniversary of the Declaration of Independence, celebrated the 4th July, 1817, the commencement of the great line of canal connecting the Hudson with Lake Erie was inaugurated. The river Hudson presented a navigable communication for vessels of a large class from New York to Albany. The object of this line of canal was to open a water communication between Albany and the northern lakes, so as to connect, by continuous water communication, the Northwestern States with the Atlantic.

In less than eight years this work was accomplished by the state of New York, with its exclusive resources.

That state alone executed and brought into operation the largest canal in the world. As first constructed, the Erie canal, with its branches, cost £2,600,000 sterling; but its magnitude and proportions being still found inadequate to the exigencies of a continually increasing traffic, its enlargement was decided upon in 1835, and about five years ago it was finally completed, at a cost of upward of £5,000,000 sterling. The total length of this canal is 363 miles, and its cost of construction per mile was therefore about £13,700.

Meanwhile the other states of the Union did not remain inactive. Pennsylvania especially rivaled New York in these enterprises, and became intersected with canals in all directions. In short, these works were undertaken to a greater or less extent in most of the Atlantic and some of the Western States; and the American Union now possesses a sytem of internal artificial water comunication amounting to nearly 4500 miles, executed with a degree of skill and perfection rarely surpassed by any similar works constructed in the states of Europe.

According to M. Michel Chevalier, whose work on this subject supplies most voluminous and valuable details,* the extent

---

* " Histoire et Déscription des Voies de Communication aux Etats Unis, et des Travaux d'Art qui en dépendent," par Michel Chevalier : Paris, 1840–1843.

of canals which were in operation in the United States on January 1, 1843, was 4333 miles. There was a further extent projected, but not executed, amounting to 2359 miles. The total cost of executing the canals which were completed was, according to M. Chevalier, £27,870,964, being at the average rate of £6,432 per mile.

If that portion remaining to be constructed could be executed at the same rate, its cost would be £15,173,088.

This extent of artificial water communication, compared with the population, exhibits, in a striking point of view, the activity and enterprise which characterize the American people.

It appears, from what has been stated, that in the United States, the population of which, according to the census of 1840, was 17,069,493, there was one mile of canal navigation for 3,939 inhabitants. Now, in the United Kingdom, there are only 3000 miles of canal navigation. The population, according to the census of 1840, was twenty-seven millions. There is, therefore, only one mile of canal to every 9000 inhabitants. The extent of canal navigation, therefore, in America, bears a proportion to the population greater than in the United Kingdom, in the ratio of 9 to 4.

In France, the entire length of canal navigation is 2700 miles, with a population of thirty-five millions. There is, therefore, one mile of canal for every 12,962 inhabitants. The canal navigation, therefore, in France, bears a less proportion to its population than in the United States, in the ratio of 13 to 4, very nearly.

RIVER NAVIGATION.

The river navigation of the United States is on a scale commensurate with the extent of their territory. The division of the country east of the Alleghanies, forming the Atlantic States, is drained by a vast number of rivers, of the first and second class, all navigable for vessels of considerable burden, the principal of which are the Hudson, the Delaware, the Susquehanna, the Connecticut, the Potomac, the James, the Roanoke, the Savannah, and, to the southward, the Altamaha and the Alabama.

The western division is drained by the Mississippi and its hundred tributaries, navigable for vessels of great tonnage for several thousands of miles.

Besides the internal communication supplied by rivers, properly so called, a vast apparatus of water transport is derived from the geographical character of the extensive coast, stretching for about four thousand miles, from the Gulf of St. Lawrence to the delta of the Mississippi, indented and serrated in every part with natural harbors and sheltered bays, fringed with islands, forming sounds, throwing out capes and promontories, which inclose arms of the sea, in which the waters are free from the roll of the ocean, and which, for all the purposes of internal navigation, have the character of rivers and lakes. The lines of communication, formed by the vast and numerous rivers, are completed in the interior by chains of lakes, presenting the most extensive bodies of fresh water in the known world.

Whatever may be the dispute maintained among the historians of art as to the conflicting claims for the invention of steam navigation, it is an incontestible fact that the first steamboat practically exhibited for any useful purpose, was placed on the Hudson, to ply between New York and Albany, in the beginning of the year 1808. From that time to the present, this river has been the theatre of the most remarkable series of experiments on locomotion on water ever recorded in the history of man.

The Hudson rises near Lake Champlain, the easternmost of the great chain of lakes or inland seas which extend from east to west across the northern boundary of the United States. The river follows nearly a straight course southward for two hundred and fifty miles, and empties itself into the sea at New York. The influence of the tide is felt as far as Albany, above which the stream begins to contract. Although this river, in magnitude and extent, is by no means equal to several others which intersect the States, it is nevertheless rendered an object of great interest by reason of the importance and extent of its trade. The produce of the state of New York, and that of the banks of the lakes Ontario and Erie, are transported by it to the city; and one of the most extensive and populous districts of the United States is supplied with the necessary imports by its waters. A large fleet of vessels is constantly engaged in its navigation; nor is the tardy but picturesque sailing vessel as yet excluded by the more rapid steamer. The current of the Hudson is said to average nearly three miles an hour; but as the ebb and flow of the tide are felt as far as Albany, the passage of the steamers between that place and

CHAP. XVI.] INLAND TRANSPORT IN THE U. STATES. 313

New York may be regarded as equally affected by currents in both directions. The passage, therefore, whether in ascending or descending the river, is made in the same time.

This river is navigable by steamers of a large class as far as Albany, nearly 150 miles above New York.

Attempts have been made, but hitherto without much success, to push the navigation a few miles higher, as far as the important town of Troy. The impediments arising however from the shallowness of the river appear to be so serious, that Albany has continued, and probably will continue, to be the limit of steam navigation in this direction.

The steam navigation of the Hudson is entitled to attention, not only because of the immense traffic of which it is the vehicle, but because it forms a sort of model for most of the the rivers of the Atlantic states. This navigation is conducted, as will be seen, in a manner and on a principle altogether different from that which prevails on the Mississippi and its tributaries.

In the steam-vessels used on these rivers, no other strength or stability is required than is sufficient to enable them to float and bear a progressive motion through the water. Not having to encounter the agitated surface of an open sea, they are supplied with neither rigging nor sails, and are built exclusively with a view to speed. Compared with sea-going steamers, they are slender and weak in their structure, with great length in proportion to their beam, and a very small draft of water.

The position and form of the machinery are affected by these circumstances. Without the necessity of being protected from a rough sea, the engines are placed on the deck in a comparatively elevated situation. The cylinders of large diameter and short-stroke, almost invariably used in sea-going ships, are rejected in these river boats, and the proportions are reversed —a comparatively small diameter and a stroke of great length being adopted. It is but rarely that two engines are used. A single engine, placed in the centre of the deck, drives a crank placed on the axle of the enormous paddle-wheels. The great magnitude of these latter, and the velocity imparted to them, enable them to perform the office of fly-wheels, and to carry the engine through its dead points with but little perceptible inequality of motion. The length of stroke adopted in these engines supplies the means of using the expansive principle with great effect.

The steamers which navigate the Hudson are vessels of great magnitude, splendidly fitted up for the accommodation of passengers; and this magnitude and splendor of accommodation have been continually augmented from year to year to the present time.

In the following table I have given the dimensions of nine steamers which were worked on the Hudson previously to 1838:

Names.	Length of Deck.	Breadth of Beam.	Draft.	Diameter of Wheel.	Length of Paddles.	Depth of Paddles.	Number of Engines	Diameter of Cylinder.	Length of Stroke.	Number of Revolutions.	Part of Stroke at which Steam is cut off.
	Ft.	*Ft.*	*Ft.*	*Ft.*	*Ft.*	*In.*		*In.*	*Ft.*		
De Wit Clinton	230	28	5·5	21	13·7	36	1	65	10	29	¾
Champlain....	180	27	5·5	22	15	34	2	44	10	27·5	¾
Erie..........	180	27	5·5	22	15	34	2	44	10	27·5	¾
North America	200	30	5	21	13	30	2	44·5	8	24	½
Independence.	148	26	..	..	..	..	1	44	10	..	
Albany........	212	26	..	24·5	14	30	1	65	..	19	
Swallow......	233	22·5	3·75	24	11	30	1	46	..	27	
Rochester....	200	25	3·75	23·5	10	24	1	43	10	28	
Utica.........	200	21	3·5	22	9·5	24	1	39	10	..	
Providence....	180	27	9	..	..	..	1	65	10	..	
Lexington.....	207	21	..	23	9	30	1	48	11	24	
Narragansett..	210	26	5	25	11	30	1	60	12	2	½
Massachusetts.	200	29·5	8·5	22	10	28	2	44	8	26	
Rhode Island..	210	26	6·5	24	11	30	1	60	11	21	

Within the last ten years considerable changes have been made in the proportion and dimensions of the vessels navigating this river; all these changes having a tendency to augment their magnitude and power, to diminish their draft of water, and to increase the play of the expansive principle. Increased length and beam have been resorted to with great success. Vessels of the largest class now draw only as much water as the smallest drew a few years ago: 4ft. 6in. is now regarded as the maximum. In the following table I have exhibited the dimensions and other particulars of nine of the most efficient and most recently built steamers plying on the Hudson and its collateral streams; and by a comparison of this with the former table, it will be seen to what an extent the dimensions and efficiency of these vessels have been increased.

CHAP. XVI.] INLAND TRANSPORT IN THE U. STATES. 315

Name of Vessel.	Dimensions of Vessel.				Engine.			Paddle-wheel.		
	Length.	Beam.	Depth of Hold.	Tonnage.	Diameter of Cylinder.	Length of Stroke.	Number of Strokes.	Diameter.	Length of Bucket.	Depth of Bucket.
	ft.	*ft. in.*	*ft. in.*		*in.*	*ft.*		*ft. in.*	*ft. in.*	*in.*
Isaac Newton......	333	40 4	10 0	..	81	12	18½	39 0	12 4	32
Bay State..........	300	39 0	13 2	..	76	12	21½	38 0	10 3	32
Empire State	304	39 0	13 6	..	76	12	21½	38 0	10 3	32
Oregon	305	35 0	..	..	72	11	18	34 0	11 0	28
Hendrik Hudson ...	320	35 0	9 6	1050	72	11	22	33 0	11 0	33
C. Vanderbilt	300	35 0	11 0	1075	72	12	21	35 0	9 0	33
Connecticut........	300	37 0	11 0	..	72	13	21	35 0	11 6	36
Commodore........	280	33 0	10 6	..	65	11	22	31 6	9 0	33
New World........	376	35 0	10 0	..	76	15	18	44 6	12 0	36
Alida..............	286	28 0	9 6	..	56	12	24½	32 0	10 0	32

It is not only in dimensions that these vessels have undergone improvements. The exhibition of the beautifully finished machinery of the English Atlantic steamers did not fail to excite the emulation of the American engineers and steam-boat proprietors, who ceased to be content with the comparatively rude though efficient structure of the mechanism of their steam-boats. All the vessels more recently constructed are accordingly finished and even decorated in the most luxurious manner. In respect of the accommodations which they afford to passengers, no water communication in any country in the world can compare with them. Nothing can exceed the splendor and luxury of the furniture. Silk, velvet, and the most expensive carpeting, mirrors of immense magnitude, gilding and carving, are used profusely in their decorations. Even the engine-room in some of them is lined with mirrors. In the Alida, for example, the end of the room containing the machinery is composed of one large mirror, in which the movements of the highly-finished machinery are reflected.

All the new and largest class of steamers, such as the Isaac Newton, the Hendrik Hudson, the New World, the Oregon, and the Alida, are capable of running from twenty to twenty-two miles an hour, and make, on an average, eighteen miles an hour without the least effort. These extraordinary speeds are obtained usually by rendering the boilers capable of carrying steam from forty to fifty pounds pressure above the atmosphere, and by urging the fires with fanners, worked by an independent engine, by which the furnaces can be forced to any desired extent.

It is right to observe here that this extreme increase of speed is obtained at a disproportionately increased consumption of fuel. When the speed is increased, the space through which the vessel must be propelled per minute is increased in the same proportion: and, at the same time, the resistance which the moving power has to overcome is augmented in the ratio of the square of the speed. Hence, the effect to be produced by the moving power per minute, is increased by two causes : first, the actual resistance which it has to overcome is augmented in the ratio of the square of the speed; and, secondly, the space through which the moving power has to act against this resistance in each minute is increased in the ratio of the speed. Thus, the total expenditure of moving power per minute will be augmented in the proportion of the cube of the speed.

Let us suppose the speed to be increased, for example, from eighteen to twenty-one miles an hour : the power to be expended per minute to produce this effect must be increased in the ratio of the cube of 18 to the cube of 21, or, what is the same, in the ratio of the cube of 6 to the cube of 7, that is, in the ratio of 216 to 348, or as 3 to 5 very nearly.

Hence, if the furnaces could be worked with equal economy, an increased consumption of fuel per hour would be necessary in the proportion of 3 to 5; but the waste incurred by urging the blowers so as to produce a sufficiently vivid combustion is so great, that it is practically found that the consumption of fuel is increased in a much higher ratio than that which results from the increased resistance, and indeed in some cases that the increase of three or four miles an hour on eighteen miles will cause nearly triple the consumption of fuel.

Much of the efficiency of these engines arises from the application of the expansive principle; but to this there has been hitherto a limit, owing to the inequality of the action of the piston when urged by expanding steam on the crank. When the steam is cut off at less than half-stroke, the force of the piston is diminished before the termination of the stroke to less than one half its original amount. This inequality is aggravated by the relative position of the crank and connecting rod, the leverage diminishing in nearly the same proportion as the power of the piston diminishes. On this account it has not been found generally practicable to cut off the steam at less than half-stroke.

A recent improvement, invented by Captain Ericsson, is directed to remove this defect. The steam is worked successively in two cylinders of different magnitudes, as in the engines of Woolf and Hornblower, but without allowing the action of the first piston to impair the effect of the second; and the arrangement of the connection between the piston and the crank-shaft is such, that, notwithstanding the expansion of the steam to from twenty to thirty times its original volume, the action on the crank is more uniform than in the common crank engine, even when worked without expansion.

The effect of this arrangement is reported to be a saving in the consumption of fuel of very large amount. A small trial engine of ten-horse power is stated to have been worked by the consumption of 15 lbs. of coal per hour, being at the rate of $1\frac{1}{2}$ lb. per horse per hour.*

It must be observed, in relation to the navigation of these eastern rivers, that the occurrence of explosions is almost unheard of. During the last ten years, not a single catastrophe of that kind has occurred on them, although cylindrical boilers ten feet in diameter, and composed of plating $\frac{5}{16}$ths of an inch thick, are commonly used with steam of fifty pounds pressure above the atmosphere.

It will be seen by the table given above, that the paddle-wheels used on these rivers have extraordinary magnitude. There is nothing particular in their construction. The split paddle-board, which was adopted about ten years since, has been discontinued, and has given way to the simple and continuous paddle-board. These boards, however, are generally placed alternately at greater and less distances from the centre, somewhat like a break-joint. Wooden spokes, with cast-iron centre pieces, are generally adopted.

The steam is universally worked with expansion, the valves for its admission and emission being moved independently of each other. A separate engine is generally provided for driving the blowers, and a cylindrical fan-blower is employed for each boiler. Some of these blowers are ten feet in diameter, being driven by a crank placed on their axle, which receives its motion from the small independent engine.

The great power developed by these river engines is due, not

* I have since received from Captain Ericsson a more exact report of the performance of the model engine of ten-horse power. It appears that, in long-continued work, its average consumption of fuel is 25 lbs. per hour, or 2·5 lbs. per horse power. This is considered excessive by the inventor, and ascribed to the small dimensions of the engine. An engine of larger power is now being constructed at New York, which, it is expected, will work with much greater economy of fuel.

so much to the magnitude of their cylinders, as the pressure of steam used in them. The New World, one of the most recently constructed boats, has a cylinder seventy-six inches in diameter, and fifteen feet stroke. The steam has forty pounds pressure in the boiler, and is cut off at half-stroke. The wheels, which are forty-five feet in diameter, make sixteen revolutions per minute. The speed of the circumference of the wheel will, therefore be twenty-five miles an hour; so that, if the speed of the boat be twenty miles an hour, we have the difference, five miles, giving the relative movement of the edge of the paddle-boards through the water.

To ascertain the power developed by these engines, let us suppose the mean effective pressure on the piston, taking into account the vacuum produced by the condenser, and supposing the steam to be cut off at half-stroke, to be 40 lbs. per square inch, the area of the piston being 4536 square inches, and the stroke 15 feet; the piston moves through 30 feet during each revolution of the wheels; and since 16 revolutions take place per minute, we shall find the effective force developed by the piston by multiplying its area, 4536, by twice the length of the stroke, which is 30, and by 16, which is the number of revolutions per minute. This product multiplied by 40, the number of pounds effective pressure per square inch, gives 87,091,200 lbs. raised one foot high per minute as the power developed by the engine. This is equivalent, according to the ordinary mode of expressing steam power, to 2640 horse power.

Whatever allowance, therefore, may be made for friction, &c., it is clear that the effective power thus obtained must be greater than any thing hitherto executed on water.

The increase of the dimensions of these vessels and their machinery has been attended with a greatly augmented economy of fuel.

On comparing the Hendrik Hudson, for example, with the Troy, a vessel formerly well known, plying between New York and Albany, it has been found that when the speed of the former is reduced to an equality with that of the latter, the trip between New York and Albany being performed in the same time, the former consumed thirteen tons of coal while the latter consumed twenty; yet the displacement of the Hendrik Hudson, owing to its increased dimensions, is nearly twice that of the Troy.

The ease with which these vessels of extraordinary length and beam and small draft move through the water is very remarkable. The results of their performance show that the resistance per square foot of immersed midship section is not perceptibly increased by the increased length of the vessel, and the consequently augmented surface and friction. This anomaly has not been explained, but it is certain that the increased length does not diminish the effect of the moving power in any perceptible degree.

Practical evidence of the economy arising from this increase of power and dimensions is supplied by the fact that the proprietors of the Hudson steamboats reduced their tariff for passengers, as well as for freight, as they increased the size of their vessels.

Previously to 1844, the lowest fare between New York and Albany, one hundred and forty-five miles, was four shillings and fourpence (one dollar). At present the fare is two shillings and twopence, and for an additional sum of the same amount the passenger can command the luxury of a separate state-room. When the splendor and magnitude of the accommodation is considered, the magnificence of the furniture and accessories, the cheapness and luxuriousness of the table (each meal, supplied on the most liberal scale, costing only two shillings and twopence), it will be admitted that no similar example of cheap locomotion can be found in any part of the world. Passengers may there be transported in a floating palace, surrounded with all the conveniences and luxuries of the most splendid hotel, at the rate of twenty miles an hour, for less than one-sixth of a penny per head per mile!

It is not an uncommon occurrence, during the summer, to meet individuals on board these boats, who have lodged themselves there permanently during a certain part of the season, instead of establishing themselves, as is customary, at some of the hotels in the towns on the banks of the river. Their daily expenses in the boat are as follows:

	s.	d.
Fare	2	2
Exclusive use of state-room, &c.	2	2
Breakfast, dinner, and supper	6	6
Total daily expense for board, lodging, attendance, and traveling 150 miles at from 18 to 20 miles an hour	10	10

Such accommodation is, on the whole, more economical than an hotel. The state room is as luxuriously furnished as the most handsome bed-room, and is more spacious than the room in packet ships similarly designated.

To obtain an adequate notion of the form and structure of one of the first-class steamboats on the Hudson, let it be supposed that a boat is constructed similar in form to a Thames wherry, but above three hundred feet long, and twenty-five or thirty feet wide. Upon this, let a platform of carpentry be laid, projecting several feet upon either side of the boat, and at stem and stern. The appearance to the eye will then be that of an immense raft, from two hundred and fifty to three hundred and fifty feet long, and some thirty or forty feet wide. Upon this flooring let us imagine an oblong, rectangular wooden erection, two stories high, to be raised. In the lower part of the boat, and under the flooring just mentioned, a long, narrow room is constructed, having a series of berths at either side, three or four tiers high. In the centre of this flooring is usually, but not always, inclosed an oblong, rectangular space, within which the steam machinery is placed, and this inclosed space is continued upward through the structure raised on the platform, and is intersected at a certain height above the platform by the shaft or axle of the paddle-wheels.

These wheels are propelled, generally, by a single engine, but occasionally, as in European states, by two. The paddle-wheels are usually of great diameter, varying from thirty to forty feet, according to the magnitude of the boat. In the wooden building raised upon the platform already mentioned, is contained a magnificent saloon devoted to ladies, and to those gentlemen who accompany them. Over this, in the upper story, is constructed a row of small bedrooms, each handsomely furnished, which those passengers can have who desire seclusion, by paying a small additional fare.

The lower apartment is commonly used as a dining or breakfast room.

In some boats, the wheels are propelled by two engines, which are placed on the platform which overhangs the boat at either side, each wheel being propelled by an independent engine; the wheels, in this case, acting independently of each other, and without a common shaft or axle.* This leaves the entire space in the boat, from stem to stern, free from machinery. It is impossible to describe the magnificent "*coup d'œil*" which is presented by the immense apparent length when the communication between them is thrown open. Some of these boats,

---

* The steamboat, Empire, which was recently lost by collision with another vessel, was thus constructed.

as has been already stated, are upward of three hundred feet long, and the uninterrupted length of the saloons corresponds with this.

This arrangement of machinery is attended with some practical advantages, one of which is a facility of turning, as the wheels, acting independently of each other, may be driven in opposite directions, one propelling forward and the other backward, so that the boat may be made to turn, as it were, on its centre. Although, from the great width of the Hudson, no great difficulty is encountered in turning the longest boat, yet cases occur in which this power of revolution is found extremely advantageous.

Another advantage of this system is, that when one of the two engines becomes accidentally disabled, the boat can be propelled by the other.

The general appearance of the Hudson steamers is represented in the annexed engraving of the "Iron Witch."

No spectacle can be more remarkable than that which the Hudson presents for several miles above New York. The skill with which these enormous vessels, measuring from three to four hundred feet in length, are made to thrid their way through the crowd of shipping, of every description, moving over the face of these spacious rivers, and the rare occurrence of accidents from collision, are truly admirable. In a dark night these boats run at the top of their speed through fleets of sailing vessels. The bells through which the steersman speaks to the engineer scarcely ever cease. Of these bells there are several of different tones, indicating the different operations which the engineer is commanded to make, such as stopping, starting, reversing, slackening, accelerating, &c. At the slightest tap of one of these bells, these enormous engines are stopped, or started, or reversed by the engineer, as though they were the plaything of a child. These vessels, proceeding at sixteen or eighteen miles an hour, are propelled among the crowded shipping with so much skill as almost to graze the sides, bows, or sterns of the vessels among which they pass.

The difficulty attending these evolutions by a vessel such as the New World, for example, one hundred and twenty-five yards long and twelve yards wide, may be easily imagined; and the promptitude and certainty with which an engine whose pistons are seventy-six inches in diameter, and whose stroke is five yards in length, is governed, must be truly surprising.

The navigation of the other rivers of the Atlantic States differs

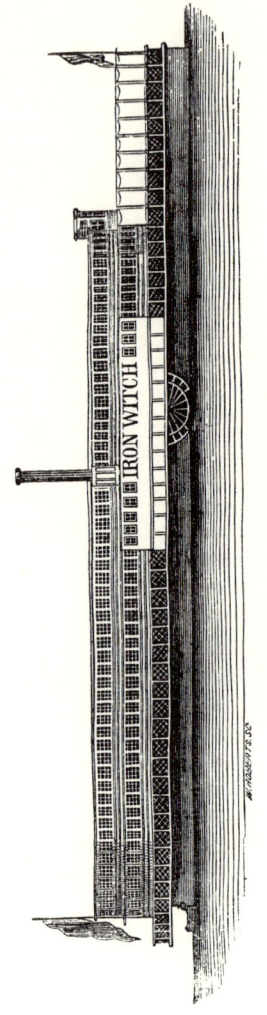

STEAM-BOAT IRON WITCH.
BUILT AT NEW YORK, AFTER THE DESIGN OF CAPTAIN ERICSSON.

in nothing from that of the Hudson and its collateral branches, except in the extent of their traffic and the magnitude and power of the steamers. The engines, in all cases, are constructed on the condensing principle; and although steam of forty or fifty pounds above the pressure of the atmosphere is frequently used, it is worked expansively, and a good vacuum is always sustained behind the piston by means of the condenser.

The steam navigation of the Mississippi is conducted in a manner entirely different from that of the Hudson and the Eastern rivers. Every one must be familiar with the lamentable accidents which happen from time to time, and the loss of life from explosion which continually takes place in these regions.

These accidents, instead of diminishing with the improvements of art, appear rather to have increased. Engineers, disregarding the heart-rending narratives continually published, have done literally nothing to check the evil; and it may be almost said to be a disgrace to humanity, that the legislature of the Union has not ere this interposed its authority to check abuses, which are productive of such calamities.

In a Mississippi steam-boat the cabins and saloons provided for the accommodation of the passengers, though less magnificently furnished, are as spacious as those already described in the boats on the Hudson. They are, however, erected on a flooring or platform, six or eight feet above the deck of the vessel. Upon this deck, and in the space under the cabins and saloons allotted to the passengers, are placed the engines, which are of the coarsest structure. They are invariably worked with high-pressure steam without condensation; and in order to obtain that effect which, in the boats on the Hudson, is due to the vacuum, the steam is worked at an extraordinary pressure. I have myself frequently witnessed boilers of the most inartificial construction worked with steam of the full pressure of 120 lbs. per square inch; but more recently this pressure has been increased, the ordinary working pressure being now 150 lbs., and I am assured, on good authority, that it is not unfrequently raised to even 200 lbs. The boilers are cylindrical, of large diameter, and of the rudest kind. When returning flues are constructed in them, the space left is so small, that the slightest variation in the quantity of water they contain, or in the trim of the vessel, causes the upper flues to be uncovered, and the intense action of the furnace in this case soon renders them red-hot, when a frightful collapse is almost inevitable. The red-hot iron, no longer able to resist the intense pressure, gives way, the boiler explodes, and the scalding water is scattered in all directions, often producing more terrible effects than even the fragments of the boiler, which are projected around with destructive force.

Another frequent cause of explosion in these boilers, is the quantity of mud held in suspension in the waters of the Mississippi below the mouth of the Missouri. As the water in the boiler is evaporated, the earthy matter which it held in suspension remains behind, and accumulates in the boiler, in the bottom of which it is at length collected in a thick stratum. This produces effects similar to those which take place in marine boilers, in consequence of the deposition of salt. This earthy stratum collected within the boiler being a non-conductor, the heat proceeding from the furnace is interrupted, and, instead of being absorbed by the water, is accumulated in the boiler-plates, which it ultimately renders red-hot. Being thus softened, they give way, and the boiler bursts. The only preventative remedy of this catastrophe is, to blow the water out of the boiler from time to time, before a dangerous accumulation of mud takes place, in the same manner as marine boilers are blown out to prevent the accumulation of salt. The engine-drivers and captains, however, rarely attend to this process. They are too intently bent upon obtaining speed, and, to use their own phrase, " going ahead." They do not hesitate to endanger their own lives and those of the passengers, rather than allow themselves to be outrun by a rival boat.

Not only the Mississippi, but the Ohio, the Missouri, the Illinois, the Red River, and, in a word, all the tributaries of the Father of rivers, are navigated for many thousands of miles by this description of boats, worked with the same reckless disregard of human life.

The magnitude and splendor of these boats is little if at all inferior to those of the Hudson. They are, however, constructed more with a view to the accommodation of freight, as they carry down the river large quantities of cotton and other produce, as well as passengers, to the port of New Orleans. Many of these vessels are three hundred feet and upward in length, and are capable of carrying a thousand tons freight, and three or four hundred deck passengers, besides the cabin passengers. The traffic in goods and passengers of the entire extent of the immense valley of the Mississippi is carried by these vessels, except that portion which is floated down by the stream in a species of raft called flat boats.

This line of steam navigation is continued up the Mississippi, branching east and west along its great tributaries. The Ohio carries it eastward as far as Pittsburgh in Pennsylvania. A canal connects the Ohio at Cincinnati with Lake Erie. The navigation of the Upper Mississippi is continued by the Illinois river to a port near Lake Michigan, with which it is connected by a canal extending to Chicago, on the western shore of that lake. Here commences the great chain of Lake steam navigation, which extends across the northern division of the States, traversing Lakes Michigan, Huron, Erie, and Ontario, and being continued along the St. Lawrence to Montreal and Quebec. The lakes are connected by canals, and the navigation is effected by steam-boats having submerged propellers at their stern, constructed almost universally according to the principle of Captain Ericsson. Upward of fifty vessels propelled by this improved method are now (1849) working between Chicago and Quebec, carrying grain and other products. Chicago is by this means converted into a port of great importance. This transit is further facilitated by the improvements recently made in the navigation of the St. Lawrence.

By the Erie canal, connecting the lake of that name with the head of the Hudson navigation at Albany, the circuit of navigaiton round the United States is completed.

Notwithstanding the facilities for coast navigation which are offered along the Atlantic shores from New York southward, successful efforts have been directed to establish a parallel inland communication by the Potomac and the Hudson. A line of inland steamers, also driven by Ericsson's propellers, are established between the Potomac and New York by Chesapeake Bay, the Delaware, the Chesapeake and Delaware canal, the Delaware and Raritan canal, and the Raritan river, and by these means the same line of communication is extended to the shores of New England and Long Island Sound.

A project is introduced, and likely to be carried into effect, for enlarging the Great Erie canal, so as to admit of steamers impelled by the same means. When this shall be effected, the entire extent of the States, from Washington, by New York, Albany, the great Northern Lakes, and the Mississippi, to New Orleans, will be surrounded by a continuous chain of inland steam navigation. The importance of this internal communication in the event of a war must be apparent.

Although the limits of the subject of this work would naturally confine it to inland communication, it will not be without interest to exhibit here the particulars of some of the steam-vessels intended for sea navigation. I have accordingly given, in the following table, the dimensions of some of those which have been most recently constructed, or are in process of construction:

326   RAILWAY ECONOMY.   [CHAP. XVI.

Name and Route of Vessel.	Dimensions of Vessel.				Engine.				Paddle-wheel.			
	Length.	Beam.	Depth of Hold.	Tonnage.	Diameter of Cylinder.	Length of Stroke.	Number of Strokes.		Diameter.	Length of Bucket.	Depth of Bucket.	
	Ft.	*Ft. In.*	*Ft. In.*		*In.*	*Ft. In.*			*Ft. In.*	*Ft. In.*	*In.*	
PANAMA, Panama and San Francisco	200	33 6	20 0	....	70	8 0	17		26 0	8 9	30	
PACIFIC, New York and Liverpool	280	45 6	24 0	....	95	9 0	16½		35 0	11 6	34	
ANTARCTIC, Do.	280	45 6	24 0	1750	96	10 0	16½		35 0	12 0	32	
WASHINGTON, New York, Southampton, and Bremen.	230	39 0	32 0	1850	72	10 0	12		35 0	7 6	36	
HERMANN, Do.	235	40 0	33 0	850	72	10 0	12		36 0	8 0	36	
SOUTHERNER, New York and Charleston	196	32 0	22 0	1000	67	8 0	14		31 0	7 7	30	
NORTHERNER, Do.	206	33 0	22 0	1250	70	8 0	14		31 0	7 7	30	
CHEROKEE, New York and Savannah	212	35 0	22 0	1250	75	8 0	14		31 0	8 0	30	
TENNESSEE, Do.	212	35 0	22 0	1100	75	8 0	14		26 0	8 0	30	
OREGON, Panama and Oregon	200	34 0	20 0	1050	70	8 0	14		26 0	9 0	30	
CALIFORNIA, Do.	200	33 0	26 0	2300	70	8 0	15		26 0	9 0	30	
FRANKLIN, New York and Havre	260	42 0	26 0	....	94	8 0	15		34 0	12 0	30	
ATLANTIC, New York and Liverpool	280	46 0	32 0	2800	95	9 0	..		35 0	12 0	32	
UNITED STATES, New York, New Orleans, and Chagres	250	40 0	34 6	....	80	9 0	16		35 0	9 0	36	
CRESCENT CITY, Do.	220	34 0	17 6	....	80	9 0	16		32 0	8 0	30	
EMPIRE CITY, Do.	230	38 0	17 6	....	83	9 0	..		32 0	8 6	30	
GEORGIA, Do.	260	45 0	34 6	....	90	8 0	..		36 0	10 0	30	
OHIO, Do.	260	47 0	34 6	....	90	8 0	16		36 0	10 6	30	
FALCON, Do., touching at Havanna	206	32 0	22 6	2419 3/2	60	5 0	..		31 0	7 8	13	
POWHATAN	254	45 0	26 6	2398 5/2	70	10 0	..		31 0	10 0	30	
SUSQUEHANNA } Government vessels	252	45 0	26 6	2398 5/2	70	10 0	..		31 0	9 6	34	
SARANAC	215	38 0	23 6	1459 5/2	60	9 0	..		27 0	9 0	30	
									Screw Propellers.		*No. of Blades.*	
SAN JACINTO	215	38 0	23 0	....	62¾	4 0	..		14 0	5 0	6	
CAROLINIAN, Philadelphia and Charleston	175	28 0	18 0	660	44	3 0	..		11 0			
PHILADELPHIA, Do.	192	33 0	18 6	....	56	3 6	19		27 0	9 0		
ISABEL, Charleston and Havannah	222	33 0	21 0	1115	72	8 0	16		31 0	8 0		
REPUBLIC, Baltimore and Charleston	200	30 0	18 6	800	54	6 0	..		25 6	8 0		

RAILWAYS.

The phenomena of transport so unexpectedly developed on the opening of the Liverpool and Manchester Railway, and the miracles of swift locomotion there exhibited, had no sooner been announced, than the Americans, with their usual ardor, resolved to import this great improvement; and projects of passenger railways, on the vast scale which characterizes all their enterprises, were immediately put forth.

Some lines of railway in isolated positions, around coal works and manufactories, had been, as in England, already for some years in operation. It was not, however, until after 1830 that the railway system began to assume in America the character which it had already taken in England. A few years were sufficient to bring it into practical operation in several parts of New England and in the State of New York; and once commenced, its progress was extremely rapid. A system nearly 9000 miles in length of railway in different parts of the Union was projected. A great portion of this, however, has not yet been brought into operation, and a part not even commenced. The total length of railways now in actual operation, exclusive of some lines about the mining districts and private establishments, amounts to something more than 6000 miles. More than 4000 miles of these were in operation as early as 1843, before England or any other country of Europe possessed railway communication at all approaching to the same extent.

As might naturally have been expected, the chief theatre of railway enterprise has been the Atlantic States. The Mississippi and its immense tributaries serve the purposes of commerce and intercommunication for the Western States so efficiently, and the population is comparatively so thinly spread over them, that many years will probably pass away before any considerable extent of railway communication will be established in that vast territory. Nevertheless, there are detached examples of railways serving local purposes in different parts of the Mississippi valley. Thus there are in the State of Mississippi five short railways; in Louisiana ten; a few in Florida, Alabama, Illinois, Michigan, Indiana, and Ohio. These are, however, detached and single, and form nothing approaching to a system. They are generally constructed to connect populous towns with the nearest adjacent navigable rivers.

To the traveler in these wilds, the aspect of such artificial lines of transport in the midst of a country a great portion of which is still in the state of native forest is most remarkable, and strongly characteristic of the irrepressible spirit of enterprise of its population. Traveling in the back woods of Mississippi, through native forests where, till within a few years, human foot never trod, through solitudes the stillness of which was never broken even by the red man, I have been filled with wonder to find myself drawn on a railway by an engine driven by an artisan from Liverpool, and whirled at the rate of twenty miles an hour by the highest refinements of the art of locomotion. It is not easy to describe the impression produced as one sees the frightened deer start from its lair at the snorting of the ponderous machine and the appearance of the snake-like train which follows it, and when one reflects on all that man has accomplished within half a century in this region.

Of the total length of railways which overspread the territory of the Union, more than the half are constructed in the States of Pennsylvania, New York, and those of New England. The principal centres from which these lines of communication diverge are Boston, New York, and Philadelphia.

A considerable extent, though of less importance, diverges from Baltimore; and recently lines of communication of great length have been constructed, from Charleston in South Carolina, and from Savannah in Georgia.

From Boston three trunk lines issue; the chief of which passes through the State of Massachusetts to Albany, on the Hudson. This line of railway is two hundred miles in length, and appears destined to carry a considerable traffic. Its ramifications southward, through the smaller states of New England, are numerous, chiefly leading to the ports upon Long Island Sound, which communicate by steamboats with New York. The first branch is carried from Worcester, in Massachusetts, to New London on the Sound, where it meets a short steam ferry which communicates with Greenport, at the eastern extremity of Long Island, from which another railway, nearly 100 miles long, is carried to Brooklyn, which occupies the shore of that island immediately opposite New York, and communicates with the latter city by a steam ferry.

Thus there is a continued railway communication from Boston to New York, interrupted only by two ferries.

Another branch of the great Massachusetts line is carried south from Springfield, through Hartford to New Haven; and a third from Pittsfield to Bridgeport, both the latter places being on the Sound, and communicating with New York by steamboats.

The second trunk line from Boston proceeds southward to Providence, and thence to Stonington, from which it communicates by a ferry with the Long Island Railway. This trunk line throws off a branch from Foxburgh to New Bedford, where it communicates by ferries with the group of islands and promontories clustered round Cape Cod.

A third trunk line proceeds from Boston through the State of Maine.

Notwithstanding the speed and perfection of the steam navigation of the Hudson, a railway is now being constructed on the east side of that river to Albany, which which will be opened in the course of 1850. The section terminating at New York is already in operation.

From Albany an extensive line of railway communication, 323 miles in length, is carried across the entire State of New York to Buffalo, at the head of Lake Erie, with branches to some important places on the one side and on the other. This line forms the continuation of the western railway, carried from Boston to Albany, and, combined with this latter, completes the continuous railway communication from the harbor of Boston to that of Buffalo on Lake Erie, making an entire length of railway communication, from Boston to Buffalo, of 523 miles.

The branches constructed from this trunk line are not numerous. There is one from Schenectady to Troy, on the Hudson, and another from Schenectady to Saratoga; another from Syracuse to Oswego, on Lake Ontario; and another from Buffalo to the falls of Niagara, and from thence to Lockport.

Not content with this fine line of communication to the Western Lakes, the commercial interests of New York have projected, and in part constructed, a more direct route from New York to Buffalo, independent of the Hudson.

The disadvantage of this river as a sole means of communication is, that, during a certain portion of the winter, all traffic upon it is suspended by frost. In this case, the line of railway communicating already from Bridgeport and New Haven to Albany has been resorted to by travelers. However, it may be regarded as certain, that the intermediate traffic of the State of New York along the direct line of railway now in progress from that city to Buffalo, will very speedily be sufficient for the support of an independent line of railway.

The immediate environs of New York are served by several

short railways, as is usual, indeed, in all great capitals where the railway system of transport prevails.

The line connecting that city with Harlem is analogous in many respects to the Greenwich and Blackwall lines at London, and the Versailles and St. Germain lines at Paris. It is supported by a like description of traffic. The New York line, however, has this peculiarity, that it is conducted through the streets of the capital upon their natural level, without either cutting, tunnel, or embankment. The carriages, on entering the town, are drawn by horses, four horses being allowed to each coach; each coach carrying from sixty to eighty persons, and being constructed like the railway coaches in general in the United States.

The rails along the streets are laid down in a manner similar to that which is customary at places where lines of railway in England cross turnpike roads on a level. The surface of the rail is flush with the pavement, and a cavity is left for the flange to sink in.

Other short railways, from New York to Patterson, Morristown, and Somerville, require no particular note.

The great line of railway already described, from Boston to New York, is continued southward from that capital to Philadelphia. There are here two rival lines; one of which, commencing from Jersey city on the Hudson, opposite the southern part of New York, is carried to Bordentown, on the left bank of the Delaware, whence the traffic is carried by steamboats a few miles further to Philadelphia. The rival line commences from South Amboy in New Jersey, to which the traffic is brought from New York by steamers plying on the Raritan river, which separates New Jersey from Staten Island. From Amboy, the railway is continued to Camden, on the left bank of the Delaware opposite Philadelphia.

By far the greater part of the traffic between New York and Philadelphia is carried by the former line.

Philadelphia is the next great centre from which railways diverge. One line is carried westward through the State of Pennsylvania, passing through Reading, and terminating at Pottsville, in the midst of the great Pennsylvanian coal-field. There it connects with a network of small railways, serving the coal and iron mines of this locality. This line of railway is a descending line toward Philadelphia, and serves the purposes of the mining districts better than a level. The loaded trains descend usually with but little effort to the moving power, while the empty wagons are drawn back.

The passenger traffic is chiefly between Reading and Philadelphia.

Another line of railway is carried westward through the State of Pennsylvania, passing through Lancaster, Harrisburg, the seat of the legislature, Carlisle, and Chambersburg, where it approaches the Baltimore and Ohio Railway. The length of this railway from Philadelphia to Chambersburg is 154 miles. The former, to Pottsville and Mount Carbon, is 108 miles, the section to Reading being 64.

A great line of communication is established, 400 miles in length, between Philadelphia and Pittsburg, on the left bank of the Ohio, composed partly of railway and partly of canal. The section from Philadelphia to Columbia, 82 miles, is railway. The line is then continued by canal, for 172 miles, to Holidaysburg. It is then carried by railway 37 miles to Johnstown, from whence it is continued 104 miles further to Pittsburg by canal.

The traffic on this mixed line of transport is conducted so as to avoid the expense and inconvenience of transhipment of goods and passengers at the successive points where the railway and canals unite. The merchandise is loaded, and the passengers accommodated in the boats adapted to the canals, at the dépôt in Market-street, Philadelphia. These boats, which are of considerable magnitude and length, are divided into segments, by partitions made transversely and at right angles to their length, so that each boat can be, as it were, broken into three or more pieces. These several pieces are placed each on two railway trucks, which support it at its ends, a proper body being provided for the trucks adapted to the form of the bottom and keel of the boat. In this manner the boat is carried in pieces, with its load, along the railways. On arriving at the canal, the pieces are united so as to form a continuous boat, which, being launched, the transport is continued on the water.

On arriving again at the railway, the boat is once more resolved into its segments, which, as before, are transferred to the railway trucks, and transported to the next canal station by locomotive engines.

Between the dépôt in Market-street and the locomotive station, which is situate in the suburbs of Philadelphia, the segments of the boats are drawn by horses, on railways conducted through the streets. At the locomotive station the trucks are formed into a continuous train, and delivered over to the locomotive engine.

As the body of the trucks rests upon a pivot, under which it is supported by the wheels, it is capable of revolving, and no difficulty is found in turning the shortest curves; and these enormous vehicles, with their contents of merchandise and passengers are seen daily issuing from the gates of the dépôt in Market-street, and turning without difficulty the corners at the entrance of each successive street.

The southern line of railway communication is continued from Philadelphia to Baltimore, interrupted only by a steam ferry over the Susquehanna.

The management of these steam ferries is deserving of notice. It is generally so arranged, that the time of crossing them corresponds with a meal of the passengers. A platform is constructed, level with the line of rails, and carried to the water's edge. Upon this platform rails are laid, on which the wagons which bear the passengers' luggage, and other matters of light and rapid transport, are rolled directly upon the upper deck of the ferry-boat, the passengers meanwhile passing under a covered way to the lower deck.

The whole operation is accomplished in five minutes. While the boat is crossing the spacious river, the passengers are supplied with their breakfast, dinner, lunch, or supper, as the case may be. On arriving at the opposite bank, the upper deck comes into contact with a like platform, bearing a railway upon which the luggage wagons are rolled. The passengers ascend by a covered way, and, resuming their places in the railway carriages, the train proceeds.

Baltimore is the next centre of railway movement. One line issues northward to Harrisburg in Pennsylvania, where it unites with the Philadelphia and Chambersburg line. A great line of western railway is projected to be carried from Baltimore to the left bank of the Ohio, to some point near Wheeling. This line, however, is as yet finished only so far as Cumberland, 153 miles. This place is at the foot of the Alleghany range, which is crossed by the great national, an excellent Macadamized roadway, which continues the communication 126 miles further, to Wheeling, on the Ohio. The ascent is gradual, and constructed on good engineering principles.

The railway, when completed, will cross this ascent by a series of inclined planes, all of which but one will be worked by locomotive engines. This will probably be worked by means of a stationary engine. Nothing, however, is done as yet toward the realization of this part of the project.

Baltimore is connected with Washington, the seat of the federal legislature, by an excellent line of railway, nearly forty miles in length. From this point the great southern line of communication is continued by steam-boats on the Potomac to the left bank of that river near Fredericksburg, in Virginia, a distance of about fifty miles. Here the line of railway communication is resumed and continued through the State of Virginia, passing through Richmond and Petersburg, being continued southward to Halifax, on the frontiers of North Carolina.

Another line of communication southward is formed by steamboats on the Chesapeake, which ply between Baltimore and Norfolk, from which place a line of railway is carried to the frontiers of North Carolina, near Halifax, running into the great artery just mentioned, at Weldon. From Halifax the great southern railway is continued through North Carolina to Wilmington, a seaport near the southern limits of that state.

Thus is completed so far a continuous line of railway communication running north and south through the Atlantic States, commencing at Portland in the State of Maine, passing successively through Boston, Providence, New York, Philadelphia, Baltimore, Washington, and Richmond, and terminating at Wilmington, the total length of which is nearly 1000 miles. From Wilmington the communication with Charleston is maintained by steam-boats, which ply along the coast.

Charleston in South Carolina, and Savannah in Georgia, are the points from which other great lines of railway communication issue westward. That which proceeds from Charleston is carried across South Carolina to Augusta, on the confines of Georgia, throwing off a branch northward to Columbia, the capital of the state.

The length of the main line to Augusta is 134 miles.

From Augusta the line of railway is continued westward through Georgia, passing through Madison and Decatur to the left bank of the Tennessee river, throwing off a branch to Athens, the seat of the university.

From Savannah the line of railway passes through Georgia and Macon, and unites with the former line at Decatur.

These lines of railway communication are continued westward to the left bank of the Alabama river, on which the transport is continued by steam-boats to Mobile, and thence to New Orleans, and by another line to the Tennessee, by which the navigation is continued through the Mississippi valley to the left bank of its great tributary, the Ohio.

When the expenditure involved in the construction and maintenance of the railways of the United Kingdom is considered, the financier, the statistician, and the economist will naturally ask how, with a population so sparse and a territory so vast, a system of communication so extensive, could be established and sustained ? If the great mass of the passenger lines in England have cost at the rate of forty thousand pounds per mile, and the profits gained even on the most successful among them do not exceed seven per cent., while the average profits of all do not much exceed half that rate—how, it may be asked, can this stupendous system of American railways, with a traffic comparatively so insignificant, among a people where profits on capital are high and the rate of interest from six to ten per cent., be made to answer.

This difficulty is explained, partly by the general nature of the country, partly by the mode of constructing the railways, and partly by the manner of working them.

With certain exceptions, few in number, the tracts of country over which these railways pass form nearly a dead level. Of earth-work, therefore, there is but little. Occasionally, low embankments and shallow cuttings are all the difficulties the engineer has to surmount. Of works of art, such as viaducts and tunnels, there are almost none. Where the lines have to be conducted over streams or rivers, bridges are constructed, in a rude but substantial and secure manner, of timber, which is supplied from forests at the road-side, subject to no other cost save that of hewing it. The station-houses, booking-offices, and other buildings are likewise slightly and cheaply constructed of timber.

On some of the best lines the timber bridges are constructed with stone piers and abutments supporting arches of truss-work. The cost of such bridges varies from 46s. per foot for 60 feet span to £6 10s. per foot for 200 feet span, for a single line, the cost for a double line being 50 per cent. more. This includes the road work and rails, but not the masonry of the piers and abutments.

A bridge of this kind is constructed on the Philadelphia and Reading Railway, the length of which is 1800 feet, and the cost of which was £8600.

Where the railways strike the course of rivers of great breadth, such as the Hudson, the East River, the Delaware, the Susquehannah, or the Potomac, the transport is continued, as already explained, by steam ferries.

But, besides the facilities afforded for the formation of railways by the flat and level character of the country, and the boundless supply of timber at a trifling cost, a further and much larger economy is effected, as compared with European lines, by the method of construction.

Formed to supply a very limited amount of traffic in proportion to their length, the American railways are, generally, single lines. Sidings are of course provided at convenient stations, in which one train waits until the train in the contrary direction has passed. Collision is impossible, for the first train which arrives must, by the rules of the road, move into the siding. This arrangement would be attended with inconvenience, on lines where a frequent passage of trains takes place; but on the principal American lines, the fast trains seldom pass in each direction more than twice a day, and the time and place of their meeting is perfectly regulated. In fact, no inconvenience is felt or complained of from this cause in the practical working of the lines. In cases where the traffic is so considerable as to require them, double lines have been constructed.

In the structure of the roads themselves, principles have been adopted which have been attended with great economy compared with European lines—the application of which was rendered admissible by the lightness of the traffic and the moderate speed contemplated. In laying out these lines, the engineers did not, as in England, impose on themselves the difficult and expensive condition of excluding all curves but those of a large radius. On the other hand, curves having a radius of one thousand feet are usual; and occasionally curves of five hundred feet, and even less, are allowed. Nor are the gradients restricted to the same low limits as with us. Acclivities rising at the rate of one foot in a hundred and thirty, are considered a moderate ascent; and there are not less than fifty lines in which the gradients are laid down at a rate varying from one in a hundred to one in seventy-five. Nevertheless, these lines are worked without difficulty by locomotives, without the expedient either of assistant or stationary engines. The consequences of this have been to diminish the cost of earth-work, bridges, and viaducts, even in parts of the country where the character of the surface is least favorable. But the chief source of economy in the construction of these lines has arisen from the structure of the road surface. In many cases where there is a light traffic, the rails consist of flat bars of iron two and a half inches broad, and from five to seven tenths of an inch thick—nailed or spiked down to planks of timber laid longitudinally on the road in parallel lines, at the proper width, so as to form what are called continuous bearings. Some of the most profitable lines, and those of which the maintenance has proved the least expensive, have been constructed in this manner.

The structure of the road, however, varies in its character according to the traffic. Rails are sometimes laid down weighing from twenty-five to thirty pounds per yard. In some cases of still greater traffic, the rails are laid on transverse sleepers of wood, in the same manner as on the European railways; but, in consequence of the comparative cheapness of wood and high price of iron, the strength necessary for the road is obtained by reducing the distance between the sleepers, so as to supersede the necessity of giving greater weight to the rails.

In all cases where augmented traffic may be expected from the increase of population and commerce, the earth-work and structures on the lines are made so as to admit of a double line of rails, whenever they may be required.

In the working of the railways, the same attention to the economy rendered necessary by their limited traffic is observable. The engines are strongly built, perfectly safe, and sufficiently powerful; but they are destitute of much of that elegance of exterior, and luxurious beauty of workmanship, which are seen upon the British locomotives. The fuel used to work them is generally wood. On certain lines, however, in the neighborhood of coal-mines—such, for example as the Philadelphia and Pottsville Railway, which penetrates into the great coal-fields of Pennsylvania—coal is the fuel used. The use of coke is nowhere resorted to. Its expense would make it inadmissible; and in a country so thinly inhabited, the smoke proceeding from coal or wood is not objected to.

The ordinary speed, stoppages included, is fourteen or fifteen miles an hour. Independently of other considerations, the light structure of most of the railways would not allow of a greater velocity without considerable danger; on some of the better constructed lines, I have, however, freqently traveled at the rate of twenty-five miles an hour, when at full speed. This is not uncommon on some of the New England lines—on the railway from Baltimore to Washington, and some of the southern lines; as, for example, that between Charleston and Augusta in Georgia, the Columbia line in South Carolina, and the line from Augusta to the University of Athens in Georgia.

Notwithstanding the apparently feeble and unsubstantial structure of some of the lines, accidents to passenger trains are scarcely ever heard of in America. With an experience of nearly twenty thousand miles of railway traveling in the United States, I have never encountered an accident of any kind, or heard of a fatal or injurious one. This security may be explained by the moderate speed of the trains, and the absence of a highly active traffic.

In some cases of lightly constructed roads, where the bars spiked down on the planks are not kept in good order, an accident, called (from its analogy to a catastrophe common on American rivers) *snagging*, is said sometimes to have happened. In this case the iron bar, worn thin and unspiked, gets detached from the plank, and as the wheels pass upon it, springs up and pierces the bottom of the carriage, to the great danger of the passengers. I have, however, never met with a well authenticated case of this kind.

The form and structure of the carriages is a source of considerable economy in the working of the lines. The passenger carriages are not distinguished, as in Europe, by different modes of providing for the ease and comfort of the traveler. There are no first, second, and third classes. All are first class, or rather all are of the same class. The carriage consists of a long body like that of a London omnibus, but much wider, and twice or thrice the length. The doors of exit and entrance are at each end; a line of windows being placed at each side, similar exactly to those of an omnibus. Along the centre of this species of caravan is an alley or passage, just wide enough to allow one person to walk from end to end. On either side of this alley are seats for the passengers, extending crossways. Each seat accommodates two persons; four sitting in each row, two at each side of the alley. There are from 15 to 20 of these seats, so that the carriage accommodates from 60 to 80 passengers. In cold weather, a small stove is placed near the centre of the carriage, the smoke-pipe of which passes out through the roof; and a good lamp is placed at each end for illumination during the night. The vehicle is perfectly lighted and warmed. The seats are cushioned; and their backs, consisting of a simple padded board, about six inches broad, are so supported that the passenger may at his pleasure turn them either way, so as to turn his face or his back to the engine. For the convenience of ladies who travel unaccompanied by gentlemen, or who otherwise desire to be apart, a small room, appropriately furnished, is sometimes attached at the end of the carriage, admission to which is forbidden to gentlemen.

It will occur at once to the engineer, that vehicles of such extraordinary length would require a railway absolutely straight: it would be impossible to move them through any portion of a line which has sensible curvature. Curves which would be altogether inadmissible on any European line are nevertheless admitted in the construction of American railways without difficulty or hesitation, and through these the vehicles just described move with the utmost facility. This is accomplished by a simple and effectual arrangement. Each end of this oblong caravan is supported on a small four wheeled railway truck, on which it rests on a pivot; exactly similar to the expedient by which the fore-wheels of a carriage sustain the perch. These railway carriages have in fact two perches, one at each end; but instead of resting on two wheels, each of them rests on four. The vehicle has therefore the facility of changing the direction of its motion at each end; and in moving through a curve, one of the trucks will be in one part of the curve while the other is at another—the length of the body of the carriage forming the *cord* of the intermediate arc! For the purposes they are designed to answer, these carriages present many advantages. The simplicity of the structure renders the expense of their construction incomparably less than that of any class of carriage on an European railway. But a still greater source of saving is apparent in their operation. The proportion of the dead weight to the profitable load is far less than in the first or second-class carriages, or even than the third-class on the English railways. It is quite true that these carriages do not offer to the wealthy passenger all the luxurious accommodation which he finds in our best first-class carriages; but they afford every necessary convenience and comfort.

In several of the principal American cities, the railways are continued to the very centre of the town, following the windings of the streets, and turning without difficulty the sharpest corners. The locomotive station is, however, always in the suburbs. Having arrived there, the engine is detached from the train, and horses are yoked to the carriages, by which they are drawn to the passenger dépôt, usually established at some central situation. Four horses are attached to each of these oblong carriages. The sharp curves at the corners of the streets are turned, by causing the outer wheels of the trucks to run upon their flanges, so that they become (while passing round the curve) virtually larger wheels than the inner ones. I have seen, by this means, the longest railway carriages enter the dépôts in Philadelphia, Baltimore, and New York, with as much precision and facility as was exhibited by the coaches that used to enter the gateway of the Golden Cross or the Saracen's Head.

The paucity of official, or other authentic information respecting the American railways, renders it difficult to discover with precision either the cost of constructing or working them collectively, or even the actual length of railway under traffic. M. Michel Chevalier ascertained from the most authentic sources, that on the 1st of January, 1843, the total length projected was 9076 miles, of which 4235 miles were completed and under traffic.

Since that date, a considerable extent of railways has been completed. The following table, showing the lines completed in June, 1849, the length to be completed, and the expense of construction, so far as they could be ascertained, may be considered as presenting the most complete and authentic statement of the actual condition of the railways of the United States which can be supplied:

TABULAR REPORT of the Railways of the United States, showing the Extent of the Lines completed and under Traffic in June, 1849; the Length of Lines projected but not completed; the Cost of Construction and Plant, where such Particulars can be ascertained; the last Dividends, and the average Prices of Shares.

Name of Company.	Length of Line.	Length of Branches.	Miles finished.	Cost of Road and Equipment.	Cost per Mile.	Dividends in 1848.	Price of Shares.
				£.	£.		
Atlantic and St. Lawrence	146	..	36	In progress.	..	..	78 *a* 81
Androscoggin and Kennebeck	55	..	6	In progress.	..	..	70
Albany and Schenectady..	16⅞	..	16⅞	356,932	22,222	1 5–9	82
Auburn and Rochester....	78	..	78	587,671	7,555	8	86
Auburn and Syracuse....	26	..	26	250,197	9,622	2 9–10	80 *a* 81
Attica and Buffalo.......	31½	..	31½	182,514	5,777	4¼	..
Alleghany and Portage...	36	..	36	..	..	..	Leased to
Albany and W. Stockb...	38¼	..	38¼	427,711	11,111	..	Western
Bangor and Oldtown.....	11¾	..	11¾	..	..	..	Railroad.
Boston and Lowell.......	25¾	1¾	27½	447,486	16,266	8	116¼
Boston and Maine........	74¾	5	79¼	793,740	10,000	8½	105¾
Boston and Worcester....	44⅝	22	66⅝	1,033,421	15,555	8½	108¼
Boston and Providence...	41	6½	47½	673,579	14,177	6½	91
Bristol Branch...........	12	..	12	..	..	..	..
Boston, Concord, and Montreal	90	..	38	In progress.	..	..	..
Berkshire...............	21	..	21	133,333	6,333	7	..
Buffalo and Niagara......	22	..	22	55,643	2,555	6 1–3	..
Baltimore and Susquehanna	36	..	36	..	..	..	..
Beaver Meadow.........	26	..	26	..	..	..	..

Name of Company.	Length of Line.	Length of Branches.	Miles finished.	Cost of Road and Equipment.	Cost per Mile.	Dividends in 1848.	Price of Shares.
				£.	£.		
Baltimore and Ohio......	..	..	178				
Baltimore and Washington Branch...............	..	..	31	2,919,320	13,844	..	40 *a* 41
Calais and Baring........	3	..	3	..	..	..	..
Concord	34	..	34	..	..	..	..
Cheshire	54	..	54	423,435	7,846	..	72
Connecticut and Passump.	115	..	40	4,644	..	..	85
Connecticut River........	50	2	52	352,929	6,777	8	97¼
Cape Cod Branch........	28	..	28	130,470	4,644	..	62
Corning and Blossburgh ..	..	..	40	..	..	..	..
Cayuga and Susquehanna	28¼	..	28¼	..	..	..	..
Camden and Amboy.....	61						
Trenton Branch........	6¼	.	96¼	711,111	7,333	..	130 *a* 135
New Brunswick Branch	29						
Columbia................	82	..	82	..	..	..	..
Camden and Woodbury ..	9	..	9	..	..	..	..
Cumberland Valley	..	..	52	..	..	..	..
Carbondale and Honesdale	26	..	26	..	..	..	..
Chesterfield	12	..	12	33,333	3,000	..	..
City Point	9¼	..	9¼	43,526	3,535	..	..
Central of Georgia	191	..	191	..	..	..	..
Central of New Jersey....	63	..	36	..	..	..	..
Dorchester and Milton....	3¼	..	3¼	25,283	7,800	..	..
Detroit and Pontiac.......	25	..	25	..	..	..	..
Eastern	54	19¾	73¾	..	..	8	99½
Essex (Salem to Law.)...	22½	..	22½	93,683	4,155	..	..
Erie and Kalamazoo	33	..	33	..	..	..	..
Fall River	42	..	42	254,662	6,066	7½	86
Fitchburg	49¼	6¾	56	654,584	11,622	8½	112½
Franklin	..	..	22	63,136	3,006	..	..
Greensville and Roanoke	21	..	21	..	..	..	..
Germantown Branch.....	6	..	6	..	..	..	88 *a* 90
Gaston and Raleigh......	96	..	96	..	..	..	..
Georgia(Augusta to Attica)	171	..	171	..	..	..	..
Harrisburgh and Lancaster	37	..	37	..	..	..	88 *a* 90
Hartford and New Haven	62	..	62	..	..	..	104 *a* 105
Housatonic	74	..	74	..	..	..	86½
Hudson and Berkshire ...	31½	..	31½	181,996	5,888	..	..
Hickford and Gaston	21	..	21	..	..	..	..
Hazleton and Lehigh	10	..	10	..	..	..	..
Jackson and Brandon	13	..	13	..	..	..	..
Lexington and West Cambridge	6½	..	6½	56,151	8,644	..	..
Lowell and Lawrence....	12½	..	12½	62,944	5,033	..	..
Long Island	98¼	..	98¼	483,032	4,911	..	23½
Lockport and Niagara	23	..	23	49,111	2,154	..	..
Lewiston................	3¼	..	3¼	7,483	2,288	..	..
Lykens Valley...........	16	..	16	..	..	..	..
Little Schuylkill	23	..	23	..	..	..	..
Louisa	50	..	50	105,364	2,107	..	..
Lexington and Frankfort..	29	..	29	100,000	3,466	..	..
Little Miami.............	84	..	84	336,311	4,000	..	..
Machias Port	8	..	8	..	..	..	..
Morris and Essex	23	..	23	..	..	..	..
Mauch Chunk and R. Run	36	..	36	..	..	..	..
Mine Hill and Sc. Haven..	25	..	25	..	..	..	136
Mount Carbon	7	..	7	..	..	..	..
Mount Carbon and Point Carbon	2½	..	2½	..	..	..	..
Mill Creek..............	6	..	6	..	..	..	..
Montgomery and West Point...................	67	..	67	..	..	..	..

Name of Company.	Length of Line.	Length of Branches.	Miles finished.	Cost of Road and Equipment.	Cost per Mile.	Dividends in 1848.	Price of Shares.
				£.	£.		
Madison and Indianapolis	86	..	86	..	..	..	110
Mad River and Lake Erie	102	..	102	..	..	..	..
Mansfield and Sandusky..	..	..	56	245,804	4,378	..	..
Michigan Central........	..	..	221	..	..	..	..
Michigan Southern.......	..	..	70	..	..	..	..
Macon and Western......	..	..	101	..	..	..	..
Mississippi	..	..	30	..	..	..	..
Nashua and Lowell......	..	..	14½	116,680	8,044	10	..
Northern (Ogdensburg) ...	..	..	12	Unfinished.	..	..	..
„ (Concord to Lebanon)	..	..	69	..	..	..	80½
New Bedford and Taunton	..	..	20	110,903	5,555	6	..
Norfolk County..........	..	..	26	138,108	5,310	..	57½
New York and New Haven (14 miles Harlem branch)	..	..	62	..	..	..	90
New Haven Canal	..	..	28	..	..	..	..
Norwich and Worcester ..	59	7	66	486,184	7,355	..	37
New York and Harlem...	..	..	80¼	795,458	9,911	..	58½
New York and Erie......	..	..	200	..	..	..	61 *a* 62
New Jersey	..	..	29	..	..	..	107 *a* 108
Newcastle and Frenchtown	..	..	17	..	..	..	..
New Orleans and Carrollton	..	..	5½	..	..	..	..
Old Colony	37¼	7¾	45	462,423	10,266	6½	80⅝
Oswego and Syracuse....	..	..	41	..	..	..	..
Portland, Portsmouth, and Saco	51	..	51	300,000	5,866	6	96½
Peterborough and Shirley	12	..	12	46,291	3,844	..	..
Pittsfield and New Adams	18¾	..	18¾	99,501	5,333	..	..
Providence and Worcester	43½	..	43½	416,421	9,555	..	82½
Providence and Stonington	50	..	50	..	..	..	..
Patterson and Hudson River	16½	..	16½	..	..	..	..
Philadelphia and Trenton	28	..	28	..	..	10	130 *a* 140
Philadelphia, Wilmington, and Baltimore	97	..	97	1,371,967	14,666	..	54
Philadelphia City	6	..	6	..	..	..	..
Philadelphia, Germantown, and Norristown.	17	..	17	..	..	..	..
Philadelphia and Reading	93	..	93	..	..	..	29¾
Penn Township..........	2	..	2	..	..	..	..
Petersburg	59	..	59	210,302	3,564	..	..
Portsmouth and Roanoke	..	..	76½	337,586	4,546	..	..
Pontchartrain	4½	..	4½	..	..	..	..
Point Hudson, Jackson, and Clinton................	28	..	28	..	..	..	..
Rensselaer and Saratoga..	25	..	25	155,962	6,222	..	..
Richmond, Fredericksburg, and Potomac	75¾	..	75¾	327,556	4,324	..	..
Richmond and Petersburg	22	..	22	194,996	8,863	..	..
Sullivan.................	28	..	28	..	..	..	..
South Shore.............	11½	..	11½	56,832	4,933	..	33½
Stony Brook.............	13	..	13	54,813	4,222	..	..
Saratoga and Washington	40	..	40	210,749	5,266	..	..
Syracuse and Utica	53	..	53	437,341	8,235	..	..
Schenectady and Troy ...	20½	..	20½	146,591	7,132	..	..
Saratoga and Schenectady	22	..	22	73,564	3,333	..	..
Summit	2	..	2	..	..	..	..
Schuylkill Valley	14	..	14	..	..	..	..
Shamokin	22	..	22	..	..	..	..
Swatara.................	4	..	4	..	..	..	..
South Carolina Main Stem	136	..	..	..	..	..	..
Columbia Branch	..	68½	242	1,320,817	5,444	..	..
Camden Branch	..	37½	..	..	..	..	..
Sangamon and Morgan ...	53	..	53	..	..	..	..

342   RAILWAY ECONOMY.   [Chap. XVI.

Name of Company.	Length of Line.	Length of Branches.	Miles finished.	Cost of Road and Equipment.	Cost per Mile.	Dividends in 1848.	Price of Shares.
				£.	£.		
Taunton Branch.........	..	..	11	67,796	6,133	..	..
Tonawanda.............	43½	..	43½	216,636	4,977	..	..
Troy and Greenbush.....	6	..	6	60,806	10,200	..	..
Tuckahoe James River...	4¾	..	4¾	15,405	3,333	..	..
Tallahasse and Port L ...	..	..	26	..	..	..	..
Tuscumbia and Decatur ..	..	..	44	..	..	..	..
Utica and Schenectady...	78	..	78	702,597	9,000	10	120 a 121
Vermont and Massachusetts	69	..	69	..	..	..	45½
Vermont Central.........	121	..	69	..	..	..	53½
Vicksburg and Clinton....	..	..	46	..	..	..	..
Western	117¾	..	117¾	1,772,323	15,044	8	105
West Stockbridge........	2¾	..	2¾	9,226	3,333	..	..
Worcester and Nashua...	45	..	45	..	..	..	52
Wrightsville, York, and Gettys..................	..	..	13	..	..	..	..
Whitehaven and Wilkes..	..	..	20	..	..	..	..
Williamsport and Elmira	..	..	26	..	..	..	..
Westchester Branch	..	..	10	..	..	..	..
West Feliciana	..	..	24	..	..	..	..
Westchester and Potomac	..	..	32	113,203	3,538	..	..
Wilmington and Weldon	..	..	150	..	..	..	..
Westminster Branch	..	..	10	..	..	..	..
Western and Atlantic....	..	..	100	..	..	..	..
York and Maryland Line	..	..	21	..	..	..	..
Total length......	4789¾	184¼	6565¼*				

* The lengths of lines projected is given in this Table only so far as they have been ascertained. It will be observed that in numerous cases lengths are given as completed without any corresponding number in the first column. In such cases it must be understood that the lengths projected are unascertained.

From this table it appears, that the total length of the railways completed and under traffic in the United States in the present year (1849) is 6565 miles.

The cost of construction and plant of 2842 miles of these is known, and amounts in the aggregate to £23,104,909, which is at the average rate of £8129 per mile.

If we assume that the remainder of the railways under traffic, amounting to 3723 miles, have cost the same average sum per mile, then it will follow that the total cost of the railways completed, amounting to 6565 miles, has been £53,386,885.

It appears, therefore, on this supposition, that above 6500 miles of railway have been constructed in the United States, at a cost of 53 millions, while 5000 miles of railway in the United Kingdom have cost 200 millions.

I have not been able to obtain any reports from which

CHAP. XVI.] INLAND TRANSPORT IN THE U. STATES. 349

the movement of the traffic on the American railways collectively can be ascertained with precision; but I have obtained the necessary statistical data relating to nearly twelve hundred miles of railway in the States of New England and in that of New York, from which I have been enabled to calculate all the circumstances attending the working of these lines. I have, accordingly, given these in the following table:

TABULAR ANALYSIS of the average daily Movement of the Traffic on Twenty-eight principal Railways in the States of New England and in the State of New York during the Year 1847.

	Passenger Traffic.				Goods Traffic.			
	No. booked.	Mileage.	Receipts.	Mileage of Trains.	Tons booked.	Mileage.	Receipts.	Mileage of Trains.
			£.					
Albany and Schenectady	630	9,787	65	136			32	62
Utica-Schenectady.	733	37,600	300	406			111	360
Syracuse-Utica....	544	21,550	169	288			38	151
Auburn-Rochester.	518	24,200	197	400			37	212
Tonawanda	367	13,000	92	212			23	40
Attica-Buffalo	358	9,850	61	162			19	48
Saratoga—Schenectady	146	2,068	22	54	1730*	65,550*	4	4
Troy-Schenectady .	189	3,840	20	140			8	9
Reussalaer-Saratoga	181	2,625	24	680			12	26
Troy and Greenbush	545	3,090	21	131			25	19
New York and Harlem	4,336	17,000	133	450			80	170
New York-Erie....	326	12,400	60	246			102	191
Boston-Worcester .	1,640	39,672	180	580	775	29,450	221	459
Western	1,062	48,952	296	648	752	76,580	471	1,408
Norwich-Worcester	434	8,158	67	326	249	7,858	64	204
Connecticut River..	650	6,454	42	203	122	2,210	28	64
Pittsfield-N. Adam .	98	11,048	9	45	29	469	6	31
Boston-Providence .	1,338	19,680	133	464	240	5,310	69	143
Trenton	297	3,234	20	60	83	910	10	19
New Bedford	268	4,460	40	173	53	930	13	53
Stoughton Branch .	46	482	3	11	22	238	3	4
Lowell	1,328	26,050	120	452	770	19,450	139	194
Nashua	618	8,540	41	81	414	6,130	49	55
Boston-Maine	1,995	34,500	189	625	330	9,880	106	200
Fitchburg	1,342	21,920	98	434	670	14,230	119	192
Eastern	2,240	34,910	203	557	112	3,190	30	93
Old Colony	1,068	13,420	73	288	117	2,048	24	77
Fall River	474	8,860	46	219	79	1,718	18	72
	23,981	437,350	2,723	8,091	6,547	248,351	1,861	4,560

* The reports do not supply the tonnage and mileage of these railways separately, and the above numbers are estimated by analogy with the other American railways.

				Miles.
Total length of the above railways in the State of New York				490
,,	,,	,,	States of New England..	670
			Total....	1160

				£.
Average cost of construction and stock per mile in the State of New York....				7,010
,,	,,	,,	States of New England	10,800
			General average....	9,200

	Receipts.	Expenses.	Profits.
Total average receipts, expenses, and profits per day in the State of New York	1654	684	970
,, ,, ,, States of New England	3040	1505	1535
Totals....	4694	2189	2505

	Per Mile of Railway per day. £.	Per Mile run by Trains. s. d.	Per Cent. per Annum on Capital.
Receipts	4·05	7 5	16·1
Expenses	1·89	3 5½	7·5
Profits	2·16	2 11½	8·6

Expense per cent. of receipts................................... 46·8

Average receipts per passenger booked	27·0 d.
Average distance traveled per passenger	18·2 miles
Average receipts per passenger per mile	1·47 d
Average number of passengers per train	54·0
Total average receipts per passenger train per mile	7s.
Average receipts per ton of goods booked	5s. 8½ d.
Average distance carried per ton	38·0 miles
Average receipts per ton per mile	1·8 d
Average number of tons per train	54·5
Total average receipts per goods train per mile	8·2 s.

The railways, of the traffic of which I have here given a synopsis, include the most active and profitable enterprises of this kind in the United States. We can not, therefore, infer from the results obtained, the corresponding movement on the remaining lines. It will appear by the table given in page 403, of the entire system of American railways, that the dividends, exclusive of those contained in the preceding analysis, are in general small, and in many instances nothing. It is therefore probable that, in the aggregate, the average profits on the total amount of capital invested in the railways do not exceed, if they equal, the average profits obtained on the capital invested in English railways.

The extraordinary extent of railway, constructed at so early a period, in the United States, has been by some ascribed to the absence of a sufficient extent of communication by common roads. Although this cause has operated to some extent in certain districts, it is by no means so general as has been supposed. In the year 1838, the United States mails circulated over a length of way amounting on the whole to 136,218 miles, of which two thirds were land transport, including railways as well as common roads. Of the latter there must have been about 80,000 miles in operation, of which, however, a considerable portion was bridle roads. The price of transport in the stage coaches was upon an average 3·25 d. per passenger per mile, the average price by railway being about 1·47 d. per mile.

The great extent of internal communication, by railways and canals, in America, in proportion to its population, has been a general subject of admiration. The population of the United States in 1840 amounted to 17 millions, and if its rate of increase during the ten years commencing at that epoch be equal to the rate during the preceding ten years, its present population must be about 23 millions. There are, as I have stated, about 6500 miles of railway in actual operation within the territory of the Union. This, in round numbers, is at the rate of one mile of railroad for every 3200 inhabitants.

In the United Kingdom, there are in operation 5000 miles of railway, with a population of 30 millions, which is at the rate of one mile for every 6000 inhabitants.

It would therefore appear that, in proportion to the population, the length of railway communication in the United States is greater than in the United Kingdom in the proportion of 6 to $3\frac{1}{5}$. The result of this calculation, however, requires considerable modification.

Of the entire extent of railway constructed in the United States, by far the greater portion, as has been already explained, consists of single lines constructed in a light and cheap manner, which in England would be regarded as merely serving temporary purposes; while, on the contrary, the entire extent of the English system consists not only of double lines, but of railways constructed in the most solid, permanent, and expensive manner, adapted to the purposes of an immense traffic.

If a comparison were to be instituted at all between the two systems, its basis ought to be the capital expended and the traffic served by them; in which case the result would be somewhat different from that obtained by the mere consideration of the length of the lines.

It is not, however, the same in reference to the canals, in

which, it must be admitted, that America far exceeds, in proportion to her population, all other countries.

There is no country where easy and rapid means of communication are likely to produce more beneficial results than in the United States. Composed of twenty-six independent republics, having various, and in some instances opposite interests, the American confederacy would speedily be in danger of dissolution, if its population, scattered over a territory so vast, were not united by communications sufficiently rapid to produce a practical diminution of distance. In this means of intercommunication Nature has greatly aided the efforts of art, for certainly no country in the world presents such magnificent lines of natural water communication.

To say nothing of the streams which intersect the Atlantic States, and carry an amount of inland steam navigation wholly unexampled in Europe, we have the gigantic stream of the Mississippi, intersecting the immense valley to which it gives its name, with innumerable tributaries, navigable by steam-boats having a tonnage of first-rate ships for many thousands of miles, and traversing territories which present immense tracts of soil, of the highest degree of fertility, as well as sources of mineral wealth which are as yet unexplored.

On the American railways, passengers are not differently classed, or admitted at different rates of fare, as on those in Europe. There is but one class of passengers and one fare. In one or two instances, second and third-class carriages were attempted to be established, but it was found that the number of passengers availing themselves of the lower fares and inferior accommodation was so small that they were discontinued. The only distinction observable among passengers on railways is that which arises from color. The colored population, whether emancipated or not, are generally excluded from the vehicles provided for the whites. Such travelers are but few; and they are usually accommodated either in the luggage van or in the carriage in which the guard or conductor travels.

Railways in America have been generally constructed, as in England, by joint-stock companies, with which, however, the state interferes much more largely than in England. In some cases, a major limit to the dividend is imposed by the law which constitutes the company. In some, the dividends are allowed to augment; but when they exceed a certain limit, the surplus is divided with the state. In some, the privilege granted to the companies is limited to a certain period. In some, a right of revising and restricting the tariff periodically is reserved to the state.

But little merchandise is transported on the American railways, the cost of transport being greater than goods in general are capable of paying; nevertheless, a tariff, regulated by weight alone, without distinction of classes, is fixed by law for merchandise.

In the States of New England the legislature does not interfere with the rate of fare or the tariff of charges imposed by the companies; but there is a provision in all the railway acts, that after ten years from the date of the opening of each railway, dividends are not to exceed ten per cent., and that if the profits should be such as to produce a greater dividend, the tariff must be reduced so as to bring the dividend to that limit. In some few cases of the New England railways, as, for instance, in the line from Boston to Providence, this period is only four years.

In the State of Pennsylvania, the charters granted to the several railway companies differ very much in their conditions. In some, an average limit is named, which the fares and tonnage are not to exceed; in others, an average maximum tariff is fixed. These maxima are different on different lines.

Besides these major limits imposed on the fares, there is also, in certain cases, a major limit imposed on the dividends, which in some cases must not exceed twelve, and in others fifteen per cent. In some cases, the dividends above a certain amount are subject to a tax, payable to the state.

With the exception of this tax upon dividends which exceed a certain amount, and which only prevails in the State of Pennsylvania, no special tax is imposed on the American railways and canals. Sometimes, however, they are subject to the same taxes on their lands and buildings to which other proprietors are liable, in some cases they are exempted from them.

In several of the largest states, such as New York, Pennsylvania, and Virginia, the acts constituting the railway companies contain a clause reserving an absolute power of modifying them from time to time as the legislature may see fit. In no case, however, has this clause been yet brought into practical operation, and it is generally regarded as the mere theoretical expression of the unlimited sovereignty of the state.

In some of the states the grants to the railway companies are for an unlimited time. In the northern states, however, their period varies from 50 to 100 years.

In some of the latter grants an exclusive privilege is given to the companies of making railways through certain districts.

Nothing can be more simple, expeditious, and cheap than the means of obtaining an act for the establishment of a railway company in America. A public meeting is held, at which the project is discussed and adopted. A deputation is appointed to apply to the legislature, which grants the act without expense, delay, or official difficulty. The principle of competition is not brought into play, as in France; nor is there any investigation as to the expediency of the project, with reference to future profit or loss, as in England. No other guarantee or security is required from the company than the payment by the shareholders of a certain amount constituting the first call. In some states, the nonpayment of a call is followed by the confiscation of the previous payments; in others, a fine is imposed on the shareholder; in others the share is sold, and if the produce be less than the price at which it was delivered, the surplus can be recovered from the shareholder by process of law. In all cases, the acts creating the companies fix a time within which the works must be completed under pain of forfeiture. The traffic in shares before the definitive constitution of the company is prohibited.

Although the state itself has rarely undertaken the execution of railways, it holds out in most cases inducements in different forms to the enterprise of companies. In some cases, the state takes a great number of shares, which is generally accompanied by a loan made to the company, consisting in state stock delivered at par, which the company negotiate at its own risk. This loan is often converted into a subvention.

In many cases the companies obtain the land gratuitously, or for a nominal price.

When the price becomes a matter of consideration, the land is valued by a jury, as in England.

Several states have made a condition that foreign capital shall be excluded under penalty of forfeiture or fine against the companies.

CHAPTER XVII.

BELGIAN RAILWAYS.

THE Belgian state railways, though in their total length not exceeding 350 miles, are an object of vast importance considered in relation to the entire system of railroads now spread over the continent of Europe.

They are a subject of further interest to the statistician and the historian from the date and the circumstances of their construction.

The small state of Belgium had but just established its independence and been acknowledged by the great powers of Europe, when the statesmen to whom its government was confided, seeing the isolation in which it stood, and the somewhat contemptuous regards cast upon it by the powers of the north and east, from whom its recognition had been reluctantly extorted, resolved to confer upon it, by an effort of enterprise and art, that influence which was denied to it by its insignificant territory, its small population, and limited commerce.

The first administration under the newly appointed sovereign was scarcely installed, therefore, when it was determined to signalize its inauguration by a grand project, tending to establish relations with other states, and calculated to produce such reciprocal dependence as would be a strong guarantee for the maintenance of general tranquillity and respect for the independence of the new state. It was, in a word, resolved to overspread the territory with a system of railway communication, which should render this small kingdom the great highway for a large share of the commerce and personal intercourse between some of the chief countries of Europe.

It was proposed to construct two great trunk railways forming a cross, the intersection of which should be at Malines. The length of the cross was to extend from Ostend to Liege, and to be continued through the Prussian territory by Aix-la-Chapelle to Cologne.

The transverse line was to be carried at right angles to this from north to south, extending from Antwerp through Brussels by Mons to the French territory near Valenciennes, to which city it was to be continued.

Thus it will be perceived, that Malines, and not Brussels, was to be the great focus of these lines of communication. Several secondary lines or branches were to complete the network.

The EASTERN LINE, extending from Malines to Cologne, by Louvain, Tirlemont, Landen, Waremme, Liege, and Verviers, near the Prussian frontier, was to have a branch to St. Trond.

The WESTERN LINE, from Malines to Ostend, by Termonde, Ghent, and Bruges, was to have a branch from Ghent to Lille and Courtrai.

The NORTHERN LINE, from Malines to Antwerp, was to have a lateral line from Antwerp to Ghent, to be continued to Lille, so as to afford a direct communication between Ghent, Ostend, Lille, and Antwerp, without the circuitous route afforded by the trunk lines intersecting at Malines.

The SOUTHERN LINE, extending from Malines through Brussels to Mons, was to throw off a branch at Brain-le-Comte to Charleroi, to be carried from thence to Namur.

The total length of the entire system was to be 347 miles.

This magnificent project was no sooner announced, than it was adopted by the legislature, and received with enthusiasm by the people.

The date of the law sanctioning it was the 1st May, 1834; and the statesmen to whom the country was indebted for it were MM. Lebeau and Rogier.

Independently of those considerations which affected the relations of the new state with the other powers of Europe, the internal commerce of Belgium prompted such an enterprise.

The revolution of 1830 having separated that country from Holland, it lost the mouth of the Scheldt as an issue for its commerce. The communication with the German states could not be maintained by sea, and was attended with expense by land on common roads, which rendered it impracticable. The coal-producing provinces of Liege, which before the revolution supplied the Dutch markets, were now isolated and unable to share the supply of the interior with the coal district of Mons. An effectual and cheap communication with the ocean on the one side, and with the frontier next to the Rhine on the other, so as to traverse the kingdom from east to west, would be necessary to restore the prosperity of Liege. It was first proposed to accomplish this by means of a canal; but MM. Lebeau and

Rogier were sufficiently clearsighted to perceive, even at that early epoch, the important part which railways were destined to play in the commerce and politics of Europe, and how much more such a system would conduce to the national prosperity and political importance of their country.

It was resolved to construct the system of railways thus projected at the national expense, and to work them under national management. The execution of the project was commenced on the 1st June, 1834. Within two years, portions of the system were completed and opened for traffic. The length open in 1840 was 190 miles, and the entire system was completed within the next four years at the following rates:

	Length in Operation. Miles.
In 1841	212.
1842	246
1843	300
1844	347

The stimulus which this system of communication impressed upon the commerce of Belgium may be inferred from the following table, showing the progressive development of the home and foreign trade of that country from 1836 to 1845:

TABULAR STATEMENT of the progressive Increase of the Commerce of Belgium during Ten Years ending December 31, 1845.

Year.	Imports.		Exports.	
	Value of Goods entered.	Value of Goods delivered for Consumption.	Value of Belgian and foreign Goods.	Value of Belgian Goods.
	£.	£.	£.	£.
1836	8,356,000	7,488,000	6,620,000	5,792,000
1840	9,856,000	8,224,000	7,340,000	5,584,000
1841	11,088,000	8,400,000	8,464,000	6,164,000
1842	11,536,000	9,368,000	8,080,000	5,684,000
1843	11,784,000	8,656,000	8,884,000	6,248,000
1844	12.308,000	8,152,000	11,344,000	6,980,000
1845	12,640,000	9,344,000	12,408,000	7,312,000

The value of the imports and exports at the port of Antwerp in 1839 was £5,600,000; in 1841 it had risen to £6,640,000, and in 1843 it amounted to £9,080,000.

The production of coal in Belgium was doubled in the ten years ending 1845.

From 1831 to 1835, the average annual export of cast-iron

was 3887 tons. In the next five years the average annual amount was 7478 tons.

After 1840, when the railways were nearly completed, this branch of commerce was nearly quintupled; its average amount, in the six years ending December, 1845, being 35,000 tons.

The same rapid progression is observable in the other branches of commerce.

The average importation of raw cotton, previous to 1835, was 4400 tons. In the five years ending 31st December, 1846, its average annual amount was 7353 tons.

Previous to 1835, the average annual import of wool was 2973 tons. In the five years ending 31st December, 1846, its annual average amount was 4066 tons.

Let us now consider the expenditure by which the agent which was so mainly instrumental in thus extending Belgian commerce was created.

The general character of the country was favorable to the construction of railways; but much more stress has been laid on this circumstance, by those who desire to explain the early advance made in this improvement by Belgium, than is due to it. It is true that those parts of the country between Brussels and the ocean are generally level, and that but little earth-work or works of art necessary to bestride valleys or penetrate hills were required; but, on the other hand, the country was intersected by numerous rivers and canals, which necessitated the construction of as many bridges and aqueducts.

The country, however, has a very different character between Brussels and the Prussian frontier. The ground there presents obstacles requiring works of art of an expensive and difficult character.

From Louvain to Ans, the line passes through an undulating country, and is carried by cuttings of an average depth of fifty feet, alternating with embankments of an average height of sixty-six feet, up a gradual inclination to a summit nearly five hundred feet above the station at Louvain. In this section of the line there is a tunnel which measures upward of one thousand yards, besides numerous aqueducts, bridges, and viaducts, by which the canals and common roads are conducted over and under the railway.

From Ans to Liege, the country falls along the side of the valley of the Meuse, by a steep declivity. Here, in a length of 2300 feet, there is a fall of 360 feet.

The descent is effected by two inclined planes, worked by

two stationary engines of 360 horse power. The average gradient of these planes is one in 33. The prevailing gradient between Louvain and Liege is from one in 340 to one in 250, with the exception of a few short gradients constructed at one in 150. The curves upon this line have generally a large radius, with the exception of a few points where they are laid down with a radius of about a quarter of a mile.

It is not found in the working of the line that these curves are dangerous, or produce any appreciable resistance to the tractive power.

The Belgian railways are distinguished from those of England and France by the circumstance of passing common roads, wherever it is possible to do so, by level crossings. By this expedient considerable expense in the original construction is saved in bridges and viaducts; and, notwithstanding the great traffic on the Belgian lines, no serious accidents have been produced by it. It is to be considered, however, that, the speed of the trains being less than on the English railways, the liability to accident is proportionally diminished.

The extraordinary expedition with which the Belgian railroads were completed, has been mainly caused by the circumstance of their having been executed by the state, and the execution being conducted under the superintendence of a special railway committee, invested with adequate powers. By this expedient, innumerable official formalities were avoided. The two engineers, MM. Simons and Deridder, who had proposed the project, were invested with the general direction of the works; full powers were given them to form contracts, purchase land, and make other definitive arrangements necessary for carrying on the works, without reference to higher official powers.

On the 1st January, 1848, the amount which had been expended on the construction of the Belgian railways, and the stock employed in working them, was £6,406,476, of which the following were the details:

	£.
Construction of the road	4,800,270
Buildings and machinery for the inclined planes	59,544
Buildings and appendages of the stations	402,949
Dependencies of the stations	84,772
Management and office expenses	205,773
Rolling stock	853,168
	£6,406,476

But of this sum, a part had been expended in land for the way and works, which was subsequently found to be in excess. A portion of this was accordingly resold, which produced £46,865. Deducting this from the above expenditure, the remainder will be £6,359,611; which is, therefore, the actual amount of capital invested in the construction of the Belgian railways, consisting of 353 miles, including all the works and the rolling stock.

The cost per mile, therefore, of this system, with its working stock, has been £18,016.

The amount of the rolling stock, the total cost of which was, as appears by the above estimate, £853,168, was, on the 1st January, 1848, as follows:

Locomotive engines.......................... 153
Tenders..................................... 154
Passenger coaches........................... 751
Goods wagons 2915
Post-offices 14
Wagons used in the service of the railway 394

An increase of 192 goods wagons was ordered, which were delivered in 1848.

In the following table I have exhibited the classified receipts, the expenses, and profits, with the relation of them to each other, on the Belgian railways, during the seven years ending 31st December, 1847:

TABULAR ANALYSIS of the Receipts, Expenses, and Profits arising from the Traffic carried on the Belgian Railways during the Seven Years ending December 31, 1847.

	1841.	1842.	1843.	1844.	1845.	1846.	1847.
Number of miles open............	210	246	300	347	347	347	353
	£.	£.	£.	£.	£.	£.	£.
Passengers	164,550	187,372	219,288	246,664	255,736	277,488	278,716
Passengers' baggage	5,088	11,916	13,632	15,788	16,860	19,364	21,200
Goods carried by passenger trains.	13,600	16,332	24,808	35,980	40,364	39,884	42,096
Goods carried by goods trains.....	57,684	70,676	92,016	132,920	167,024	188,784	232,504
Carriages, horses, cattle and sundries	8,328	12,168	11,904	9,868	16,148	19,716	18,928
Total receipts....	249,250	298,464	361,648	441,220	496,132	546,236	593,444
Working expenses	181,586	188,012	219,064	230,616	252,864	289,830	372,756
Profits...........	67,664	110,452	141,584	210,604	243,268	256,406	220,688
Expenses per cent. of receipts	72	63	61	52	51	53	63

CHAP. XVII.]   BELGIAN RAILWAYS.   355

Having explained, in the preceding chapters of this volume, the manner in which the movement of the traffic of the carrying stock and the engines can be deduced from the respective quantities and mileages of these, when properly recorded, it will not be necessary here to go through the details of the calculations by which these important statistical data are obtained. I shall, therefore, give the principal results, in the following table, without the arithmetical processes by which they are found:

SYNOPSIS of the Movement on the Belgian Railways, computed from official Documents, during the Four Years ending Dec. 31, 1847.

LOCOMOTIVE POWER.	1844.	1845.	1846.	1847.
Total average daily mileage of engines.				
With goods	1,452	2,071	2,788	3,483
With passengers	2,778	2,571	2,765	3,001
Total	4,230	4,642	5,553	6,484
Total average hours of engine standing daily with steam up without running	489	472	559	588
Total daily average consumption of coke.	lbs.	lbs.	lbs.	lbs.
In lighting and steaming	37,540	40,916	46,105	50,973
In standing with steam up	10,432	10,421	12,337	14,539
In working trains	125,687	136,657	166,270	195,893
Total	173,659	187,994	224,712	261,405
Number of engines employed	143	148	151	154
Average daily mileage per engine	29·6	31·4	36·8	42·2
Average number of engines lighted daily	63·0	67·4	75·0	84·0
Average number of miles run by each engine lighted	67·2	69·0	74·0	77·0
Average hours standing daily with steam up without working per engine	7·7	7·4	7·5	7·0
Average consumption of coke per engine lighted.	lbs.	lbs.	lbs.	lbs.
In lighting and steaming	595	610	613	607
In standing with steam up	165	155	165	173
In working trains	1,995	2,039	2,217	2,332
Total	2,755	2,804	2,995	3,112
Average consumption per hour when standing with steam up	21·4	20·9	22·0	24·7
Average consumption per mile when drawing trains	29·7	29·9	30·0	30·3
Average consumption per running mile, including standing and lighting	40·0	41·6	40·0	37·1
PASSENGER TRAFFIC.				
Total average daily number booked.				
1st class	904	1,089	1,138	1,132
2d class	2,390	2,660	2,837	2,486
3d class	5,425	5,685	6,032	6,469
Total	8,719	9,510	10,007	10,087
Total average daily mileage.				
1st class	39,080	37,236	41,652	42,567
2d class	68,274	65,638	73,446	67,939
3d class	116,492	96,937	110,155	115,772
Total	223,846	199,811	225,253	226,278

	1844.	1845.	1846.	1847.
PASSENGER TRAFFIC—*continued.*				
Total average daily receipts.	£.	£.	£.	£.
1st class	174	192	209	214
2d class	243	255	274	254
3d class	254	249	269	283
Total	671	696	752	751
Total average receipts per passenger booked.	d.	d.	d.	d.
1st class	46·2	42·3	44·1	45·2
2d class	24·3	23·0	23·2	24·6
3d class	11·3	10·5	10·7	10·5
General average..	18·5	17·5	18·0	18·0
Total average number of miles traveled per passenger booked.				
1st class	43·2	36·9	36·8	37·6
2d class	28·5	24·7	25·9	27·4
3d class	21·4	17·1	18·3	17·8
Average	25·6	20·9	22·5	22·6
Total average receipts per passenger per mile.	d.	d.	d.	d.
1st class	1·42	1·24	1·21	1·21
2d class	0·85	0·93	0·90	0·90
3d class	0·53	0·62	0·58	0·59
Average	0·72	0·84	0·80	0·80
Average number of passengers drawn by each engine.				
1st class	14·1	14·6	15·0	14·1
2d class	24·6	25·6	26·5	22·6
3d class	42·0	37·8	39·8	38·6
Total	80·7	78·0	81·3	75·3
Average receipts per mile run of passenger trains.	s.	s.	s.	s.
1st class	1·26	1·50	1·51	1·43
2d class	1·75	1·98	1·98	1·69
3d class	1·83	1·94	1·94	1·89
Total	4·84	5·42	5·43	4·98
Total number of passenger carriages used....	586	643	700	735
Total average daily mileage of all the passenger carriages	16,806	20,568	17,972	21·007
Average daily mileage per carriage	28·7	32·0	25·6	28·6
Average number of passengers carried by each coach	13·5	9·7	12·6	10·75
Average number of passenger carriages drawn by each engine	6·05	8·0	6·5	7·0
Average composition of a passenger train.				
Passenger coaches	6·05	8·00	6·5	7·0
Baggage-vans	0·81	1·06		
Parcel-vans	1·01	1·32		
Horse-boxes	0·09	0·09		
Carriage-trucks	0·30	0·24	2·3	2·7
Cattle-wagons	0·10	0·10		
Post-offices	0·16	0·16		
Prison-vans	0·04	0·05		
Wagons in the service of the railway,.	0·10	0·18		
Total number of vehicles	8·66	11·2	8·8	9·7

BELGIAN RAILWAYS.

Goods Traffic.	1844.	1845.	1846.	1847.
Total average daily number of tons booked ..	1,264	1,771	2,016	2,634
Total average daily mileage of goods........	56,756	83,420	94,000	115,817
Average number of miles carried per ton	44·8	47·0	47·0	43·8
Average number of tons drawn by each engine	38·0	40·0	33·7	33·2
Average receipts per mile run of goods trains	5·17s.	4·41s.	3·36s.	3·65s.
Total average daily mileage of goods wagons	23,102	38,728	54,087	70,008
Total number of wagons used	1,783	2,073	2,400	2,707
Average daily mileage of each wagon	13·4	18·7	22·5	25·9
Average number of goods wagons drawn by each engine	15·74	18·7	19·4	20·1
Average number of tons carried per wagon ..	2.46	2·15	1·74	1·66
Total daily average receipts for goods........	375l.	456l.	517l.	639l.
Average receipts per ton booked.............	5s. 10d.	5s. 2d.	5s. 1½d.	5s. 2d.
Average receipts per ton per mile............	1·57d.	1·32d.	1·32d.	1·34d.

From the important results brought together in the preceding table, we collect the following summary conclusions, in round numbers.

1st. On the Belgian railways each locomotive is worked every other day, runs 75 miles, is kept standing with steam up for 7 hours, and consumes a ton and a half of coke.

2d. Each passenger engine draws 80 passengers, with baggage, parcels, mails, &c.; the receipts amounting to 5s. per mile, exclusive of a small amount due to baggage, &c.; the train consisting of from eight to ten vehicles. Each first-class passenger travels on an average 37 miles, each second-class passenger 26 miles, and each third-class passenger 18 miles. The receipts proceeding from each first-class passenger are 3s., from each second-class passenger 2s. 2d., and from each third-class passenger, 1s. 6d.

3d. Each passenger coach runs about 28 miles a day, and carries about 11 passengers.

4th. Each goods engine draws on an average 20 goods wagons, drawing 34 tons of goods. Each ton of goods is transported on an average 44 miles, and the receipts for each mile run by the goods engines are 5s. 2d.

To compare the quantity of traffic with the extent of the railway, it will be necessary to suppose it uniformly carried over the whole length of the lines, and to calculate the quantity which would, in that case, pass over every mile. The results are exhibited in the following table:

TABLE showing the average Amount of Traffic carried daily over each Mile of the Belgian Railways during the Four Years ending December 31, 1847.

	1844.	1845.	1846.	1847.
Passengers, 1st class	113	107	120	120
„ 2d class	196	189	212	193
„ 3d class	336	279	317	328
Total	645	575	649	641
Passenger engines	8·00	7·40	7·95	8·50
Passenger carriages	48·4	59·3	51·7	59·5
Tons of goods	163·6	240·5	271·0	328·0
Number of goods engines	4·18	5·96	8·3	8·5
Number of goods wagons	66·5	111·4	156·0	198·0

This would, therefore, be the movement of the traffic on the Belgian railways, if it were uniformly carried over the whole extent of the lines, and throughout all seasons of the year. A great variation, however, takes place, both locally and according to the change of season.

The official reports published by the Belgian government supply the means of ascertaining both these variations. In the annexed diagram I have exhibited the local variation of the goods and passenger traffic on every section of the Belgian railways. The variations of the passenger traffic are marked by the continuous lines; those of the goods traffic by the dotted lines; the heights in each case representing the quantity of the traffic which passes over each section of the line.

It will be observed that each sort of traffic is subject to very great local variation; the passenger traffic rather more so than the goods.

The section between Brussels and Malines is obviously exceptional, having a much larger proportion of passenger traffic than any other section of the line. This is easily explained by the configuration of the Belgian railways. Malines forms the intersection or focus of the four great trunk lines, and the great predominance of traffic exhibited in the diagram arises from that portion of the traffic which proceeds from Brussels to feed all these, and which returns to Brussels from them.

The same exceptional character appears in the goods traffic between Antwerp and Malines, which is explained in the same manner. The merchandise arriving at or departing from Antwerp necessarily travels over the section of the line between Antwerp and Malines, either departing from or arriving at the common focus of the trunk lines at Malines.

CHAP. XVII.] BELGIAN RAILWAYS. 359

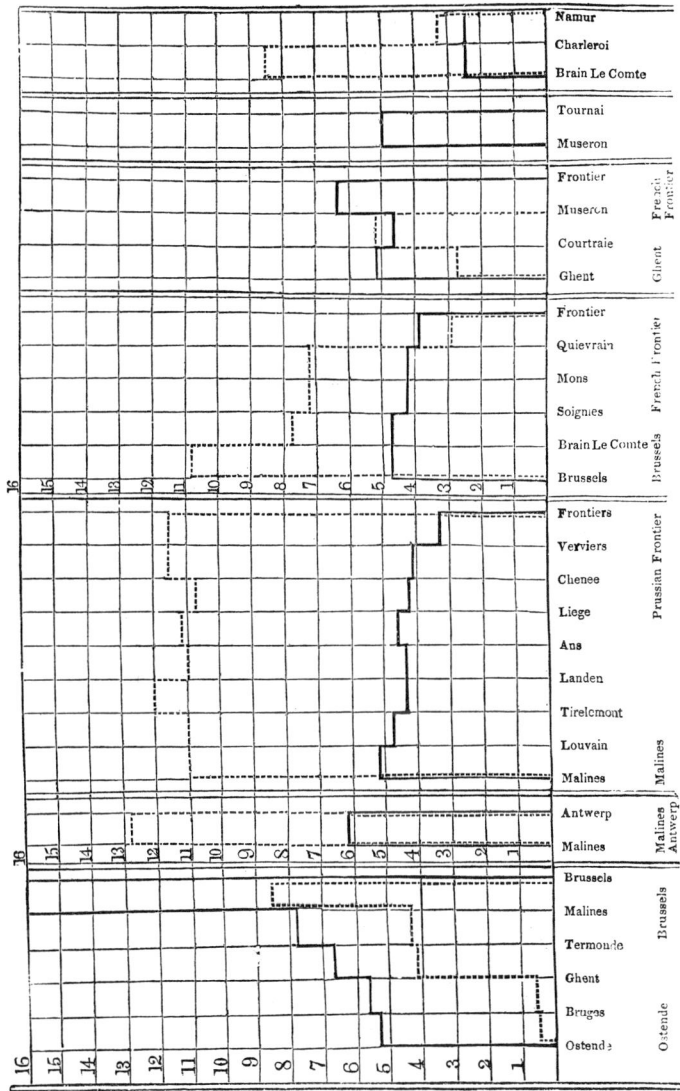

Another exceptional character in the goods traffic is exhibited between Charleroi and Brain-le-Comte, which is to be attributed to the coal trade of the former district.

The variation of the daily traffic with the change of seasons is exhibited in the same manner in the annexed diagram, in which, as before, the continuous lines represent the passenger traffic, and the dotted lines the goods traffic. It will be observed that the latter is much more uniform and independent of the seasons than the former.

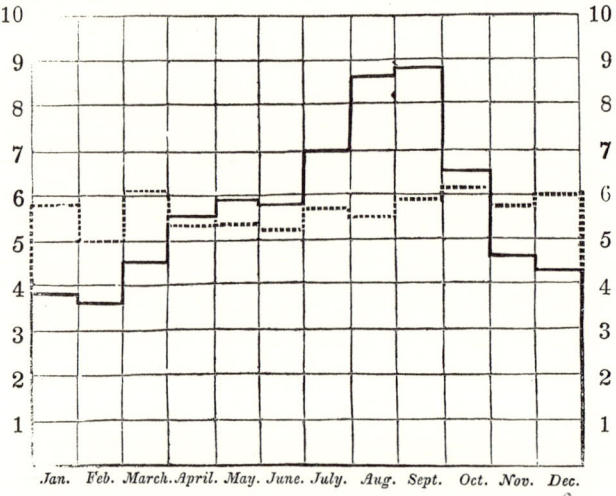

August and September form the great traveling season for passengers; the quantity of traffic of this kind being in these months more than double its amount in the four months commencing in November and ending in February.

The proportion in which each of the three classes of passengers supplies traffic to the railways, is exhibited in the following table (see page 361) for the four years ending 31st December, 1847.

But the preceding details, important as they are, do not form all the valuable information which can be deduced from the reports of the railway department of the Belgian government.

In order to ascertain the proportion in which the business of the railway is supplied by traffic classified according to the distances it is transported, tables have been published showing the

TABLE showing the Number of each Class of Passengers in every 100 booked, the Share of each Class in every 100 Miles traveled, and the Share contributed by each Class to every £100 Receipts on the Belgian Railways during the Four Years ending December 31, 1847.

	Year.	1st class.	2d class.	3d class.	Totals.
Number of passengers of each class in every 100 booked.	1844	10·75	27·66	61·59	100
	1845	11·50	28·20	60·30	100
	1846	11·36	28·36	60·28	100
	1847	11·22	24·64	64·14	100
Share of each class in every 100 miles traveled.........	1844	17·40	30·50	52·10	100
	1845	18·60	32·86	48·54	100
	1846	17·27	32·60	48·90	100
	1847	18·80	30·10	51·10	100
Average amount contributed by each passenger to every £100 of receipts..........	1844	26	36	38	100
	1845	27	37	36	100
	1846	28	36	36	100
	1847	28	34	38	100

quantity of each class of objects of traffic booked which have been carried to distances within certain assigned limits.

These voluminous tables have supplied me with the means of computing the number of units booked which were carried over distances under 20 miles, between 20 and 40 miles, 40 and 60 miles, and so on. I have also given, in the following table, the quantity of locomotion which each class of such objects demanded:

TABULAR ANALYSIS of the Traffic on the Belgian Railways, classified according to the Distances over which the Objects of Transport were severally carried, showing the Proportion of 1000 Objects booked of each Class which was carried over each specified Distance, and also showing the Proportion per 1000 of the Mileage of each Class assignable to each specified Distance.

Passengers:	Under 20 Miles.	From 20 to 40.	From 40 to 60.	From 60 to 80.	From 80 to 100.	Above 100.	Total.
1st class.							
Number	253	349	174	130	77	17	1000
Mileage	79	253	204	231	174	59	1000
2d class.							
Number	411	345	128	75	34	7	1000
Mileage	167	328	198	175	100	32	1000
3d class.							
Number	510	303	100	63	20·2	3·8	1000
Mileage	237	329	176	171	68	19	1000
Total.							
Number	392	332	134	89	44	9	1000
Mileage	161	303	193	192	114	57	1000

		Under 20 Miles.	From 20 to 40.	From 40 to 60.	From 60 to 80.	From 80 to 100.	Above 100.	Total.
Baggage—Tons.	Number	257	315	125	158	113	32	1000
	Mileage	69	207	135	256	234	99	1000
Parcels—Tons.	Number	247	304	170	154	84	41	1000
	Mileage	72	201	182	249	174	122	1000
Carriages.	Number	71	268	196	175	206	84	1000
	Mileage	15	125	156	207	310	187	1000
Horses.	Number	24	133	144	534	122	43	1000
	Mileage	5	55	101	593	167	79	1000
Goods—Tons.	Number	343	289	108	135	113	12	1000
	Mileage	108	206	138	243	266	39	1000
Cattle (large)—Head.	Number	253	301	135	303	8	0	1000
	Mileage	77	203	160	542	18	0	1000
Cattle (small)—Head.	Number	137	316	386	156	3	2	1000
	Mileage	45	220	456	265	7	7	1000

This table supplies some curious and important inferences, which are probably applicable more or less to all railway traffic; but we have no means of testing this, owing to the insufficiency of the official reports of other railways.

It appears that 40 per cent. of all the passengers booked are for distances under 20 miles, and that 73 per cent. are for distances under 40 miles.

Those who are booked for distances under 20 miles employ 16 per cent. of the mileage, and those who are booked for distances under 40 miles employ 46 per cent. of all the mileage.

It further appears that only 5 per cent. of all the passengers booked travel distances above 80 miles, and that they together supply only 17 per cent. of the mileage.

With respect to goods, conclusions very nearly similar follow. 34 per cent. of the goods booked are carried distances under 20 miles, while 63 per cent. are carried distances under 40 miles. Those which are carried distances under 20 miles employ, however, less than 11 per cent. of the mileage, while those carried distances under 40 miles employ only 31 per cent. It further follows, that only 12 per cent. of all the goods booked are carried distances above 80 miles, but that this quantity employs 30 per cent. of the mileage of the railways.

The class of objects which are carried the greatest distances, and which employ the greatest amount of mileage, are horses. Of these 50 per cent. are carried distances from 60 to 80 miles, and employ 60 per cent. of the mileage.

The larger class of cattle are also carried to considerable distances, 30 per cent. being carried to distances from 60 to 80 miles, employing 54 per cent. of the mileage.

The proportions in which the different classes of traffic contributed to the revenue of the Belgian railways is exhibited in the following table:

TABLE showing the Share of every £100 of gross Revenue contributed by each Class of Traffic on the Belgian Railways, during the Four Years ending December 31, 1847.

	1844.	1845.	1846.	1847.
Passengers	55	51·5	51·0	47·0
Baggage	3·5	3·4	3·5	3·5
	58·5	54·9	54·5	50·5
Money parcels	0·3	0·3	0·3	0·3
Carriages	1·8	1·6	1·5	1·2
Horses	1·1	0·7	0·7	0·7
Parcels	8·0	8·1	7·3	7·1
Goods	29·6	33·7	34·6	39·2
Sundries	0·7	0·7	1·1	1·0
	41·5	45·1	45·5	49·5
Total	100·0	100·0	100·0	100·0

In the following table I have exhibited the proportion of every £100 expended, which has been chargeable to the usual heads of direction, way and works, locomotive power, carrying expenses, and sundries:

ANALYSIS of the Proportion in which the working Expenses of the Belgian Railways were distributed, under the specified Heads, in the Four Years ending 1847.

	Direction and Management.	Maintenance of Way and Works.	Locomotive Power.	Carrying Expenses.	Collection and Sundries.	Total.
Year 1844	6·3	24·3	49·3	16·6	3·5	100
„ 1845	6·5	25·7	48·7	15·7	3·4	100
„ 1846	5·4	25·1	51·7	14·6	3·2	100
„ 1847	3·7	31·4	50·1	12·3	2·5	100
Mean	5·47	26·62	49·96	14·80	3·15	100

Finally, I have compared in the following table the receipts, expenses, and profits with the length of the lines, the movement upon them, and the capital invested in them:

SYNOPSIS of the Proportion between the Receipts, Expenses, and Profits, and the Length of Line worked, the Movement of the Trains, and the Amount of Capital on the Belgian Railways during the Seven Years ending December 31, 1847.

	Total average daily Amount.	Amount per Mile of Railway.	Amount per Mile run by Trains.	Amount per Cent. of Capital.
Year 1841.	£.	£.	s. d.	
Receipts....	683	3·25	5 4	6·56
Expenses...	498	2·37	3 11	4·78
Profits	185	0·88	1 5	1·78
Year 1842.				
Receipts....	820	3·33	6 0	6·72
Expenses...	516	2·10	3 9½	4·24
Profits	304	1·23	2 2½	2·48
Year 1843.				
Receipts....	994	3·31	6 3	6·68
Expenses...	602	2·00	3 10	4·05
Profits	392	1·31	2 5	2·63
Year 1844.				
Receipts....	1234	3·50	5 9½	7·20
Expenses...	634	1·80	3 0	3·71
Profits	600	1·70	2 9½	3·49
Year 1845.				
Receipts....	1363	3·90	5 11	7·95
Expenses...	694	2·00	3 0	4·05
Profits	669	1·90	2 11	3·90
Year 1846.				
Receipts....	1500	4·30	5 5	8·75
Expenses...	796	2·30	2 11	4·65
Profits	704	2·00	2 6	4·10
Year 1847.				
Receipts....	1630	4·6	5 0	9·32
Expenses...	1022	2·9	3 1½	5·85
Profits	612	1·7	1 10½	3·47

It appears from this table, therefore, that the gross receipts have never exceeded 8 per cent. on the capital, and the net profits have never exceeded 4 per cent.

CHAP. XVII.]   BELGIAN RAILWAYS.   365

To exhibit the average speed on the Belgian railways, I have calculated in the following table, from the published time-tables, the rate of progress on several of the principal lines; showing, as in former chapters, the average speed when in actual motion, and the reduction of this produced by the stoppages. It appears that the average speed in actual motion, one line taken with another, is 25 miles, and that the average speed including stoppages is 18 miles.

We have seen in Chap. X., that on the English railways the average speed in motion is 32 miles, and the average speed including stoppages, $24\frac{1}{2}$ miles.

TABULAR ANALYSIS of the Movement of the Passenger Traffic on the principal Belgian Lines of Railway, showing the average Speed, Stoppages, &c., of each Class of Trains.—N.B. An average Loss of Five Minutes is allowed for each Stoppage, except in particular Cases where a greater Delay is fixed by the Programme. This is intended to include the Time lost in coming to Rest and getting up Speed.

Name of Railway.	Train.	Distances traveled.	Time.	No. of Stoppages.	Average Speed including Stoppages.	Average Speed in Motion excluding Stoppages.
		Miles.	h. m.		Miles.	Miles.
Brussels to Valenciennes...............	1st class	57·75	2 35	7	22·45	27·90
,, ,,	2d class	57·75	2 50	9	20·40	27·80
,, ,,	3d class	57·75	3 50	13	15·12	21·00
Brussels to Cologne...	.. ..	149	9 15	22	16·10	22 00
Brussels to Verviers...	1st class	86·50	4 30	9	19·20	24·20
,, ,,	2d class	86·50	5 0	19	17·30	25·40
Brussels to Namur....	1st class	67·50	3 45	16	18·00	22·90
,, ,,	2d class	67·50	3 50	11	17·65	22·50
,, ,,	3d class	67·50	3 55	19	17·30	29·00
Brussels to Antwerp..	1st class	27·33	1 10	3	23·55	30·00
,, ,,	2d class	27·33	1 15	3	21·85	27·33
,, ,,	3d class	27·33	1 15	5	21·85	33·00
		779·74	43 10	136	18·10	24·90

In the present chapter our observations have been limited to the system of Belgian railways constructed and worked by the State. There are, however, besides these, a few lines in progress of construction in Belgium by private companies.

A grant for ninety years has been made to a company under the title of the "Great Luxembourg Railway Company," for the construction of a line of railway joining the State railway near Charleroi and Namur, to be carried across the extensive province of Luxembourg by Dinant, Neufchateau, and Arbon, and to be extended to Thionville and Metz, where it will join the Paris and Strasbourg Railway. The entire length of this system, when completed, will be about 140 miles.

The canal and mineral property of the Luxembourg Society has been purchased by this company for £260,000. The canal was intended to connect the Moselle with the Meuse, passing through a district rich in minerals, and covered with extensive forests.

With the exception of the earth-work on about ten miles of the line from Brussels to Wavre, no progress has yet been made in the realization of this project.

A grant for ninety years has been made to another company for a line of railway between Namur and Liege, following the valley of the Meuse, with a branch from Mons to Manage. The length of the main line will be about forty-four miles, and that of the branch twenty-two miles.

This railway is in progress of construction, and the branch between Mons and Manage is expected soon to be opened for traffic.

The Sambre and Meuse Railway Company have a grant for ninety years for a line joining the Sambre with the Meuse at Vereux. The entire length of the line, with three short branches, will be about seventy miles, of which twenty-five miles have been completed, and were lately opened for traffic.

The Tournai and Joubise, and Landen and Hasselt Company, have a grant for ninety years. The length of the two lines together is forty-six miles. They are completed and opened for traffic.

The West Flanders Company have a grant for ninety years for a system of railways in that province. One line will pass from Bruges to Courtrai, Ypres, and Poperinghe, passing by Thourout, Rowlers, and Menin, and forming at Courtrai a junction with the State line from Ghent to Lille and Tournai. The second line will run from Furnes through the centre of West Flanders to Thiels, where it will join the State line from Antwerp to Brussels.

Of these lines thirty-three miles are opened for traffic, the remaining sixty miles not being yet commenced.

Thus the entire system of Belgian railways in operation is as follows:

	Miles.
State lines	353
Sambre and Meuse	25
Tournai and Joubise, and Landen and Hasselt	46
West Flanders	33
Total	457

I have not been able to obtain any authentic information as to the cost of the lines constructed by companies; but if their average cost be assumed to be equal to that of the State lines, which, as we have seen, is £18,016 per mile, the total capital absorbed by the Belgian railways must be £8,233,312.

CHAPTER XVIII.

FRENCH RAILWAYS.

BEFORE the memorable epoch when the experiment of the Manchester and Liverpool Railway rendered manifest the vast capabilities of iron roads worked by steam power as means of general transport, no communication of that description existed in France, except a few lines appropriated exclusively to the mineral districts of St. Etienne and the Rive-de-Gier, near the banks of the Loire. These lines were analogous to the railways which existed from an early date in the north of England; their extent was inconsiderable, and they were for the most part single lines, worked generally by horses, but in some cases by locomotive engines of the rudest kind, such as those formerly used on our mineral lines.

When the wonderful effects developed between Manchester and Liverpool became known, and when the execution of more extensive lines of railway for the expeditious transport of passengers and merchandise had been undertaken in England, the attention of all parts of Europe was awakened to this improvement; but a general incredulity prevailed as to its practicability, except in localities where traffic and intercourse existed on a very large scale. France, sharing this skepticism, remained passive, while the neighboring small state of Belgium was overspreading her territory with that admirable network of communication we have described in the preceding chapter.

At length, in 1835, five years after the opening of the Liverpool and Manchester Railway, and when other great lines were known to be in active progress in England, a spirited and enterprising person, whose name must always remain connected with the history of French railways, M. Emile Pereire, deeply impressed with the advantages which must arise from this improvement in transport, and desiring to bring its effects, hitherto known only by hearsay, under the very eyes of the French legislature and of the population of Paris, succeeded in forming a company for the construction of a passenger line between Paris and St. Germain. An act authorizing this was obtained in July, 1835. The works were commenced and prosecuted with activity, and it was finally opened for traffic at the end of 1837.

This event, combined with the rapid progress of railways in England, forced the French legislature to direct a portion of its attention, hitherto distracted by political dissensions and the convulsions which followed the revolution of 1830, to this national improvement.

In the session of 1837, a commission was authorized to prepare a project of law on the subject of national railways, which was to be submitted to the Chambers in the following session; and it was generally understood and agreed that the construction of railways was urgent, and that the most important lines should be executed and possessed by the State, but that the branches and secondary lines might be conceded to private companies.

The report of the commission presented to the Chamber on the opening of the following session of 1838, was in accordance with these resolutions; but, in the mean while, the majority had changed its opinion, and was now opposed to the principle of the State assuming the direction and management of these enterprises. The government, nevertheless, still adhered to the original project, and was supported by the parties which then usually constituted the opposition, and was known as the Left and Extreme Left of the Chamber. The parties of the Centre and the Left Centre, distrustful and jealous of the influence with which the possession of vast patronage must invest the government, opposed the project.

This section of the Chamber was seconded in its opposition by a large and influential party representing the financial and commercial interests, which looked forward to reaping considerable profits from the operations of the Bourse resulting from the traffic in shares, if the railways were executed, as in England, by joint-stock companies. The combination of these parties prevailed, and the project of government was rejected.

During the next four years, little or no progress was made; parties continued to be distracted, and the question of the East especially engrossed the attention of statesmen.

In this interval, however, private companies came forward

and proposed to construct railways by their own resources, independent of the government, between Paris and Orleans and Paris and Rouen.

In 1838 a grant was made to a company of a lease of seventy years, on the condition of providing a capital of forty millions for the construction of a line of railway from Paris to Orleans, with branches to Corbeil, Pithiviers, and Arpajon. The company, however, had no sooner commenced their operations, than they found themselves involved in financial embarrassments, and were compelled later to obtain the authorization of the legislature to abandon their branches, except that to Corbeil. In fine, the government assisted them by guaranteeing an interest of four per cent. on their capital for forty-seven years, and extending their lease to ninety-nine years. Thus aided, the enterprise was prosecuted, and the railway finally completed.

Two companies proposed the construction of lines from Paris to Rouen: one by the right bank of the Seine, and the other by the plateau above it. A grant was first made to the latter in 1838; but the financial crisis which ensued rendered the project abortive. At length, in 1840, the project of a line by the right bank of the Seine was resumed, and a grant was made to the present Paris and Rouen Railway Company, with a lease of ninety-nine years, the result being the present railway, which, having been commenced in 1841, was opened for traffic on the 9th May, 1843.

In 1842, M. Teste, then Minister of Public Works, presented a project to the Chambers for the execution of a system of railways in which the government should co-operate with private companies. This project, with some modification, was finally adopted, and the law known as that of the "11th of June, 1842," was passed.

This law proposed a certain system of trunk lines to be executed by companies on conditions to be imposed by the State. These conditions were as follow:

1st. The government was to purchase the lands, buildings, and other property necessary for the construction of the lines; two-thirds of the expense to be paid by the departments and communes through which the railways would pass, and the remaining one-third by the State.

2dly. Leases of the railways were to be granted for limited periods to companies, who were to be required to provide the capital necessary to defray the expenses of the way and works, the rolling-stock, and all the material necessary for the working of the lines. At the expiration of their leases, provided they were not renewed, a valuation was to be made of this property, and the amount of such valuation to be paid to the companies by the State.

The police of the roads, the limitation of the tariff, and a general power of supervision and control, were reserved to the government, which was to appoint agents to represent it, and to form part of the administration of each railway, the salary of such functionaries to be paid by the companies.

The system of railways, the construction of which was contemplated by this law, was to consist of seven principal arteries —the first directed upon the Belgian frontier; the second upon one or more ports of the channel; the third upon the ocean, by one or more of the western ports; the fourth upon the Spanish frontier, by Bayonne; the fifth upon the Spanish frontier, by Perpignan, passing through the centre of France; the sixth upon the Mediterranean, by Marseilles; and the seventh upon the Rhine, by Nancy and Strasbourg.

Besides these, two trunk lines were contemplated, diverging from Marseilles; one connecting that port with Bordeaux by Toulouse, and the other connecting it with the Rhine at Mulhausen, by Dijon and Lyons.

This law had not long been promulgated, before it became manifest that capital would not flow so freely and abundantly to the French railways as the legislature appeared to expect; and that even with conditions modified in favor of those who should undertake the execution and working of the lines thus projected, no small difficulty was likely to stand in the way of the accomplishment of the object which the government and the legislature contemplated. The departments and the communes, already oppressed under a heavy burden of taxation, had neither the ability nor the will to co-operate in the enterprise, by the contribution of two-thirds, or even a much smaller part of the cost of the land. In short, it became evident that the law was impracticable; and, although not subsequently repealed, it became eventually, in a great degree, a dead letter.

Although the general outline of the system of trunk lines described in the law of 1842 has been in the main adhered to, the government has been forced to lay aside other conditions of the law, and to make the best terms it could with such companies as presented themselves, to induce them to undertake and work the railways; and even, in some cases, it has been found impracticable to accomplish this through the medium of private companies, and the government has been obliged to construct the lines provisionally, trusting to the probability of finding a company willing to work them when completed.

The first great artery of the system is that now known as the Northern Railway. This line, issuing from the northern suburbs of Paris, goes directly to Amiens, following the valleys of the rivers, such as the Oise, the Brêche, the Aré, the Somme, which run north and south. From Amiens the line is carried to Douay, where it forks; one branch being directed by Valenciennes to the Belgian frontier at Quiévrain, and the other by Lille to Calais, a sub-branch being carried from Hazebrouk to Dunkerque.

A branch is also in progress from Creil, a place between Paris and Beauvais, to St. Quentin, by Compiègne. This line was executed and nearly completed by the government, through the agency of the department of the Ponts et Chaussées; and being that part of the system projected in the law of 1842, which was attended with the most promising commercial results, it was found that, when it was proposed to offer this line to public competition, terms highly advantageous to the government could be obtained.

In fine, it was granted in September, 1845, to the present company, upon a lease of thirty-eight years, the company agreeing to provide all the expenses necessary for the establishment of the railway, and to reimburse all the expenses which had been previously incurred in its construction.

Connected with this railway, was the line extending from Amiens to Boulogne, which was constructed by a private company, on a lease of ninety-nine years.

Two short lines had been previously constructed and opened for traffic, connecting Paris with Versailles; the one by the right, and the other by the left bank of the Seine.

In carrying out the system defined in the law of 1842, these lines were adopted as the first section of the artery of communication intended to be carried through Brittany to the port of Brest. It was accordingly proposed to continue this western line, by Chartres, Laval, and Rennes, to the ocean at Brest.

No company having proposed to execute it, the government proceeded provisionally to construct it, through the agency of the department of the Ponts et Chaussées.

The section from Versailles to Chartres has been completed, and recently opened for traffic. It is worked by the government. The remaining sections of the line beyond Chartres are in progress.

The Paris and Orleans Railway, which had been previously conceded to, and nearly completed by a company, was adopted as the first stage of the two lines of communication intended to be carried from the capital to the Spanish frontier. From Orleans it was proposed to carry one of these lines, by Tours, Poitiers, and Angoulême, to Bordeaux, and from thence to Bayonne.

This line, from Orleans to Bordeaux, is in process of execution by the State. The first section, from Orleans to Tours, 71·5 miles in length, has been completed, and is now in operation. The entire line has been leased to a company for a period of twenty-eight years, on the conditions of completing the road structure, and supplying the rolling stock and all the requisites for working the line.

With a view to establish a railway communication between the centre of France, and the coal and manufacturing districts north of Lyons, on the banks of the Loire, it was proposed to construct a railway communication extending directly from those districts to the port of Nantes, intersecting the great southern line at Tours. No progress has, however, been made in this project east of Tours. The line from Tours to Nantes has been constructed by the government, and the section from Tours to Angers is now open for traffic, having been leased to a company for thirty-four years, on terms similar to those on which the grant has been made to the company of Orleans and Bordeaux. The other section, from Angers to Nantes, is in progress, and will be worked by the same company when completed.

A branch of the southern trunk line was contemplated, to be carried by Niort to Rochefort from Poitiers and La Rochelle; but this has not been conceded, or even commenced.

The continuation of this southern trunk from Bordeaux toward Bayonne still exists merely in contemplation.

The first section of the great Centre railway intended to be carried from Paris to Perpignan is completed and in operation. This section commences at Orleans, and is carried by Vierzon to Chateauroux, a distance of 90 miles, and is now in operation. A branch is thrown off at Vierzon, which proceeds eastward by Bourges to Neronde, and is intended to be continued to Nevers. This branch from Vierzon to Neronde is 38 miles in length, and is in full operation.

CHAP. XVIII.]   FRENCH RAILWAYS.   373

Great financial difficulties have been encountered in executing the southern trunk line from Paris to Marseilles. The section from Paris to Tonnerre, by Fontainbleau and Montereau, consisting of 122 miles, has been recently completed, and is now open for traffic.

The section from Tonnerre to Dijon, consisting of 90 miles, is in progress, and will speedily be completed. The section from Dijon to Chalons-sur-Saone, consisting of 43 miles, is completed, and under traffic.

The section from Chalons by Macon to Lyons is in progress. The company to whom the line from Paris to Lyons was originally conceded, on a lease of forty-one years, sinking under financial embarrassments, the Constituent Assembly, after the revolution of February, 1848, passed a law decreeing the line the property of the State, and offering shareholders certain compensation in government stock. This has been followed by various negotiations, which are still in progress, and which will probably end in the establishment of a new company on new conditions.

The continuation of this southern trunk line from Lyons to Avignon was granted to a company who, finding themselves involved in financial embarrassments, resolved in 1847, to wind up their affairs, return the funds to the shareholders, and forfeit the deposit which had been made to the government, and the expenses incurred. Nothing has since been done with this section of the line, and the government is now negotiating with companies to include it with the line from Paris to Lyons under the same contract.

This section will consist of about 150 miles.

The last section of the Marseilles line between Avignon and Marseilles, granted to a company under a lease of thirty-three years, has been completed and open for traffic, the chief part of the cost of construction having been defrayed by the State.

A branch of this line, 15 miles in length, is in progress from Rognac to Aix. The total length of the line from Avignon to Marseilles now in operation is 78 miles.

The line connecting Paris and Strasbourg has been undertaken by the State, and is now completed and in operation, as far as Chalons-sur-Marne, a distance of 107 miles. The next section, from Chalons to Nancy, making a total distance of 144 miles, will probably be in operation before the end of 1851. The remainder of the line from Nancy to Strasbourg, as well as the branches from Epernay to Rheims, and from Frouard to Forbach are in progress and in a forward state. The total length of this trunk line and branches will, when completed, be 410 miles.

This line has been leased to a company for forty-four years, on conditions similar to those already explained for the Centre line and the Orleans and Bordeaux; the company undertaking, however, the construction of the branch from Frouard to Forbach, 75 miles, at an expense of £1,680,000.

Of the lines contemplated to connect Marseilles with Bordeaux and the Rhine, nothing has been done.

The connection between Marseilles and the Rhine will be effected as far as Dijon by the great southern railway already mentioned. A branch is contemplated from Dijon by Besançon, to unite with the Strasbourg and Basle Railway at Mulhausen. Respecting this branch, however, nothing has been done.

Besides these, which constitute the principal trunk lines indicated by the legislature, several detached lines have been projected, and some executed in different localities. These, however, are generally short, and of but little importance.

The following table exhibits the length of the French railways, distinguishing those which are open for traffic, those which are in progress, and those which are projected, but not commenced:

TABULAR STATEMENT of the French Railways open, in Progress, and projected.

	Lease.			Lines.		
Passenger Railways.	Duration.	Commencement.	Termination.	Open.	In Progress.	Projected.
				Miles.	Miles.	Miles.
NORTH OF FRANCE.						
Main line from Paris to Belgian frontier at Quiévrain......	38	1845	1883	180	..	..
1st branch:						
Douay to Calais............	38			85	..	..
Sub-branch:						
Hazebrouk to Dunkirk.......	70	..	..	25·5	..	..
Lille to Moscrou............	38	1845	1883	10·5	..	..
2d branch:						
Creil to St. Quentin.........	25	1849	1874	20	43	..
AMIENS AND BOULOGNE............	99	1844	1941	77	..	..
PARIS, HAVRE, AND DIEPPE.						
Paris to Rouen..............	99	1840	1939	85	..	..
Rouen to Havre.............	99	1842	1941	55	..	..
Rouen to Dieppe............	97	..	..	31	..	..
PARIS TO VERSAILLES.						
Right bank.................	99	1837	1936	11·8	..	..
Left bank	99	1837	1936	10·5	..	..
VERSAILLES TO CHARTRES.........	..	..	..	44	..	..
CHARTRES TO RENNES, with branches from Mans to Caen and from Chartres to Alencon	..	..	..	..	292	..

CHAP. XVIII.] FRENCH RAILWAYS. 375

	Duration.	Lease. Commencement.	Lease. Termination.	Open.	In Progress.	Projected.
				Miles.	Miles.	Miles.
PARIS TO ST. GERMAIN	99	1835	1934	13	..	..
PARIS TO ORLEANS.						
Paris to Orleans	99	1838	1937	75	..	..
Corbeil branch	..	..	..	6·5	..	..
ORLEANS AND BORDEAUX.						
Orleans to Tours	27	1844	1871	71·5	..	..
Tours to Bourdeaux				..	222	..
TOURS TO NANTES.						
Tours to Angers	34	1850	1884	67	..	..
Angers to Nantes				..	52	..
CENTRE RAILWAY.						
Orleans, by Vierzon, to Chateauroux. Branch, Vierzon to Neronde by Bourges.	40	1849	1889	142	..	..
Chateauroux to Limoges	..	..	..	..	85	..
PARIS TO LYONS.						
Paris to Tonnerre	..	..	..	122	..	..
Tonnerre to Dijon	..	..	..	..	74	..
Dijon to Chalons-sur-Saone	..	..	..	43	..	..
Chalons to Lyons	..	..	..	..	80	..
LYONS TO AVIGNON	..	..	..	..	143	..
AVIGNON TO MARSEILLES	33	1848	1881	78	..	..
Branch to Aix	..	..	..	..	15	..
PARIS TO STRASBOURG.						
Paris to Chalons-sur-Marne				106·75	..	..
Chalons to Nancy						
Nancy to Strasbourg, with branches from Epernay to Rheims, and from Frouard to Forbach.	44	1855	1899	37·25	..	..
				..	266	..
STRASBOURG TO BASLE	70	1838	1908	87	..	..
MULHAUSEN TO THANN	99	1837	1936	13	..	..
PARIS TO SCEAUX	50	1845	1895	7	..	..
BOURDEAUX TO CETTE, with branch to Castres	..	..	..	..	..	326
CAEN TO ROUEN RAILWAY at two points	..	..	..	..	..	151
BEC-D'ALLIERS TO CLERMONT, with branch to Nevers	..	..	..	..	..	101
MONTEREAU TO TROYES	75	1849	1924	62	..	..
BORDEAUX TO TESTE	70	1841	1911	32·3	..	..
MONTPELIER TO NISMES	12	1844	1856	32·3	..	..
LYONS TO ST. ETIENNE	99	1827	1926	36	..	..
ST. ETIENNE TO ANDRESIEUX	..	..	..	13·5	..	..
ANDRESIEUX TO ROANNE	99	1841	1940	41·5	..	..
Total	..	..	..	1721·9	1274	577·5

Mineral Lines.

EPINAC TO THE BOURGOGNE CANAL	..	..	..	18	..	..
MONTBRISON TO MONTROND	..	..	..	10	..	..
ALAIS TO BEAUCAIRE AND GRANDE-COMBE	..	..	..	54·5	..	..
ABSCON AND ANZIN TO DENAIN	..	..	..	10	..	..
VILLARS-COTTERETS TO PORT-AUX-PERCHES	..	..	..	5·6	..	..
MONTPELIER TO CETTE	99	1838	1937	16·75	..	..
MINES OF FINS TO THE ALLIER	..	..	..	15·5	..	..
CREUZOT TO CENTRE CANAL	..	..	..	6·25	..	..
DECIZE TO NIVERNOIS CANAL	..	..	..	4·33	..	..
COMMENTRY TO MOUTLUCON	..	..	..	9·33	..	..
Total	..	..	..	150·26	..	..

It appears from this table, that the following are the total lengths of the French railways for the transport of passengers and goods, under traffic, in progress, and projected:

Under traffic	1,722 miles.
In progress	1,274 „
Total length open and in progress	2,966 „
Projected, but not commenced	577 „
Total	3,573 „

Besides these, there are, as appears by the above table, 150 miles of railway for the conveyance of coals and minerals, in many cases composed of single lines of railway of comparatively small importance.

It is difficult to ascertain with precision the actual cost of the construction of the French railways, owing to the manner in which they have been executed, and to the great variety of arrangements which have been made between the government and the companies to which they have been leased. In some cases, as in the Northern Railway, the companies have reimbursed, or have undertaken to reimburse the State the entire expense incurred in the construction of the line. In other cases, however, these expenses remain to the charge of the State, and the companies undertake to provide only the remainder of the capital.

I have, however, been able to ascertain, from the published reports of the railway companies and from the official documents published by the government, the actual cost of construction of the following lines, with sufficient approximation to supply the basis of a general average estimate of the cost of the entire system, completed and in progress.

SYNOPSIS of the Length and Cost of Construction of Fifteen of the principal French Railways.

Name of Railway.	Length under Traffic.	Total Expenses of Construction and Working Stock.	Average Cost per Mile.
	Miles.	£.	£.
North	321	7,216,596	22,481
Amiens and Boulogne	77	1,562,564	20,293
Paris and Rouen	85	2,682,878	31,563
Rouen and Havre	55	2,324,790	42,269
Rouen and Dieppe	31	570,440	18,400
Paris and Versailles (right bank)	11·8	740,258	62,734
„ (left bank)	10·5	690,832	65,700
Paris and Orleans	81·5	2,324,784	28,525
Orleans and Tours	71·5	1,749,628	24,470
Tours and Angers	67	1,355,916	20,239
Centre	142	3,473,812	24,463
Avignon and Marseilles	78	2,894,193	37,105
Strasbourg and Basle	87	1,788,536	20,557
Paris and St. Germain	13	996,399	76,646
Lyons and St. Etienne	36	949,866	26,385
Totals and averages	1167·3	31,321,492	26,832

The length of these fifteen lines being 70 per cent. of the total length of the lines under traffic, and 41 per cent. of the total length of those under traffic and in progress, we can not fall into serious error if we assume the average cost per mile of this extent of 1167 miles as a standard cost for the whole. This will enable us to compute the amount of capital which has been absorbed by the entire system of lines open, and the additional amount which will be absorbed by those which are in progress when completed, as well as by those which are projected, if they should be executed. The result of this computation is as follows:

Estimated Cost of the French Passenger Railways.

	£.
1722 miles open at £26,832 a mile	46,204,704
1274 miles in progress at do.	34,183,968
	80,388,672
577 miles projected, but not commenced, at do.	15,482,064
	£95,870,736

Hence it appears that the French lines executed, and those likely to be completed, will absorb a capital of more than eighty millions; while those which are projected, but the execution of which has not been commenced, will require nearly fifteen millions and a half.

It is probable that the estimate of the cost per mile which we have assumed is not below the truth, inasmuch as, among the fifteen lines from which it has been deduced, there are some which are exceptionally high in their cost per mile.

It will be perceived from what has been explained, that the French railway companies stand in the relation of tenants or lessees toward the state. In many cases, the government proceeded with the construction of the lines before a grant had been made, or even before the lines were submitted to competition. The surveys were all made, under the direction of the government, by the engineers of the department of the Ponts et Chaussées; the earth-work and works of art were also in some cases constructed, the iron-work of the road laid, and the buildings of the stations erected. In a word, several of the lines were already in a forward state at the epochs at which they were submitted to competition, with a view to leasing them to the companies by whom they were to be worked.

The mode in which the government proceeds to offer the leases to public competition is nearly the same as is customary with public contracts in England. A day is named on which sealed proposals previously received by the government will be opened. The minister lays on the table a sealed paper, in which is stated the maximum duration of the lease which the government has determined to grant, and it is understood that the company which offers to accept the line on the shortest lease will receive the preference; but government does not bind itself to select the shortest lease proposed, if other circumstances appear to render another proposal preferable.

The effect of this system of competition, combined with the railway mania which prevailed at the epoch at which the principal concessions were offered, has had the effect of greatly abridging the period for which the leases of some of the principal lines have been granted. Instead of ninety-nine years, which were granted to the earlier companies, the more recent leases have been limited to periods varying from thirty to forty years.

The French railways in general have been opened at an epoch comparatively so recent, that they supply much more limited data for the calculations of the average results of the movement of the traffic upon them than do the railways of Belgium or those of the United Kingdom. The reports published, however, have been in general so ample as in some degree to compensate for the brief period through which they extend.

The locomotive and carrying stock, as well for passenger as for goods traffic, is in all respects similar to that which is worked on the English railways. Indeed, in many cases, the passenger carriages are constructed in a more luxurious and commodious manner, and the second-class coaches especially are provided, and furnished with more regard to public convenience.

The locomotive duty, the consumption of fuel, and other particulars relating to the engines on the French railways, give results not differing in any important respects from those which have been already exhibited with reference to the railways of the United Kingdom and of Belgium. It is found, for example, that the average distance run by each engine lighted varies from seventy to eighty miles; that the average daily mileage of each engine employed is about thirty miles; and that the average consumption of fuel per mile run, including that which is consumed in lighting and standing, is about forty pounds.

As an example of the manner in which the rolling stock is utilized on the French railways, and of the very complete reports published of the railway statistics in that country, I give the following synopses, deduced from the reports of the Northern Railway Company, which works the traffic of three hundred and twenty miles of lines, being nearly 20 per cent. of all the lines under traffic:

FRENCH RAILWAYS.

TABULAR SYNOPSIS of the average daily Movement of the Locomotive Stock of the North of France Railway during the Year 1848.

	Passenger Engines.	Goods Engines.
Number employed	113	64
Their total mileage	3,476	1,782
Average distance traveled per engine	30·7	27·8
Total mileage of trains	3,083	1,522
Number of trains per 100 drawn by two engines	12·75	17·25
Equivalent number running over entire line	10·8	5·5

Total number of engines lighted daily	57·5
Average distance traveled per engine lighted	92 miles.
Number of lbs. of coke consumed daily	246,600
Number of lbs. per mile run	46·7

TABULAR SYNOPSIS of the average daily Movement of the Carrying-Stock on the North of France Railway during the Year 1848.

	Number employed.	Total Mileage.	Distance traveled per Vehicle.	Average Number composing a Train.	Equivalent Number running over the entire Line and Branches.
PASSENGER STOCK.					
Saloon carriages	--	10	--	0·0033	0·03
1st class coaches	102	4,235	41·6	1·37	13·2
2d " "	183	6,354	34·7	2·06	19·8
3d " "	199	6,020	30·3	1·95	18·8
Totals and averages	484	16,619	34·4	5·3833	51·83
Baggage and parcel-vans	97	6,200	64·0	2·010	19·30
Carriage and diligence-trucks	78	1,430	18·3	0·464	4·46
Horse-boxes	50	480	9·6	0·155	1·50
Milk-wagons	--	706	--	0·228	2·20
Post-offices	--	493	--	0·160	1·50
Totals	709	25,928	34·9	8·4003	80·79
GOODS STOCK.					
Flat-wagons		24,260		16·000	75·600
Covered-wagons for sugar and merchandise		5,972		3·900	18·600
Ditto for cattle and merchandise	3,119	9,356	12·8	6·150	29·200
Sheep-wagons		259		0·170	0·810
Wagons for transport of turn tables		5		0·003	0·015
Totals and averages	3,119	39,852	12·8	26·223	124·225

In the last column of this table is exhibited the relation between the movement of the rolling stock and the extent of the railway. The numbers in it express the number of vehicles of each kind which would have run over the whole length of the railway per day, if the movement of the rolling stock were uniformly distributed over it.

In the following table is presented a synopsis of the passenger traffic on several of the principal railways of France, during the year 1848, together with the average results of the whole.

It is necessary, however, to observe that this year, 1848, was exceptional as regards the French railways more especially; the traffic having suffered a considerable diminution, and on several having been totally suspended for a certain interval, by the events of the Revolution.

TABULAR SYNOPSIS of the average daily Movement of the Passenger Traffic, and the Revenue proceeding from it on the principal French Railways during the Year 1848.

	Number booked.	Total Average daily Mileage.	Average Receipts.	Receipts per Passenger booked.	Average Distance traveled per Passenger.	Average Receipts per Passenger per Mile.
Northern.			£.	s. d.	Miles.	d.
1st class	514	29,555	188	7 3½	57·5	1·52
2d class	1,705	66,836	318	3 10¾	39·2	1·17
3d class	4,375	114,187	350	1 7¼	26·1	0·74
Totals and averages	6,594	210,578	856	2 7¼	31·9	0·98
Boulogne and Amiens.						
1st class	78	4,149	30	7 8½	53·2	1·74
2d class	184	7,089	38	4 2	38·5	1·30
3d class	227	5,084	21	1 9½	22·4	0·96
Totals and averages	489	16,322	89	3 4	32·6	1·23
Paris, Rouen, and Havre.						
1st class	325	14,625	102	6 3	45·0	1·67
2d class	1,030	32,445	170	3 3½	31·5	1·25
3d class	1,959	56,419	220	2 3	28·8	0·94
Totals and averages	3,314	103,489	492	2 11½	31·2	1·08
Rouen and Dieppe.						
1st class	18·4	520	3·43	3 7½	28·25	1·54
2d class	89·0	2,194	11·05	2 5½	24·65	1·20
3d class	112·6	2,209	8·25	1 5½	19·61	0·89
Totals and averages	220·0	4,923	22·73	2 0¾	22·09	1·12

FRENCH RAILWAYS. 381

	Number booked.	Total Average daily Mileage.	Average Receipts.	Receipts per Passenger booked.			Average Distance traveled per Passenger.	Average Receipts per Passenger per Mile.
				£.	s.	d.	Miles.	d.
*Paris and St. Germain.								
1st class	7·2	93	0·6		1	8	13·0	1·47
2d class	330·0	3,861	17·9		1	1	11·7	1·11
3d class	2065·0	20,133	74·5		0	8½	9·75	0·87
Totals and averages	2402·2	24,087	93·0		0	9	10·03	0·9
*Paris and Versailles (right).								
1st class	7	77	0·6		1	8	11·00	1·74
2d class	404	4,194	23·10		1	1½	10·38	1·30
3d class	1,888	16,048	73·0		0	9¼	8·50	1·08
Totals and averages	2,299	20,319	97·6		0	10¼	8·83	1·16
Paris and Orleans.								
1st class	473	29,799	175		7	5	63·0	1·42
2d class	912	38,031	187		4	1¼	41·7	1·18
3d class	2,253	44,159	130		1	2	19·6	0·71
Totals and averages	3,638	111,989	492		2	8¼	30·7	1·05
Marseilles and Avignon.								
1st class	69	2,567	17·5		5	0½	37·2	1·62
2d class	393	11,043	56·0		2	10	28·1	1·21
3d class	1,378	29,214	96·0		1	5	21·2	0·80
Totals and averages	1,840	42,824	169·5		1	10	24·72	0·89
Strasbourg and Basle, and Mulhausen and Thann.								
1st class	116	3,190	21·4		3	0½	27·5	1·62
2d class	565	10,057	51·0		1	9½	17·8	1·21
3d class	1,300	19,240	63·0		1	6	14·8	0·81
Totals and averages	1,981	32,487	135·4		1	4½	16·40	0·97
Grand totals and general averages.								
1st class	1,607	84,575	538		6	8	52·43	1·53
2d class	5,612	175,750	872		3	1¼	31·20	1·19
3d class	15,557	306,693	1,036		1	4	19·72	0·81
Totals and averages	22,776	567,018	2,446		2	1¾	24·9	1·03

* Strictly speaking, the class denominated 1st on these lines, corresponds with the saloon class on other French railways, and is scarcely analogous to 1st-class passengers generally. Hence the exceptionally small proportion of these passengers.

It will be desirable to show, as we have done with respect to the railway traffic elsewhere, the proportion in which the different classes of passengers have contributed to the business of the railways.

This is done in the following table for several of the principal lines, and the average result of the whole is given:

TABLE showing the Proportion of Business supplied to the principal French Railways by the several Classes of Passengers, and the Proportion in which they contributed to the Receipts.

	Number of each Class in every 100 booked.	Share of each Class in every 100 Miles traveled.	Share of each Class in every £100 Receipts.
North of France.			
1st class	7·8	14·0	22·0
2d class	25·8	31·7	37·3
3d class	66·4	54·3	40·7
Total	100·0	100·0	100·0
Boulogne and Amiens.			
1st class	16·0	25·5	33·7
2d class	37·5	43·5	42·7
3d class	46·5	31·0	23·6
Total	100·0	100·0	100·0
Paris, Rouen, and Havre.			
1st class	9·8	14·1	20·7
2d class	31·1	31·3	34·6
3d class	59·1	54·6	44·7
Total	100·0	100·0	100·0
Rouen and Dieppe.			
1st class	8·4	10·5	15·2
2d class	40·0	44·5	48·6
3d class	51·6	45·0	36·2
Total	100·0	100·0	100·0
*Paris and St. Germain.			
1st class	0·3	0·4	0·6
2d class	17·5	16·1	18·4
3d class	82·2	83·5	81·0
Total	100·0	100·0	100·0
*Paris and Versailles (right bank).			
1st class	0·3	0·38	0·6
2d class	17·6	20·62	23·8
3d class	82·1	79·00	75·6
Total	100·0	100·0	100·0

* See note to table at p. 381.

	Number of each Class in every 100 booked.	Share of each Class in every 100 Miles traveled.	Share of each Class in every £100 Receipts.
Orleans.			
1st class	13·0	26·6	35·6
2d class	25·1	34·0	38·1
3d class	61·9	39·4	26·3
Total	100·0	100·0	100·0
Marseilles and Avignon.			
1st class	3·8	6·0	10·3
2d class	21·4	25·8	33·1
3d class	74·8	68·2	56·6
Total	100·0	100·0	100·0
Strasbourg and Basle,			
1st class	5·9	10·0	15·8
2d class	28·5	30·8	37·8
3d class	65·6	59·2	46·6
Total	100·0	100·0	100·0
General averages.			
1st class	7·0	14·9	21·9
2d class	24·6	30·9	35·6
3d class	68·4	54·2	42·5
Total	100·0	100·0	100·0

By comparing the mileage and receipts of the passengers with the mileage of the engines or trains, the average number of passengers carried by each train, and the average receipts per train per mile, may be ascertained. This is exhibited in the following table :

TABULAR ANALYSIS of the daily Movement and daily average Receipts of the Passenger Traffic on the undermentioned French Railways for the Year 1848.

	Average daily Mileage of Passenger Trains.	Average daily Mileage of Passengers.	Average Number of Passengers per Train.	Average Receipts per Train per Mile run.
				s. d.
Northern	3,083	210,578	68·0	6 9¾
Boulogne and Amiens	616	16,322	26·5	4 9
Paris, Rouen, and Havre	2,677	103,489	38·7	5 0
Rouen and Dieppe	330	4,923	14·9	2 3
Paris and St. Germain	182	24,087	132·0	10 3
Paris and Versailles (right)	154	20,319	132·0	12 6
Paris and Orleans	1,265	111,989	88·5	0
Orleans and Tours	565	75,710	134·0	6 11
Strasbourg and Basle	841	32,487	38·6	3 6½
Avignon and Marseilles	740	42,824	58·0	5 1
Totals and averages	10,453	642,728	61·4	7 2¼

To ascertain the proportion in which each class of objects of transport contributed to the gross revenue of the railways, it is only necessary to compare the receipts proceeding from each class with the gross receipts.

The results of such a comparison for some of the principal railways are given in the following table:

TABLE showing the Share of every £100 of gross Revenue contributed by each Class of Traffic on the under-mentioned French Railways.

	North of France.	Orleans.	Paris and Rouen.	Rouen and Havre.
Passengers	49·40	48·20	46·70	37·60
Baggage	1·47	5·55	2·51	1·92
	—— 50·87	—— 53·75	—— 49·21	—— 39·52
Parcels	8·86	3·47	10·72	8·95
Horses	0·27	0·45	0·24	0·02
Carriages	0·67	1·02	0·44	0·03
Mails	2·22	3·39	3·65	2·67
Goods	34·25	30·64	31·40	48·00
Cattle	1·52	7·28	0·05	0·01
Sundries	1·34	..	4·29	0·80
	—— 49·13	—— 46·25	—— 50·79	—— 60·48
Total....	100·00	100·00	100·00	100·00

By comparing the mileage of the tons of goods carried, and the gross receipts produced by them, with the number of tons booked, we are enabled to ascertain all the circumstances attending the goods traffic.

These are exhibited in the following table:

TABULAR ANALYSIS of the Movement of the Goods Traffic, and the Receipts proceeding from it, on some of the principal French Railways.

Goods Traffic.	Average Number of Tons booked.	Average Mileage.	Average Distance carried per Ton.	Average Receipts per Ton.
				s. d.
Northern	1015	84,821	83·5	8 0
Paris and Orleans	713	41,653	58·5	11 0
Paris, Rouen, and Havre	1367	80,534	59·0	5 9½
Lyons and St. Etienne	190	49,300	26·0	3 10

The proportion in which the revenue of the principal lines has proceeded from passengers and merchandise is exhibited in the following table, the revenue from passengers including all the traffic carried by the passenger trains:

FRENCH RAILWAYS.

TABULAR ANALYSIS of the Total average daily Receipts, Expenses, and Profits on the principal French Railways during the Year 1848, showing the Proportion due to Passengers and Goods.

Railway.	Receipts.			Per Cent. of Total Receipts.		Expenses.	Profits.
	Per Passenger Trains.	Per Goods Trains.	Total.	For Passengers.	For Goods.		
	£.	£.	£.			£.	£.
Northern	1053	627	1680	62·5	37·5	803	877
Boulogne and Amiens ..	147	18·3	165·3	89·0	11·0	102	63·3
Paris, Rouen, and Havre	671	348	1019	65·5	34·5	832	187
Rouen and Dieppe	36·4	17·8	54·2	67·2	32·8	47·5	6·7
Paris and St. Germain ..	93	00	93	..	..	69	24
Paris and Versailles	96·5	00	96·5	..	..	63·5	33
Paris and Orleans	634	384	1018	62·4	37·6	642	376
Orleans and Tours	196	208	404	48·6	51·4	252	152
Centre	235	97	332	70·5	29·5	218	114
Strasbourg and Basle ...	149	73	222	67·0	33·0	168	54
Avignon and Marseilles.	189	7·3	196·3	96·5	3·5	152	44·3
Lyons and St. Etienne..	119	366	485	24·6	75·4	273	212
Totals and averages	3618·9	2146·4	5765·3	62·8	37·2	3622	2143·3

By comparing the receipts, expenses, and profits with the movement of the trains, the length of the lines worked, and the expense of their construction, we obtain the proportion of these assignable to each mile run by the trains, each mile of the railway open, and each £100 of the capital expended. This is exhibited in the following table:

TABULAR ANALYSIS of the Proportion of the Receipts, Expenses, and Profits on the French Railways, chargeable per Mile run by Trains, per Mile of Lines worked, and per Cent. of Capital expended.

Railway.	Per Mile of Trains.			Per Mile of Railway.			Per Cent. per Annum of Capital.		
	Receipts.	Expenses.	Profits.	Receipts.	Expenses.	Profits.	Receipts.	Expenses.	Profits.
	s. d.	s. d.	s. d.	£.	£.	£.			
Northern	7 3½	3 6	3 9½	5·24	2·50	2·74	8·50	4·07	4·43
Boulogne and Amiens	..	..	..	2·14	1·32	0·82	3·87	2·39	1·48
Paris, Rouen, and Havre	..	..	..	7·28	5·93	1·35	7·43	6·06	1·37
Rouen and Dieppe	..	..	..	1·75	1·53	0·22	3·45	3·03	0·42
Paris and St. Germain	10 3	7 8	2 7	7·15	5·31	1·84	3·36	2·49	0·87
Paris and Versailles	12 6	8 3	4 3	8·17	5·38	2·79	13·00	8·55	4·45
Paris and Orleans .	9 6	6 0	3 6	12·50	7·87	4·63	16·00	10·08	5·92
Orleans and Tours.	8 8½	5 4	3 4½	5·64	3·52	2·12	9·15	5·70	3·45
Centre............	..	..	..	2·34	1·54	0·80	3·76	2 47	1·29
Strasbourg and Basle	5 3½	4 0	1 3½	2·22	1·68	0·54	4·25	3·21	1·04
Avignon and Marseilles..........	..	..	..	5·25	3·60	1·95	2·47	1·92	0·55
Lyons and St. Etienne	..	..	..	13·50	7·50	5·91	18·60	10·50	8·10
	7 6	4 3	3 3	5·30	3·33	1·97	7·20	4·52	2·68

The average speed of the passenger trains on the principal French lines is exhibited in the following table:

TABULAR ANALYSIS of the Movement of the Passenger Traffic on the French Lines of Railway, showing the average Speed, Stoppages, &c., of each Class of Trains.—N.B. An average Loss of Five Minutes is allowed for each Stoppage, except in particular Cases where a greater Delay is fixed by the Programme. This is intended to include the Time lost in coming to Rest, and getting up Speed.

Railway	Train	Distance traveled.	Time.		No. of Stoppages.	Average Speed including Stoppages.	Average Speed in Motion excluding Stoppages.
		Miles.	h.	m.		Miles.	Miles.
Paris to Calais............	Mail	235·0	8	0	10	29·35	34·60
,, ,,	1st class	235·0	9	25	23	25·40	32·40
,, ,,	3d class	235·0	12	30	33	18·85	25·40
Paris to Boulogne........	1st class	168·3	6	45	15	25·00	29·30
,, ,,	2d class	168·3	7	10	21	23·50	33·10
Paris to Havre...........	Night M.	140·0	6	45	1	20·70	20·70
,, ,,	1st class	140·0	6	5	22	23·00	34·25
,, ,,	3d class	140·0	7	5	28	19·75	30·85
Paris to Orleans	1st class	75·00	3	15	4	23·10	25·80
,, ,,	2d class	75·00	4	0	17	18·72	28·85
Orleans to Tours.........	..	64·50	3	55	15	16·50	24·25
Tours to Angers	1st class	39·75	3	0	5	13·25	15·30
,, ,,	2d class	39·75	5	30	13	7·20	8·65
Paris to Chalons-sur-Marne	1st class	106·75	4	38	10	22·95	28·10
,, ,,	2d class	106·75	4	50	12	22·10	26·65
,, ,,	3d class	106·75	5	0	14	21·35	28·00
Totals and averages..	....	2075·85	97	53	243	21·20	26·95

CHAPTER XIX.

GERMAN RAILWAYS.

THE Germanic States are the only extensive theatre of railway enterprise which now remains to be noticed, and under this term I would be understood to include all that portion of Central Europe which is situate east and north of the Rhine.

The system of railways executed and in progress upon this part of the Continent is very unequally distributed, in accordance with the unequal distribution of population, commerce, and industry. A tract, east of the frontier of the kingdom of the Netherlands, having a length of about four hundred miles measured east and west, and a breadth of about two hundred miles measured north and south, is covered with a close network of railways, most of which are completed and in operation, and the remainder in active progress.

This system includes Prussia Proper and its provinces, the kingdoms of Hanover and Saxony and their dependencies, and Brunswick and the other northern duchies. These form an extensive basin of population, commerce, and industry, subordinate and tributary to which all the other systems of railways in the Germanic States may be considered. These latter systems consist of four distinct trunk lines, running north and south in parallel directions.

The first follows the course of the Rhine, commencing at Cologne, and terminating for the present at Bâle. This system is completed and in full operation from Mayence and Frankfort to Bâle, and from Cologne to Bonn, the link between Bonn and Mayence being still incomplete.

Short branches are thrown off from this trunk line at various points, to reach principal centres of population which do not lie in its direct course, such as Baden, Manheim, and Spires.

The second of these tributary lines which run north and south is the Würtemburg Railway, which has for its point of departure Stuttgard, the capital of that kingdom. From this the line proceeds northward to Heilbronn, to which point it is complete and in operation. From Heilbronn, it is proposed to continue it to Frankfort; and a branch is also projected to connect Stuttgard with Carlsruhe.

From Stuttgard, the line is carried southward by Ulm to Frederickshafen, on Lake Constance. This part is also nearly completed. It is proposed to continue the line southward from a point on the opposite shore of the lake, crossing the Alps, by the pass of the Splugen, and descending by the western shores of the Lago Maggiore into the plain of Piedmont, terminating on the field of Marengo, under the walls of Alexandria. Here this line would join the Piedmont system of railways, and thus communicate at once with Turin and Genoa.

A continuous line of railway communication would thus be made from Genoa to Cologne, and thence to the principal ports of the Baltic, the Sound, the German Ocean, and the Channel, by means of the extensive network of railways already described as overspreading the northern section of the Germanic States, and by the Belgian lines.

The third great tributary to which we have referred is that which traverses the kingdom of Bavaria, having Munich as its point of departure. From Munich it proceeds northward, by Augsburg, Donauworth, Nüremberg, Bamberg, and Lichtenfels, to Hof, where it unites with the Saxon railways, and ultimately reaches Leipsic; being thus connected with the great northern system already mentioned. This northern trunk of the Bavarian system throws off several branches east and west. From Augsburg a branch is in progress, intended to be carried to Lindau, on the shores of Lake Constance. This is completed and opened as far as Kaufbeuren, the remainder being in progress. Another branch proceeds westward from Augsburg, and unites with the Würtemburg Railway at Ulm. From Nüremburg a branch is projected (but not yet commenced), to be carried eastward, and to terminate on the left bank of the Danube, at Ratisbon. From Bamberg a branch is in progress westward, to be carried through Würzburg to Frankfort on the Maine, and there to unite with the great Rhenish trunk. From Lichtenfels a link is projected, but not yet commenced, to pass through Cobourg and Meiningen to Cassel. Finally, it is intended to carry a branch eastward from Hof to Pilsen in Bohemia, and from thence, by two branches to Prague on the one side, and to Budweis, the terminus of an Austrian mineral line, on the other.

The Bavarian trunk line for the present terminates at Munich, but it is designed to carry it southward and eastward. The southern trunk will traverse the Tyrol, passing through Innspruck and Bautzen, following the pass of the Alps to Trent, and terminating finally at Verona, where it will unite with the railway connecting Venice and Milan.

When this project shall be realized, a continuous railway communication will be in operation between the Adriatic and the ports of the Baltic, the Sound, the German Ocean, and the Channel, the course being through the Tyrol, Bavaria, and either through the Rhenish states, or through Prussia, according as it is desired to reach the German Ocean or the Baltic.

The eastern trunk will be carried from Munich to Saalsburg, on the frontiers of Austria, where it will fork; one branch being carried to the Linz and Gmünden line at Lambach, and the other to the Vienna and Trieste line at Brück. When this project is realized, an unbroken railway communication will be formed from Vienna westward to Munich, and from thence, by Augsburg, Ulm, and Stuttgard, to the Rhine at Frankfort.

The fourth tributary of the northern basin is that which traverses Austria north and south, having Vienna for its point of departure, and throwing off numerous and important branches. This line proceds south from Vienna by Glognitz, Gratz, Cilli, to Laybach, and terminates at Trieste. The line is already open and in operation to Laybach, with the exception of a short distance presenting some engineering difficulties near Glognitz. The section between Laybach and Trieste crosses the Julian Alps, and will be attended with some engineering operations of an expensive kind.

Of the branches from this southern trunk of the Austrian line, one of the most important is that which has been already mentioned, connecting Brück with Saalsburg and Munich. Another proceeds eastward from Neustadt, and is completed as far as Oderberg. It is intended to be continued to Pesth; and the last section of it, connecting Stahlweissenberg with Pesth, is in operation. From Vienna, several short lines to neighboring places of resort, such as Laxenberg, Brück, and Stokerau, are completed and in operation.

The trunk line is carried northward from Vienna by Gandserndorf, Lundenburg, and Prerau, to Oderburg, on the confines of Upper Silesia, where it unites with the extensive system of northern lines already adverted to. This northern trunk throws off several extensive and important branches. The first proceeds eastward from Gandserndorf to Presburg and Pesth, throwing off a sub-branch to Tyrnau. It is completed and in operation as far as Presburg, as is also the last section between Waitzen and Pesth, and the sub-branch to Tyrnau, the intermediate sections being in progress.

From Pesth the line is continued eastward into Hungary as far as Debreczen, about half its length, terminating at Sczolnok, being completed and in operation.

Another branch of the northern trunk is carried westward from Lundenberg, passes the field of Austerlitz at Brünn, and is continued from thence to Bohm-Tribau in Moravia. Another branch proceeds eastward from Prerau by Olmutz, and unites with the former at Bohm-Tribau. From Bohm-Tribau this line proceeds further eastward by Kollin to Prague, from whence it is continued northward to Dresden, following the valley of the Elbe, where it unites with the great northern system already described. Short branches are thrown off from Prague to Lana and to Saatz.

The branch lines from the Austrian northern trunk, extending across the entire territory of Bohemia, are complete and in full operation, with the exception of a short section near Dresden, between Pirna and Aussig.

This Austrian system of railways thus carried north and south, and which is now completed, except the short section between Labach and Trieste, forms an almost unbroken line of railway communication between Trieste and the various ports of the Baltic, the Sound, and the German Ocean, and presents various routes according to to destination aimed at. If the ports of the German Ocean be desired to be reached, the branch diverging eastward at Lundenberg will be adopted, by which the traveler will pass pass through Bohemia, Saxony, and Western Prussia, touching at Prague, Dresden, Leipsic, Magdeburg, and arriving ultimately at Hamburg. If it be desired to reach the ports of the Baltic or the Sound, he will pursue the Austrian trunk line to Oderburg, on the frontiers of Silesia, where he will enter on the Prussian-Silesian system, and will pass by Breslau, Frankfort on the Oder, and Berlin to Stettin.

Berlin is the common centre and point of departure of the extensive system of northern railways. From this capital seven trunk lines will ultimately diverge, five of which are completed and in operation. The first of these connects Berlin with Hamburg, passing through Wittenberg, and following the right bank of the Elbe.

The second connects Berlin with Hanover and Dusseldorf,

on the right bank of the Rhine, passing through Magdeburg, Brunswick, Minden, and Hamm, and throwing off various branches in its course.

The third proceeds from Berlin, by Potsdam, to Kothen, Halle, Weimar, Gotha, and Cassel. From Halle, a link connects it with Leipsic, and this is continued from Leipsic to Dresden. A shorter course, however, has been opened between Berlin and Dresden, by a link formed with the Berlin and Kothen line just mentioned, proceeding from Jüterbogt to Riesa, passing through Herzburg.

The fourth line diverging from Berlin, and which may be considered as the continuation of the Berlin and Hamburg line, passes through Frankfort on the Oder, and is carried through Upper Silesia, by Bunslau, Breslau, and Oppeln, to Kosel, where it forks, one branch going to Cracow, and the other uniting with with the Austrian northern trunk at Oderburg, on the frontier. This Silesian trunk line by Berlin and Cracow throws off various branches of more or less importance, connecting it with the principal centres of population and industry on the one side and the other. A most important branch, proceeding northward from this line, is intended to be carried from Breslau by Posen to Dantzic and Königsberg; and another is projected from Frankfort to Posen, uniting with this latter.

The fifth line diverging from Berlin proceeds northward to Stettin, from whence it is carried at right angles by Stargard to Posen.

The two remaining lines diverging from Berlin have not yet been commenced. One will proceed northward to Strelitz, and the other eastward to Bromberg, in the grand duchy of Posen, uniting at this point with the Breslau and Dantzic line already mentioned.

A great number of lines are projected, but not yet commenced, in the tract of country between the Weser and the German Ocean, which will be seen by reference to the table of railways completed and projected, which we shall presently give.

Dresden and Hanover form two secondary centres of divergence of this northern Germanic system. From Dresden three trunks diverge; one, which has been already mentioned, follows the valley of the Elbe to Prague; another proceeds eastward, by Bautzen to Kohlfurt, where it unites with the Silesian trunk line connecting Berlin with Breslau, throwing off a branch to Zittau; the third trunk, which diverges from Dresden, proceeds westward to Leipsic, first following the right bank of the Elbe, which it crosses at Riesa. A branch proceeds from Riesa to Chemnitz, now in operation, which is to be continued to Zuickau, and to join the Saxon-Bavarian line at Werdau.

From Hanover three trunk lines issue, all of which are in operation : one directed to Bremen, following the right bank of the Weser; another by Celle and Luneburg to Harburg, on the left bank of the Elbe, opposite Hamburg.

The third trunk proceeding from Hanover, being the continuation of the great line from Berlin westward, strikes the Elbe at Minden, and is continued by Hamm and Duisburg to Cologne. This line throws off several branches. One which proceeds from Minden, and which is in progress, will pass through Osnabruck and Lingen to Emden. Another proceeds from Hamm eastward by Padderborne to Cassel, where it is connected with the line which traverses the duchies of Anhalt, and is continued to Halle, Leipsic, and Dresden. Another branch of this trunk line connects Hamm with Munster. At Dortmund the line forks; one branch proceeding to Dusseldorf by Elberfeld, and the other to Dusseldorf by Duisburg. At Cologne this unites with the Belgian railways, which open a communication to the ports of the Netherlands and to the French system of railways.

The progress of the construction of the Germanic railways for the last five years, including those which are merely projected, as well as those which are in progress or contemplated, is exhibited in the following table :

TABLE showing the Progress of the Railways in the Germanic States during the Five Years ending December 31, 1849.

RAILWAYS.	1845.	1847.	1849.
	Miles.	*Miles.*	*Miles.*
Completed and in operation	1,588	2,828	4,542
In process of construction	2,917	2,138	800
Total completed and in process of construction	4,505	4,966	5,342
Decided to be constructed and sanctioned by the state	..	1,299	
Total constructed, in progress, and decided on	..	6,265	3,114
Projected or contemplated, but not finally decided on or sanctioned by the state	..	1,921	
Total constructed, in progress, sanctioned, and contemplated	..	8,186	8,456

CHAP. XIX.] GERMAN RAILWAYS. 393

In order to present a complete view of the present state of the railways constructed and in progress in the Germanic States, I have collected in the following table the railways classed as they are in operation, in progress, or merely projected, according to the most recent documents. The lengths assigned to the lines open and in progress are generally exact, being taken from official reports. The lengths of the lines projected are in some cases taken only from measurement on the maps and charts.

TABLE showing the Railways of the Germanic States, distinguishing those which were in operation, those which were in progress, and those which were projected but not commenced in 1849.

RAILWAYS.	Length of Line.		
	Completed.	In progress.	Projected.
	Miles.	*Miles.*	*Miles.*
Altona—Kiel	65·5		
Branches to Gluckstadt and Rendsburg	31·10		
Amsterdam—Rotterdam—Arnheim	100·0		
Annaburg—Bochnia		100·0	
Arnheim—Duisburg			70·0
Arnheim—Zwolle			40·0
Augsburg—Ulm			45·0
Bamberg—Francfort-on-Maine			230·0
Bavarian Railway (Lindau—Hof)	288·4		
Branch: Augsburg—Munich	37·4		
Berlin—Hamburg	176·0		
Berlin—Stettin—Posen	184·20		
Berlin—Dantzic			350·0
Berlin—Potsdam—Magdeburg	90·0		
Berlin—Kothen—Bernburg	109·6		
Berlin—Breslau	241·3		
Branch: Handsdorf—Glognu	43·75		
Breslau—Fribourg	35·6		
Branch: Konigszeit—Schwednitz	5·75		
Breslau—Kozel	78·0		
Breslau—Bromberg			182·0
Brieg—Niesse	81·0		
Budweis—Gmünden	122·0		
Canstadt—Esslingen	6·3		
Cassel—Francfort-on-Maine		130·0	
Cologne—Duisburg	39·0		
Cologne—Herbestal	53·30		
Cologne—Bonn	18·4		
Constance to Alexandria by Splugen			260·0
Copenhagen—Roskild—Kersoer	20·0		50·0
Delfzyl—Meppel—Arlingen			160·0
Dresden—Lobau—Zittau	63·1		
Dresden—Prague	20·0	60·0	
Dusseldorf—Dortmund	34·1		
Dusseldorf—Maestricht			70·0
Flensburg—Rensburg—Husum			65·0
Francfort-on-Maine—Wiesbaden	25·3		
Francfort—Hanau	25·0		
Francfort—Soden	10·0		
Francfort—Fribourg—Efringen	224·5		
Branches: Baden—Kehl	25·0		
Gendserndorf—Pesth	57·0	74·0	
Göttingen—Cassel			28·0

394   RAILWAY ECONOMY.   [Chap. XIX.

RAILWAYS.	Length of Line.		
	Completed.	In progress.	Projected.
	Miles.	*Miles.*	*Miles.*
Halle—Weimar—Cassel	160·0		
Halle—Göttingen—Brunswick			108·0
Hamm—Munster	16·0		
Hamm—Duisburg	50·0		
Hamm—Cassel	36·0	54·0	
Hanover—Bremen	64·0		
Hanover—Harburg	64·0		
Hanover—Brunswick	40·5		
Hanover—Hamm	95·0		
Hildesheim—Celle	30·5		
Hof—Pilsen			90·0
Jütebogt—Riesa	70·0		
Kosel—Cracow	92·0		
Kosel—Annaburg	19·70		
Kotzbus—Goyatz	22·0		
Lana—Budweis		80.0	80·0
Leipsic—Dresden	71·3		
Leignitz—Lissa			40·0
Lichtenfels—Gerstung			80·0
Lundenburg—Prague	216·5		
Lingen—Zwolle			60·0
Lingen—Munster			40·0
Lubeck—Schwerin			40·0
Lubeck—Hamburg—Kiel			79·0
Magdeburg-Brunswick	57·2		
Branches: Oschersleben—Halberstadt	18·6		
Wolfenbittle—Harzburg	27·6		
Magdeburg—Leipsic	72·5		
Manheim—Spires	10·0		
Manheim—Metz		50·0	
Mecklenburg-Schwerin—Hagenau	18·4		
Middleburg—Dusseldorf			170·0
Minden—Emden			120·0
Munich—Lambach			200·0
Munich—Verona			260·0
Nieustadt—Oderburg	32·0		
Nüremberg—Fürth	3·5		
Odenburg—Raab			45·0
Oswiectin—Warsaw	161·0	50·0	
Pesth—Diebrizen	40·0	60·0	
Pesth—Stalweisseuberg	40·0		
Prague—Lana	41·0		
Prague—Saatz	35·0		
Presburg—Tyrnau	20·0		
Prerau—Annaburg	34·2		
Riesa—Meissen	16·0		
Riesa—Guben			80·0
Rotterdam—Utrecht			30·0
Schwerin—Rostock			42·0
Vienna—Brünn—Bohm	174·4		
Vienna—Stockerau	13·8		
Vienna—Brück	25·5		
Vienna—Trieste	259·0	92·0	
Branch: Mödling—Laxenburg	5·75		
Würtemburg Railway (Heilbronn—Stuttgart—Frederickshafen)	107·3	50·0	
Total	4542·30	800·0	3114·0

The proportion in which this extent of railway communication in operation, in progress, and projected, to Jan. 1, 1847, was shared among the several States of Germany (excluding the kingdom of the Netherlands), is shown in the following table:

TABLE showing the Proportions in which the German Railways on January 1, 1847, were distributed among the several States.

	Open.		In progress.		Adopted.		Contemplated.	
	Miles.	Miles per Cent. of total Length.	Miles.	Miles per Cent. of total Length.	Miles.	Miles per Cent. of total Length.	Miles.	Miles per Cent. of total Length.
Austria	725·60	25·62	231·39	10·79	160·0	12·41	296·00	15·39
Prussia	1,141·60	40·54	572·50	26·65	628·34	47·91	778·23	40·56
Duchies of Anhalt	52·20	1·85	..	..	..	..	..	..
Kingdom of Saxony	178·16	6·32	149·70	6·98	4·64	0·36	9·28	0·48
Saxon Duchies....	13·92	0·49	44·10	2·05	88·10	6·84	18·53	0·96
Bavaria	151·17	5·33	448·00	20·70	44·10	3·41	331·80	17·26
Würtemburg......	24·33	0·86	149·70	6·98	32·48	2·52	118·20	6·16
Grand Duchy of Baden..........	161·14	5·66	35·80	1·67	..	..	124·00	6·45
Grand Duchy of Hesse	34·90	1·23	44·10	2·05	40·06	3·15	2·32	0·12
Nassau...........	23·70	0·84	3·48	0·17	..	..	74·30	3·86
Free city of Francfort	5·80	0·20	10·44	0·49	..	..	..	..
Electorate of Hesse	..	..	179·80	8·46	3·62	0·28	..	..
Duchy of Brunswick............	75·80	2·58	..	..	6·63	0·51	..	..
Kingdom of Hanover.	59·50	2·10	155·70	7·29	246·93	19·19	..	..
Schamberglippe...	..	..	15·59	0·73	..	..	..	..
Free cities of Hamburg, Lubeck, and Bremen	9·28	0·34	2·32	0·12	..	..	18·54	0·96
Duchy of Mecklenburg	46·40	1·64	95·10	4·44	..	..	69·50	3·62
Duchy of Holstein and Lavensburg..	124·50	4·40	9·28	0·43	44·10	3·42	80·30	4·18
	2,828·0	100·0	2,138·0	100·0	1,299·0	100·0	1,921·0	100·0

The German railways have been constructed in some cases by companies, and in others by the government. Those of the grand duchy of Baden, the kingdoms of Würtemburg, Bavaria, and Hanover, the empire of Austria, the duchy of Brunswick, and the principailties of Hesse, have been, with a few exceptions, constructed and are worked by the States. Even in the few cases where the construction of particular lines was confided to companies, the governments have generally redeemed them.

In Prussia, the State has abstained from any direct interference with the construction or working of the railways, but has extended encouragement to the private companies by whom the extensive system of lines which cover its territory has been executed. In cases where the traffic did not offer sufficient encouragement to stimulate private enterprise, the government has extended its aid, either in the shape of subvention, or by taking certain shares in the line, or in guaranteeing a minimum rate of interest on capital. The government, however, reserves a power of redemption at the end of thirty years, on the condition of paying to the railway proprietors a capital equal to twenty-five times the average amount of the dividends enjoyed by the shareholders for the preceding five years. The State would, in that case, assume the responsibilities and debts of the company, but it would at the same time take possession of their entire assets, as well as the reserve fund. The State engages meanwhile, not to permit parallel and competing lines to be constructed. The government also retains a power of controlling the tariff.

Constructed with a view to a traffic comparatively limited, and resembling closely in their commercial conditions the roads of the United States, the German railways have been constructed, in general, on principles analogous to those which have been found to answer so well in America. The vast expenditure for earth-work and costly works of art, such as viaducts, bridges, and tunnels, by which valleys are bestridden and mountains pierced to gain a straight and level line in the English system, have not been attempted; and the railways have been carried more nearly along the natural level of the country, the cost of earth-work having been generally limited to that of short cuttings and low embankments. Curves of comparatively short radius have also been admitted, so that the railways might wind along those levels which would offer the most economical conditions of construction.

The following table will illustrate the general characters of the lines as to gradients and curves, compared with those which prevail in England:

GERMAN RAILWAYS.

TABLE showing the prevailing Gradients and Curves on the principal Railways of the Germanic States, as well as the exceptional Gradients of steeper Acclivities, and the exceptional Curves of shorter Radius, where they occur.

Names of Railways	Gradients.		Radii of Curves.		Observations.
	Prevailing.	Exceptional.	Prevailing.	Exceptional.	
	One in	*One in*	*Miles.*	*Yards.*	
Baden Railway (Manheim—Francfort)	200	..	0·56	196([1])	([1]) Six curves have radii under 400 yards. Line absolutely straight.
Nüremberg—Fürth	525	..	..	..	
Munich—Augsburg	300	..	..	1100	
Bavarian State lines	200	43	0·37	328	
Wurtemburg State lines..	100	45	..	..	
Budweis—Linz	46	15	0·011	18	Mineral lines worked by horse power.
Linz—Munden	22	..	0·09	..	
Austrian Northern	300	..	0·5	620	
Vienne—Glognitz	280	130	1·0	..	
Murzuchslag—Trieste....	130	50([2])	0·18	200([2])	([2]) At the passage of the Semmering.
Vienna—Prague	150	..	0·18	..	
Prague—Dresden	100	..	0·18	..	
Breslau—Oppela	300	..	1·11	950	
Breslau—Fribourg	200	..	1·17	1030([3])	([3]) On the Schweidnitz branch.
Lower Silesia	300	200	0·7	..	
Berlin-Frankfort-sur-Oder	114	..	0·65	..	
Berlin—Stettin	230	..	0·56	..	
Berlin—Potsdam	300	..	0·9	..	
Anhalt	300	..	0·7	..	
Magdeburg—Leipsic	300	..	0·58	..	
Magdeburg—Halberstadt..	300	..	0·7	..	
Dusseldorf—Elberfeld	130	30([4])	0·7	600	([4]) Self-acting plane.
Cologne—Belgian frontier	200	38([5])	0·7	350([8])	([5]) Inclined plane. ([8]) At Aix-la-Chapelle station.
Leipsic—Dresden	200	..	0·7	430([9])	([9]) At Leipsic station.
Saxon—Bavarian	200	..	0·5	..	
Saxon—Silesian	140	55([6])	0·4	..	([6]) At Dresden station.
Brunswick—Harzburg....	170	46	0·7	..	
Brunswick—Magdeburg ..	400	..	0·8	..	
Brunswick—Hanover	360	..	0·8	750([10])	([10]) At Lherte station.
Hamburg—Bergedorf	500	100([7])	..	..	([7]) At Hamburg station.
Francfort—Wiesbaden	270	..	0·5	..	

In the first and third columns of this table are given the characteristic or prevailing gradients and radii; and in the second and fourth columns are given those which occur only exceptionally, where the character of the ground rendered them inevitable. In some cases, as, for example, in the section of the railway constructed from Brunswick to Harburg, on the left bank of the Elbe, facing Hamburg, the prevailing gradient is 1 in 166; but in one section of this line extending over a distance of about five miles, being the section between Hamburg and the station of Weinenburg, there is a series of gradients which vary from 1 in 100 to 1 in 50. No practical difficulty, however, is encountered in the regular working of this part of the line by locomotives without assistant engines. Trains of an average gross weight of sixty or seventy tons are drawn over this section by locomotives whose weight does not exceed eighteen tons, having six coupled wheels of 4 feet 9 inches diameter.

In some cases, where circumstances favor the expedient, self-acting planes are resorted to. An example of this occurs on the railway between Dusseldorf and Elberfeld, where a descent of a mile and a half toward Elberfeld occurs with a gradient of 1 in 30. At first this plane was worked by a stationary engine and endless rope. This, however, was soon discontinued, and the traffic of the line has since been worked in the following manner. The descending train, accompanied by its engine, is attached to the upper part of the endless rope, and the ascending train, also accompanied by its engine, at the same time to the lower part. Both engines continue to work, the one ascending and the other descending; and the one train arrives at the top of the plane, when the other train arrives at the bottom. Thus the two engines are made to co-operate in drawing the ascending train, while the weight of the descending train aids in the operation. The regularity of this process requires that the trains moving in different directions should be ready to start from the top and bottom of the inclined plane at the same moment.

Accidental delays in the movement of the trains are subject to interrupt this; and to meet such exigencies a reserve engine is kept with its steam up at the top of the incline. When a train, being late, arrives at the bottom of the plane, and requires to ascend it without the aid of a descending train, the reserve engine at the top of the plane is hooked on to the endless rope, and descending in this manner, co-operates with the engine attached to the train, and draws it up to the top. In this way the regularity and continuity of the service is maintained.

The economy of construction of the German railways is further promoted by the conditions observed in the construction of the lines. Although a sufficient quantity of land has been invariably purchased, and earth-works and works of art, in most cases, constructed of sufficient width to lay a double line, one line only has been made, except in the immediate neighborhood of great centres of population and industry, where a traffic sufficient to employ a double line might be counted on.

The gauge of the railways, with one or two exceptions, is

CHAP. XIX.]   GERMAN RAILWAYS.   399

the same as that which is generally adopted in England, that is to say, 4 ft. 8½ in. between the inner edges of the rails. The form and weight of the rail varies according to the traffic, and to the varying judgment and discretion of the engineers. Rails consisting of simple iron bars nailed down on longitudinal planks of wood, such as have been extensively adopted in America, have been used in some cases, among which may be mentioned a section of the Vienna and Glognitz Railway, the section first constructed of the Leipsic and Dresden line, and a mineral line in Austria worked by horse power, between Budweis, Linz, and Gmunden. On the Leipsic and Dresden lines, these have been removed and replaced by heavier rails, and it is probable a like change has already taken place in the rails on the Vienna and Glognitz line; so that the only German railway on which this system of iron bars is used as rails is at present the mineral line above mentioned.

A rail of the form used on the Great Western Railway, representing an inverted U, supported on continuous bearings, and connected by transverse sleepers at regular intervals, has been adopted on four lines of railway in Germany, viz., the Baden, the Berlin and Frankfort, the Magdeburg and Leipsic, and the Upper Silesian lines. On the two last, however, they have lately been removed, and now are continued only on the two former railways.

The single and double T rails have obtained more favor, and are adopted, in one form or other, on several of the German lines; but the form of rail which is most prevalent is that which passes in Germany under the name of the American rail, the transverse section of which is represented in the annexed cut.

In the following table (see page 400) is exhibited the details of the construction of the principal German lines. The letters in the first column indicate the form of the rail. That which corresponds to the rail on the Great Western Railway is expressed by W, the single T rail is expressed by T, and the double T rail by TT.

The form represented in the preceding section is expressed by A, and the flat iron bar by B. In the second column is represented the inclination of the table of the rail inward; and in the third and fourth its length and weight. The weight of the chairs is exhibited in the next two columns; and in the succeeding column the nature of the supports of the rails is denoted.

In the first of these columns, the letter L indicates longitudinal and continuous bearings, S transverse sleepers at regulated distances, D stone blocks, and T L implies longitudinal continuous bearings with transverse ties at regulated distances. In the last column of the table is given, where it could be obtained, the play allowed between the flanges of the wheels and the inner edge of the rails, which varies according to the curves admitted on the lines:

TABLE showing the Dimensions, Weight, and Form of the Rails and their Supports on the principal Railways of the Germanic States.

Name of Railways.	Rails.				Weight of Chairs.		Support of Rails.		Play for Flanges.
	Form.	Inclination.	Length.	Weight per Yard.	Joint.	Common.	Sort.	Distance between Sleepers or Transverse Beams.	
		One in	Feet.	lbs.	lbs.	lbs.		Feet.	Inches.
Baden Railway: (Manheim—Francfort)..	W	24	14·75	52·50	3·3	..	L	7·37	..
Würtemburg State lines...	A	18	15·00	53·50	7·1	..	S	2·50	..
Nüremberg—Fürth	T	8	14·40	28·00	13·6	11·1	D	2·40	..
Munich—Augsburg	T	..	14·75	45·00	21·0	17·3	S	2·80	..
Bavarian State lines......	TT	40	16·75	47·50	25·3	19·7	D & S	2·80	0·70
Budweis—Linz	B	..	9·33	5·00	..	..	L	6·20	..
Maine—Neustadt.........	A	18	18·25	52·00	12·3	..	L }	4·14	..
Neustadt—Glognitz.......	B	18	..	31·00	..	..	L }		..
Austrian Northern........	T	24	15·55	42·50	19·8	13·6	S	2·60	0·55
Upper Silesian	A	16	18·50	53·50	3·5	..	S	3·10	0·55
Breslau—Fribourg........	A	16	18·50	60·00	..	..	S	3·00	..
Berlin—Francfort	W	16	..	50·00	..	..	L	4·10	0·55
Berlin—Stettin	A	16	18·50	50·50	..	..	S	2·66	0·27
Berlin—Potsdam	T	..	15·45	45·00	23·7	17·5	S	3·10	0·55
Anhalt	TT	32	..	49·00	..	..	S	3·10	0·70
Magdeburg—Leipsic	A	16	18·50	52·50	..	..	S	3·10	0·27
Magdeburg—Halberstadt..	A	16	15·40	59·00	..	..	TL	3·10	..
Dusseldorf—Elberfeld.....	T	..	15·00	49·50	17·5	16·4	TL	2·70	..
Cologne—Belgian frontier.	T	..	..	51·50	22·7	20·4	S	3·10	..
Cologne—Bonn...........	A	..	15·40	63·00	23·8	..	S	3·10	..
Leipsic—Dresden.........	A	20	..	51·60	..	..	S	2·33	..
Saxon—Bavarian.........	A	16	17·90	59·00	..	..	S	3·00	0·55
Brunswick—Magdeburg...	A	..	15·00	63·50	11·3	..	S	3·00	0·55
Brunswick—Hanover.....	A	..	17·90	64·50	..	..	S	3·00	0·27
Hamburg—Bergedorf.....	A	..	..	61·50	..	..	..	..	..
Altona—Kiel.............	A	..	..	56·50	..	..	..	..	..
Francfort—Wiesbaden....	TT	..	15·40	59·00	24·2	21·0	S	3·00	..
Manheim—Francfort	A	..	16·40	70·00	..	..	S	2·73	..

The cost of construction of the system of German railways is, as might be expected from these and other local circumstances, incomparably less than in other parts of Europe, and will not exceed in a considerable proportion that of the railways of the United States. I have given in the following table the estimated expense of the construction of the railways, obtained from the most authentic sources, up to the year 1847:

TABLE showing the estimated Cost of Construction of the Railways of the Germanic States completed, in Progress, and Projected.

Railways.	Lines constructed by the State.		Lines constructed by Companies.		Totals and Averages.	
	Total Cost.	Cost per Mile.	Total Cost.	Cost per Mile.	Total Cost.	Cost per Mile.
	£.	£.	£.	£.	£.	£.
Completed..........	10,080,858	12,554	20,507,539	10,122	30,588,397	10,813
In progress	16,992,867	14,624	11,335,531	11,613	28,328,398	13,203
Adopted but not commenced...........	7,844,844	12,038	6,074,301	9,387	13,919,145	10,715
Contemplated but not adopted...........	5,828,571	11,631	13,758,676	9,689	19,587,245	10,186
	40,747,140	13,069	51,676,047	10,197	92,423,187	11,289

It appears from the preceding statement, that the capital absorbed by the railways which had been completed up to the date of the reports we have quoted, which are the most recent we have obtained of an authentic and exact character, was at the average rate of something less than £11,000 per mile; but it is probable that these lines had not yet absorbed their full amount of capital. It appears further, that the estimated expenses of the lines in progress were greater than those which had been executed, being at the average rate of upward of £13,000 per mile. We shall probably not depart widely from the truth, if we estimate the entire extent of railways in the German States, constructed and to be constructed, at the rate of £13,000 per mile, including in that amount the cost of stock as well as the cost of construction. This rate of expense is scarcely one third of the cost per mile of the English railways.

The expenditure of thirty millions, which had been made previously to 1847, had been spread over nine years, being at the average rate of three millions and one third per annum, 2828 miles of railway having been then completed. In the three years ending 31st December last, 1720 miles of additional lines had been opened, being at the average rate of 570 miles per annum, which, being estimated at £12,000 per mile, would give an annual expenditure by the German States of £6,800,000 per annum, being just double the average annual expenditure of the preceding nine years. It is, however, to be observed here, that although the average expenditure of the nine years preceding 1847 was only three millions and one third, yet the chief part of this expenditure had been incurred within the last four of these nine years; and, consequently, it is probable that the entire rate of expenditure in the three years ending 31st December, 1849, did not on the whole much exceed the average annual expenditure of the years immediately preceding.

The comparatively low rate of cost of the German railways has arisen from several causes, some of which we have already indicated. The absence of expensive earth-works and works of art, while it caused a considerable diminution of the cost of construction, might be expected to create difficulties in the working of the lines. Nevertheless, the German engineers were reassured on this subject by what they had witnessed in several parts of the United States, and more especially on the line which connects Boston and Albany. They did not, therefore, hesitate to admit a system of gradients and curves, where the character of the country rendered it necessary, which are nowhere seen on the railways of England, France, or Belgium.

The low comparative cost of construction of the German railways was also influenced by the low price of the land occupied by the lines and stations, the low price of materials, and the low rate of wages of manual labor. In order to render manifest how far these causes operated, I have exhibited, in the following table, the average cost per acre of the land, and the average wages per day of the laborers employed in earth-work on the principal lines:

TABLE showing the average Cost of Land per Acre, and the average Wages of Earth-work Laborers per Day on the principal German Railways.

Railways	Cost of Land per Acre.	Wages of Laborers per Day.
	£.	d.
Baden	143·0	14·5
Upper Silesia	47·0	7·8
Berlin—Francfort	69·2	
Anhalt	63·0	
Berlin—Stettin	46·0	15·6
Magdeburg—Leipsic	53·5	
Dusseldorf—Elberfeld	70·0	13·0
Cologne—Belgian frontier	95·5	15·6
Saxon—Silesian	53·0	
Nüremberg—Fürth	--	9·5

It would be important to ascertain the proportion in which the cost of construction of the German lines has been shared among the different heads of expenses, such as the cost of land, the road structure, the stations, and the stock. I have not been

GERMAN RAILWAYS.

able to obtain, in every case, complete data for this purpose; but in the following table the expenses of construction and stock of several of the principal lines are exhibited under their respective heads:

TABLE showing the Cost of Construction per running Mile of each of the principal German Railways, with the Share of the total Expenses assigned to each Head.

Railways.	Surveys and Land.	Earth-work, Works of Art, and Fences.	Road Structure.	Stations, including Purchase of Land for them.	Stock.	Direction and Management.	Total.
	£.	£.	£.	£.	£.	£.	£.
Baden	1,445	3,478	2,625	1,957	1,983	276	11,764
Nüremberg—Fürth	829	163	1,800	438	593	354	4,177
Munich—Augsburg....	1,042	3,485	2,966	318	810	434	9,055
Austrian Northern	745	2,030	3,190	642	1,092	104	7,823
Berlin — Frankfort-sur-Oder	920	1,365	2,272	1,178	1,384	399	7,518
Berlin—Stettin	550	1,770	1,835	750	975	388	6,268
Berlin—Potsdam	1,940	2,110	2,760	2,222	3,300	194	12,526
Berlin—Kothen	607	2,020	2,485	582	1,052	304	7,050
Magdeburg-Halberstadt	616	650	2,170	733	895	299	5,273
Bonn—Cologne	1,965	885	2,118	839	1,610	..	7,417
Saxon—Bavarian......	1,085	3,850	1,854	990	1,248	303	9,330

The sufficiency of single lines for the maintenance of the traffic generally throughout the German States will at once suggest the fact, that the amount of the traffic is small comparatively with that which prevails on the English and some of the continental lines. The mode of working the traffic has generally relation to its amount. On the single lines, sidings are provided, as in America, at convenient intervals, and trains proceeding in contrary directions run into these, the first which arrives waiting for the passage of that which is about to meet it. No practical inconvenience ensues from this, since the traffic does not require the frequent departures which are necessary upon English, French, and Belgian railways. On the German railways, three departures per day for passenger trains, and one or two for mixed trains of passengers and goods, are generally sufficient.

In passing from railway to railway under the administration of different companies, or through the territory of different states, the passengers are generally obliged to change carriages; but arrangements are in most cases made, by which they may book their places and obtain tickets to their ultimate destination, so that no further payment of fare or examination of luggage is necessary. Thus, at the Berlin station of the Anhalt railway, tickets and baggage may be booked for Brunswick, and the passengers will then be carried through without further trouble, except occasionally changing carriages.

On the German railways there are, as on those in England, three classes of passengers, the first, second, and third, and in some cases even a fourth class, with corresponding degrees of accommodation in the vehicles of transport; but no such classification prevails as to the trains. There are no express, or first and second-class trains, as in England, distinguished from third-class trains. Passengers of all the classes are indifferently taken in each.

There are mixed trains, by which goods and passengers are indifferently carried, and in general these only take goods. On a few railways, however, there are trains exclusively devoted to merchandise. The "mixed trains" on the German railways, mean those which carry passengers and goods indifferently.

In order to show the movement of the trains which generally prevails on the German railways, I have exhibited in the following table the number of each kind running daily in each direction, on fifteen principal railways. In the first column is indicated by the letter T such as run through from terminus to terminus over the entire length of the lines, and by the letter I such as ply to intermediate stations. The numbers in the other columns indicate the number of those respectively which start from each station daily.

TABLE showing the Number of Trains daily which depart from each of the Termini of the under-mentioned principal German Railways, distinguishing those which go from Terminus to Terminus from those which ply to intermediate Stations.

Railways.	Indication of Distance.	Number of Trains.		
		Passenger Trains.	Mixed.	Goods.
Altona—Kiel	T	2	-	1
Berlin—Hamburg	T	2	1	1
Berlin—Stettin	T	2	-	1
Berlin—Magdeburg	T	4	-	-
Berlin—Kothen	I	2	2	-
Magdeburg—Leipsic	T	3	2	-
" "	I	-	1	-
Halle—Eisenach	T	2	1	-
" "	I	-	1	-
Brunswick—Hartzburg	T	-	4	-
Leipsic—Dresden	T	3	2	-
Leipsic—Reichenbach	T	3	2	-
Berlin—Breslau	T	2	-	-
" "	I	1	2	-
Breslau—Myslowitz	T	1	2	-
Cologne—Hamm	T	2	-	-
" "	I	2	1	-
Manheim—Fribourg	T	3	-	1
" "	I	6	-	1
Vienna—Leipsic	T	2	-	1

It will be seen from this table, that, in general, on the German lines the number of trains daily in each direction does not exceed four. The railways which form exceptions to this are short lines diverging from chief cities, such as Vienna, Berlin, or Leipsic, which serve as excursions for the population of these towns, analogous to the Greenwich, Blackwall, and other short lines diverging from London, or the Versailles and St. Germain lines from Paris.

When railways in the German states were first brought into operation, considerable difficulty was encountered in obtaining locomotive power and carrying stock, and engineers were sent by their respective governments to England and America, for the purpose of obtaining the information, and making contracts for engines and vehicles of transport.

A considerable stock was soon obtained, and a still greater number were ordered. Before the end of 1845, 237 engines had been delivered by the principal engine-builders in England, of which 168 were supplied by Messrs. Stephenson of Newcastle, and Messrs. Sharp and Roberts of Manchester. Upward of 30 were then under order in England, but not yet delivered, 57 engines had been obtained from the manufactory of Messrs. Norris of Philadelphia, 43 from the Belgian manufacturers, and 25 from Messrs. Meyer and Co. of Mullhouse, in France.

The senior partner of Messrs. Norris of Philadelphia was induced to remove to Germany, and to establish a factory of locomotive engines near Vienna, from which a considerable number of engines have already been obtained.

The expense and disadvantage of importing soon, however, stimulated domestic talent and industry; and there are now established in Germany several extensive factories for the construction of locomotive engines, among which may be mentioned those of Messrs. Kessler at Carlsruhe, Hirschau at Munich, the factory of the Vienna and Glognitz Railway, that of Mr. Norris at Vienna, the Wyener and Neustadt factory near Vienna, that of Borsig at Berlin, and several others of minor importance at Berlin, Magdeburg, Aix-la-Chapelle, Chemnitz, &c.

Before the end of 1845, 125 engines had been delivered from the German factories, to which a large number has since been added.

In the following table are shown the dimensions of the engines generally used on the principal German railways:

TABLE showing the Dimensions of the Locomotive Engines used on the principal German Railways.

	Baden.		Bavaria.		Austria.	
	ft. *in.*		*ft.* *in.*		*ft.* *in.*	
Diameter of cylinders	0	13	0	13	0	12	0	13
Stroke of pistons	0	18	0	24	0	24	0	25
Diameter of driving-wheels	5	6	6	0	5	0	4	2
Diameter of supporting-wheels	3	7	3	7	3	0	2	7
Diameter of boiler	3	1	3	4	3	4	3	8
Length of boiler	12	0	12	4	9	0	12	6
Number of tubes	150		121		111		115	
Internal diameter of tubes	0	1·6	0	1·6	0	1·60	0	2·00
Fire-box, length	3	2	3	10				
,, breadth	3	2	3	6				
,, height	4	0	3	10				
Heating surface of fire-box	60 sq. ft.		57½ sq. ft.		54 sq. ft.		59½ sq. ft.	
Heating surface of tubes	765 ,,		658 ,,		463 ,,		775 ,,	
Total heating surface	825 ,,		715½ ,,		517 ,,		834½ ,,	
Weight of engine	18 tons.		17·2 tons.		14·6 tons.		17 tons.	

Table [B] referred to in page 407.

TABLE showing the Magnitude and average Cost of the Vehicles of Transport used on the principal German Railways.

Designation of Vehicles.	No. of Places.	Cost of Construction.	Cost per Place.
PASSENGER STOCK.		£.	£.
Four-wheeled carriages—1st class	18	276	15·3
,, ,, 2d class	30	217	7·24
,, ,, 3d class	36	166	4·6
Six-wheeled carriages—1st class	32	346	10·8
,, ,, 2d class	40	287	7·17
,, ,, 3d class	40	235	5·9
Six-wheeled do. 1st class	48	485	10·1
,, ,, 2d class	60	338	5·64
,, ,, 3d class	60	279	4·66
Eight-wheeled American do.—1st class	70	545	7·8
,, ,, 2d class	70	472	6·75
,, ,, 3d class	120	332	2·78
GOODS STOCK.	Capacity.		Cost per Ton.
	Tons.		
Four-wheeled baggage-wagons	4·5	113	25·2
Six-wheeled do.	7·5	181	24·2
Four-wheeled goods wagons uncovered	4·5	69·6	15·4
Four-wheeled do. covered	4·5	77·0	17·1
Six-wheeled do. uncovered	7·5	99·5	13·25
Eight-wheeled do. covered	12·5	311·0	24·9
Eight-wheeled do. uncovered	12·5	261·0	21·0
Horse-boxes	..	111	
Carriage-trucks	..	89	
Eight-wheeled cattle-wagons	..	260	

The vehicles of transport for passengers and goods on the German railways are very various.

Passenger carriages similar to those used in England, Belgium, and in France, are adopted on many German lines. The passenger vehicles used in the United States, already described in Chapter XII., are also extensively used. These carriages measure from 25 to 35 feet in length, and accommodate from 70 to 120 passengers. The goods wagons, of like construction, are capable of carrying upward of twelve tons.

There are also passenger vehicles supported on six wheels, and consisting of six compartments, each first-class compartment accommodating eight, and each second or third-class compartment accommodating ten passengers.

In the Table [B] (see page 406) are given the dimensions, capacity, and cost of construction of the several classes of vehicles for the transport of passengers and goods on the principal German lines.

In order to show the movement of traffic in passengers and goods on the German railways, I have obtained such official returns as have been published for the year 1846, which is the latest period for which returns have been made. These are given in the following table; the passenger and goods traffic being distinguished, and the quantity, mileage, and receipts of each class being given:

TABULAR ANALYSIS of the average daily Traffic in Passengers and Goods on the under-mentioned German Railways during the Year 1846.

Railways.	Length.	Passenger Traffic.			Goods Traffic.		
		Number of Passengers booked.	Mileage.	Receipts.	Number of Tons booked.	Mileage.	Receipts.
				£.			£.
1. Altona—Kiel	65·50	1,084	24,635	77·5	220	4,550	72·0
2. Baden — Manheim — Fribourg	142·00	6,230	82,013	258·0	275	23,850	189·0
3. Bavarian: (Munich—Donauworth)	63·00	1,108 }	37,140	{ 67·5	60·0 }	5,740	{ 27·4
Nüremberg — Neumarket)	81·00	1,254 }		56·3	55·6 }		18·0
4. Berlin—Anhalt: (Berlin—Kothen)	99·00	937	51,520	186·0	133·0	10,750	95·0

408   RAILWAY ECONOMY.   [Chap. XIX

	Length.	Passenger Traffic.			Goods Traffic.		
Railways.		Number of Passengers booked.	Mileage.	Receipts.	Number of Tons booked.	Mileage.	Receipts.
				£.			£.
5. Berlin—Hamburg	176·00	184	6,152	19·4	..	505	8·0
6. Berlin—Potsdam--Magdeburg.................	90·00	1,380	28,600	103·0	..	2,150	19·4
7. Berlin — Stettin — Stargard	104·20	1,222	43,200	136·0	154·0	4,870	77·0
8. Brunswick Railway	61·50	1,540	21,620	68·0	..	5,430	48·0
9. Breslau — Schweidnitz — Fribourg	41·35	645	15,900	46·0	166·0	2,550	33·0
10. Cologne—Minden: (Cologne—Duisburg)	39·00	1,852	18,120	75·5	..	200	3·5
11. Dusseldorf —Elberfeld...	16·25	976	11,472	47·8	154·0	2,130	37·3
12. Gluckstadt—Elmshorn ..	10·40	265	1,910	6·0	43·3	177	2·8
13. Hamburg—Bergedorf	10·00	519	4,600	15·3	..	..	1·4
14. Hanoverian Railway: (Hanover — Brunswick Hildesheim—Celle)...	71·00	1,040	22,250	70·0	186·0	4,145	36·6
15. Austrian Northern: (Vienna—Brünn—Olmutz Leipsic—Stockerau) ...	188·00	2,016	90,640	336·0	432·0	31,840	398·0
16. Leipsic—Dresden	71·30	1,338	44,850	156·0	166·0	11,700	112·0
17. Lower Silesian: (Breslau—Berlin ...... Kohlfurt—Gorlitz)....	240·00	1,523	45,120	188·0	123·0	8,450	109·0
18. Nüremberg—Fürth	3·50	1,450	4,900	13·0	..	..	0·06
19. Breslau—Myslowitz	124·00	1,069	35,280	102·0	198·0	6,380	101·0
20. Austrian States Railway: (Murzusclag—Cilli.......	144·00	1,090	26,400	110·0	221·0	8,720	109·0
Olmutz—Prague)........	152·00	860	39,360	164·0	181·0	10,640	133·0
21. Rendsburg—Neuminster .	20·80	214	3,500	11·8	28·0	410	6·5
22. Rhenish Railway: (Cologne—Belgian frontier)	53·30	1,490	33,300	154·0	521·0	16,280	129·0
23. Saxon—Bavarian: Leipsic—Reichenbach) ..	65·50	835	23,350	75·0	189·0	7,100	68·0
24. Saxon—Silesian: (Dresden—Lobau).......	49·30	418	9,200	32·0	..	1,254	12·0
25. Taunus Railway: (Francfort—Wiesbaden) .	28·30	2,180	28,150	98·0	22·0	123	10·3
26. Vienna—Glognitz: (Trunk line)	49·90	3,350	48,720	203·0	233·0	7,440	93·0
Vienna—Brück	25·50	158	1,776	7·4	15·0	264	3·3
27. William's Railway: (Kosel—Ratisbor)	19·70	131	1,356	8·6	25·0	348	5·5
	2304·40	39,768	778,634	3061·1	3800·0	176,263	1915·7

From the results of this table we can deduce the average distance over which each passenger and each ton of goods was carried, the average receipts obtained per head or per ton booked, and the average receipts per head or per ton per mile.

These are exhibited in the following table:

CHAP. XIX.] GERMAN RAILWAYS. 409

TABLE showing the average Distance carried and the average Receipts obtained, per Head or per Ton per Mile, from the Passengers and Goods transported on the principal German Railways under-named during the Year 1846.

Railways.	Passengers.			Goods.		
	Average Distance traveled per Passenger.	Average Receipts per Passenger booked.	Average Receipts per Passenger per Mile.	Average Distance carried per Ton.	Average Receipts per Ton booked.	Average Receipts per Ton per Mile.
	Miles.	*d.*	*d.*	*Miles.*	*d.*	*d.*
Altona—Kiel	22·7	17·2	0·75	20·7	78·0	3·80
Baden — Manheim—Fribourg	13·2	10·0	0·75	87·0	165·0	1·90
Munich—Donauworth Nuremberg—Neumarket	15·75	12·6	0·80	50·0	94·0	1·90
Berlin—Anhalt	55·0	47·5	0·87	81·0	172·0	2·12
Berlin—Hamburg	33·0	25·3	0·75	..	..	3·80
Berlin—Postdam--Magdeburg	20·7	17·9	0·86	..	..	2·16
Berlin—Stettin—Stargard	35·4	26·8	0·75	31·6	120·0	3·80
Brunswick Railway	14·5	10·6	0·75	..	..	2·11
Breslau — Schweidnitz — Fribourg	24·6	17·0	0·69	15·4	48·0	3·10
Cologne—Minden	9·75	9·8	1·00	..	..	4·20
Dusseldorf—Elberfeld	11·75	11·8	1·00	13·9	58·0	4·20
Gluckstadt—Elmshorn	7·20	5·4	0·75	41·0	15·6	3·80
Hamburg—Bergedorf	8·9	7·0	0·80	..	..	..
Hanoverian Railway	21·3	16·1	0·75	22·3	47·0	2·11
Austrian Northern	45·0	40·0	0·89	74·0	222·0	3·0
Leipsic—Dresden	33·6	28·0	0·83	70·0	161·0	2·3
Lower Silesian	29·7	29·8	1·00	69·0	213·0	3·1
Nuremberg—Furth	3·0	2·1	0·64	..	..	..
Breslau—Myslowitz	33·1	22·9	0·69	32·2	123·0	3·8
Austrian States	24·2	24·2	1·00	39·5	118·0	3·0
Olmutz—Prague	45·6	47·2	1·03	58·0	173·0	2·9
Rensburg—Neuminster	16·3	13·2	0·81	14·6	57·0	3·9
Rhenish Railway	22·4	24·8	1·11	31·0	59·0	1·9
Saxon—Bavarian	28·0	21·5	0·77	37·6	86·0	2·3
Saxon—Silesian	22·0	18·4	0·85	..	..	2·3
Taunus Railway	13·0	10·8	0·83	..	112·0	..
Vienna–Glognitz (trunk line)	14·5	14·5	1·00	32·0	96·0	3·0
Vienna—Bruck	11·2	11·2	1·00	17·6	53·0	3·0
William's Railway	10·5	16·2	1·56	13·9	53·0	3·0
General averages	19·6	18·5	0·93	46·4	121·0	2·6

It will be observed, in these results of the passenger traffic, that the average receipts per passenger per mile very little exceed the tariff for the third-class passengers. This is explained by the fact that the third class constitutes a very large proportion of the entire number of passengers booked, a much larger proportion than prevails on the railways worked in the western states of Europe.

To demonstrate this, I have given in the following table the proportion of each class of passengers booked for the principal German railways:

TABULAR ANALYSIS showing the Number of Passengers belonging to each Class in every 100 booked on Sixteen of the principal German Railways.

	1st Class.	2d Class.	3d Class.	Total.
Nüremberg and Fürth	3·42	24·37	72·21	100·00
Vienna and Glognitz	5·28	25·54	69·18	100·00
Breslau and Opeln	1·10	15·55	83·35	100·00
Breslau and Fribourg	1·00	14·00	85·00	100·00
Berlin and Francfort-sur-Oder	0·97	17·93	81·10	100·00
Berlin and Stettin	1·80	26·89	71·31	100·00
Berlin and Potsdam	8·16	23·84	68·00	100·00
Berlin and Kothen	2·88	31·44	65·68	100·00
Magdeburg and Leipsic	1·80	22·55	75·65	100·00
Dusseldorf and Elberfeld	2·00	17·74	80·26	100·00
Bonn and Cologne	3·08	33·69	63·23	100·00
Cologne and Herbestal	13·74	35·08	51·18	100·00
Leipsic and Dresden	3·32	19·70	76·98	100·00
Nüremberg and Hof	0·72	11·64	87·64	100·00
Hamburg and Bergedorf	0·70	9·68	89·62	100·00
Francfort and Wiesbaden	1·65	11·22	87·13	100·00
General averages	3·60	22·40	74·00	100.00

It follows, therefore, that there are not four passengers in every hundred on the German railways that take the first-class places, and that 74 per cent. of all the passengers booked belong to the third class.

The following are the average fares chargeable per mile on the three classes of passengers on the German lines:

                    d.
1st class .... 1·62
2d class .... 1·13
3d class .... 0·79

The following are the average tariffs per mile for other objects of transport on the German railways:

                    d.
 Carriages .... 8·1
 Horses .... 5·0
 Cattle per head .... 1·56
 Sheep per head .... 0·18

Goods: *d.*
 Not classed per ton .... 6·85
 1st class .... 3·47
 2d class .... 2·53
 3d class .... 2·40

The traffic on the German railways, as elsewhere, is subject to variation arising from local circumstances.

This variation is shown in the following table in which the receipts per mile of railway and per cent. of capital in the four years terminating 31st December, 1846, on eighteen of the principal German railways, are given:

TABLE showing the average Receipts per Mile and per Cent. of Cost of Construction on the under-mentioned Railways during the Four successive Years ending December, 1846.

Railway.	Receipts per Mile of Railway.				Receipts per Cent. of Capital.			
	1843.	1844.	1845.	1846.	1843.	1844.	1845.	1846.
	£.	£.	£.	£.	£.	£.	£.	£.
Nüremberg—Fürth	1,300	1,300	1,390	1,410	24·75	24·75	26·48	26·85
Vienna—Glognitz	1,898	2,000	2,120	2,428	8·70	9·15	9·70	11·10
Austrian—Northern	806	863	1,050	1,420	8·15	8·73	10·60	14·35
Upper Silesian (Breslau—Myslowitz)	489	487	..	599	12·40	12·35	..	15·20
Breslau—Fribourg	..	560	643	696	..	7·82	8·97	9·74
Berlin—Francfort	840	862	..	..	10·56	10·84	..	..
Berlin—Stettin	682	744	623	752	9·48	10·35	8·64	10·44
Berlin—Potsdam	1,625	1,728	..	..	12·96	13·80	..	..
Berlin—Kothen	1,085	1,085	977	1,030	14·46	14·46	13·00	13·72
Magdeburg—Leipsic	1,352	1,395	1,420	1,600	15·20	15·50	15·78	17·80
Magdeburg—Halberstadt	495	548	634	760	7·85	8·70	10·08	12·06
Dusseldorf—Elberfeld	1,310	1,353	1,618	1,932	5·65	5·84	6·98	8·34
Bonn—Cologne	..	980	1,058	1,110	..	10·90	11·76	12·35
Cologne—Herbestal	1,068	1,528	1,704	1,940	4·60	6·58	7·35	8.35
Leipsic—Dresden	1,185	1,210	1,270	1,380	9·35	9·53	10·00	10·86
Saxon—Bavarian	743	683	483	802	7·98	7·32	5·18	8·60
Hamburg—Bergedorf	716	660	595	600	5·34	4·91	4·43	4·46
Francfort—Wiesbaden	1,376	1,385	1,478	1,610	11·85	11·95	12·75	13·90

I have obtained exact returns of the gross receipts on upward of two thousand miles of all the railways open in the German States in the years 1845 and 1846, later than which there are no published returns. The results of these reports are as follows:

	1845.	1846.
Total length of railways to which the returns refer......Miles	2,348	2,738
Gross receipts	£1,433,061	2,049,231
Receipts per mile of railway	612	748
Receipts per cent. of capital, taking cost of construction at £12,500 per mile	4·9	6·0

It appears therefore, that, although upon some few of the most frequented of the railways the receipts bear a considerable proportion to the cost of construction, yet on the average of the whole they did not, according to the last returns, exceed 6 per cent. on the capital expended. The proportion in which they have been produced by passenger and goods traffic has been, on an average, in the ratio of 61 per cent. from passengers, and 39 per cent. from goods.

I have not been able to obtain exact returns of working expenses, more recent than 1844. In the following table is given the details of these expenses, together with their ratio to the gross receipts, for eighteen of the principal lines for that year:

CHAPTER XX.

RAILWAYS IN RUSSIA, ITALY, AND SPAIN.

Of the railways in operation, in progress, and contemplated in other countries, a brief notice will suffice.

Russia, carried along by the tide of public opinion in Europe, found herself compelled, by a due regard to the interests of her people, to consecrate a part of her exertions and her capital to the construction of the new lines of communication. An attempt was first made to attract private capitalists to these projects, and special advantages were offered to companies who might be disposed to undertake the construction of the lines of railway contemplated in Russia. The emperor, besides guaranteeing to the shareholders a minimum profit of 4 per cent., proposed to give them gratuitously all the lands of the state through which the railways should pass, and to place at their disposal, also gratuitously, the timber and raw materials necessary for the way and works which might be found upon the spot. It was further proposed to permit the importation of rails and the rolling stock free of duty. Russian proprietors also spontaneously came forward, and not only agreed to grant such portion of their land as the railways might pass through gratuitously, but further to dispossess themselves temporarily of their serfs, and surrender them to the use of the companies on the sole condition that they should be properly supported while employed.

By a special ukase, dated February 13, 1842, it was decreed, that the railway which was to unite the two capitals of St. Petersburg and Moscow should be constructed exclusively at the expense of the State, in order to retain in the hands of the government, and in the general interest of the people, a line of communication so important to the industry and the internal commerce of the empire. The local proprietors equally agreed to surrender to government gratuitously the lands necessary for the works of this line.

The system of railways contemplated in Russia is composed of five principal trunk lines, one of which, connecting Warsaw with Cracow, is completed and in operation, and has been already noticed in the last chapter, in connection with the German railways: the length of this line is 168 miles. The second will connect Warsaw with St. Petersburg: the extent of this would be, when executed, 683 miles. The third will connect St. Petersburg with Moscow; this line is in active progress: its length will be about 400 miles.

Besides these, authorization was given to a company by a ukase dated July, 1843, to construct a railway for the transport of goods between the Wolga and the Don, the length of which would be 105 miles.

In the actual execution of this magnificent system of railway communication, no considerable progress has been yet made, with the exception of the line already mentioned between Warsaw and Cracow.

A short line of railway connecting St. Petersburg with Tsarkoé-soéla, having an analogy to the Greenwich and Richmond lines, which diverge from London, and the Versailles and St. Germain lines from Paris, was completed and opened for traffic in April, 1838. The traffic on this line has hitherto amounted to about seven hundred passengers per day.

The railway connecting the Don and the Wolga was opened for traffic in 1846; but this line is exclusively for merchandise, and is worked by horses.

In southern Russia a line of railway is projected between Kief and Odessa, the surveys of which have been made by Belgian engineers; but no progress in its construction has yet been effected.

A railway has been projected also between St. Petersburg and Cronstadt, and another between St. Petersburg and Baltishport, in Esthonia, to be constructed and worked by a company with a guarantee of four per cent. by the government.

In Italy a few short lines of railway only have been executed, connecting the chief states with neighboring places. They are as follows:

	Miles.
Naples to Portici, opened Oct. 1839	5
Portici to Castelmare, with branch to Nocera	$21\frac{3}{4}$
Naples to Capua	$23\frac{1}{2}$
Milan to Treviglio	18
Milan to Monza	12
Venice to Vicenza	40
Leghorn to Pisa	$12\frac{1}{2}$
Florence to Empoli, Ponte Dera, Pisa, and Sienna	
Pisa to Lucca and San Salvador	
Florence to Prato	$10\frac{1}{2}$

In the kingdom of Sardinia, railways exist as yet only in prospect. It is intended to carry two lines from Turin, one directed on Genoa by Alexandria, and the other on Milan by Vercelli and Novara. The political distractions, however, of the last two years have suspended these projects.

In Spain only one railway of eighteen miles in length, connecting Barcelona with Mataro, has been constructed. Others have been projected and even conceded to companies, the principal of which is that between Madrid and Valencia. The political distractions of the country, however, have suspended all such projects.

CHAPTER XXI.

COMPARISON OF RAILWAY TRANSPORT IN DIFFERENT COUNTRIES.

HAVING investigated in the preceding chapters the conditions of railway communication in the different countries of the globe where this species of locomotion has been adopted, we shall now bring into juxtaposition the results of our calculations, and show the comparative progress which different people have made in this important art, and distinguish what has been actually done from what is in progress and likely to be accomplished. I shall not notice here the projects which exist only in contemplation, many of which will probably never be executed.

In making such a comparison it is especially necessary to consider not merely the length of railway reported to be in operation or in progress, but the capital which has been invested in its construction; for two lines of communication receiving the common denomination of railways may differ from each other extremely in their utility and value. Such a line of communication as that which connects, or lately connected, Portsmouth (Virginia) with Weldon (North Carolina), and that which con-

CHAP. XXI.] RAILWAY TRANSPORT GENERALLY. 417

nects London and Birmingham, both receive the common name of railway, nearly in the same manner as a log cabin of a Missouri settler and the palace of Blenheim receive the common denomination of "dwelling-house." The most exact measure of the relative utility or efficiency of two lines of railway is their cost. It is not, however, to be forgotten that, even in adopting this test, regard must be had to the relative cost of land, material, and manual labor.

The extent of railway communication, and the expense of its construction, may be compared either with the population to whose commerce it is appropriated, or to the territorial extent of the country through which it is carried.

In the following table I have given, according to the most recently published reports, the population, the extent of territory, the extent of railway open and in progress, and the capital invested in the one, and to be invested in the other in those countries where railways have been established.

TABLE showing the Population, Extent of Territory, and Extent of Railway in Operation and in Progress, in the several Countries of the World where Railways have been constructed.

Countries.	Population.	Extent of Territory.	Population per Square Mile.	Extent of Railway open.	Extent of Railway in Progress.	Capital invested in Railways open.	Capital to be invested in Railways in Progress.
		Sq. Miles.		*Miles.*	*Miles.*	£.	£.
United Kingdom	27,019,558	121,050	223·0	5,000	4,500	200,000,000	100,000,000
Germanic States, including Denmark and Holland	45,753,640	268,548	170·0	4,542	800	56,775,000	10,000,000
United States	17,104,615	1,642,536	10·4	6,565	200	52,000,000	2,000,000
France	35,400,486	204,708	173·0	1,722	1,189	45,812,000	15,350,000
Belgium	4,335,319	11,256	382·0	457	200*	8,000,000	3,600,000
Russia	54,092,300	1,892,478	28·6	200	470*	3,000,000	7,500,000
Italy	47,696,338	312,774	152·0	170	470*	3,000,000	8,300,000
Totals & averages	231,312,256	4,453,350	52·0	18,656	7,829	368,567,000	146,750,000

* Statistiches Jahrbuch für 1847, von Karl August Muller: Leipsic, 1848.

The data supplied by this table will enable us to compare the length of railways and the railway capital of each country, with its population and its territory. This is done in the following table.

COMPARISON of the Extent of Railways in Operation, and the Amount of Railway Capital, with the Population and Territorial Extent of the Countries which possess them.

Countries.	Length of Railway per Million of Population.	Length of Railway per 1000 Square Miles of Territory.	Amount of Railway Capital per Head of Population.	Railway Capital per Square Mile of Territory.	Share of each Country in every 100 Miles of Railway open.	Share of each Country in every £100 of Capital expended.	Share of each Country in every 100 Miles of Railway in Progress.	Share of each Country in every £100 of Capital to be expended.
	Miles.		£.	£.				
United Kingdom	185·00	41·3	7·400	1,652·00	26·80	54·10	57·50	68·16
Germanic States, including Denmark and Holland	99·50	16·9	1·240	212·00	24·34	15·27	10·20	6·82
United States	384·00	4·0	3·050	31·70	35·17	14·10	2·55	1·37
France	48·30	8·3	1·310	227·00	9·12	12·75	15·20	10·40
Belgium	105·20	40·5	1·850	705·00	2·45	2·16	2·55	2·45
Russia	3·70	0·10	0·055	1·59	1·07	0·81	6·00	5·13
Italy	3·57	0·54	0·063	9·60	0·91	0·81	6·00	5·67
Totals and averages	80·5	4·18	1·600	83·00	100·0	100·00	100·00	100·00

Some of the results of this table are very remarkable.

In the proportion which the length of railway bears to the population, the several countries stand in the following order:

1. United States.
2. United Kingdom.
3. Belgium.
4. Germanic States.
5. France.
6. Russia.
7. Italy.

In the proportion which the length of railway bears to the extent of territory, these countries stand in the following order:

1. United Kingdom.
2. Belgium.
3. Germanic States.
4. France.
5. United States.
6. Italy.
7. Russia.

In the proportion of the railway capital to the population, the following is the order in which they stand:

1. United Kingdom.
2. United States.
3. Belgium.
4. France.
5. Germanic States.
6. Italy.
7. Russia.

In the proportion which the railway capital bears to the extent of territory, the following is the order:

1. United Kingdom.
2. Belgium.
3. France.
4. Germanic States.
5. United States.
6. Italy.
7. Russia.

Chap. XXI.] RAILWAY TRANSPORT GENERALLY. 419

The following is the order in which they stand with reference to the actual length of railway open:

1. United States.
2. United Kingdom.
3. Germanic States.
4. France.
5. Belgium.
6. Russia.
7. Italy.

And the following is their order in relation to the capital expended in railways:

1. United Kingdom.
2. Germanic States.
3. United States.
4. France.
5. Belgium.
6. Russia.
7. Italy.

While the total length of railway in operation in the United States exceeds the length open in the United Kingdom in the proportion of about 4 to 3, the capital invested in railway communication in England exceeds that invested in the United States in the ratio of about 4 to 1.

It will also be observed that, of the aggregate amount of capital invested in railways in all the countries of the globe, England possesses more than the half, or 54 per cent.; while the length of railways constructed with this capital is less than 27 per cent., or little more than one quarter of the aggregate length.

This will exhibit, in a striking manner, the superior efficiency of the mode of construction in England.

Of all the railways in progress in every part of the world, more than the half, or $57\frac{1}{2}$ per cent., are in England; and of the entire amount of capital to be invested in these, about 68 per cent. is to be invested in England.

It appears from the results of the preceding tables, that the entire amount of capital actually invested in railway communication in all the countries of the world is three hundred and sixty-eight millions and a half; and that with this, upward of eighteen thousand six hundred miles of railway have been constructed, and that the capital to be invested in seven thousand eight hundred miles of railway in progress will amount to nearly one hundred and forty-seven millions.

It would have been desirable to have exhibited a comparative view of the average movement of the traffic upon the railways in operation in different countries at a corresponding epoch. Unfortunately we have no documents to enable us to do this with all the precision which might be wished. I have, however, collected in the following table as many data as are supplied by authentic documents for nearly corresponding epochs. The

420 RAILWAY ECONOMY. [Chap. XXI.

railways on which the traffic reported has been carried do not in general include all the lines open in the respective countries; nevertheless, they will afford some approximation to a comparison of the extent of intercommunication by railway. In some cases, also, I have been obliged to obtain the numerical results by estimation. These I have indicated in the table:

COMPARATIVE VIEW of the Movement of the Traffic on a Portion of the Railways in operation in the United Kingdom, United States, Belgium, France, and Germany.

	United Kingdom.	United States.	Belgium.	France.	Germanic States.
Year reported	1847.	1847.	1847.	1848.	1846.
Length of railway	*miles.* 3036	*miles.* 1160	*miles.* 353	*miles.* 1090	*miles.* 2304
Average cost of construction and stock per mile	£. 40,000	£. 9200*	£. 18,000	£. 26,800	£. 11,000
Per mile of railway per day:	£.	£.	£.	£.	£.
Receipts	7·6	4·05	4·6	5·30	2·16
Expenses	3·0†	1·89	2·9	3·33	1·04
Profits	4·6†	2·16	1·7	1·97	1·12
Expenses per cent. of receipts	40·0†	46·8	63·0	63·0	48·3
Profits per cent. of capital	4·2†	8·6	3·44	2·68	3·72
	s. d.	s. d.	s. d.	s. d.	s. d.
Receipts per mile of trains	7 0	7 5	5 0	7 6	..
Receipts per passenger booked	2 0	2 3	1 6	2 1·75	1 6·5
Distance traveled per passenger	*miles.* 15·75	*miles.* 18·2	*miles.* 22·6	*miles.* 24·9	*miles.* 19·6
	d.	d.	d.	d.	d.
Receipts per passenger per mile	1·54	1·47	0·8	1·03	0·93
Number of passengers per train	50	54	75·3	61·4	..
Per cent of passengers booked:					
1st class	13·8	100	11	7·0	3·6
2d class	39·5	..	24·0	24·6	22·4
3d class	46·7	..	65	68·4	74·0
	s. d.	s. d.	s. d.		s. d.
Receipts per ton of goods booked	3 2·2	5 8·5	5 2	..	10 1
Distance carried per ton	*miles.* 22·5	*miles.* 38	*miles.* 43·8	..	*miles.* 46·4
	d.	d.	d.		d.
Receipts per ton per mile	1·67	1·8	1·34	..	2·6
Number of tons per train	..	54·5	33·2	..	..
Average speed of passenger-trains in miles per hour:					
Stoppages included	24·5	15·0‡	18·10	21·2	20·0
Stoppages excluded	32·0	..	24·90	27·0	24·2

* The average cost of the American railways taken collectively per mile is only £8129. Those to which the present report refers include among them the most expensive in the States.

† The estimated limit, see page 263. ‡ By estimation.

CHAPTER XXII.

THE RELATION OF RAILWAYS TO THE STATE.

RAILWAYS, when first brought into operation, were regarded as exceptional modes of conveyance, suitable to particular localities and particular conditions of commerce and intercourse. As their powers were gradually developed, it became evident that they were destined to play a more important part in the business of transport, and that they must ultimately become the general, if not the only means by which the internal movement and commerce of peoples, and even the intercommunication of people and people, would be conducted. Under this point of view, the question of their relation with the State became one of capital importance.

Hitherto the public highways in all countries have been regarded as within the special domain of government. By government and by the legislature they were controlled and regulated; and it was natural, therefore, to conclude that the same system of regulation and control must be extended to the new ways of communication, by which they seem destined to be superseded.

Between the common high roads, however, and the railways, an important difference was not slow to unfold itself. The superintendence and control of the State over the highways had been limited to their maintenance and superintendence, and to the regulation of their police. The carrying business conducted upon them was always in the hands of the public, and was regulated and controlled by the wholesome influence of competition.

The operation of the same principle of competition was contemplated in the infancy of railways, as is apparent from the provisions in the legislative enactments by which the companies have been incorporated. It was expected that the public should be admitted to exercise the business of carriers upon them, subject to certain specified regulations and by-laws.

It soon became apparent, however, that this new means of transport was attended with qualities which must exclude every indiscriminate exercise of the carrying business. A railway, like a vast machine, the wheels of which are all connected with each other, and whose movement requires a certain harmony, can not be worked by a number of independent agents. Such a system would speedily be attended with self-destruction. The organization of a railway requires unity of direction and harmony of movement, which can only be attained by the combination of the entire carrying business with the general administration of the road. Hence it followed, as a necessary consequence, as has been already explained, that the companies originally established for the construction of a road only, became, in spite of themselves, the exclusive carriers upon it; and hence arose inevitably as many local monopolies of transport as there were separate and independent companies.

This evil was speedily aggravated by amalgamation. The very same principles and conditions which rendered it indispensable that each company should have the sole direction and management of the entire movement of transport upon its own line, rendered it scarcely less expedient that systems of lines running into each other should either voluntarily establish a code of regulations to secure their mutual harmony, or that they should coalesce so as to form fewer companies of greater magnitude. Both of these expedients have been resorted to. Lesser, placed near greater companies, have coalesced with them. A great number of small monopolies have, by the operation of the affinities of commercial interest, been drawn together, and have become a small number of great monopolies; and so indispensable has a certain unity of management and harmony of movement proved to be to the efficiency of the entire system, that, where amalgamation has not been effected, the device of the Clearing-house has been invented to surmount, as far as is practicable, those difficulties which might arise from the absence of unity of direction and management of intercommunicating lines.

Such were the circumstances out of which sprung those colossal monopolies among which the territory of the United Kingdom is parceled out, and by which the entire internal commerce, and correspondence, and personal intercourse of its people are conducted.

A great variety of relations have arisen out of a like state of things in other countries, according to the local circumstances attending the form of government, and the social and commercial condition of the people.

In some the State has taken upon itself the entire charge of the construction and working of the railways. This is the case, for example, in Belgium and Hanover, in some of the Northern Duchies, in the Grand Duchy of Baden, in Würtemburg, Bavaria, and Austria. It is true that a few isolated lines in these several states had been conceded to companies before the great question of the relation between the State and the railways had been raised; but these cases, besides being exceptional, have gradually been diminished in number by the governments respectively redeeming the property in the roads.

In other countries, a mixed system has been pursued. Some railways have been constructed and furnished by the State, but farmed by companies on terminable and frequently short leases, the State maintaining a certain control regulated by the clauses of the leases. In some cases, the railways have been constructed and stocked by the companies themselves, who hold the property under a lease of more or less extended duration; but still the State is represented in the administration of the railway by the presence of an agent, who is invested with almost unlimited control over the working of the lines. In France, this agent was established under the name of a Royal Commissioner, and one such functionary was nominated to form part of the administration of each railway company. Besides this, the government appoints the police of the road, all these functionaries, however, of every grade, being paid by the company. On the expiration of the leases, the State is usually bound to reimburse to the company the estimated value of the movable stock attached to the establishment; and the company, on the other hand, is bound to sustain this movable stock in a satisfactory and efficient state pending the lease.

In cases where the State has adopted the policy of leaving the construction and management of the railways to private companies, it has nevertheless intervened, by means of subvention or other encouragement, to stimulate private enterprise in those cases in which the lines run through localities where the commerce is deemed insufficient to produce the average profit on the capital invested. In different countries this object is accomplished by different expedients.

In some, a subvention in money is directly given; in others, the State takes a certain proportion of the shares, supplying the corresponding amount of capital on favorable terms; in others, the State guarantees a minimum amount of interest on the capital to be invested; in others, the companies are favored by the free importation of stock and materials, by the gratuitous use of the land, and by exemption from taxation.

The authority of the State is, in almost all cases, asserted, and in many periodically exercised. Thus a power of revising the tariff at stated intervals, such as every three or five years, is often reserved. This is the case in some of the railway enterprises in the United States.

The case of the English railway companies is, in several respects, peculiar. The spirit of the laws and traditions renders the State averse from interference in commercial enterprises, and somewhat reserved even in the exercise of that control over them, which would seem to be indispensable to the general interests.

Powers of an unusually extensive and durable character were therefore readily granted to all railway companies in this country, and monopoly after monopoly grew up, fostered by the legislature, and favored by the public. Monopoly, however, was not slow to develop some of its customary evils, and complaints and remonstrances followed. Abuses were signalized, and a reaction in public opinion was manifested. Railway directors, who had been previously the objects of unbounded laudation, now became the subjects of distrust and censure, and a general demand of some efficient system of control was put forth.

This demand was opposed by railway directors and parties under their influence, who went so far as to deny the right of parliament to interfere with their concerns, assimilating their establishments to those of banks, insurance offices, dock companies, and other industrial associations. These parties indignantly rejected all control, and even complained of the system of publishing periodical reports, partial and imperfect as it has been, which the law and public opinion has exacted from them, as a grievance. They declared that any interference with the affairs of railway companies, or any compulsory publication of their proceedings, or any report of the state of their financial concerns, is a violation of the rights of capital as gross and unjustifiable as would be the same measures if adopted in reference to the mercantile transactions of Rothschild's, Baring's, or any other private establishment. They admit that government may so far interfere as to provide for the safety and convenience of the public in traveling. But beyond this, they denounce all legislative or State intervention in their affairs. They complain that the temper evinced by parliament and the press is such as ought to be directed only against the greatest enemies of social progress, instead of the promoters, as they justly enough claim to be, of one of the most signal instruments for the advancement of civilization that modern times have witnessed. Such a temper, they contend, must produce a corresponding feeling on the part of railway directors; and it is declared that, if such a system of annoyance and improper interference be continued, it must result either in raising a spirit of opposition on the part of railway interests, which, considering the magnitude of the property at stake, can not be lightly regarded, or inducing an apathy and indifference in the administration of railways; in either case being the cause of great injury and inconvenience to the public.

To all this it is answered, that bodies which possess the almost exclusive control of the intercourse of the country, including the conveyance of persons and goods, the service of the post-office, and the movement of the troops, have none of the qualities, and ought to have none of the privileges, attaching to private commercial establishments; that, therefore, it would be a great error to regard the British railways as speculations important to none but the shareholders; that they, on the contrary, involve interests public, political, and social, of the greatest magnitude; that they have not been created, as the advocates of their complete independence pretend, by the unaided efforts of individuals; that they owe their origin and existence to the will of the legislature, expressed in their various acts of incorporation, and that to the legislature they must be held, in a peculiar degree, responsible; that they have been intrusted with privileges and powers almost without precedent; and that, in fine, it is incumbent on parliament to see that these powers are properly exercised, and to amend the laws which regulate them in such a manner as may from time to time be deemed expedient.

It is further contended, that the duty of legislative interference is rendered more imperative by the enormous amount of money which railway companies have raised under parliamentary authority. Not only has a capital been raised amounting to a quarter of the national debt, which amount will be augmented by at least 50 per cent. within a short period, but loans have been obtained by the companies to vast amounts, under the direct sanction, and subject to the conditions, of special acts of parliament. The debentures representing these loans, as well as the railway shares, are transferable from hand to hand with as much facility as the unfunded debt, with which they enter into direct competition.

Of late years, moreover, the interests involved in railway property have assumed an importance which has introduced it into marriage settlements, wills, and other family arrangements, almost as generally as the public securities. It would therefore, it is contended, be preposterous to maintain that property of such an amount and such character should be left to the uncontrolled management of bodies so fleeting and so little responsible as the boards of railway directors.

It is further maintained by the advocates of government control, that shareholders are a fleeting and mutable body, liberated from many of the responsibilities and obligations which attach to property of a more permanent character. A share-market has been created as well in the chief commercial towns as in the capital, where transactions to an enormous amount take place. Not only are permanent investments made in railway securities which have become matters of settlement, bequest, and inheritance, but large speculations are daily made, with a view to profit, by traffic in a description of property peculiarly liable to sudden and extraordinary fluctuations, fluctuations so extreme that the capital of a single railway has been known to fall in value within the brief period of two months to the amount of three millions sterling. These violent and sudden variations in the value of the securities of one railway produce sympathetic effects in all the others, and always arise from the want of confidence entertained by the public in the representations made by the directors of railway companies of their financial condition.*

Since, however, the necessity of establishing an independent body, invested with definite powers to examine and check the railway accounts, is admitted by all persons beyond the immediate circle of railway directors, and those in their employment and under their influence, and even by some among those directors themselves, it will not be necessary to enter further into this discussion. It may be assumed that the establishment of such a controlling body is demanded by public opinion; the only points to be considered being the authority from which its nomination must emanate, and the nature and extent of its powers.

The appointment of such a body can only be made by the directors, the proprietors of railways, not being directors, or the State.

That railway directors should nominate the body which is to control themselves, would be an outrage on common sense, which public opinion indignantly rejects.

The appointment of an efficient and independent board of

* Third Report of Select Committee of House of Lords, June, 1849.

control by railway proprietors, exercising its powers over railway directors, would be attended with many practical difficulties. The railway proprietors are a very numerous body, scattered over the country, and even over the world, varying extremely in age, sex, and condition. It is difficult to imagine how such a body could ever be brought into any real co-operation otherwise than by the agency and influence, direct or indirect, of the directors themselves. The body of proprietors have already nominated the directors, and must be presumed to have selected the individuals for that office whom they regarded as best entitled to their confidence. To call on the same proprietors to elect other individuals to be placed in a sort of antagonism to the former, and invested with powers to check and control them, would be to require them to place over those individuals, in whom they have manifested the greatest confidence, others, in whom they must necessarily have less.

The impracticability of attaining such an object is in some degree illustrated by the effect of the system of audit hitherto pursued. It is well known that on the presentation of each half year's report, auditors are appointed by the meeting of shareholders, to examine and to check the balance-sheet. The witnesses produced before the House of Lords, consisting of public accountants, eminent railway directors, and others, distinguished by special knowledge on such subjects, were unanimous in declaring this system of audit to be destitute of all efficiency.

Mr. Swift (says the report), a witness whose confidential connection with the Northwestern Railway Company gives great weight to his testimony, declared such an audit to be "moonshine against dishonest directors." Mr. King, who had been secretary to two companies, said, the audit was "a complete farce," to which he could not attach the slightest value or importance. Sir John Easthope declared that he could never consent to become a director again unless an effective audit were established, and that if such audit be not entirely independent of the directors, it would be better to have no audit at all. Mr. King said that a shareholder ought not to be an auditor, "inasmuch as it would place him in an invidious position. He would, in some way or other, be connected with the directors, and would probably be chosen, or suggested, or recommended, by them to the shareholders."

A board of railway control properly constituted would represent, not the interest of the shareholders only, but that of the public; and among the abuses which it would become its duty to check, would be more especially those which affect that portion of the public who are not shareholders. The misapplication of capital and financial malversations, which have been already sometimes practiced by directors, having the effect of producing factitious changes in the marketable value of railway securities, of which changes the directors themselves, who thus brought them about, have largely availed themselves, are examples of this. So far, then, as such a board of control would represent the interests of the public in general, as contradistinguished from those of railway proprietors in particular, it ought legitimately to derive its appointments and authority from the State, which represents the public.

But, whatever may be the origin of such a controlling or auditing body, it is agreed on all hands that it must be perfectly independent of the directors in the exercise of its functions. If such independence can be shown to be compatible with any system of election by shareholders, no legitimate objection can perhaps be brought against it; and it would, in such case, be exempted from those inconveniences which are supposed to attend such a body when deriving its nomination and authority from the government.

Whatever may be the nature of the functions and limits of the powers to be conferred upon the body proposed to be created for the control or audit of railway management, its objects may be briefly and clearly stated.

They must be to supply railway shareholders, and the public in general (any of whom may at any moment become railway shareholders), with the means of obtaining an assurance of the honesty and of estimating the ability of the railway management. This object will be attained partly by the confidence which the public may entertain in the persons appointed to compose such a board, and partly by the publicity which may be given to the accounts and proceedings of the railway managers.

One of the objects most strongly insisted upon in the measure proposed in the House of Lords for an independent system of railway audit in the session of 1849, was to secure greater uniformity and more detailed explanation in the system of financial accounts issued by the directors to the shareholders. These accounts naturally arrange themselves under the two heads of capital and revenue.

It was proposed that the capital account should be twofold, or, to state it more correctly, a single account consisting of triple columns.

The first column would consist of a clear and detailed statement of the amounts of capital which the company had been authorized to raise, stating the purposes to which these amounts respectively had been directed by the legislature to be applied.

The second column would contain a statement of the extent to which the company had exercised these powers. It would state the amounts respectively which had been raised under each authorization, assigning them to their respective heads, and showing the purposes for which they were destined.

The difference between the totals of these two columns would show the amount of the unexhausted power with which the company was still invested.

The third column would contain a clear and detailed statement of the capital which had been actually expended, stating the objects to which it had been appropriated, and showing clearly that these objects were those for which parliament had authorized the capital to be raised.

The difference between the totals of the second and third columns would show the portion of the capital raised which had been still unexpended.

One of the abuses against which legislative interference had been invoked, was the misappropriation of capital by railway directors. This misappropriation was twofold. In some cases the directors would apply the capital which the company had been authorized to raise for one purpose to another, still, however, being legitimately capital. Thus, capital authorized to be raised for the construction of a particular branch of the trunk line, would be applied to the purchase of steamboats, or to the improvement or construction of docks.

Such proceedings involved a double violation of the spirit of the law. Not only was capital applied to a purpose not authorized by parliament, but works, the construction of which was sanctioned by parliament, and ordered to be executed within a given limit of time, were left either incomplete or not commenced.

But the most frequent and scandalous misapplication of capital, whether considered in itself or its consequences, had been the appropriation of capital to the purposes of revenue, and more especially to the payment of dividends.

Railway directors are usually large holders of shares, frequently obtained by allotment, and at a much lower rate than the current market price.

Thus situated, they have a direct interest to raise the market, and to avail themselves of such elevation to dispose of shares.

This object is accomplished by the misappropriation of capital for the purpose of swelling the dividends beyond the amount which they would have reached if paid legitimately out of profits.

When a rise has been produced by these means, and the directors avail themselves of it, they dispose of their allotted shares at a large profit. This spurious price is of course only temporary, and the market soon declines. The deluded public loses precisely to the extent to which the directors and those in their confidence gain. Thus the fortunes of the widow and orphan, and the accumulations of industry and thrift, are fraudulently transferred to swell the colossal fortunes of individual directors, who by such means suddenly rise from stations comparatively obscure to almost fabulous wealth.

It may be most truly replied, that proceedings such as these are rare, that directors in general are persons altogether incapable of such malpractices, and that it would be unjust to stigmatize a large, respectable, and intelligent body of men, to the unwearied exertions and talents of many of whom the world is indebted for the successful issue of the most signal improvement of modern times, because of the misconduct of some individuals among them. To this it is answered, that unreserved and complete publicity of all the details of the management of the affairs of each company can alone do justice to the respectable and independent majority of directors. Such a publicity will enable every one who possesses the necessary information to judge not only of the honesty but of the ability of the management, and without such publicity there can be no test by which the public at large can know the integrity or skill with which any railway establishment is conducted.

An intelligent and experienced witness, long connected with railway affairs, declared, before the Committee of the House of Lords, that practices of misapplying capital, such as had prevailed in certain cases, would lead at some period to "total ruin, and in the mean while to great confusion, and an entire misapprehension of the value of each undertaking."

Another said, that there was "no safety for bondholders or shareholders, unless the separation of capital from revenue was observed, and that any deviation from it must falsify the accounts and deprive the public of the means of measuring the value of such undertakings."

An experienced accountant stated, that under the present

system "there is no security that capital and income snall be kept distinct, and that the practical consequence is, that the purchaser who buys shares does so in ignorance of the true state of the company's affairs, and is led to give a higher price than the thing is worth, under the belief that the dividends declared come *bonâ fide* out of profits. Any balance under such a system, may be struck which may suit the purpose of the directors; any dividend may be declared, and the public may be deceived to any extent desired."

"If capital," says the Report of the Lords' Committee, "be unduly brought to increase income, or ordinary expenditure be unduly carried to the account of capital, the apparent balances may be varied at pleasure, a fallacious and fraudulent value may for a time be given to shares, greatly profitable to all proprietors desirous of selling, but leading to results fatal to the interests of the more important class who invest permanently; for the sake of a deceptive present gain the value of the reversion will be sacrificed. Cases may easily be contemplated, and undoubtedly have occurred, in which the future profitable working of the line may thus be endangered, and the public interests connected with the maintenance of railways be placed in jeopardy, if not sacrificed."*

To guard against this and similar abuses, shareholders have always had a certain power at reasonable times to examine the books of the company, but this power has proved, as might easily have been foreseen, illusory. It is not by individual shareholders going to a railway office, and demanding journals and ledgers, and running over their pages, that any real estimate of the state of the affairs of the company can be ascertained. This is a proceeding which individual shareholders will never be induced to undertake, nor, if they did, would any satisfactory result ensue. Practiced accountants alone can form a satisfactory estimate of the financial condition of the company, and even they could only accomplish this by an elaborate examination of the books; such an examination as individual shareholders could never effect by the means provided in the acts of incorporation.

But whatever powers may be conferred upon the controlling or auditing body, and from whatever source it may derive its appointment and authority, its influence will be unavailing unless the most ample and unreserved publicity be given to the details of the railway management, and with such publicity the

* Third Report of the Lords' Committee, June, 1849.

task of the auditors or controllers will be rendered comparatively easy. Their duties will in such case be reduced in effect to mere verification of the disbursements by the vouchers; for, by such means, the public at large would be converted into one great and unquestionable Board of Audit. Railway affairs would, in a word, be placed under the immediate operation of public opinion. Railway directors, instead of demanding, as they now do, half-yearly votes of confidence from their blindfolded constituents, would receive the intelligent approbation of a well-informed public.

In all the discussions which have hitherto taken place on this question of railway control, a stress much too exclusive has been placed on the fidelity and accuracy of the report of the financial condition of the company, as if the honesty and integrity of the management were all that could be required to satisfy the railway proprietors and the public. The degree of ability and skill with which the affairs of the railway may have been conducted, seems to be wholly left out of view. This is a grave error. Honesty is happily a much more ordinary quality than ability, and there is much stronger ground for distrusting the skill shown in the management of the enterprise of a railway than the integrity of those to whom the management is confided.

It is not, therefore. sufficient, for the satisfaction of public opinion, to publish an authenticated report of the financial condition of each railway company.

Such details of its management must also be given as may enable all persons competently informed to form an estimate of the skill and ability with which its affairs have been conducted. They must be in a condition to judge whether the capital has been duly utilized; but, to place them in this condition, a much more ample report of the business of the company must be published than any which has hitherto been issued by railway companies in England, or even on the Continent, where the periodical reports are more detailed. The Belgian government alone puts forth a complete and satisfactory annual report of its management. We do not maintain that the exposition annually supplied to the public by the Belgian government of the administration of the State railways may not be susceptible of improvement, or that it may not contain some needless detail. It can not, however, be denied that it demonstrates the possibility of placing the affairs of railway management under the operation of public opinion.

The report should be annual, and not half-yearly, as is the practice in England; because the traffic runs through its periodical phases, and completes them with the revolution of the seasons. Half-yearly reports, therefore, supply imperfect inferences; and it is only by comparing two such reports successively issued that correct average results can be obtained.

While I would therefore propose greater amplitude in detail of the railway reports, I would suggest that they should be published annually and not half-yearly, and as soon after the commencement of each year as might be practicable, giving the details of the management and working of the railway for the preceding year.

Such a report might consist of the following heads:

SECTION I.
CONSTRUCTION AND STOCK.

Sums which the company has been empowered to raise.—Sums actually raised under such powers.—Sums expended, specifying in detail the objects to which they have been appropriated, and the sources from which they have been derived.

SECTION II.
EXPENSES.

This section should contain a detailed statement of the current expenses of the management and working of the railways, each class of disbursement being assigned to its proper head—such as direction and management, way and works, locomotive power, carrying expenses, &c.

SECTION III.
RECEIPTS.

This section should contain a detailed statement of the revenue of the company, assigning distinctly the amount of revenue proceeding from each object of traffic, such as passengers, distinguished by classes, baggage, parcels, horses, carriages, mails, and all objects carried by passenger trains; goods and live stock, classed according to their tariff.

The receipts should also be stated according to the parts of the line from which they have proceeded; thus the amount received for each class of traffic at each station should be given.

The receipts should also be classified according to the period of the year at which they have been realized, their amounts being separately stated for each successive month.

In cases where a graduated tariff has been established, diminishing as the distance to which the objects of transport are carried is increased, the receipts should also be classified according to the distances to which the objects of transport producing them have been severally carried, so as to show the amounts of revenue which have proceeded from long traffic and short traffic.

Such a statement is supplied in the reports of the Belgian railways.

SECTION IV.

THE MOVEMENT OF THE TRAFFIC.

This section should contain a statement of the quantity and mileage of the several classes of traffic. Thus the number of passengers of each class booked and the total mileage of each class should be given. In like manner, the quantity and mileage of each object of transport conveyed by passenger trains, such as baggage, parcels, mails, horses, and carriages, should be stated. The comparison of the quantity of these with their mileage would give the average distance over which each passenger and other object of traffic was carried.

A like statement should be given for the various classes of goods traffic, showing in each case the quantity booked and its mileage.

The quantity booked at each section of the line should be distinctly given, to show the variation of the traffic on different parts of the railway; and the quantity in each month, to show the variation of the traffic according to the seasons.

SECTION V.

THE MOVEMENT OF THE LOCOMOTIVE STOCK.

This section should contain a statement of the quantity of the locomotive stock, enumerating the engines with the circumstances of their origin, construction, age, former services, and their current mileage. The distances run by each engine during the year should be stated, as well as the total distance it has run since first put upon the road. The consumption of fuel should be given, distinguishing that which is consumed in lighting and getting up steam, and standing, and in profitable work. The consumption of oil and other materials, and the cost of repairs, should also be given. All these details are supplied annually in the reports of the Belgian railways.

SECTION VI.

THE MOVEMENT OF THE CARRYING STOCK.

This section should contain a statement of the entire stock of vehicles of transport used during the year, distinguishing them according to classes, and giving their mileages respectively.

Also a statement of the consumption of materials, cost of repairs, &c.

SECTION VII.

MOVEMENT OF TRAFFIC COMPARED WITH MOVEMENT OF LOCOMOTIVE AND CARRYING STOCK.

By comparing the movement of the different classes of traffic with the movement of the various classes of vehicles of transport to which they are respectively appropriated, we can obtain the average load carried by each vehicle, and by comparing them with the movement of the locomotive stock, we can obtain the average load drawn by each engine. Data are thus obtained by which numerous economical problems of the highest importance can be solved. It is by these means that we can ascertain the extent to which the moving stock of the railway has been utilized.

SECTION VII.
RECEIPTS AND EXPENSES COMPARED WITH THE MOVEMENT OF THE TRAFFIC AND ROLLING STOCK.

By this comparison may be ascertained the proportion of the expenses chargeable to each class, and even to each individual object of traffic. By comparing such expenses with the receipts arising from each object of traffic, the profit or loss arising from each class of traffic can be ascertained.

By this means a numerous class of important problems can be solved which are intimately connected with the questions of the tariff, and by which alone the future tariff can be advantageously regulated.

SECTION IX.
THE MOVEMENT OF THE TRAFFIC AND ROLLING STOCK COMPARED WITH THE EXTENT OF THE RAILWAY.

The comparison made in this section would show the extent to which the railway itself has been utilized. It would indicate the proportion in which the traffic has been distributed over it, showing the quantity of profitable load as well as of dead weight which has been transported between station and station on every part of the line. This would also indicate the extent to which the local supply of traffic may have been cultivated, and would direct the attention of managers and the public to the still unsatisfied exigencies of the districts through which the railways may be carried.

It must not be supposed that a report containing details such as I have enumerated here, is either difficult or impracticable.

Many of them are regularly supplied in the annual reports of most of the continental railway companies, and all of them, and many others still more minute, are contained in the annual railway report of the Belgian government. It is true, that the existing arrangements of the English railways do not afford the means of recording some of these statistical facts, but nothing would be more easy than to organize in this country, as elsewhere, the means of recording them.

In order to show the extent to which the movable stock of the railway has been utilized, it is essential to supply the means of comparing the movement of the rolling stock with the movement of the traffic. It is by such a comparison alone that the average amount of loads carried by the different vehicles of transport can be accurately ascertained. This will be easily comprehended from the preceding part of this volume.

If we know the distance which any class of vehicles of transport have traveled within the year, and also know the distance over which each class of objects of transport to which such vehicles are appropriated have been carried, the comparison will immediately supply the means of ascertaining the average load carried by each vehicle, and this average load is the only exponent of the extent to which each class of vehicle has been utilized.

To accomplish this it would be necessary to keep separate mileage accounts of the traffic and of the rolling stock. In the case of the traffic, its mileage can be immediately ascertained from the record of the receipts, inasmuch as each sum received represents the transport of a given object to a given distance.

In the case of the vehicles of transport, the manner in which the mileage has been hitherto kept on continental lines is not as simple and satisfactory as could be desired. The places of departure and arrival of each vehicle are registered, and reports from the different stations are received, the comparison of which supplies the means of computing the mileage.

Nothing, however, would be more easy than to attach to each vehicle of transport a *counter*, which would become a self-acting register of the aggregate space over which each vehicle has run. These counters, when required in large numbers, could be constructed at a small expense. They are not liable to derangement, and would relieve the railway administration from the clumsy and expensive method of observing and registering the movement of the stock, and, in fine, would accomplish the object with greater certainty and accuracy. The counters, as commonly constructed, run up to a million of revolutions of the wheels, which, with a wheel ten feet in circumference, would, in round numbers, extend to about two thousand miles.

Similar instruments might be attached to the engines, by which a register of their mileage would be kept. In this manner an account recorded of the movement of the entire rolling stock would be obtained at a nominal expense, nothing more being necessary than to provide agents who would attend to and record the indications of the counters.

The expenses, besides being recorded under the usual heads of direction, way and works, locomotive power, carrying expenses, &c., should also be distributed according to some principles such as those which have been explained in Chap. XII.,

CHAP. XXII.] RAILWAYS AND THE STATE. 437

so as to enable the managers of the road to ascertain the cost at which each object of traffic has been transported. It is by a comparison of this cost with the tariff, that the profit arising from each object of traffic is ascertained. Data would thus be also obtained, by which the managers could ascertain what increased expense would be produced by any given increase of the distance to which each object of traffic is transported, and hence would arise the data necessary for the formation of a graduated tariff, diminishing in its rate per mile according as the distances to which the objects of traffic respectively are transported are increased.

These, and a multitude of other practical problems, involving the most important economical principles in railway management will at once suggest themselves as arising out of the circumstances here adverted to, and the solution of which would be altogether impossible unless data, such as those here described, could be obtained.

No such data can be obtained, however, from the present system of railway accounts, nor is it possible for directors and managers themselves to obtain the means of solving such economical problems.

Connected with each railway administration, a statistical bureau should be established for organizing and recording these classes of data.* Such bureaus are already established in connection with several of the best conducted continental railways, and although their operations have not been in all cases conducted so efficiently as could be desired, they are, nevertheless, attended with the best effects.

It can not escape observation that, by the publication of such ample and detailed reports as I have here proposed, the functions of the board of audit, about which so much discussion has taken place, would be stripped of much of their invidious character, and less difference of opinion would prevail as to the source from which they might derive their nomination and authority.

---

* The business of such a bureau, and indeed that of other departments in the railway administration, would be materially facilitated and expedited by the adoption of "FULLER's *Calculating Scale*," which is an improvement on the sliding rule, the uses and application of which it has enlarged so as to become almost a new instrument. In all statistical inquiries, where rates percentages and arithmetical reductions are necessary, it supplies the place of a table of logarithms, and gives the results with much greater expedition, and with sufficient accuracy for all practical purposes.

It is sometimes contended that railways, being commercial companies, whose concerns affect only their respective shareholders, publicity should not be exacted from them, and that the shareholders alone have a right to be informed of the affairs of their administration and management; but to this it may be answered, that nothing short of publicity can bring such information to the knowledge of bodies so large and fluctuating as those of railway shareholders. By what means, short of general publicity for example, could a body like the proprietors of the Northwestern Railway, acquire a clear, full, and satisfactory knowledge of the affairs of that vast enterprise?

Besides, it may be answered, the shares being matters of daily bargain and sale in the public market, every individual who may become a purchaser has a claim to a full knowledge of the state of the affairs of the company into which he is about to enter.

In fine, considering the questions which have been agitated for some months respecting the great railway enterprises of the country, in all their bearings and relations, no expedient appears so likely to remedy the evils which have formed the subject of universal complaint and remonstrance, to revive public confidence, and to restore railway property to its just value in the public market, as a system of publicity such as is here recommended.

INDEX.

ACCIDENTS, 265, 335; chances of, 265; causes of, 273; rules to prevent, 277; fog signals, 278; analysis of cases produced by imprudence, 282; precautions against, 283; plain rules to avoid, 284.
American electric telegraph, 302.

Baggage, 128.
Baggage vans, 91.
Belgian railways, 349; register of, 72; locomotive stock, 73; mileage of engines, 75; carrying stock, 92; mileage of, 94; goods wagons, 131; number of passengers carried by each train, 171; transport of horses and carriages, 174; expenses of locomotive power, 215; analysis and expenses of carrying stock, 220; proportional expenses of station for goods, 228; estimated station expenses, 330; analysis of general expenses, 230; receipts, expenses, and profits, 247; encouragement to complete loads, 261; length, 349; description, 350; constructed by state, 351; Belgian commerce, 351; character of the country, 352; curves, 353; gradients, 353; cost of construction, 353; cost per mile, 354; rolling stock, 354; locomotive power, passenger traffic, 357; goods traffic, 357; traffic compared with extent of railway, 357; local variations of traffic, variations of traffic with seasons, 360; percentage of number, mileage, and receipts of passengers, 361; traffic according to distance, 361; proportions of revenue contributed by traffic 363; proportion of expenses chargeable to usual heads, 363; comparison of receipts, expenses, and profits, with length of line, 364; speed, 365; passenger traffic, 365; constructed by companies, 365; estimated cost of, 367.
Brighton and South Coast railway, coke, 82; number of passengers per engine, 172; distance traveled per passenger, 172; number of passenger coaches in each train, 173; departures, 175; expense of locomotive power, 218; estimated general working expenses, 233. (See British railways.)
British railways, mileage of passenger coaches, 98, 152; passenger traffic, 154; 158, 163; length of, 166; speed, 177; goods mileage, 185; estimated working expenses of, 233; receipts on, 235; proportion per cent. of receipts from each class of passengers, 237; from traffic in general, 241; proportion of receipts to length, traffic, and capital, 243; daily receipts per mile, 243; proportion of receipts to increase of railways, 244; proportion of receipts to capital, 264; accidents on, 267. (See Great Western, Northwestern, Southeastern, Southwestern, and Brighton Railways, Receipts, Expenses, Profits, Locomotive, Carrying stock, Capital.)

Capital of railways in United Kingdom, 68; and revenue, 116; account, 116; of all the railways in the world. (See Belgian, French, German and United States Railways.)
Carriage, service of, 52; trucks, 91, 192; dépôt, 120; station, 126; sheds, 138.
Carriages 136, 192; weight of augmented, 58; passenger, 90; passenger of Northwestern, 97; cost of, 112; mixed, 261; on railways of the United States, 387.
Carrying stock, 89; weight of augmented, 58; Belgian, 92; North of France, 92; Northwestern, 92, 97, 110; register of, 93; mileage, 94, 95, 96, 98; number necessary to stock railway, 98, 170; railway manufactories of, 108; of English railways, 112; question as to deterioration, 114; average load, 168; number, 170; expenses, 220, 230; analysis of expenses of, in Belgium, 220, 221; mixed carriages, 261.
Cattle wagons, 92.
Chairs, 208; expenses of repair, 207.
Clearing house, 140; bankers', 141; companies associated in, 143; goods traffic and live stock, 146; passenger traffic, 147; parcels, 148; carrying stock, 149; statistics, 151; capable of extension, 151; passengers recorded in,156.
Coal, consumed in making coke on British railways, 84.
Coke, 80; fabrication of, 80; quantity produced from coal, 81; consumption of on Great Western, 81; on Northwestern and Brighton and South Coast, 82; on British railways, 89.
Counter, to register mileage, 436.
Cost of railway traveling compared with old mode, 164.
Crusades, influence on art of transport, 45.

Dead weight drawn by each engine, 105.
Derailment, 279.

440 INDEX.

Engine, 127, 132; weight of augmented, 58; passenger, 71; goods, 71; to ascertain mileage, 73; can not be used indefinitely, 74; to determine average number of miles run by, after lighting, 75; number lighted on Belgian railways, 75; on Orleans railway, 75; reserve, 76; assistant on bank, 76; number of times lighted on Belgian railways, 82; require three days a week for cleaning, 83; useful service of, on Belgian lines, 83; total annual and daily mileage on foreign railways, 83; useful service of, on Northwestern, 83; fixed, 127; station, 134; stable, 135; number of passengers drawn by, 172; action of at high speeds, 178; relation between mileage of and receipts, 262. (See Locomotive.)

Engine drivers, distance driven by, on Northwestern, 85.

Expenses, 191; objects of analysis of, 194; relation of to services, 198; of direction and management, 201; way and works, 204; causes of repair of iron work of road, 207; locomotive power, 211; of locomotive power, how distributed among carrying stock, 214; carrying, 220; recapitulation of various heads of, 225; stations, 226; chargeable independently of distance, 226; proposal of M. Teisserenc to fix common measure for expenses of stations, 258; estimated, of stations on Belgian railways, 230; measures for increased economy of, 233; gross expenses classified, 250; decreased by increasing distance of transport, 256; means of diminishing, 262; on Belgian railways, 353. (See British, Belgian, United States, and German railways.)

Fog signals, 278.

Foreign railways, carrying stock, 96; mileage, 83, 96.

French revolution, its influence on internal commerce, 46; roads, 46; canal navigation, 311.

French railways, 367; introduced by M. E. Pereire, 367; St. Germains line, 368; commission appointed by Chambers, 368; Paris and Orleans and Paris and Rouen lines, 369; law of 11th June, 1842, 369; description of, 369; length of, completed, in progress, and projected, 374; cost of construction, 376; estimated cost of all the, 377; companies tenants of State, 377; mode of receiving tenders for leases, 377; locomotive and carrying stock, 378; locomotive duty and consumption of fuel, 378; average daily movement of locomotive stock of North of France, 379; of carrying stock, 379; relation between movement of rolling stock and extent of railway, 380; passenger traffic, 380; receipts, 380; proportion of business and receipts supplied by several classes of passengers, 382; daily movement and daily receipts of passenger traffic, 383; share of every £100 by each class of traffic, 384; movement of goods traffic, and receipts from it, 384; receipts, expenses, and profits, 385; proportion of receipts, expenses, and profits per mile, of trains and of lines, and per cent. of capital, 385; speed 386.

Fuel, consumed in working railways, 77; economy of on Belgian lines, 78; register of on Belgian lines, 79; sources for economizing, 80, 142.

German railways, 387; description of, 387; summary of length completed, in progress, and projected, 392; detail of lines, 392; constructed by companies and government, 395; on similar principles to American, 396; gradients and curves, 397; cost of construction, 401; cost per mile, 403; causes of low rate of cost, 402; self acting planes, 398; rails, 400; prices of land and labor, 402; proportion of cost shared between land, road, stations, and stock, 403; mode of working traffic, 403; passengers, 404; mixed trains, 404; movement of trains, 404; movement of traffic 413; distance traveled and receipts, 407; proportion of passengers, 410; fares, 410; tariffs, 410; local variations of traffic, 411; gross receipts per mile and per cent. of capital, 412; proportion of receipts from passengers and goods, 411; working expenses, 411; receipts, expenses and profits, compared with length of railway, proportion per ct. of expenses to receipts and of receipts and profits to capital, 412; speed, 413; percentage of miles in the several states in reference to territorial surface, 417.

Goods engines, 71, 132; wagons, 92, 131; carrying stock, mileage of, 98, 187; number of carrying stock on Northwestern, 99; movement of on Northwestern, 99; station, 120, 131; accounts, 146; mileage, 183, 187.

Goods traffic, 182; clearing house, 145; mileage, 184, 190; distance per ton, 184; 213; augmentation, 187; compared with development of railways, 188. (See British, Belgian, German, and United States railways.)

Goods wagons, average load, 99.
Grease, (yellow), 137.
Grease-box, 137.

Great Western: coke, 81; number of passengers drawn by each engine, 172; distance traveled by each passenger, 172; departures, 175; expenses of locomotive power, 219; estimated general working expenses, 233. (See British railways.)

Horses, 126, 174.
Horse-boxes, 51, 126, 174.
Horse-power, compared with steam-power, 163, 188.

Inclined plane, 127.
Italian railways, 404.

Load, average of passenger carriages, 168; of goods wagons, 99.

INDEX.   441

Live stock: clearing house, 146; mileage, 184.
Locomotive power, 71; stock, 71; Belgian stock, 72; quantity of, independent of length of line, 86; depends on mileage, 87; or on amount of receipts, 88; number of locomotives on British railways, 88; mileage, 88; railway locomotive manufactories, 108; stock of Northwestern, 111; dépôt, 120; expense of, 211, 230. (*See* Engine, British, Belgian, French, German, and United States railways.)
London retail dealers, 133.
London fruit, 134.
Lost luggage office, 128.
Luggage, 128, allowed, 122; free, 122.

Mileage, definition of, 87.
Morrison, K., suggests clearing house, 141.

Napoleon, roads projected and executed by, 46.
Navigation developed earlier than internal commerce, 46. (*See* United States.)
North of France Railway, carrying stock of, 92; mileage of passenger vehicles, 96, 97; goods wagons, 131; number of passengers carried by each train, 171; average daily movement of locomotive stock, 172. (*See* French railways.)
Northwestern, investigation of durability of rails by, 63; coke, 82; service of engines, 84; engine drivers, 85; carrying stock, 93, 97, 106, 110; movement of carrying stock, 99; manufactories, 108; locomotive stock, 111; goods wagons, 131; goods engines, 132; goods trains, 133; number of passengers drawn by each engine, 172; distance traveled per passenger, 172; departures, 175; persons and horses employed, 190; expenses of locomotive power, 219; estimated general working expenses. (*See* British railways, Expenses, Receipts, Profits.)

Orleans Railway, mileage of engines, 75

Parcels, 123, 133.
Parcel vans, 91.
Passenger engines, 71; station, 120.
Passenger carriages, load, 168.
Passenger traffic, 152; mileage account, 100; clearing house, 147; mileage of, 152, 169; augmentation of, 162, 167, 186; comparative, per mile, 167: decrease, 168. (*See* British, French, Belgian, German, and United States Railways.)
Post offices, 91.
Profits, 235; may be increased by increasing distance of transport, 259; and regulating tariff of empty transport and incomplete loads, 260. (*See* British, Belgian, French, German, and United States railways.)

Rails, gradual wear, 56–63; means of calculating duration, 56; weight augmented, 58; recommended by Stephenson and Locke, 59; modes of support, 59; durability of, investigated, 60, 207; expenses of repair, 204; reserve fund for relaying, 65; on United States railways, 342.
Railways, organization of administration of, 52; newly constructed require frequent repair, 55; erroneous opinion as to durability, 57; date of modern, 56; projects sanctioned by parliament, 67; extent to which used by rolling stock, 103; proprietors carriers on, 108; development of compared with traffic, 166, 188; length of British, 166; trains classified, 176; accidents on, 265; in different countries, 416; population, extent of territory, extent of railway and capital in countries where railways exist, 417; comparison of length of railways and capital with population and territory, 418; relation of to State, 421; in some countries constructed and worked by State, 423; in others a mixed system, 423; case of English railway companies peculiar, 424; demand of system of control, 424; right of parliament to interfere, 424; necessity of control, 425; nomination of Board of Control, 426; parliamentary evidence on audit system, 427; objects of control, 428; reports of House of Lords, 431; details necessary in railway accounts, 433; advantages of complete record of railway affairs, 433; necessity of publishing such record, 438; (*See* British, Belgian, French, German, United States, Russian, Italian, and Spanish railways.)
Receipts, 235; on British railways, 235; on what gross receipts depend, 247; relation between variation in and tariff, 248; means of augmenting, 257; relation between mileage of engines and, 262; on Belgian railways, 364. (*See* Belgian, British, French, German, and United States railways.)
Register of locomotive stock, 71; of Belgian railways, 72.
Repairs, chief objects of annual repairs of way, 55.
Reserve fund for relaying permanent way, 65.
Revenue and capital, 115.
Roads only in two sevenths of inhabited parts of globe, 42; Roman and Egyptian, 42; constructed by Semiramis, 43; in ancient Greece, 43; of the Phœnicians, and Carthaginians, 43; ancient Roman, 44; constructed by Romans, 44; projected and made by Napoleon, 46; in western Europe after peace of 1802, 46; French, 47; English, 48; Roman, in England, 48.
Rolling stock, maintenance and reproduction of, 107; on Belgian railways, 353.
Rules (plain) to avoid accidents, 284.
Russian railways, 414.

Sleepers, 60; material, 60; distance, 60;

magnitude, 60; investigation as to durability, 61; expenses of repair, 207.
Spanish railways, 416.
Southeastern: departures, 175; estimated general working expenses, 233. (*See* British railways.)
Southwestern: departures, 175; estimated general working expenses, 233. (*See* British railways.)
Speed, 176, 336, 365, 386, 413; depends on stoppages, 175; injurious effects of high, 179.
Stations, 119; service of, 52; passenger, 121; goods, 131; engine, 134; carriage and wagon, 136; intermediate, 138; number, 138; expenses, 226.
Statistical bureau, 437.
Stock, valuation of, 118.
Stoppages, injurious effects of, 176.

Tariff, 195, 235, 247; goods, 182, 306; relation between variation of tariff and receipts, 248; skill required to adjust, 252; may be reduced by increasing distance of transport, 257; on empty transport and incomplete loads, 260.
Telegraph (Electric), 38, 296; discovery of phenomena subservient to, 296; conductors and non-conductors, 297; effects used as signals, 297; mode of operation, 299; in United States, 302; sub-marine, 304; in England, 306; tariff of charges, 306; subscription intelligence rooms, 307; in Prussia, 307; extent in England, 308; project of East India Company, 308; cost of construction, 308.
Tenders, number of, should be equal to engines, 88.
Traffic, compared with development of railways, 165. (*See* British, Belgian, French, German, and United States railways.)
Trains, increase in speed of, 58; increase in number and weight of, 58; composition of, 99; arrangements of, 126; arrival, 128; for poorer classes, 161; number of passengers carried by each, 171; classified, 176; express, 180.
Transport, improved, influence of on civilization, 25; requisites of, 26; advantages, 26; confers value on things valueless, 29; augments commerce, 30; parliamentary evidence as to, 31; augments rent and profit of farmer, 33; importance of speed as regards persons, 34; importance of improved transport to operative classes, 34; enlarges area of supply and of residence for large towns, 35; importance in military affairs, 37; diminishes chances and duration of war, 37; tends to diffusion of knowledge and increase of civilization, 38; effect of rapid, exhibited in journalism, 38; retrospect of progress of, 41; influence of Crusades on, 45; impediments by fiscal exactions, 46; on English roads, 49.
Traveling (railway) compared with old mode, 163, 188.

United Kingdom: canal navigation, 311; railway in proportion to population, 343.
United States: transport in, 308; canal navigation, 309; river navigation, 311; Hudson steamers, 313; Ericsson's engine, 316; steamers of other rivers, 323; Ericsson's propellers, 325; seagoing steamers, 326; railways introduced, 327; length of, 327; description of, 328; mixed lines, 328; steam ferries, 334; mode of construction of railways, 335; mode of working, 336; speed on, 336; accidents, 337; cariages, 337; curves, 338; railways completed, in progress, and projected, 339; cost of construction, 342; dividends and price of shares, 339; roads, 345; extent of railways and canals in proportion to population, 345; passengers on railways, 346; railways constructed by companies, 346; little goods traffic, 347; conditions imposed by States on railway companies, 347; railway act, 348; inducements by States to companies, 348.

Valuation of stock, 118.
Vehicles (public) in connection with railways, 121, 128, 132.
Vehicles of transport. (*See* Carrying stock.)

Wagons station, 136.
Way and works, 53; service of, 52; wear, 53; expenses of, 204, 230.
Way (permanent), with given traffic, when relaid, 54; reserve fund for relaying, 54.
Wheels, 136

THE END.